AF796618

Faulkner

A Comprehensive Guide to the Brodsky Collection

Volume II: The Letters

Edited by
Louis Daniel Brodsky
and
Robert W. Hamblin

UNIVERSITY PRESS OF MISSISSIPPI
JACKSON

PS
3511
.A86
Z78334
v.2

Center for the Study of Southern Culture Series

Copyright © 1984 by Louis Daniel Brodsky
All Rights Reserved
Manufactured in the United States of America

Library of Congress Cataloging in Publication Data
(Revised for vol. 2)
Main entry under title:

Faulkner, a comprehensive guide to the Brodsky Collection.

(Center for the Study of Southern Culture series)
Includes index.
Contents: v. 1. The biobibliography—v. 2. The letters.
1. Faulkner, William, 1897–1962—Bibliography—Catalogs. 2. Faulkner, William—1897–1962—Manuscripts—Catalogs. 3. Faulkner, William, 1897–1962—Miscellanea—Catalogs. 4. Faulkner, William, 1897–1962—Correspondence. 5. Novelists, American—20th century—Correspondence. 6. Brodsky, Louis Daniel—Library—Catalogs. I. Brodsky, Louis Daniel. II. Hamblin, Robert W.
Z8288.F38 1982 [PS3511.A86] 016.813′52 82-6966
ISBN 0-87805-159-7 (set)

Faulkner

A Comprehensive Guide to the Brodsky Collection

Volume II: The Letters

CONTENTS

LIST OF ILLUSTRATIONS

ACKNOWLEDGMENTS

We are much indebted to all of the many individuals who graciously assisted us in the production of this volume. We are particularly grateful to the correspondents, or their representatives, for allowing us to print the contents of the enclosed letters.

We especially want to express our sincere thanks to Jill Faulkner Summers, the daughter and executrix of William Faulkner, for her continuing cooperation on the series of which this book is a part.

We are also extremely grateful to William Ferris and Ann J. Abadie, Director and Assistant Director, respectively, of the Center for the Study of Southern Culture at the University of Mississippi, for their ongoing support of our work.

The following individuals not only granted permission for the use of materials but also courteously responded to numerous inquiries and offered many helpful suggestions: Frances Commins Bennett, Dorothy B. Commins, Ruth Ford, Araminta Stone Johnson, James W. Silver, and Emily Whitehurst Stone. To each of these persons we extend our heartfelt thanks.

Others who provided permissions or pertinent information include Jean A. Adams, Stanley Belkin, Edmund Berkeley, Jr., Joseph Blotner, E. P. Bollier, Mary Winslow Chapman, Jack Cofield, Carvel Collins, Diana Crump, Albert Erskine, Clifton Fadiman, Regina K. Fadiman, John V. Fleming, Larry E. Grisvard, Warren R. Howell, Victoria F. Johnson, Donald S. Klopfer, Bertha Kranz, Stephen N. Limbaugh, Jr., Jay Martin, Mary P. Massey, Ward L. Miner, Phillip E. Mullen, Michael Plunkett, Craig Tenney, Janet A. Thompson, and Phyllis Cerf Wagner. We deeply appreciate their cooperation and assistance.

Several of our friends and colleagues supplied friendly encouragement and tangible support. We wish to thank especially William Boozer, Fredson Bowers, Dolores Cleve, Gray Cole, Louis Dollarhide, David Farmer, Fred Goodwin, Rolla E. Gordon, John Gulla, Evans Harrington, Glenn Horowitz, Maribeth Needels, Maurice Neville, Janice Nunnelee, John Pilkington, Henry Sessoms, Lewis P. Simpson, Bill W. Stacy, Thomas M. Verich, James G. Watson, James W. Webb,

Pat Williams, Harriet Yeargain, Williams Young, and James K. Zink.

We again express our admiration and thanks to Paul Lueders, Master Photographer, our partner from the beginning, for the pride and care he lavished on the illustrations for this book.

We are extremely grateful to Charlotte and Saul Brodsky for providing crucial funding and indispensable personal support for this project. We also thank the American Council of Learned Societies and the Grants and Research Funding Committee of Southeast Missouri State University for supplying research and travel funds. We appreciate, too, the financial aid contributed by Biltwell Company, Inc., of St. Louis.

We have reserved the acknowledgment of our greatest debt until last. To our immediate families, especially our beloved wives Jan and Kaye, we express our deepest love and gratitude.

INTRODUCTION

THIS VOLUME PRINTS almost five hundred letters from the private collection of William Faulkner materials assembled by Louis Daniel Brodsky. Included are one hundred and twenty-nine letters and telegrams by Faulkner, as well as correspondence by his wife Estelle, his daughter Jill, his great-aunt 'Bama McLean, his lifelong associate Phil Stone, his editor and confidant Saxe Commins, his agent Harold Ober, his friends Ruth Ford and Jim Silver, and various scholars, critics, and collectors, among them Carvel Collins, Richard P. Adams, Robert Coughlan, Linton Massey, William B. Wisdom, Robert Daniel, Lawrance Thompson, Clifton Fadiman, and Ward Miner. As such a listing demonstrates, the writers of these letters represent an impressive cross-section of individuals closely connected with Faulkner's personal life and literary career. While the letters contained herein do not present anything approaching the complete story of either that life or the career, they do supply essential information, much of it previously unrecorded, which serves to clarify and extend the critical understanding of Faulkner's life and work.

The Faulkner letters printed here complement those collected by Joseph Blotner in *Selected Letters of William Faulkner.* Readers familiar with that volume will quickly note further mention of various subjects, events, and personages.[1] What the present work does, in effect, is to fill in some of the missing or omitted pieces in Blotner's volume. What emerges is not so much a new and different Faulkner as one perceived in fuller detail and thus greater depth.

One segment of Faulkner's life which is significantly illuminated by his letters in this volume is the period from 1951 to 1957. These years, though belonging to the time of his greatest public acclaim, were among the most difficult in Faulkner's life, marked as they were by illness, personal unhappiness, and self-doubt. Experiencing the decline of his physical prowess (a decline made more acute by recurring

[1] Approximately one-fourth of the Faulkner letters in this volume appeared, in part or in whole, in *Selected Letters of William Faulkner* (New York: Random House, 1977). Since one purpose of the present work is to supply a comprehensive record of the letters in the Brodsky Collection, it has seemed appropriate to include even the letters which have been previously published.

pains from an earlier back injury, as well as by the increasingly enervating effects of his already severe alcoholism), and fearing a corresponding loss of his creative powers, Faulkner reacted with a despondency at times bordering on despair. Not altogether atypical of his attitude during this period is the letter he wrote to Saxe Commins in January 1956, in which Faulkner confessed that although work on *The Town* was progressing nicely, "I still have the feeling that I am written out though, and all remaining is the craftsmanship, no fire, no force." He continued, "My judgment might be extinct also, so I will go on with this until I know it is no good. I may even finish it without knowing it is bad, or admitting it at least." This fear of being past his prime had been building in Faulkner for some time, and his growing sense of unhappiness was undoubtedly related in part to this anxiety concerning his art.

Another element, equally debilitating, in Faulkner's distress was a persistent feeling of entrapment in an unhappy marriage. Just when Faulkner's relationship to Estelle turned sour is a matter of conjecture, but as early as the 1930s, in his affair with Meta Carpenter, Faulkner demonstrated his inclination to seek sexual gratification and love outside marriage. By the 1950s the incompatability between Faulkner and Estelle had become nearly total. As a partial solution to this problem Faulkner began to spend more and more time away from Rowan Oak, and he occasionally allowed himself to dream of a complete break. He wrote Commins on July 29, 1952: "We talked some of my giving myself six months of absence, getting completely away from here and all my familiar life. I think now it will take more than that. I think now I may, to save my soul, something of peace, contentment, save the work at least, quit the whole thing, give it all to them, leave and be done with it." In a letter to Commins dated October 25, 1952, Faulkner noted: "This is a terrible situation; never can I remember ever being so unhappy and downhearted and despaired. I have done no work in a year, am living on my fat, will begin soon to worry about money, and I do not believe I can work here. I must get away."

To assuage his pain and grief, Faulkner turned not only to frequent periods of drunkenness but also to extended love affairs with Joan Williams, Jean Stein, and Else Jonsson. While he found a degree of happiness in each of these relationships, ultimately these liaisons proved scarcely less troubling than his marriage. Joan, whom Faulkner adopted as his protégé, was very reluctant to become his lover and, as Faulkner pointed out in a letter to Commins on March 14, 1954, never quite overcame her concern for traditional mores. By contrast, Jean impressed Faulkner as a free, untrammeled spirit. In the letter just mentioned Faulkner commented: "[Jean] came to me in St. Moritz almost exactly as Joan did in Oxford. But she has none of the emotional conventional confusion which poor Joan had. This one is so uninhibited that she frightens me a little." Faulkner ended with words which implied the hope of a continuing, blissful relationship. "She is charming, delightful, completely transparent, completely trustful. I will not hurt her for any price. She doesn't want anything of me—only to love me, be in love." As it turned out, however, Jean proved as unwilling as Joan to perpetuate a relationship with Faulkner and, like Joan before her, soon married another man. In Else's case, the circumstances of time and geography prohibited the development of anything more than a casual romance.

A slightly amusing, if somewhat pathetic, episode from 1951 provides a poignant illustration of Faulkner's personal and domestic dilemma during this period. In late January and again in February Faulkner sought Saxe Commins' assistance in securing the address of Elliot Paul, a fellow writer. Although he did not explain why he needed Paul's address, Faulkner indicated that he wanted to spend the last two weeks of April in Europe. He added that he was sharing this information in strictest confidence; he wanted his family in Oxford to think that he would be in New York working on his play-novel, *Requiem for a Nun.* Nevertheless, just in case he could not conceal the European trip from his family, he would need a "good covering reason" to explain the visit. Fortunately, Robert Haas soon provided the necessary excuse by suggesting that Faulkner use some time in France to tour World War I battlefields and thus refresh his memory for the writing of key scenes in *A Fable.* Finally, in early April, after more than two months of meticulous and mysterious plotting, Faulkner explained to Commins that he hoped Paul could supply the name of an "obscure" Paris hotel, "so I wont be too well known." He added, "You can see by now what all this is leading to." What it led to was a rendezvous with Else Jonsson, whom Faulkner had met the previous November in Stockholm during the Nobel Prize festivities. Faulkner's elaborate scheming to effect this brief romantic interlude (the first of possibly four such meetings with Mrs. Jonsson) suggests not only the extent of Faulkner's unhappiness but also the degree of intrigue and deceit he was willing to employ in order to escape that unhappiness.

Supplementing Faulkner's correspondence regarding his marital problems and his extramarital affairs are the letters written by Estelle Faulkner. The Brodsky Collection contains forty-five letters which Mrs. Faulkner wrote to Saxe and/or Dorothy Commins between 1951 and 1966, plus four letters she addressed, from 1954 to 1966, to a close family friend, Professor James W. Silver, and another letter she wrote from Santa Monica, California, in 1936 to her two eldest children, Malcolm and Victoria Franklin. Taken collectively, these letters, none previously published, shed impressive new light upon Estelle's character and attitudes; but several of the letters to Saxe and Dorothy Commins are especially revealing, since Estelle, like Faulkner, came to depend upon the Comminses as intimate friends and advisers during some extremely difficult times.

The personality profile which surfaces from Estelle's letters is that of a bright, creative, and refined (even somewhat pampered) woman who deeply loves her husband and children, yet who is continually plagued with extended periods of self-doubt and insecurity. In a letter to Dorothy Commins in 1966, Estelle remarked, "The fact that I've sold paintings, aroused the doubt lately that people bought them because I am Mrs. William Faulkner—I feel that I must prove Estelle Oldham—an individual with a certain amount of talent." One suspects, particularly in view of the use of the maiden name in the above statement, that Estelle had lived with these feelings of inferiority for many years.

Interestingly, both Estelle's need for recognition and her insecurity are mirrored in her handwriting.[2] Her noticeable use of long slashes in forming such letters as *f, l,* and *t;* her similarly unorthodox shaping of other letters, especially *b, e, h, th,* and *w;* her unconventional employment of dashes instead of periods; and her frequent disdain of standard paragraph indentation suggest both an independence of will and a strong desire to call attention to herself. However, the dominant characteristic of Estelle's graphology is the disconnected letters. Very few of her words are written in a continuous, flowing pattern. For example, in her typical signature "Estelle," only the *st* and the *ell* are joined. In this practice, too, one notes an idiosyncrasy, an exaggerated commitment to self, but that self is one which is fragmented, not successfully integrated with the outside world.

Predictably, both the happy and tragic aspects of Estelle's life are reflected in the contents of her letters. She records the simple, everyday joys of tending the house and grounds at Rowan Oak, entertaining guests, preserving jams and jellies, and going fishing; and she delights in the wedding of her daughter, the birth of grandchildren, and the achievements of her husband. But the somber side of her life, too, may be perceived in her remarks about her dying mother, her

[2] I am grateful to Jay Martin, Bing Professor of English at the University of Southern California and Lecturer in the Department of Psychiatry and Human Behavior in the University of California, Irvine, Medical School, for assisting me in the analysis of Mrs. Faulkner's handwriting.

unstable son, and her estranged husband. Concerning the behavior of the last, Estelle at times exhibits a surprising sense of detachment and objectivity. Though deeply distressed by her knowledge of Faulkner's affairs with Joan Williams and Jean Stein, Estelle could assume an impressive degree of understanding and even forgiveness. She wrote Commins in March 1954: "I am much too old and poised (I hope) to give vent to personal animosity—In fact, am not sure that I feel any—Certainly I do not blame Joan—In all probability, had I been an aspiring young writer and an elderly celebrity had fallen in love with me—I would have accepted him as avidly as Joan did Bill." In the same letter Estelle observed, "Bill's article, 'Mississippi,' in next month's *Holiday* explains the two Bills—He is so definitely dual I think—Perhaps artists must needs be." Regarding Faulkner's later affair with Jean Stein, Estelle wrote to Commins on November 5, 1956: "I know, as you must, that Bill feels some sort of compulsion to be attached to some young woman at all times—it's Bill—At long last I am sensible enough to concede him the right to do as he pleases, and without recrimination—It is not that I don't care—(I wish it were not so)—but all of a sudden [I] feel sorry for him—wish he could know without words between us, that it's not very important after all."

Beside Faulkner's frequently selfish and self-pitying remarks, Estelle's comments seem remarkably magnanimous. Of course, one must acknowledge the possibility that in her letters to Commins Estelle was seeking, either consciously or subconsciously, to manipulate Faulkner indirectly by influencing his trusted friend. Faulkner's warning to Commins in a May 1952 letter may be pertinent here. "In ten minutes," Faulkner wrote, "[Estelle] can have you believing that black is white. Of course, in eleven minutes you know better, but sometimes it is too late by then." Unquestionably there is an element of self-interest in Estelle's letters,[3] as in Faulkner's. Moreover, one cannot emphasize too strongly that the Estelle letters in the Brodsky Collection (with one exception) date from the later years of her life and thus do not mirror the early, developing stages of her alienation from Faulkner. Still, even if Estelle's letters to the Comminses seem designed to interpret her situation to her own best advantage, or even if they express an acquiescence deriving, not from nobility or charity, but from a weary resignation to a time-inured circumstance, these letters nonetheless reveal the poignant and even heroic efforts of a

[3]Evidence of a possible degree of dissimulation in Estelle's letters to the Comminses is the fact that there is no mention of her alcoholism until November 5, 1956, that is, not until *after* she has gotten the problem under control through the assistance of Alcoholics Anonymous. Faulkner occasionally mentions Estelle's drinking problem in his letters to Commins, but significantly Estelle does not.

suffering individual to preserve and protect her own pride and dignity, as well as endure her unfortunate and unhappy condition.

The inescapable question raised by both Faulkner's and Estelle's letters about their marriage concerns why they did not secure a divorce. Both, by their own admissions, seriously considered legal separation from time to time. For several years, apparently, it was concern over the effect a divorce might have upon their daughter Jill that led the couple to avoid, or at least postpone, a separation. As Estelle wrote to Commins on February 28, 1954, "I'll do *anything* that is best—The only thing that I shudder at and might try to evade, is a divorce—and *that,* only on Jill's account."[4] Similarly, Faulkner stated in his letter to Commins postmarked October 25, 1952: "I am afraid that, if I came up [to Princeton], E. would insist on some public formal separation and so forth, so that every time Jill entered a class room or the dining room [at Pine Manor], she would think: *All these people know that my parents have separated,* and it would ruin her year, even if she herself did not do something in desperation. So I dont see much hope until after she graduates. . . ." Even after Jill's graduation and subsequent marriage, however, the Faulkners maintained their union. Again one wonders why. Was it simply that Estelle had at long last become totally resigned to living with Faulkner on his own terms, and that he, having been granted what amounted to complete freedom, no longer needed a divorce? Or was it that Faulkner and Estelle had willingly if reluctantly succumbed to that same conventionality about which he had chided Joan Williams? Or was it perhaps that Faulkner still longed, if subconsciously, to punish Estelle for betraying him to marry her first husband, Cornell Franklin, so many years before? Or, to acknowledge quite another possibility, could it be that, despite the suffering and cruelty they had imposed upon one another over the years, Faulkner and Estelle did indeed continue to love one another? Or, if their love had actually expired, were they still somehow compelled to preserve that union which symbolized the memory of their youthful, ideal love? Faulkner wrote in *The Wild Palms* about a fictional relationship which may owe more to his marriage than critics have been disposed to admit: "*Between grief and nothing I will take grief.*" In any event, that statement stands as an ironic, self-fulfilling prophecy of the eventual judgment both Faulkner and Estelle would make, for better or worse, about their marriage.

Another vastly significant group of letters in this volume is the

[4]On occasion Estelle used her concern for Jill's welfare as an argument *for* divorce. On February 11, 1954, she wrote to Commins: "I was just on the verge of writing Bill that I was suing for divorce—I still believe it the only wise thing to do—on his account, as well as Jill's and mine."

correspondence of Saxe Commins. Faulkner's principal editor at Random House from the publication of *Absalom, Absalom!* in 1936 until his death in 1958, Commins performed with competence and insight a variety of editorial functions, ranging from assisting Faulkner in his selection of a title for *Knight's Gambit,* to writing the promotional copy for *A Faulkner Reader,* ordering the stories in *Big Woods,* and providing the emotional support which enabled Faulkner to complete the frequently-delayed *A Fable.* This last effort undoubtedly represents Commins' greatest achievement as Faulkner's editor. Commins not only provided expert advice regarding the technical aspects of the novel, but he and his wife Dorothy also opened their home at 85 Elm Road in Princeton to Faulkner as a writing haven during an extended period of emotional and artistic distress. Testimony concerning Commins' contribution to *A Fable* is succinctly expressed in Estelle Faulkner's letter to Commins dated April 19, 1954: "*A Fable* owes its completion to your untiring, loving work with Bill those last weeks in Princeton—I realize, only too well, that he was in no emotional nor physical condition to do it without *you.*"

But Commins' services to Faulkner went far beyond mere professional concerns. Indeed, during the last decade of the editor's life Commins became Faulkner's dearest personal friend and confidant. As noted previously, it was Commins to whom both Faulkner and Estelle frequently turned for advice regarding their troubled marriage. It was Commins, too, who looked after Faulkner's suits and pipes, monitored his checking account and invested his earnings, booked his airline flights and hotel rooms, accepted awards on his behalf, signed documents as his attorney-in-fact, and served as his intermediary in numerous other personal and professional dealings. On April 13, 1951, Faulkner named Commins "to act as my literary executor and as editor for all my past and future literary work," an appointment which recognized the central role Commins had assumed in Faulkner's life and career. In all of his relationships to Faulkner, Commins ever proved the loyal and faithful friend, often putting the writer's interests and well-being above his own personal health and concerns.

There is no better evidence of Commins' dedication to his friend than the occasion in 1952 when he journeyed to Oxford to attend a gravely-ill Faulkner. The author, disillusioned over his unhappy home situation and suffering the severe aftereffects of his back injury, had turned to alcohol to alleviate his pain. When the problem became too great for Estelle to handle, she contacted Commins for assistance, and he responded immediately, arriving in Oxford late on the evening of October 7. As he recorded in his personal diary periodically throughout the night and in two letters written the following morning, Commins was shocked to find Faulkner in a drunken stupor and mumbling incoherently, his body viciously bruised from the many falls he had taken on the stairs. After nursing Faulkner through the long night, Commins wrote to his wife Dorothy and to his Random House colleagues, Robert Haas and Bennett Cerf, describing Faulkner's tragic condition. "This is more than a case of acute alcoholism," Commins explained to Dorothy. "It is a complete disintegration of a man." To Haas and Cerf he added: "I shall have to stay here until something effective can be decided upon. The decisions, God help me, will have to be mine. Please rely on my judgment."

Recognizing that Faulkner could not be left in such a dangerous condition and that he was too seriously ill to travel to New York for treatment, Commins consulted with an Oxford physician and arranged to have Faulkner admitted to a Memphis hospital. At midmorning on October 8 Commins, Estelle, and her son Malcolm Franklin left Oxford with Faulkner for the trip to Memphis. As Franklin drove and Estelle sat in the front seat beside him, Commins ministered to Faulkner in the back seat, occasionally bribing him with a tin of beer into continuing the journey. Only after Faulkner had been safely delivered to the hospital and placed under the care of professionals, did Commins catch an afternoon flight for a return to Princeton and, as he put it, "the amenities of publishing."

Back at Random House, Commins conferred with Cerf and Haas about the best course of action to follow. Faulkner's life, Commins felt, might well be hanging in the balance. The only solution, since Faulkner resisted extended hospitalization, was to get the writer away from his unhappy situation in Oxford and seek to protect him from his self-destructive tendencies. Commins and Dorothy offered their home as a retreat. Faulkner accepted their invitation, arriving in Princeton in mid-November 1952. After a few days at the Comminses' residence, he checked into a room at the Princeton Inn. Thus began a pattern which would continue until Commins' death. Faulkner's malaise would lead to uncontrolled drinking, Commins would nurse him back onto his feet again, and Faulkner would resume his writing, sometimes under Commins' watchful eye at Random House or in Princeton.

As instructive as the Saxe Commins letters are those written by Phil Stone, the Oxford lawyer and self-styled literary critic who was a principal influence upon Faulkner during his formative years. Shortly after Faulkner's death in July 1962 Stone contemplated producing a book of his reminiscences about Faulkner. That book was never written, but Stone's letters, published here for the first time, preserve many of the incidents and opinions which would undoubtedly have provided the substance of such a work.

Throughout his career Stone maintained an office file of his correspondence regarding Faulkner. That file, a considerable portion of which was destroyed by fire in 1942, included letters written to Stone by various individuals and carbon copies of Stone's letters to those persons and others. The Stone letters were dictated to and typed by his various secretaries, including (to name only those who may be identified from materials in the Brodsky Collection) Mary Stone, Estelle Patton, and Elaine Hoffman. Each letter was hole-punched at the top and fastened in its folder with a two-pronged metal clasp. In accordance with usual office procedure, the materials in each folder were stacked in chronological order, with the most recently received (or filed) letter occupying the topmost position. The Brodsky Collection contains several letters which survived the 1942 fire (in some instances the burned edges offer lingering evidence of the conflagration), as well as a presumably-complete file, occupying three large folders, of the correspondence from 1949 to 1962. Brodsky has also managed to recover some additional Stone letters from recipients.

While the ninety-nine Stone letters in this book represent only a part of his voluminous correspondence on Faulkner, they nonetheless supply crucial information which helps to clarify Stone's complex relationship to Faulkner. The story of that relationship, as it is usually told, is greatly oversimplified. The account prevalent in Oxford over the years has held that Stone was exceedingly possessive toward his protégé and that, once Faulkner had outgrown and escaped Stone's influence, the older man became extremely jealous and even vindictive over Faulkner's success. Joseph Blotner has documented the additional fact that Stone's failure to repay a personal loan of $6,000 from Faulkner in 1939 further contributed to the alienation of the two friends.

Although Stone's proprietary attitude and the default on the loan were definitely factors in the estrangement of Stone and Faulkner, these details do not tell the whole story. For one thing, such explanations ignore the evidence that Stone apparently genuinely believed that Faulkner had come to be greatly overrated, particularly in view of the work he had produced after 1940. As Stone wrote to Ward Miner on September 29, 1952, "After all, the Nobel Prize was for work [Faulkner] did between 1928 and 1940 and he has done very little since then of the same stature as the work of that period. I think now that he never will and I think his great success and the adulation that has followed it has really been a misfortune." In the same letter Stone acknowledged that Faulkner "is good, probably the best of the lot in contemporary American fiction, but he is just not as good as his present worshippers think he is." Ten years earlier Stone had expressed the same notion, but with greater clarification, in a letter to Robert Daniel.

> The truth is that none of the contemporary novelists have the stuff that the old ones seem to have had although in the last book which Hemingway wrote, he seems to have been better than ever before. The present day boys seem to make a virtue of being half undressed. I am not talking about their literary morals but about their performances. They, especially Faulkner, seem to make virtues of all their literary faults and seem to think that it is a cardinal sin to be coherent. They usually copy all the faults of James Joyce (who had something of genius) and very few of Joyce's virtues. I am reminded of what Oscar Wilde said about Zola when he said that Zola had said genius was never clever and that Zola had proved that if he could not be a genius, he could at least be dull. Our contemporary novelists seem to prove that if they cannot be geniuses they can at least be obscure and incoherent.

Coming from an individual who championed such modern experimentalist poets as Ezra Pound, T. S. Eliot, Conrad Aiken, and the Imagists, the above passage exhibits a notable insensitivity to twentieth-century writers of fiction. For example, what is one to think of the critical acumen of a reader who prefers *For Whom the Bell Tolls* to Hemingway's earlier novels or who appears only grudgingly to admit that Joyce possessed "something of genius"?[5] Actually, as his letters clearly reveal, Stone's taste in fiction, quite unlike his attention to poetry, was narrow and traditional. In the letters there is scarcely any mention of modern novelists; rather it is the "old masters" such as Balzac, Thackeray, Fielding, and DeFoe whom Stone holds up for emulation.

This conventional bias in favor of the eighteenth- and nineteenth-century realists influences Stone's judgments when he identifies the specific weaknesses in Faulkner's work. Stone lists three of these de-

[5] In at least one instance Stone expressed a more favorable view of Joyce. In a letter to Carvel Collins dated August 16, 1954, Stone commented: "What you said about Joyce having a great deal to do with [*The Sound and the Fury*] is true but the reason it is true is because about that time, in the late 'teens and early 'twenties I was drilling into Bill that Joyce was a pioneer and that fiction would never again be the same after *Ulysses*. In fact, when the portions of *Ulysses* were published in *The Little Review* I gave them to Bill to read and talked to him endless hours about it." More typical, however, seems to be Stone's remark in his July 19, 1962 letter to Elizabeth Grosch: "I did steer [Faulkner] into Joyce and Ezra Pound, but I told him by all means not to use Joyce as a model."

fects in a letter to Clifton Fadiman dated April 6, 1956.[6] First of all, Stone insists, Faulkner has no mastery of style, but only "a personal mannerism" which he imposes on any and every subject, whether appropriate or not. Moreover, Faulkner has "no sense of overall design"; hence "his novels are merely a collection of episodes." Finally, Stone notes, most of Faulkner's characters are "mere puppets" who "come out at the end of the book almost exactly like they came in." All such observations, of course, are grounded in the realistic canons of verisimilitude and the well-plotted novel. While Stone may have been mistaken in his judgments (though, in all fairness, one must concede that better critics than Stone have faulted Faulkner at one time or another for these same tendencies), the point being emphasized here is that Stone's censure of Faulkner was based, at least in part, on particular critical presuppositions and distinctions and was not altogether the result of wounded vanity or subconscious guilt. Ultimately Stone may have proved an unreliable critic of Faulkner's work,[7] but that fact may derive from philosophical and not necessarily personal causes.

Yet there were, undeniably, strong personal feelings which divided Stone and Faulkner—even one particular source of agitation which has received almost no attention. Reference here is to the men's opposing views on integration and the race question. Both Stone and Faulkner, one should not forget, came of age in a South dominated by a belief in white supremacy and committed to a regional, as opposed to a national, perspective. It is hardly surprising that the young Faulkner did not totally escape the prejudices of this tradition. For example, a cartoon which Faulkner drew for a proposed high school yearbook in 1913 shows Miss Ella Wright, his history teacher, preparing to grind out punishment from a "demerit mill" for a fierce, bearded figure standing beside her. The culprit is identified as Abraham Lincoln. At Lincoln's feet, and with the president's obvious approval, a bully holding aloft a Union flag and brandishing a knife is attacking a much smaller, unarmed figure holding a Confederate flag. The caption, printed in Faulkner's juvenile hand, reads:

[6]The first two of these characteristics Stone had previously delineated in his letter to Malcolm Cowley dated April 30, 1945.

[7]Not all of Stone's judgments, of course, were wrongheaded; indeed, some of his remarks were quite perceptive. To Carvel Collins (August 16, 1954) Stone defended the assigned order of the separate sections of *The Sound and the Fury,* noting how the story gradually "unfold[s] like a flower" and adding, "This is just exactly the effect Bill was trying to get." To Robert Coughlan (October 6, 1954) Stone stressed Faulkner's "deliberate withholding of information" and linked the practice to a desire to make "the reader feel that he is sharing himself in working out the solution." To James B. Meriwether (May 28, 1957) Stone identified Faulkner as "just about the best there is when it comes to writing a short story."

"Them's my sentiments."[8] While these words are doubtless intended as a commentary on the way Miss Wright (and many other Southerners) taught history (that is, from a Confederate point of view), there is at least the possibility that the caption also expresses Faulkner's own personal bias. Another Faulkner drawing, produced in the 1920–21 *Ole Miss,* the university yearbook, shows a graceful white couple dancing in front of a Negro jazz band, probably W. C. Handy's. The blacks in this drawing are depicted in grotesque caricature; the profiled head of one musician is strikingly ape-like. Even in his first Yoknapatawpha novel, *Sartoris,* published in 1929, Faulkner shows little disposition to treat blacks as anything other than buffoons or crafty, shiftless servants who plot to deceive their white "betters." While it would be a gross distortion ever to identify Faulkner, at any stage of his life, with "racist" beliefs and attitudes, there can be little doubt that in his early work he occasionally fell victim to the false and stereotypic impressions which many whites of that period held regarding blacks.

But Faulkner's views toward blacks dramatically, if gradually, shifted. In his description of the Negro church service at the end of *Soldiers' Pay* and in his characterization of Dilsey in *The Sound and the Fury,* Faulkner had already demonstrated that he was capable of treating blacks with great admiration and sensitivity. In the 1930s the Negro question became an increasingly central issue in Faulkner's fiction. In such works as "Dry September," "That Evening Sun," *Light in August, Absalom, Absalom!,* and *The Unvanquished* Faulkner significantly expanded his sympathetic treatment of Negroes, effectively dramatizing their exploitation and even murder at the hands of white supremacists and movingly depicting blacks' yearnings for dignity and equality. With *Go Down, Moses* in 1942 and *Intruder in the Dust* in 1948 Faulkner moved beyond mere dramatization of the racial problem to offer broad principles of social reform. After winning the Nobel Prize in 1950, Faulkner applied some of the award money toward the payment of college tuition for deserving black students. He also utilized the public forum that accompanied his world-wide fame to speak out against injustice and archaic racial patterns and to promote the cause of integration. In perhaps his strongest public statement he vehemently condemned the 1955 lynch-type murder of Emmett Till, a fourteen-year-old black youth, near Greenwood, Mississippi, concluding that "if we in America have reached that point in our desperate culture when we must murder children, no matter for

[8]This cartoon has been reproduced in Hamblin and Brodsky, *Selections from the William Faulkner Collection of Louis Daniel Brodsky* (Charlottesville: University Press of Virginia, 1979), p. 19.

what reason or what color, we don't deserve to survive, and probably won't."[9] In addition to his public pronouncements, Faulkner collaborated behind the scenes with noted Mississippi liberals James W. Silver and P. D. East to oppose segregationists and effect changes in attitudes and laws.[10] It was during this period that Melvin B. Tolson, a black author keenly concerned with civil rights issues, mailed a book of his own poems to Faulkner with the inscription, "To William Faulkner— / A rock in a weary land."[11]

As several of the letters in this present volume demonstrate, Phil Stone had difficulty in first recognizing and then accepting Faulkner's liberalized view of Negroes. As late as September 30, 1952, in a letter to Robert Coughlan, Stone characterized Faulkner as "truly a Southerner" in contrast to his townsman, newspaperman Phil "Moon" Mullen, "a Yankee who only came here in 1933." To distinguish between "authentic Southerners" and outsiders, Stone cited the race issue: "Even yet, Moon does not seem to understand that the situation in the South about negroes voting is not just a matter of denying equal rights to negroes, but that it is a natural attempt to prevent happening what has happened once before and what we have reason to think will happen again, complete negro domination." Stone concluded with the caustic challenge, "When you Yankees get your negro population up to 50% and we get ours down to 10%, we shall be glad to join you in helping the negroes get equality."

In 1955, when the Memphis *Commercial Appeal* published a verbal exchange about Mississippi schools between Faulkner and segregationist Dave Womack, a member of the Mississippi House of Representatives, Stone significantly sided with Womack. On March 28 Stone wrote to the legislator: "Of course you people are doing the best you can down there [in Jackson] and any one of you knows more about this subject in ten minutes than Bill does or ever will know in a lifetime. So don't take him seriously." Increasingly, Stone's later correspondence contains volatile remarks regarding integration and, by implication, Faulkner's defense of it. In 1957, when George Thatcher, owner of the Dixie Press in Gulfport, Mississippi, asked Stone to help get Faulkner's permission for a reissue of *The Marble Faun,* Stone retorted: "Since [Faulkner] has taken the position he has in turning his back on his own people and his native land, I don't care

[9]See James B. Meriwether, ed., *Essays, Speeches & Public Letters by William Faulkner* (New York: Random House, 1965), p. 223.

[10]For a discussion of Faulkner's involvement with Silver and East in producing *The Southern Reposure,* a satiric, pro-integrationist newspaper, see *Faulkner: A Comprehensive Guide to the Brodsky Collection,* I, pp. 252–253.

[11]See *Faulkner: A Comprehensive Guide to the Brodsky Collection,* I, pp. 250–251.

to ask him anything." Perhaps predictably, Stone's negative judgments about Faulkner the writer and Nobel laureate seem to intensify in direct proportion to Faulkner's activities in support of integration.

It would be a mistake, however, to assume that Faulkner and Stone ever abandoned their deep attachment to one another. Faulkner's continuing loyalty toward Stone is reflected in the dedication of the successive volumes of the Snopes trilogy to Stone, as well as the gift of a presentation copy of *The Reivers* to Stone and his wife less than a month prior to Faulkner's death. Stone likewise retained his strong emotional ties with Faulkner. In discussing his possible collaboration on a magazine piece about Faulkner in April 1950, Stone wrote to Carvel Collins: "If there is anything in the world I do not want to do it is commercialize on my friendship with Bill, one of the finest things in my whole life." Stone consistently indicated to Collins, Coughlan, and others that he would take no money for providing reporters and publishers information on Faulkner.[12] Even the book of memoirs which Stone considered producing after Faulkner's death would be intended solely for the sake of literary history; any money that such a book might generate, Stone insisted, should go to Jill Faulkner. Moreover, though Stone allowed himself considerable latitude in attacking Faulkner's character and behavior, he sometimes took issue with others who claimed the same privilege. Thus, on September 30, 1952, Stone defended Faulkner's character in a letter to Robert Coughlan, who had mailed to Stone the manuscript of his *Life* magazine feature on Faulkner. Coughlan, in Stone's view, had placed too much emphasis on Faulkner's drinking. Furthermore, Stone added, "You say nothing at all about his patience, kindness and tolerance toward young children and old people and his very sincere liking for them." Finally, most significantly, Stone's letters to various individuals following Faulkner's death clearly reveal that a genuine love for Faulkner had survived all the disagreements between the two men. For example, on July 11, 1962, Stone wrote to Hubert Starr: "I had no idea that Bill's death would hit me as hard as it did but I have not gotten over it yet." After two brief paragraphs of casual remarks, Stone added: "Pardon this being so short but I still don't have a lot of pep for writing letters because of Bill." It would appear that Stone's rejection of Faulkner was not quite so total as the popular myth contends.

[12] As Joseph Blotner has pointed out, Stone violated this general principle on at least one occasion, in 1959 when he sold some of the Faulkner manuscripts in his possession to the University of Texas. See *Faulkner: A Biography* (New York: Random House, 1974), pp. 1719–1720.

One additional group of letters which deserves special mention is the file of correspondence relating to Ruth Ford's involvement with *Requiem for a Nun* and other Faulkner works, most notably *Light in August*. Nearly fifty such letters are printed here, most of which derive from Miss Ford's association with Arnold Weissberger and Aaron Frosch, the New York theatrical lawyers who represented the actress and her husband Zachary Scott for several years. The letters selected for inclusion in this volume present a detailed history of the stage production of *Requiem for a Nun*—from its opening in Bournemouth, England, on November 11, 1957, through its month-long engagement at the Royal Court Theatre in London, its American premiere at the Shubert Theater in New Haven, Connecticut, on January 7, 1959, its subsequent failure on Broadway after only forty-three performances, and its planned revival by Miss Ford and various associates, either as a touring road show or in an adapted reading version suitable for presentation to college audiences. These letters record not only the financial and theatrical history of the play but also the strong personal and emotional attachment which sustained Miss Ford's devotion to *Requiem for a Nun* for more than a decade. Other letters in this grouping document the Scotts' acquisition (in partnership with Harvey Breit) of the movie rights to *Light in August* in 1959 and their extensive but unsuccessful efforts to arrange for a quality film, preferably to be directed by noted filmmaker Jean Renoir, based on that novel.

There are other impressive letters contained in this volume which, while not as important as the ones cited above, nevertheless piece out significant areas of Faulkner's life and career. Some thirty letters and memoranda from the files of Warner Bros. mirror Faulkner's complicated dealings with that film studio in the 1940s. A letter Faulkner wrote to a friend in Memphis in 1924 provides an interesting self-portrait from the period when Faulkner thought of himself as a rising poet. A sequence of seven letters documents Faulkner's involvement with President Dwight D. Eisenhower's People-to-People Program. A letter by Robert Daniel describes the first major exhibition of Faulkner's work—that mounted by Daniel at Yale University in 1942. A letter by Lawrance Thompson represents, in effect, an unpublished contemporary review of *A Fable;* and another letter, by Ward Miner, presents a first-person account of Faulkner's appearance at the Twentieth Century Masterpieces festival in Paris in 1952. Correspondence by James W. Silver and others discusses Faulkner's participation in the controversial meeting of the Southern Historical Association in Memphis in 1955.

In short, the letters published in this volume significantly contribute to the expanding and shifting mosaic still being fashioned from the artifacts which have survived to document Faulkner's complex life and career.

Robert W. Hamblin
Cape Girardeau, Missouri
August 10, 1983

EDITORIAL NOTES

THE LETTERS IN THIS VOLUME are arranged in chronological order. Such an arrangement is employed to enable the reader to follow the constantly refracting interplay of events, personages, actions, and ideas. Individuals who prefer to read the letters in units relating to particular topics or persons may, of course, utilize the index to locate such groupings.

For purposes of correlation, letters listed in *Faulkner: A Comprehensive Guide to the Brodsky Collection, Volume I: The Biobibliography,* have been assigned the same catalogue numbers in this present volume. Letters added to the collection since the compilation of the previous volume are indicated by an "S" (Supplement) prefix.

For the most part the editors have retained the stylistic idiosyncrasies of the various letter writers. For example, Faulkner's use of comma splices and British spellings, Estelle Faulkner's employment of dashes instead of periods, and the loose punctuation of many of Phil Stone's long, flowing sentences (typed by secretaries but presumably edited by Stone) have not been corrected in transcription. Similarly, the varied handling of titles—some italicized, some placed in quotation marks, some printed in capital letters, some not punctuated at all—has been copied from the respective authors.

Exceptions have been made to this general rule only when required to prevent confusion of meaning. Punctuation has been occasionally added or altered in the interest of clarity. Obvious typographical errors and misspellings have been silently corrected. In several instances dashes have been substituted for the writers' use of spaced periods, in order to eliminate possible confusion with omissions of text marked by ellipses.

All material interpolated by the editors, such as the assignment of dates to undated letters, has been enclosed in brackets.

Footnotes have been kept to a minimum, with information generally not being repeated after the first mention. In several instances the appropriate information to allow for a full and clear documentation was unavailable.

Except for the letters written by Faulkner, no special attempt has been made to identify the place of composition, although in most cases that location is clearly implied in the contents or evidenced by postmark. In the case of Faulkner's letters, unless otherwise noted in the headnote, letter, or footnote, the place of composition should be understood by the reader to be Oxford.

The availability of additional information and the luxury of hindsight have enabled the compilers to correct several errors appearing in Volume I. In those few instances in which the two volumes do not agree, Volume II should be taken as authoritative.

All photographs used as illustrations in the present volume are included in the Brodsky Collection.

Faulkner

A Comprehensive Guide to the Brodsky Collection

Volume II: The Letters

1924

39 Letter from Faulkner to Mrs. Homer K. Jones, dated "Oxford, Miss./2 Dec. 1924," signed autograph manuscript, 1 page, with envelope addressed in Faulkner's hand and postmarked Oxford, December 4, 1924.

My dear Mrs. Jones[1]—

I seem to recall, when Mr Kelly and I were with you one evening last week,[2] giving you a copy of one of my poems.[3] Mr Kelly and I were having such a grand time then that I dont know what I wrote; whatever it was, I am sure it is undecipherable, so I am taking the liberty of sending you a correct copy of the verse, as you are interested in literature. Also this was [the] poem which I tried so unsuccessfully to recite.

I am sorry to have needlessly annoyed you about the pipe and scarf. The pipe I later found, having left it somewhere else. The muffler I had after we left you, I am reliably informed. What I am asking pardon for, is failing to call you again as I should. Almost immediately after calling you that morning I was arrested on a moral charge,[4] and by the time I was a free agent again, I had forgotten it. Please forgive me, and thank you for the whisky-and-soda. I dont know whether I drank it or not, but it was a beautiful tipple.

Please give my regards to Mr Jones.

Sincerely yours,
William Faulkner

[1] Wife of a prominent Memphis physician.

[2] At the Joneses' residence, 1508 Vinton Avenue, Memphis. For a detailed discussion of the incident described in this letter, see Louis Daniel Brodsky, "William Faulkner: Poet at Large," *Southern Review,* 18 (Fall 1982), 767–775.

[3] "Pregnacy." Both this copy and the "correct copy" Faulkner enclosed with this letter are now in the Brodsky Collection.

[4] Presumably drunkenness, although the Memphis Police Department has no record of such an arrest.

1925

588 Transcribed copy (by Robert Daniel)[1] of note from Faulkner to Vance ("Vannye") Carter Witt, dated "Something of September Friday, anyway" [probably September 11, 1925]. Written in Paris.

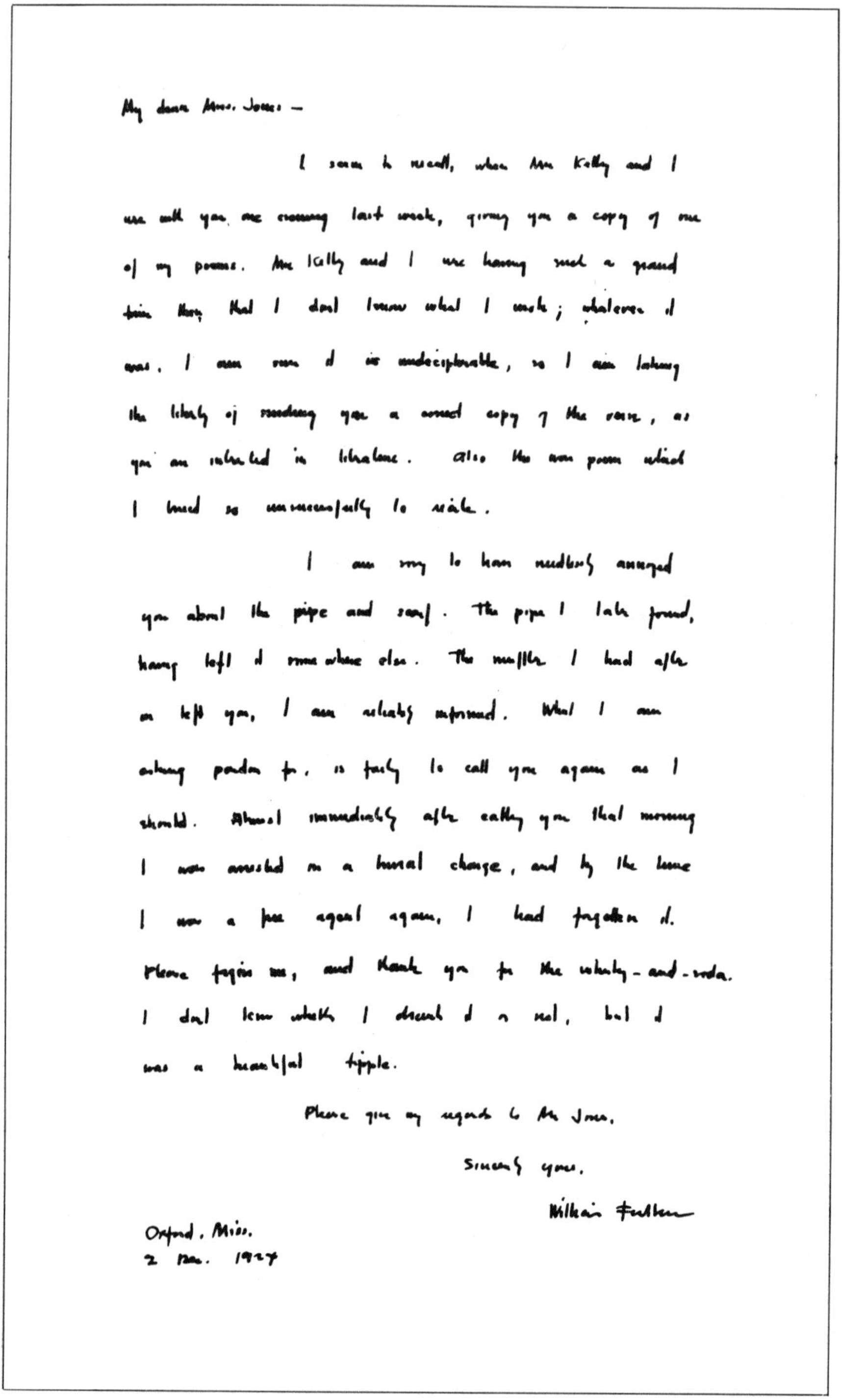

My dear Mrs. Jones —

I seem to recall, when Mr Kelly and I were with you one evening last week, giving you a copy of one of my poems. Mr Kelly and I were having such a grand time then that I don't know what I wrote; whatever it was, I am sure it is undecipherable, so I am taking the liberty of sending you a correct copy of the same, as you are interested in literature. Also the one poem which I tried so unsuccessfully to recite.

I am sorry to have needlessly annoyed you about the pipe and scarf. The pipe I later found, having left it somewhere else. The muffler I had after we left you, I am reliably informed. What I am asking pardon for, is failing to call you again as I should. Almost immediately after calling you that morning I was arrested on a burial charge, and by the time I was a free agent again, I had forgotten it. Please forgive me, and thank you for the whisky-and-soda. I don't know whether I drank it or not, but it was a beautiful tipple.

Please give my regards to Mr Jones.

Sincerely yours,

William Faulkner

Oxford, Miss.
2 Dec. 1924

1. Letter from Faulkner to Mrs. Homer K. Jones of Memphis (item 39)

Vannye, I just had a letter from Aunt Bama telling me you are in Paris. I am leaving my address,[2] so you can let me know when to call on you. The last time I saw you that I remember, I was 3 years old and crying: you and Natalie[3] had brought me home from Aunt Willie's[4] in Ripley, where I had gone to spend the night, and I lost my nerve. You held a kerosene lamp, and your hair looked like honey.[5]

William C. Falkner

[1] In 1942 Robert Daniel borrowed eight early Faulkner letters then in the possession of 'Bama McLean for use in the Faulkner exhibit which Daniel arranged for Yale University Library. Daniel's typewritten transcriptions of these letters, along with other materials relating to the Yale exhibit, were acquired by Brodsky in 1978. Four of the letters, and portions of two others, have been published in *Selected Letters of William Faulkner;* the remaining letters and excerpts appear for the first time in the present volume.

[2] Faulkner presumably left this note for Vannye at her hotel. Beneath his signature Faulkner listed his Paris address as 26 rue Servandoni.

[3] Vannye's sister.

[4] Willie Medora Falkner Carter, sister to 'Bama McLean and mother of Vannye and Natalie.

[5] For another account of this same childhood incident see *Selected Letters of William Faulkner,* p. 20.

55 Pseudonymous letter by Faulkner, from "Ernest V. Simms" to "Mr. H. Mencken, magazine orthur," dated "Paris, (France) / November 1st. 1925," carbon typescript, 1 page.

Gentlemen

Enclosed at your usual rate are poem by Wm Faulkner.[1] He wants to get a start at poetry. And I advise him to try your magazine after I made the corrections because my family is long a reader of your magazine until a train reck 2 years ago. Since I have read your magazine personally since I am not 1 of those who reads only for pleasure.

I think our Americans poets will be good as any foregner with encouragments and corrections since reading your magazine feel sure you feel the same sentiment. Give young americans chances to make good with advice and corrections say I. I onley made corrections in the above poem without changing its sentiments because the poet himself quit schools before learning to write because I have a typewritter.

I feel sure that you feel the same.

respectfully yours &etc.
/t/Ernest V. Simms

Ernest V. Simms
Baptist Young Peoples Union
care American Ambassdor
Paris (France)
(American Citizen)

[1] The poem was "Ode to the Louver." Faulkner mailed the humorous poem and letter to Phil Stone. See Brodsky and Hamblin, *Faulkner: A Comprehensive Guide to the Brodsky Collection,* I, pp. 42–45.

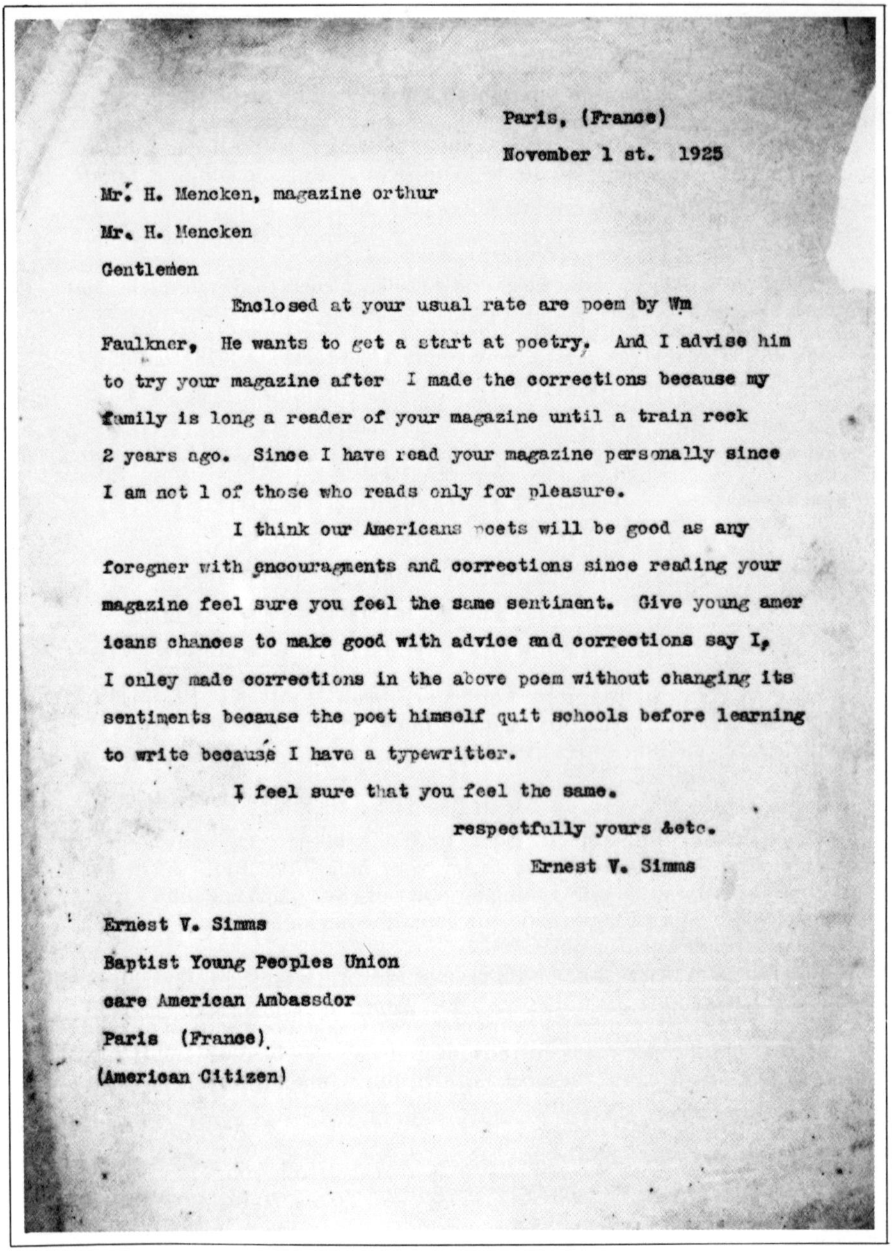

Paris, (France)

November 1 st. 1925

Mr. H. Mencken, magazine orthur

Mr. H. Mencken

Gentlemen

Enclosed at your usual rate are poem by Wm Faulkner, He wants to get a start at poetry. And I advise him to try your magazine after I made the corrections because my family is long a reader of your magazine until a train reck 2 years ago. Since I have read your magazine personally since I am not 1 of those who reads only for pleasure.

I think our Americans poets will be good as any foregner with encouragments and corrections since reading your magazine feel sure you feel the same sentiment. Give young amer icans chances to make good with advice and corrections say I, I onley made corrections in the above poem without changing its sentiments because the poet himself quit schools before learning to write because I have a typewritter.

I feel sure that you feel the same.

respectfully yours &etc.

Ernest V. Simms

Ernest V. Simms
Baptist Young Peoples Union
care American Ambassdor
Paris (France)
(American Citizen)

2. Pseudonymous letter which Faulkner mailed, along with his "Ode to the Louver," to Phil Stone (item 55)

85 Letter from Jim Crowder, of Boni & Liveright, Publishers, to Saxe Commins, April 29, 1927, signed ribbon typescript, 1 page.

Dear Commins:

What a stupid error about your book.[1] I offer you a thousand apologies. I am at once sending six copies to you, and when Faulkner returns the ones he got by mistake I'll simply return them to stock.

I meant to write and thank you for your warm and cordial letter to Donald Friede. I do hope the book has a fine circulation. I am reading it now and I am enjoying it hugely.

Yours,

/s/ Jim

[1]Through an error in packaging, six author's copies of Commins' *Psychology: A Simplification* had been mailed to Faulkner and six copies of Faulkner's *Mosquitoes* had been mailed to Commins. The story of this ironic convergence of Faulkner and Commins almost a decade before they were associates at Random House has been recorded by Dorothy Commins in *What Is an Editor?: Saxe Commins at Work* (Chicago: University of Chicago Press, 1978), p. 194.

c. 1927

588 Transcribed copy (by Robert Daniel) of letter from Faulkner to 'Bama McLean, dated "Wednesday" [probably late September 1927].

Dear Aunt Bama—

No, ma'am, I dont think I'll come to Mrs Boyle's shindig[1]—I committed the mistake of going once—wild-eyed woman that smell bad yelling "Poet, O Poet, come down from thy Mountain" while the biggest steer in Tennessee was having indigestion outside the room. But I reckon Mrs Boyle can get along without me as easily as I can without her.[2]

Grandest weather. I finished the book today.[3] Will get it off tomorrow, and next time I come up, I'll try [?] it to you. I dont know when that'll be, as I have a job of work I'll be doing this month. Painting signs.

Much love

William

[1]Tennessee poet Virginia Frayser Boyle, who (according to information supplied to Daniel by Mrs. McLean) had invited Faulkner to speak to a Book Club at the Memphis Fairgrounds during the Tri-State Fair.

[2]This paragraph is omitted from the version of this letter printed in *Selected Letters of William Faulkner,* p. 38.

[3]Presumably *Flags in the Dust.*

c. 1928

588 Transcribed copy (by Robert Daniel) of letter from Faulkner to 'Bama McLean, dated "Oxford,/Thursday" [probably Spring 1928].

Dear Aunt Bama—

I've been thinking that I'd get to Memphis again soon, and also I have been trying to get the mss.[1] in some sort of intelligible shape to send you. But neither has come to pass, so I am sending the press clippings, and when I do get the script in order, I'll send it too. Every day or so I burn some of it up and rewrite it, and at present it is almost incoherent. So much so that I've got a little weary of it and I think I shall put it away for a while and forget about it.

We are all very well; I told the family that you had almost promised to drive down and see us. We all wish you would. I have something—someone, I mean—to show you, if you only would. Of course it's a woman.[2] I would like to see you taken with her utter charm, and intrigued by her utter shallowness. Like a lovely vase. It isn't even empty, but is filled with something—well, a yeast cake in water is the nearest simile that occurs to me. She gets the days passed for me, though. Thank God I've got no money, or I'd marry her. So you see, even Poverty looks after its own.[3]

Love to Uncle Walter.

William

[1] Presumably *Flags in the Dust.*

[2] Probably Estelle Oldham Franklin, whom Faulkner married the following year.

[3] This paragraph is omitted from the version of this letter published in *Selected Letters of William Faulkner,* pp. 40–41.

1931

---

194 Western Union telegram from Faulkner to 'Bama McLean, January 19, 1931.

ALABAMA FALKNER[1] BORN SUNDAY BOTH WELL LOVE

WILLIAM

[1] Faulkner's first child, named after his beloved great aunt, Alabama Falkner McLean.

195 Western Union telegram from Holland Wilkins, Faulkner's aunt, to 'Bama McLean, January 20, 1931.

WILLIAMS BABY DIED THIS MORNING

HOLLAND

245a Letter from Phil Stone to E. Byrne Hackett, proprietor of Brick Row Book Shop, New York, June 17, 1931, unsigned carbon typescript, 2 pages.

Dear Mr. Hackett:

You doubtless remember that when William Faulkner first conceived the idea that he wanted to write I was the one who lent him books, and encouraged him. I read all of his stuff, advised and criticised, furnished him with money off and on and generally carried him forward until he was self-sustaining both financially and artistically.

He started out with the idea that he wanted to be a poet—according to the proverb that all good novelists are poets in their youth. The first book he had published was a little group of poems, "The Marble Faun," in 1924. I put up the money to pay the Four Seas Company for publishing one thousand copies[1] and this was the only edition published.

At the time I tried to sell as many copies as possible in order to get my money back. Especially I tried to interest the friends of myself and Bill's in the book and Bill autographed several presentation copies most of which we sold. Some of the people did not pay for their copies and I have on hand four autographed presentation copies besides my own. We have had several financial reverses and I am willing to sell these four copies—I would not sell my own copy, of course—if the price offered justifies.

Even at a high price these copies would be a good buy for a collector. Bill is already one of the leading figures in American literature. He is already established and his reputation is going to grow because the achievement will be forthcoming.

In addition to that he was always very stingy with autographs and has quit altogether now. He says that he is not going to give any more autographs except to me, his Mother and four or five friends. So the autographs will grow rarer and rarer and if any collectors want autographs from him they had better get them now.

Also this is the only book of verse he has had published and it is probable that it will always be the only one. He has written no verse for years and will probably never write any more.

Bill told me that a copy of "The Marble Faun" unautographed, sold not long ago for twenty-five dollars.

I am going to sell these four copies to somebody but Bill and I both remember you most pleasantly and he wanted me to give you the first chance at them. If you want them make me a price.

Also, if you wish, I will also autograph each of them since I wrote the preface and will authorize you to sell this letter with the books. This is only for you as a matter of friendship for you on the part of Bill and myself and to give you the chance to make some money and I will not do this for anyone but you or Al Delacey to whom I shall offer the books next if you are not interested.

Bill and I think of you frequently and hope that you are doing well. Whenever we come to New York again we shall come to see you.

Your friend,
[no signature]

[1]Cf. statement in Stone's letter to Robert Daniel, April 6, 1942, printed in this volume.

245b Letter from Phil Stone to Paul Leahy, book collector from Wilmington, Delaware, July 29, 1931, unsigned carbon typescript, 2 pages.

Dear Sir:

I have your letter with reference to "The Marble Faun."

I have only one copy of the first edition of "Soldiers' Pay" and would not care to sell that.

I am the man who started William Faulkner on his literary career, lent him books, encouraged him and backed him with money. I know his talent and we

L

July 29, 1931

Hon. Paul Leahy

% Ward & Gray

Delaware Trust Bldg.

Wilimington, Delaware

Dear Sir:

I have your letter with reference to "The Marble Faun".

I have only one copy of the first edition of "Soldiers' Pay" and would not care to sell that.

I am the man who started William Faulkner on his literary career, lent him books, encouraged him and backed him with money. I know his talent and we are the Closest personal friends and have been such since childhood, living here in the same town.

In 1924, in order to give him some publicity, I raised the money to pay the Four Seas Company to publish a very small book of Faulkner's verse by the title of "The Marble Faun" and wrote the preface for the same myself. Only 1000 copies were printed. In order to break even on the thing I tried to get acquaintances of his and of mine to buy the books and made autographed presentation copies of several but a few people did not take their books and I now have on hand a few of these copies besides my own. Faulkner is willing for me to sell these for what I can get in order to get back some of the money I put out.

He has not given many autographs and quit giving them sometime ago except to myself and a few very close personal friends. He says he is not going to give any more except such forthcoming books as may be published in the future and then only as regular autographed editions and announced by his publishers. Otherwise he refuses to give autographs.

He told me several months ago that an unautographed copy of "The Marble Faun" sold for $25.00. I am holding the few autographed presentation copies I have for $35.00 each. This is probably more than the book is worth but knowing the situation as I do and knowing Faulkner

3. A Phil Stone letter which survived the 1942 house fire (item 245b)

Page 2.

as I do I think the collectors will be glad before long to pick these copies up at that price. In fact, I have already sold one of the copies at that price and have refused $50.00 a copy for them.

As for the book itself and its verses it is not worth much. It is just about the average first book of poems. Its value lies in its rarety and in its autographs and should interest only someone who wants a complete edition of Faulkner's works or some collector who is buying it for a resale.

Faulkner and myself both have constant inquires for these copies and I am going to sell them to the first person who meets my price. So if you want one you had better wire me. I will not agree to hold the books because they may be sold before I hear from you.

Yours truly,

____

PS:MS

are the closest personal friends and have been such since childhood, living here in the same town.

In 1924, in order to give him some publicity, I raised the money to pay the Four Seas Company to publish a very small book of Faulkner's verse by the title of "The Marble Faun" and wrote the preface for the same myself. Only 1000 copies were printed. In order to break even on the thing I tried to get acquaintances of his and of mine to buy the books and made autographed presentation copies of several but a few people did not take their books and I now have on hand a few of these copies besides my own. Faulkner is willing for me to sell these for what I can get in order to get back some of the money I put out.

He has not given many autographs and quit giving them sometime ago except to myself and a few very close personal friends. He says he is not going to give any more except such forthcoming books as may be published in the future and then only as regular autographed editions and announced by his publishers. Otherwise he refuses to give autographs.

He told me several months ago that an unautographed copy of "The Marble Faun" sold for $25.00. I am holding the few autographed presentation copies I have for $75.00 each. This is probably more than the book is worth but knowing the situation as I do and knowing Faulkner as I do I think the collectors will be glad before long to pick these copies up at that price. In fact, I have already sold one of the copies at that price and have refused $50.00 a copy for them.

As for the book itself and its verses it is not worth much. It is just about the average first book of poems. Its value lies in its rarity and in its autographs and should interest only someone who wants a complete edition of Faulkner's works or some collector who is buying it for a resale.

Faulkner and myself both have constant inquiries for these copies and I am going to sell them to the first person who meets my price. So if you want one you had better wire me. I will not agree to hold the books because they may be sold before I hear from you.

Yours truly,
[no signature]

262 Letter from Phil Stone to Faulkner, November 2, 1931, unsigned carbon typescript, 1 page.

Dear Bill:

Try your best and see if you can't get up some buyers for the "Marble Faun." I simple must have some money.

Look around[1] too and see if you cannot find some sort of hack work I can do in the way of writing, book reviews or advertisments. I simply must add to the amount of money which I am making.

Everything here seems to be allright.

Your friend,
[no signature]

[1] Faulkner was in New York. Stone addressed this letter c/o Cape & Smith, Faulkner's publisher.

1932

284 Letter from Phil Stone to Lester C. Franklin, Chairman, Mississippi State Tax Commission, April 4, 1932, unsigned carbon typescript, 1 page.

Dear Lester:

I herewith inclose your letter of April 1st. and Income Tax Return of my friend, William Faulkner. If I understand this letter correctly the sum paid for debts is not deductible. If this is correct please send me two more blanks. Mr. Faulkner has some other taxes and expenses which he did not charge up because the present return showed that he would have to pay no tax. He is paying for a house and I will appreciate you advising me if this is deductible. Thank you.

Your friend,
[no signature]

c. 1932

588 Transcribed copy (by Robert Daniel) of letter from Faulkner to Evelyn Harter, member of the publishing firm of Cape and Smith, undated [c. 1932].

Dear Evelyn—

Your note received. I have not forgot about Mr Adler,[1] but I am still too busy writing the stuff to have time to even wonder myself how or why it gets printed. Tell him the best way I know to get published is to borrow advances from the publisher; then they have to print the stuff.

Bill F

[P.S.] Love to Louise[2]

[1] Elmer Adler, the publisher and one of the editors of *The Colophon.* In the early 1930s Adler published in *The Colophon* a series of twenty essays by well-known authors explaning how they first got published. These and related essays were subsequently collected in *Breaking into Print,* ed. Adler (New York: Simon and Schuster, 1937). Sherwood Anderson, Pearl Buck, James Branch Cabell, Theodore Dreiser, Sinclair Lewis, E. A. Robinson, Edith Wharton, and others cooperated with Adler on his series, but Faulkner characteristically did not.

[2] Louise Bonino, an associate of Evelyn Harter at Cape and Smith.

1935

376 Letter from W. M. "Mac" Reed to Mrs. F. V. B. Demarest, March 27, 1935, signed ribbon typescript, 2 pages, with envelope.

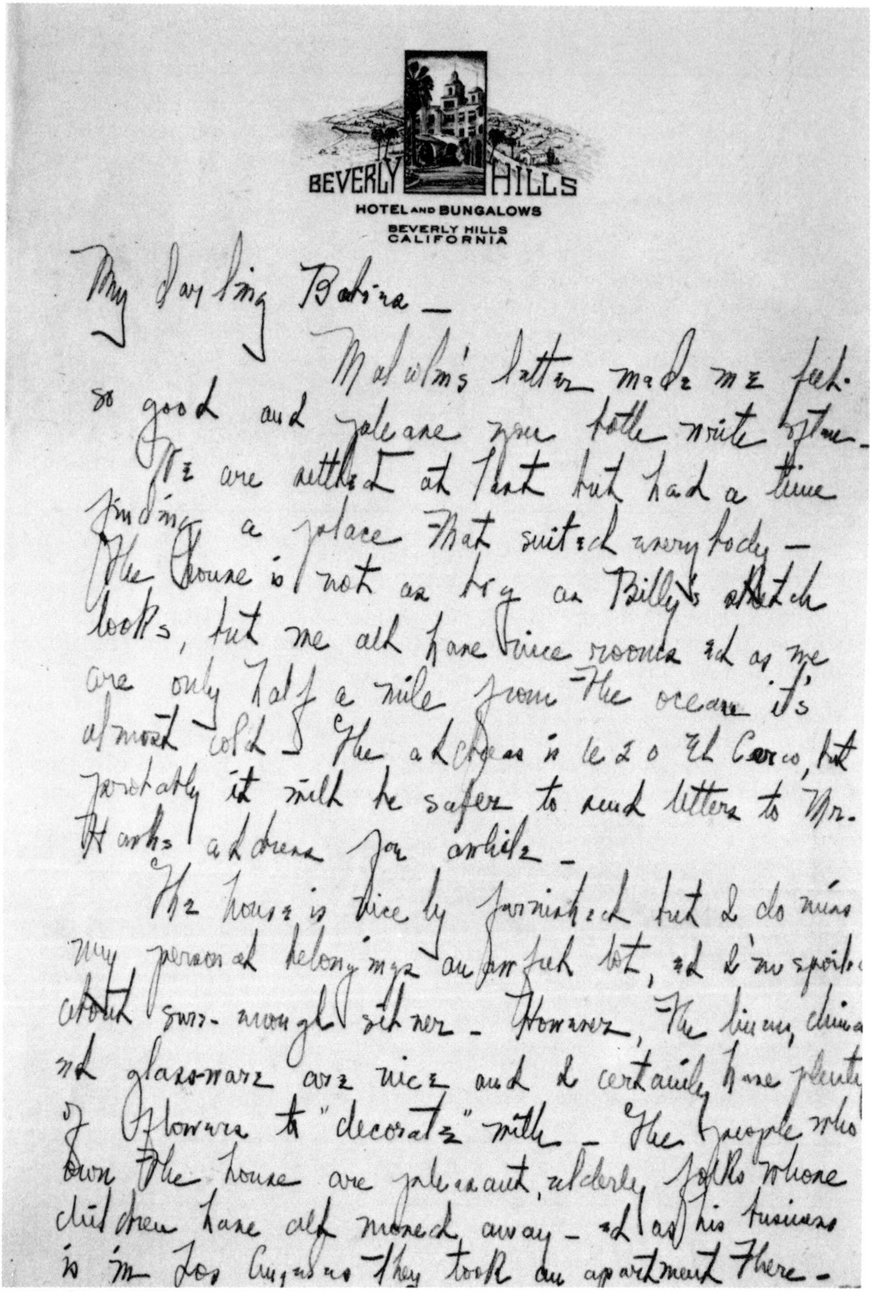

BEVERLY HILLS
HOTEL AND BUNGALOWS
BEVERLY HILLS
CALIFORNIA

My darling Babies—

Malcolm's letter made me feel so good and please you both write often—
We are settled at last but had a time finding a place that suited everybody— The house is not as big as Billy's sketch looks, but we all have nice rooms and as we are only half a mile from the ocean it's almost cold— The address is 620 El Camino, but probably it will be safer to send letters to Mr. Hawks' address for awhile—

The house is nicely furnished but I do miss my personal belongings an awful lot, and I'm spoiled about surroundings either— However, the linen, china and glassware are nice and I certainly have plenty of flowers to "decorate" with— The people who own the house are pleasant, elderly folks whose children have all moved away— and as his business is in Los Angeles they took an apartment there—

4. Letter from Estelle Faulkner to her two eldest children, July 27, 1936 (item 409)

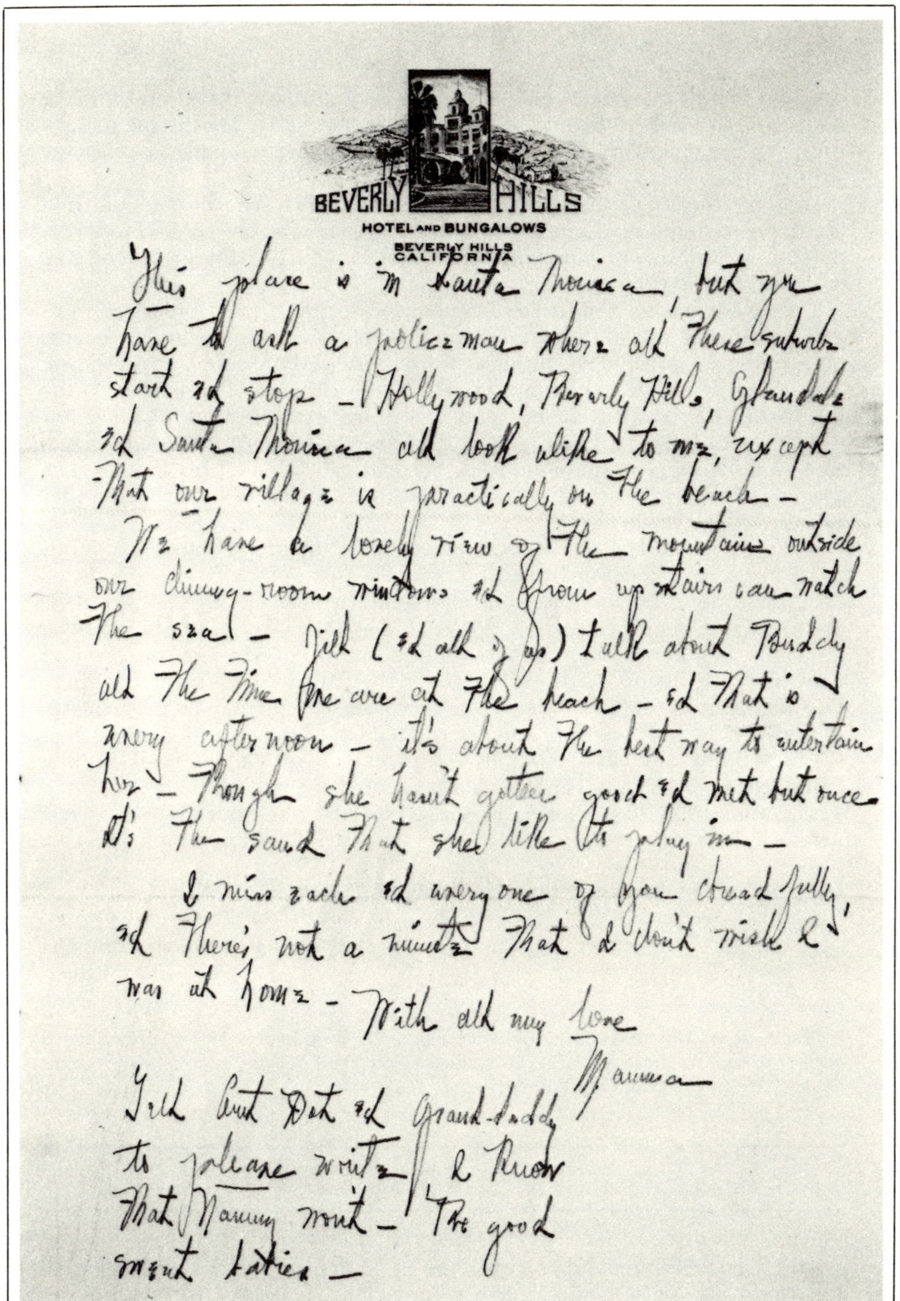
BEVERLY HILLS
HOTEL AND BUNGALOWS
BEVERLY HILLS
CALIFORNIA

This place is in Santa Monica, but you have to ask a policeman where all these suburbs start and stop — Hollywood, Beverly Hills, Glendale and Santa Monica all look alike to me, except that our village is practically on the beach —

We have a lovely view of the mountains outside our dining-room windows and from upstairs can watch the sea — Jill (and all of us) talk about Buddy all the time we are at the beach — and that is every afternoon — it's about the best way to entertain her — though she hasn't gotten good and wet but once. It's the sand that she likes to play in —

I miss each and every one of you dreadfully, and there's not a minute that I don't wish I was at home — With all my love

Mamma

Tell Aunt Dot and Grand-daddy to please write — I know that Nanny won't — the good sweet ladies —

Dear Mrs. Demarest[1]:

We are mailing to you today William's latest book, "Pylon," which was released Monday and reached us yesterday. His autograph for you bears the date of yesterday, 26th, but he made the entry just a few moments ago, fogetting the true date. It was the first time we had seen him since receiving your card last week.

We have never had any signed copies.[2] In fact, Bill has never done much of it and seems to get further away to himself as time goes on. He said today, as on other occasions when informed that you desired a book of his, "I'll be glad to do this for Myrtle."

The writer has his "Sanctuary," autographed; a gift from Bill some years ago. Surprise, it may be added. He might have thought some little favor had been rendered or some encouraging word expressed or some interest shown. The writer doesn't know but appreciates it, nevertheless. This in spite of the fact that he has not read the book nor any of his books. It wouldn't make any difference to Bill if he knew. Several of his short stories published in magazines have been genuinely enjoyed. Particularly "Thrift," his first in The Saturday Post years ago and, later, "Turn About," which was screened under title of "Today We Live."

Note the 5¢ stamps on the mailing wrapper containing your book. They came to us this morning from Kosciusko, Mississippi, to pay for medicine ordered. Only a few of this particular stamp issued—150th year since the great Polish General Kosciuszko joined forces with George Washington for the cause of liberty. Do you have a little stamp collector in your family? Kosciusko, Mississippi, is the only place in the United States named for him. Five places in the East—all having large Polish settlements—and Kosciusko, Miss., were the only towns or cities permitted to sell the stamps.

About Bill, again: His "Smoke" is in current issue of "Golden Book." It first appeared, we believe, in Harper's Magazine two or three years ago.

The amount of 51¢, shown "Brought Forward," on your account covers items we failed to extend to total on your statement last May. Think we wrote you.

Thanking you for your many kindnesses and with best wishes, we are

Sincerely,
Gathright-Reed Drug Company
By /s/ W M Reed

[1] Myrtle Ramey, a former schoolmate of Faulkner.

[2] Reed means here that his drug store has never had signed copies of Faulkner's books for sale. As the next paragraph makes clear, Faulkner did inscribe copies of his books to his dear friend "Mac" Reed.

1936

---

409 Letter from Estelle Faulkner to Malcolm and Victoria Franklin, undated, signed autograph manuscript, 2 pages, with envelope addressed in William Faulkner's hand to Malcolm Franklin and postmarked Beverly Hills, California, July 27, 1936.

My darling Babies—

Malcolm's letter made me feel so good and please you both write often—

We are settled at last but had a time finding a place that suited everybody—The house is not as big as Billy's sketch[1] looks, but we all have nice rooms and as we are only half a mile from the ocean it's almost cold—The address is 620 El Cerco, but probably it will be safer to send letters to Mr. Hawks'[2] address for awhile—

The house is nicely furnished but I do miss my personal belongings an awful lot, and I'm spoiled about sure-enough silver--However, the linens, china and glassware are nice and I certainly have plenty of flowers to "decorate" with—The people who own the house are pleasant, elderly folks whose children have all moved away—and as his business is in Los Angeles they took an apartment there—This place is in Santa Monica, but you have to ask a policeman where all these suburbs start and stop—Hollywood, Beverly Hills, Glendale and Santa Monica all look alike to me, except that *our* village is practically on the beach—

We have a lovely view of the mountains outside our dining-room windows and from upstairs can watch the sea—Jill (and all of us) talk about Buddy[3] all the time we are at the beach—and that is every afternoon—it's about the best way to entertain her—though she hasn't gotten good and wet but once—It's the sand that she likes to play in—

I miss each and every one of you dreadfully, and there's not a minute that I don't wish I was at home—

With all my love
Mamma

[P.S.] Tell Aunt Dot and Grand-daddy to *please* write, I know that Nanny won't[4]—Be good sweet babies—

[1] A facsimile of Faulkner's sketch of the house appears in Hamblin and Brodsky, *Selections from the William Faulkner Collection of Louis Daniel Brodsky* (Charlottesville: University Press of Virginia, 1979), p. 83.

[2] Film director Howard Hawks.

[3] That is, Malcolm Franklin.

[4] Reference here is to Dorothy, Lemuel, and Lida Oldham.

1941

S-1 Letter from Faulkner to "Mr. Nathan," dated "Oxford, Miss./ 18 Nov. 1941," signed ribbon typescript with two holograph revisions, 2 pages.

Dear Mr. Nathan:

Attached are a few suggestions re. the script 'THE DAMNED DONT CRY' which was sent to me.[1] I was unable to get the book here and had to order it from a dealer. When it comes, I can tell more about the story, and will then airmail to you a story outline. The following are faults as I see them in the script sent me. They could be corrected by beefing up the dialog and incidents in the script as it is. But I believe a different story line would get more of the meat out of it.

5. Faulkner, c. 1936

6. Faulkner family and guests at hunt breakfast, Rowan Oak, May 8, 1938

7. Faulkner with his daughter Jill, Rowan Oak, 1939

As I see it, the principal fault is in the plot. It fails to state a definite problem, moral, personal, or sociological, and then proceed to solve it.

The reason for this failure lies in ZELDA, assuming that this is her story, or at least that she is the principal and therefore motivating character. She has an illegitimate child, and loves it too much to repudiate it completely. Perfectly natural. She deserves no special approbation for this. She conceals the fact. That is perfectly natural too. Unmarried, the world's moral set-up would force her to do that, unless (1) She were a woman of unusual character, or (2) She were doing it for the child's good and at a sacrifice to herself, which would require character and would deserve admiration. She does it for neither of these reasons, but simply because Mrs Grundy says she must.

When the fact of the child's existence breaks, a woman of exceptional character would have risen superior to the crisis and beaten it and so have gained admiration; perhaps she would have had to choose between the child and herself and gained admiration and pity both. Or she may have been completely beaten by it and so have gained pity, even if nothing else. ZELDA does neither. She simply shrieks and faints and after a while comes to, whereupon, thanks to the frantic efforts of everybody else in the picture except her, the situation is unchanged and therefore none of it need ever have taken place. Apparently ZELDA wants a lot and she just sits and wants it until enough people rally around to attend to getting it for her.

Maybe this story is already in the script, and I just failed to see it. If this is so, and the script is an approved story line, it can be rewritten and beefed up and emphasised when necessary, changed here and there perhaps, making ZELDA consistent, and building up to a climax which she must either survive or succumb to.

DAN strikes me as being a poor sort. The worst fate ZELDA could suffer would be marrying him, even a worse fate than a woman as poor in backbone as ZELDA appears, deserves.

And there is something wrong with Engstaad. He is the only man in the lot. He is almost TYLER, but ten times the man TYLER ever will be. He is the one she should have faded out with, unless something is done with DAN, either various stages of conflict shown between DAN and ZELDA, or an undeviating fidelity despite all odds is shown between DAN and ZELDA.

I would take this script and start at page 1 and rewrite it, keeping fairly close to it when possible, but changing the incidents when necessary as I went along.

When I get the book, I will try a treatment and send it to you.[2]

/s/ William Faulkner

[1]Faulkner had been invited to revise a Warner Bros. script of Harry C. Hervey's novel, *The Damned Don't Cry* (1939).

[2]The nineteen-page treatment which Faulkner subsequently completed (now in the Brodsky Collection) was never expanded into a script.

1942

588a Letter from Ben F. Wasson, Sr., to Robert Daniel, March 16, 1942, signed ribbon typescript, 1 page.

Dear Mr. Daniel:

Mrs. Wasson requests me to write you in answer to your letter of the 12th. inst. to her.[1]

I am enclosing you the only paper Mrs. Wasson has been able to find from the pen of William Faulkner. I am of the opinion that Ben had something else by Faulkner which he carried with him to New York.

I fear this paper will not be of much value to you, but you are welcome to it for whatever it may be worth.

Ben is at sea, having left Norfolk, Va., on a plane carrier about two weeks ago, and we have not heard from him since his departure.

Yours very truly,
/s/ Ben F. Wasson

[1]Daniel wrote to Mrs. Wasson, Phil Stone, 'Bama McLean, and others to secure materials to display in an exhibit of Faulkner materials at Yale University. That exhibit, coordinated by Daniel and held in the summer of 1942, was the first major exhibit devoted to Faulkner's work and career.

588b Letter from Phil Stone to Robert Daniel, April 6, 1942, signed ribbon typescript, 2 pages.

Dear Mr. Daniel:

I have your letter of April 2 and am very much interested. Thank you for writing me.

I am afraid that I shall not be able to accomplish much with Faulkner. I shall try to get the manuscript for you but don't count on it.

About the only rare things I know of I had in our old hundred-year-old home which burned this winter. There were a lot of Faulkner's original manuscripts, letters, the original to the preface of "The Marble Faun" and many other things.

With reference to "The Marble Faun," I do not know how many copies were printed because The Four Seas Company gypped us on this thing. I put up the money to pay them to publish it in order to get Faulkner before the public and I don't think they ever did print the thousand copies they were supposed to publish. I also bought a number of these copies and had Faulkner autograph them for various people and tried to sell them to these people. It is most amusing nowadays to see some of these same people trying to get autographs out of Faulkner when they had refused to pay $1.50 for their autograph presentation copy of "The Marble Faun." I lost about twenty of these copies when our home burned.

With reference to Horace Benbow, I really suspect that I am the original of Horace Benbow. It is so much trouble getting details out of Faulkner in oral conversation that I long ago gave up trying to find out.

A. Wigfall Green is in the English Department here at the University of Mississippi (or was before he went into the Army) and is a most reliable person. However, I don't know much about his statements as to Faulkner.[1] He is not close to Faulkner and Bill has a way of telling people anything they want to know and this has been the origin for a lot of fairy tales about Faulkner. Faulkner was born in New Albany, Mississippi, lived in Ripley a while and came to Oxford as a little boy. He was not wounded in France during the last war nor was he wounded anywhere else. He never got to France although he did get a commission in the R.A.F. His wound consisted of hurting his head

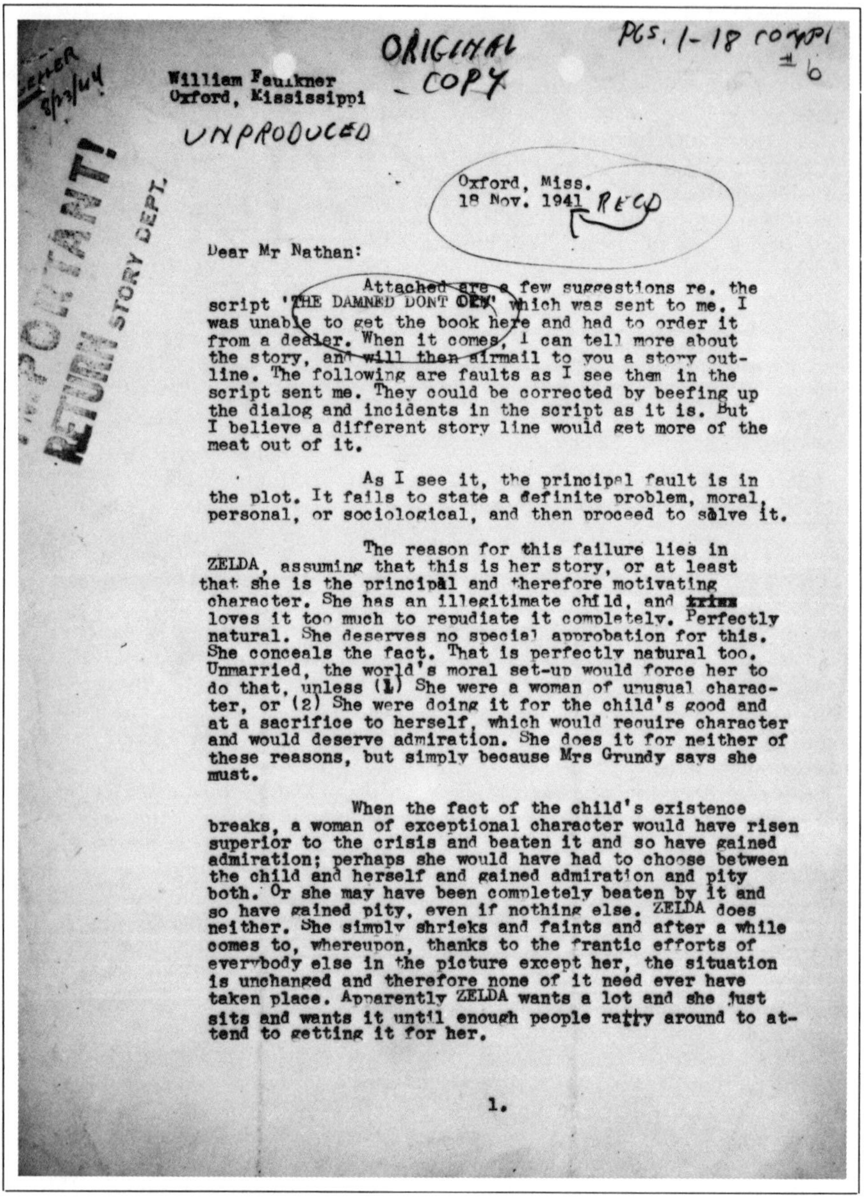

ORIGINAL COPY

PGS. 1-18 COMPL #6

William Faulkner
Oxford, Mississippi

UNPRODUCED

IMPORTANT! RETURN STORY DEPT.

Oxford, Miss.
18 Nov. 1941 RECD

Dear Mr Nathan:

Attached are a few suggestions re. the script 'THE DAMNED DONT CRY' which was sent to me. I was unable to get the book here and had to order it from a dealer. When it comes, I can tell more about the story, and will then airmail to you a story outline. The following are faults as I see them in the script sent me. They could be corrected by beefing up the dialog and incidents in the script as it is. But I believe a different story line would get more of the meat out of it.

As I see it, the principal fault is in the plot. It fails to state a definite problem, moral, personal, or sociological, and then proceed to solve it.

The reason for this failure lies in ZELDA, assuming that this is her story, or at least that she is the principal and therefore motivating character. She has an illegitimate child, and loves it too much to repudiate it completely. Perfectly natural. She deserves no special approbation for this. She conceals the fact. That is perfectly natural too. Unmarried, the world's moral set-up would force her to do that, unless (1) She were a woman of unusual character, or (2) She were doing it for the child's good and at a sacrifice to herself, which would require character and would deserve admiration. She does it for neither of these reasons, but simply because Mrs Grundy says she must.

When the fact of the child's existence breaks, a woman of exceptional character would have risen superior to the crisis and beaten it and so have gained admiration; perhaps she would have had to choose between the child and herself and gained admiration and pity both. Or she may have been completely beaten by it and so have gained pity, even if nothing else. ZELDA does neither. She simply shrieks and faints and after a while comes to, whereupon, thanks to the frantic efforts of everybody else in the picture except her, the situation is unchanged and therefore none of it need ever have taken place. Apparently ZELDA wants a lot and she just sits and wants it until enough people rally around to attend to getting it for her.

1.

8. Letter from Faulkner to Warner Bros. regarding the movie script, "The Damned Don't Cry" (item S-1)

Damned Dont ~~Die~~ Cry cont. Faulkner

Maybe this story is already in the script, and I just failed to see it. If this is so, and the script is an approved story line, it can be rewritten and beefed up and emphasised when necessary, changed here and there perhaps, making ZELDA consistent, and building up to a climax which she must either survive or succumb to.

DAN strikes me as being a poor sort. The worst fate ZELDA could suffer would be marrying him, even a worse fate than a woman as poor in backbone as ZELDA appears, deserves.

And there is something wrong with Engstaad. He is the only man in the lot. He is almost TYLER, but ten times the man TYLER ever will be. He is the one she should have faded out with, unless something is done with DAN, either various stages of conflict shown between DAN and ZELDA, or an undeviating fidelity despite all odds is shown between DAN and ZELDA.

I would take this script and start at page 1 and rewrite it, keeping fairly close to it when possible, but changing the incidents when necessary as I went along.

When I get the book, I will try a treatment and send it to you.

William Faulkner

and foot a little in a plane accident when he got drunk the day of the Armistice.

Write me for any information you want about him and I shall be glad to give it to you. From the years I spent in New Haven, I don't think its cultural level needs raising as much as does that of Oxford. After all, Faulkner is getting credit for being a much better writer than he is. I am disappointed that he has not developed into a better writer and I am afraid he has already reached his peak.

Please give my love to Arthur Head and see if you cannot persuade him to write me or to come to see me one of these days.

Yours truly,
/s/ Phil Stone
/t/ Phil Stone

[1]Green's article, "William Faulkner at Home," *Sewanee Review*, 40 (Summer 1932), 294–306, while important as one of the earliest biographical treatments of Faulkner, is erroneous in its account of Faulkner's wartime experiences.

588c Letter from Phil Stone to Robert Daniel, April 25, 1942, signed ribbon typescript, 2 pages.

Dear Mr. Daniel:

I have your letter of April 22.

There were several issues of the Oxford Magazine, three I think, and I had an article on Faulkner in all of them.[1] However, my copies of the magazine were burned when our home burned. Perhaps I can find copies somewhere else and if I can, I shall borrow them and send them to you with the understanding that you will take good care of them and return them to me as soon as you have finished with them.

The chances for getting the manuscript practically do not exist but I shall keep on trying Faulkner on it and will just do my best.

You seem to be talking about Faulkner's reputation as a writer while I am talking about his literary merit. The truth is that none of the contemporary novelists have the stuff that the old ones seem to have had although in the last book which Hemingway wrote,[2] he seems to have been better than ever before. The present day boys seem to make a virtue of being half undressed. I am not talking about their literary morals but about their performances. They, especially Faulkner, seem to make virtues of all their literary faults and seem to think that it is a cardinal sin to be coherent. They usually copy all the faults of James Joyce (who had something of genius) and very few of Joyce's virtues. I am reminded of what Oscar Wilde said about Zola when he said that Zola had said genius was never clever and that Zola had proved that if he could not be a genius, he could at least be dull. Our contemporary novelists seem to prove that if they cannot be geniuses they can at least be obscure and incoherent. Several weeks ago, Faulkner gave me a copy of his last book of short stories "Go Down Moses." I think the best prose in it is in the dedication to Aunt Caroline. What Faulkner should do is to strike out on a new vein like "The Hamlet." If he ever completes the Snopes saga, it will be the best thing that he has done yet. For several years, he has mainly been rewriting Faulkner at Faulkner's worst and I think he is all washed up unless he breaks the mold and starts over again. This disappoints me a great deal. I labored many years when Faulkner was underrated as a writer and now for several years he [has] been overrated as a writer.

Be sure to remember me again to Arthur Head and if I ever get up near New Haven, I am coming around to see him.

I don't know exactly what you are trying to put on but if you could arrange to pay the actual expenses of myself and my wife up there, we would come up there, provided I could spare the time, and give you lectures on Faulkner and his work and anything else you want. I would not want any money except the actual expenses.

Yours truly,
/s/ Phil Stone
/t/ Phil Stone

[1]The three issues of the *Oxford Magazine,* produced by Dale and Phil Mullen, appeared in 1934.
[2]*For Whom the Bell Tolls* (1940).

588d Letter from Phil Stone to Robert Daniel, May 12, 1942, signed ribbon typescript, 1 page.

Dear Mr. Daniel:

I have your letter of May 9.

I have not been able to find any copies of the Oxford Magazine nor have I been able to get the manuscript from Faulkner.

You can use anything you want to of what I said about the publication of "The Marble Faun" and you need not omit anything.

You can also use anything in the preface that you want. I wish I could be there and see the exhibit but I am afraid I would have too much to do this summer to make the trip anyway.

I almost forgot to say that it is true that Faulkner used to write out his stuff in longhand first in ink with a very minute handwriting and then type it. He still does this a little but, like most modern writers, he has gotten lazy and types most of it directly now.

Yours truly,
/s/ Phil Stone
/t/ Phil Stone

588e Letter from Robert Daniel to 'Bama McLean, July 4, 1942, signed ribbon typescript, 2 pages (1 leaf).

My dear Mrs. McLean:

You were awfully nice to write me at such length, and also to send the letters and poems—which were waiting for me on my return. It was really more convenient for me that you sent them directly here, as they had to get here by next week anyway.

Don't apologize for there not being more letters: they take a good deal of room to exhibit, and I expect the Librarian would squawk if I walked in with a bushel of them. Besides, the average tourist can be depended on to look at only a limited number. These are just right; and the notes you made are most helpful. I was also very glad to get the poems; unpublished poems are always fascinating, especially "juvenilia."

My translation of the sentence you asked about is as follows: "I would like to see you taken with her utter charm, and intrigued by her utter shallowness." I am certain of "intrigued," though would not swear to "utter."[1] I am becoming quite an expert on that cryptic handwriting after several months' practice!

I didn't know before that your name was Alabama. Didn't Mr. Faulkner have a child that died whom he named that?

By the way: it isn't a Faulkner "Day"—the exhibition will be up for at least a month, maybe more. That gives you a lot of time in which to get up here to see it. I wish you would come. I saw the Librarian yesterday, and she said that we would open it on Monday, the 13th. There are some history-books in the cases now, which the History Dept. want their classes to see before they are taken down. I have seen the page-proofs of the Catalogue,[2] and the finished copies are supposed to be here by the middle of next week. I'll send one as soon as I can; I am so sorry I was too late to include your name in the Acknowledgments.

As the show may last through August, I hope you won't mind my keeping your things that long. I have laid the letters out flat and pressed them, which is the best thing for them. We found that out with some Civil War letters that came down in the family. If kept folded, they break along the creases when they get old.

Thank you again for your additions to the show; and you'll hear from me shortly with the Catalogue.

Yours sincerely,
/s/ Robert Daniel

[1]This sentence, apparently a description of Estelle Oldham Franklin, appears in a letter Faulkner wrote to Mrs. McLean probably during the Spring of 1928. For the complete text of that letter see page 8 of this volume.

[2]Robert W. Daniel, *A Catalogue of the Writings of William Faulkner* (New Haven: Yale University Library, 1942).

588g Letter from Robert Daniel to 'Bama McLean, July 15, 1942, signed autograph manuscript, 2 pages (1 leaf).

Dear Mrs. McLean

The show opened Monday and has attracted many compliments. There are five illuminated upright cases and one flat one. I put the letters that bear on books next to the books, the poems near the volumes of poetry, and the others in the flat case with some miscellaneous items. The undergraduates are stopped first by the "stills" from the two movies, but then they go on to scrutinize everything pretty carefully. To me one of the most interesting things is the corrected galley-sheets of *Sanctuary.* You know he tells in the Introduction how he tore it down and rewrote it, and these sheets certainly prove it. (Lent by a lady in Darien, Conn.)

What are you going to do with your valuables ultimately? My collection of his books goes to the Library at Sewanee—they are going to build a Rare Book Room this winter and concentrate on Southern writers. You may think this hint disloyal, but I hate to see the Yankees get him.

Yours ever,
Robt. Daniel

c. 1942

498 Letter from 'Bama McLean to Vance Broach, undated [c. 1942], unsigned autograph manuscript, 1 page.

Believing you will be interested in this clipping,[1] as it concerns the negro woman to whom Billie dedicated "Go Down Moses," I am sending it, together with a letter he wrote Mammy's niece. The letter came to me by a lucky coincidence. My negro cook lives next door to this woman—& she hearing Mary Bell speak of it, asked to let her bring it to me. Mary B. wrote Billie to thank him "for giving Mammy such a fine funeral." (Have you been away from Dixie too long to appreciate that?)

Billie has no idea any one other than Mary B has seen this letter. For him to take the time to write to this lowly, obscure negro is an index to the real Faulkner & for that reason I wanted you to read it.

[no signature]

[1] "Rites Held for Former Slave in Novelist Faulkner's Home," Memphis *Commercial Appeal,* February 5, 1940, p. 5.

1944

S-2 Warner Bros. Inter-Office Communication from Jerry Wald to Jack L. Warner, June 17, 1944, unsigned carbon typescript, 1 page.

Dear Jack:

Here is the *first draft* on the "Don Juan" script. Last Wednesday I had Bill Faulkner put on to cut and polish the present script. He should complete his work within the next two weeks.

In revising this script I have made quite a good deal of technical changes so that what appears to me expensive looking production sets can be cheated and the picture made at a reasonable cost.

In the "Don Juan" property I feel that we have a tremendous box office picture. Basically it's nothing more than a Western laid in Spain. To me the additional values are in the color of the period and the romantic attributes of Don Juan.

[no signature]

S-3 Warner Bros. Inter-Office Communication from Jerry Wald to Alan LeMay, June 30, 1944, carbon typescript with typed signature, 1 page.

Dear Alan:

I would appreciate your reading the attached first rough draft on the script, THE ADVENTURES OF DON JUAN.

We are planning it as a vehicle for Errol Flynn and you can readily understand this combination should make for a big box-office picture.

However, somewhere along the line, this script doesn't seem to click as it should, and I was wondering if you could put your finger on the trouble.

Thanks very much.

Jerry Wald

S-4 Warner Bros. Inter-Office Communication from Jerry Wald to Steve Trilling, July 11, 1944, carbon typescript with typed signature, 2 pages.

Dear Steve:

Attached is the revised draft on DON JUAN as written by William Faulkner. I don't think it's quite right yet, but nevertheless it's a good script for budgeting.

The main trouble with this script right now is that there is considerable obscurity in it and I feel that we need a writer who has had experience doing this type of costume picture—a writer who can give us the color and romantic interest that I feel is lacking in the piece at the present time.

One thing I am positive of is that this can easily be as big a box-office picture as ROBIN HOOD.

I have outlined below what I think is wrong with the present script. I tell you these things now so that you can understand what changes I would like to have made in the final version of the story. Please read the script before considering these notes, so that you will be more familiar with my criticisms.

1. The main love story of Don Juan and Teresa seems to offer the greatest opportunity for improvement by a major change. I would look for a way to involve Teresa directly in the efforts and dangers of Don Juan, so that she becomes a key in the plot rather than a parallel effect. Don Juan's renunciation of the only woman he really loves should be made at much greater cost to Juan than the loss of the woman herself. The purpose of this will be not merely to complement the loss but to dramatize his emotional involvement in this special case among so many affairs.

Teresa, too, should be given an act of decision or sacrifice, dramatizing the special nature of her love for Juan. At present, she merely starts to love him, then is disillusioned. The sacrifice of her estates does not quite seem to fill the bill; something directly affecting Juan's interests would be better. If Teresa was properly involved and built up, I can see Juan's renunciation of her as the turning point of the climax.

2. Some of the wayside love affairs are not distinguishable from the main events.

3. The fight with Albizzi is not right at all. It is pretty late for Albizzi to crop up as Juan's superior at fencing. He has to be established much earlier in the script as the antagonist in the story along with Machiavelli—much the same way that Rathbone and Claude Rains were the heavies in ROBIN HOOD.

4. There are many other minor obscurities in the story that, if strengthened, would make the picture function much more cleanly. Don Juan's activities, too, would become less blurred if his opposition becomes more distinctly understood.

5. Don Juan's love scenes with Teresa need considerable more tenderness, while the clashes with the other women require a great deal more of comedy.

6. King Ferdinand can be given much more humor too, much along the lines of HENRY VIII. His utter frustration—not knowing how to handle the

Queen-Christopher-Don Juan set-up—forces him to turn for help to Machiavelli. In many ways, he should be a pathetic but humorous character.

All this might sound like a tremendous amount of work but actually it is a job of going through the script page by page and polishing the dialogue. It is by no means a complete rewrite.

The important point that I stress is that it does require a writer who has done and knows how to handle this type of story.

I have sent through a temp. script so that Tenny Wright and his department can get under way towards a budget. As I told you and Mr. Warner last week, there are several ways in which the production of this picture can be cheated. Instead of jumping into the cost of this type of film, I would first like to sit down with a production man and the art director and discuss ways in which several of the biggest sets can be cheated.

Sire, you have the ball.[1]

Jerry Wald

[1] *The Adventures of Don Juan* was released in December 1945, with George Oppenheimer and Harry Kurnitz being credited for the screenplay.

1945

604 Letter from Phil Stone to Malcolm Cowley, April 30, 1945, carbon typescript with typed signature, 2 pages.

Dear Mr. Cowley:

I was quite interested in reading your article on the work of William Faulkner in The Saturday Review of Literature of April 14.[1] It is the best article on his work that I have yet read. In fact it is the only one that I have read that has any great degree of accuracy and that is at all well based. However, you are all wet about a number of things.

Your statement about the phrase in *Sartoris* in the middle column on page 14[2] indicates that you missed the point that this phrase, every word of it, the very rhythm of it, was the basis of the whole novel and set the whole pitch for the entire Sartoris family. It was intentional design and good design, it seems to me.

In *The Wild Palms* and in *Absalom, Absalom,* both novels were absolutely ruined because of the fact that Faulkner apparently lacks any comprehensive sense of design. I think this lack is why his short stories are better than his novels and why his novels are mainly merely a collection of episodes. He is what I call a literary extrovert, a writer with no consistent and comprehensive theory of aesthetics.

I quite disagree with you about the merit of his later books. The trouble is that he keeps on rewriting *Sanctuary*. Except in a few books and in a few places the characters all talk like William Faulkner writes.

The Hamlet is really a part of a saga about the rise of the poor white trash in North Mississippi and it was intended to be a saga of gigantic humor. The incident about the calf[3] which ruined *The Hamlet* is simply indicative of the complete lack of aesthetic taste which Faulkner frequently shows.

His style which makes wonderful reading sometimes as to sonorous prose is

9. Phil and Emily Stone, Spring 1940

really not a style in the proper sense but merely a personal mannerism. As Willard Huntington Wright pointed out,[4] the great ones like Shakespeare and Balzac varied their styles and wrote either gently, robustly or dryly as the subject matter dictated, thus adapting the style to the subject.

Then, as I have said, Faulkner seems to severely lack a general sense of design.

There are many more things I might say but I have not the time to do so and you probably would not have the time to read them. If you are ever down this way come by Oxford and stay a few days and we shall talk the matter over. It would take several days.

No acknowledgment of this letter is necessary.

Yours truly,
Phil Stone

[1] "William Faulkner Revisited," pp. 13–16.

[2] Cowley had cited Faulkner's musing over the symbolism of the name Sartoris ("There is death in the sound of it, and a glamorous fatality. . . .") as an illustration that "[Faulkner's] taste is uncertain and sometimes almost as bad as a novelist's taste can be."

[3] The idiot Ike Snopes's love affair with the cow.

[4] In *The Creative Will: Studies in the Philosophy and the Syntax of Aesthetics* (New York: John Lane Company, 1916), a significant influence upon Stone's aesthetic theory and the source of much of the advice Stone passed on to Faulkner.

S-5 Letter from Finlay McDermid, Head, Warner Bros. Story Department, to Ed Williamson, Manager, Warner Brothers Exchange, Memphis, Tennessee, May 16, 1945, carbon typescript with typed signature, 1 page.

Dear Mr. Williamson:

I have just received a plaintive letter from one of our writers, William Faulkner, who is contemplating transportation difficulties from Oxford, Mississippi, to Los Angeles, California, and has asked our assistance in procuring Pullman reservations of some sort. Apparently he will be able to get as far as Memphis unaided. According to his letter, the best routes from Memphis are the Missouri Pacific to Fort Worth, or, alternately, by train to Kansas City and then, from either of these two junctions, the Southern Pacific to Los Angeles. I would have thought the Santa Fe or Union Pacific might be a better bet than the Southern Pacific. There is nothing that we can do about Mr. Faulkner's request from this end. I don't know whether there is anything you can do about it, but I would very much appreciate any help you can offer.

I shall write Mr. Faulkner that you will communicate with him. I would also appreciate a prompt answer as to whether you can help us in this connection.

Mr. Faulkner's address is simply: Oxford, Miss. I believe he has a large farm in the vicinity.

Yours very truly,
Finlay McDermid

S-6 Letter from Finlay McDermid to Faulkner, May 16, 1945, carbon typescript with typed signature, 1 page.

Dear Mr. Faulkner:

Upon receipt of your letter addressed to Jim Geller[1] from Oxford, Miss., I hazarded a guess that the letter was from you and had something to say about the date of your return to the studio.

I know you will be grieved, as I was, to learn that Mr. Geller is no longer with Warner Brothers, but has returned to the William Morris office. I have, however, talked to him on the telephone to give him the news about you, and he asks to be remembered.

For the time being, at least, I am handling the writers (you may remember me as the almost bald-headed guy who occasionally popped out of the Story Department door as you were on your way from the writers' building to the commissary).

I have written a letter to Ed Williamson, Manager of the Warner Bros. Exchange, 402 So. Second St., Memphis (2), Tennessee, asking him to do everything he can to assist you in procuring Pullman reservations from Memphis to Los Angeles. I also asked him to communicate with you as soon as possible. If you do not hear from him within a reasonable time, please write to me immediately and I will try some other method of helping you.

Will be delighted to have you back on the lot and will do everything we can to make your trip westward as comfortable as possible in 1945.

Sincerely,
Finlay McDermid

[1] McDermid's predecessor as head of the Story Department.

S-7 Letter from Ed Williamson to Finlay McDermid, May 18, 1945, signed ribbon typescript, 1 page.

Dear Mr. McDermid:

Immediately upon receipt of your communication dated May 16th I called Mr. William Faulkner in Oxford, Mississippi, with respect to transportation from Memphis to Los Angeles.

Mr. Faulkner stated that he had been in contact with Missouri-Pacific people here in Memphis and that they had confirmed a reservation over their lines, leaving Memphis Monday evening, June 4th, for Los Angeles.

Mr. Faulkner asked that I call the Missouri-Pacific people to make certain there would be no slip up. I just talked with the Missouri-Pacific people and they reassured me that the reservation was definite and that they had a lower berth for Mr. Faulkner leaving Memphis on the above mentioned date.

Very truly yours,
/s/ Ed Williamson
/t/ Ed Williamson

S-8 Letter from Finlay McDermid to Ed Williamson, May 23, 1945, carbon typescript with typed signature, 1 page.

Dear Mr. Williamson:

Thank you for your very prompt attention to the matter of transportation for Mr. William Faulkner.

I note that you state that he had the reservations on the Missouri-Pacific, and imagine that reservations all the way to Los Angeles were procured without trouble.

I greatly appreciate your assistance.

Very truly yours,
Finlay McDermid

S-9 Warner Bros. Inter-Office Communication from Finlay McDermid to Roy J. Obringer, June 8, 1945, carbon typescript with typed signature, 1 page.

Please return WILLIAM FAULKNER to payroll as of Thursday, June 7th.

Finlay McDermid

S-10 Warner Bros. Story Department memorandum from Finlay McDermid to Steve Trilling, July 31, 1945, carbon typescript with stationer's printed signature, 1 page.

Dear Steve:

As you know, William Faulkner is trying to break relations with Bill Herndon[1] of the McCormick Agency. Herndon has written a letter threatening legal steps against him. Faulkner has asked Obringer's advice as to what Herndon can do, but Roy would prefer to have Faulkner let things ride until Herndon actually does something and then get his own lawyer. Faulkner may be, I believe, contemplating the idea of taking another walk rather than face the general unpleasantness.

Will have to be a little careful in handling him, I imagine, during the next few weeks.

Finlay McDermid

[1]The Los Angeles agent who had negotiated Faulkner's contract with Warner Bros. Subsequently Faulkner became disenchanted with that contract and sought to sever his relationship with both the studio and the agent.

S-11 Warner Bros. Inter-Office Communication from Finlay McDermid to Steve Trilling, August 31, 1945, signed ribbon typescript, 1 page.

Dear Steve:

As you know, William Faulkner has been a quietly unhappy man during his stay in Hollywood.

He will be leaving us in September sometime, for a minimum of his customary six months' absences, and he has asked me if there would be a chance of getting a release from his contract.

While our relationship with Faulkner has been pleasant, I do feel that he has been uncomplainingly turning out scripts which nearly any Hollywood writer could have written.

I believe it would be to the advantage of Warner Bros. to re-write his agreement with us along pretty liberal lines:

1. We would like to have assurance that he would not accept work at any other studio.
2. We should have first refusal on all his story material.
3. We might have a one-picture a year commitment with him—which could be cancelled by either side and would depend upon our finding the *right* property for him or upon purchase of one of his own books.

I feel that if Faulkner could really cut loose on a story in which he was terrifically interested that we might get something pretty spectacular, but it seems a shame to waste one of the country's top novelists on routine melodramas when there are so many Hollywood writers who would be capable of turning out the same competent rough draft we get from Faulkner on this type of assignment.

What do you think?[1]

/s/ F
/t/ Finlay McDermid

[1]Trilling's reply, penciled in the left margin of this letter, reads: "Suspend & extend when returns."

S-12 Warner Bros. Inter-Office Communication from Finlay McDermid to Steve Trilling, September 8, 1945, ribbon typescript with type signature, 1 page.

Dear Steve:

I have been informed by William Faulkner—in a very mild and friendly manner—that he will not this time sign the usual extension and suspension papers.

He has no intention of working for another motion picture company, but does want to write more fiction.

I discussed the situation with Obringer, who feels we should draw up a new contract of some sort.

It is my feeling that Bill will retire to his native haunts, come what may, unless we can hold out a more tempting bid to him than his present deal offers.

Finlay McDermid

S-13 Warner Bros. Inter-Office Communication from Finlay McDermid to Roy J. Obringer, September 18, 1945, carbon typescript with typed signature, 1 page.

Dear Roy:

William Faulkner, writer, is requesting a suspension of his contract in order to write a novel.[1] We have agreed to suspend and extend his present contract with the provision that we must have a thirty-day first refusal on motion picture, radio, and television rights to any story material written by him during the suspension period.

In the event that we do not purchase said rights, Faulkner can offer the story on the open market. In the event that he receives an acceptable offer, he must, however, give us forty-eight hours exclusive of Saturdays Sundays and Holidays in which to match the offer.[2]

Faulkner will go off payroll tomorrow, September 19th. We will at that time grant six months' suspension.

Finlay McDermid

[1]*A Fable.*

[2]Such conditions, plus the relatively low salary he was being paid, contributed to Faulkner's growing conviction that his contract with Warner Bros. represented a form of bondage.

S-14 Warner Bros. Inter-Office Communication from Finlay McDermid to Steve Trilling, September 18, 1945, carbon typescript with typed signature, 1 page.

Dear Steve:
Here is a note which would assure us of first refusal on Faulkner's literary material during the remainder of his contract term which will expire July, 1950.

One advantage to writing a new contract would be the procurement of two additional years of Faulkner's exclusive motion picture services—if any—and an increased feeling of good will.

Finlay McDermid

1946

S-15 Warner Bros. Inter-Office Communication from Don Moore to Finlay McDermid, January 18, 1946, signed ribbon typescript, 1 page. From New York.

Dear Finlay:
Faulkner's illncss is as cxaggerated as Mark Twain's death once was.[1] Winchell's secretary stalled, but Random House have had letters from Faulkner in Mississippi, marveling at how well he feels in view of this reported New York nervous breakdown.

/s/ Don
/t/ Don Moore

[1] Walter Winchell had reported on his weekly radio broadcast that Faulkner was a patient in a private New York sanitarium.

S-16 Warner Bros. Inter-Office Communication from Finlay McDermid to Don Moore, January 24, 1946, carbon typescript with typed signature, 1 page.

Dear Don:
Thanks a lot for the news about Faulkner.

Finlay

S-17 Letter from Finlay McDermid to Faulkner, January 24, 1946, unsigned carbon typescript, 1 page.

Dear Bill:
Walter Winchell had you in a New York hospital—and your Hollywood friends considerably upset about two weeks ago.

I dashed off a message to our New York office to find out the name of the hospital, and have learned that Walter was talking through his hat.

During the time that I thought you were seriously ill, I talked to William Herndon in an effort to free you from him but am sorry to report that I got nowhere.

I hope the soil of Mississippi has acted as a tonic and that you are feeling tip-top.

Sincerely,
[no signature]

10. Random House, c. 1940

11. Donald Klopfer, c. 1940

12. Robert Haas, c. 1940

S-18 Letter from Finlay McDermid to Faulkner, March 4, 1946, carbon typescript with typed signature, 1 page.

Dear Bill:

I must confess with some surprise that I have had a certain amount of success in looking for an apartment for you. Things have not reached the spot where I can definitely say you will have a place to hang your hat on March 18th, but Esther Martin, one of the Warners' secretaries, does have a room and semi-bath which might be vacant by that time. She lives within ten minutes walking distance of the studio and would be very glad to have you as a tenant.

Also, one of our writers who lives at Sherman Oaks could possibly let you have a room but I do not know what the transportation problem might be.

In any case, I'll keep looking and will try to have the best available spot for you.

I trust you have managed to procure your travel reservations.

Sincerely,
Finlay McDermid

S-19 Warner Bros. Inter-Office Communication from Finlay McDermid to Steve Trilling, March 13, 1946, signed ribbon typescript, 1 page.

WILLIAM FAULKNER is supposedly returning to the studio this coming Monday. If he appears Arnold Albert has asked to have him go on THE DEALER'S NAME WAS GEORGE.

What do you think?[1]

/s/ F
/t/ Finlay McDermid

[1]Trilling's reply, written in blue ink at the bottom of McDermid's memo, reads: "If reports let me know. Then will assign." Faulkner did not report, choosing instead (with the encouragement of Harold Ober and Random House) to remain in Oxford to work on *A Fable.*

S-20 Warner Bros. Inter-Office Communication from Finlay McDermid to "Mr. Espinosa," March 19, 1946, carbon typescript with typed signature, 1 page.

The text of this memorandum is a telegraph message which Espinosa was instructed to send to Jacob Wilk, the Warner Bros. representative in New York.

SINCE J.L. WARNER IN NEW YORK, TRILLING SUGGESTS YOU DISCUSS FAULKNER MATTER WITH HIM. FOR YOUR INFORMATION AND HIS, FAULKNER NOW ON SIX MONTHS' SUSPENSION WITH UNDERSTANDING WE HAVE FIRST REFUSAL ON NOVEL.

Finlay McDermid

S-21 Letter from Finlay McDermid to Harold Ober, April 3, 1946, carbon typescript with typed signature, 2 pages.

Dear Mr. Ober:

I have not had the pleasure of meeting you but Ellingwood Kay tells me you are a straight-shooting agent, and that I may speak to you frankly and confidentially concerning Bill Faulkner's somewhat tangled affairs. I have attempted to write to Bill directly, but from the nature of the last reply I got I can see that nothing much is being accomplished by the correspondence.

On September 19th, Bill asked for and received a six-month leave of absence from his Warner contract. I explained to him that under the terms of the contract which he had signed he was not permitted to write a novel, but I had our Legal Department draw up a release granting him the right to write a novel with full rights to dispose of it in any way he chose, so long as we had first refusal of it for motion picture purposes.

Bill, however, refused to sign this agreement, stating that he had a bad case of ink poisoning. He was, of course, referring to his contract with William Herndon and contract with Warners. I assured him at the time that I understood and sympathized, but that the letter of release which I had prepared was not intended as an additional snare, but simply a means of giving him freedom to continue with his literary career.

I gather from the fact that Bill did not arrive here on March 18th as he had written he intended to do, that Jake Wilk talked to Mr. Warner in New York and secured the three-month extension which you requested. I wrote to Bill asking what his plans really were and urging him to sign the agreement which would allow him to complete his [novel. In reply, I received a denial that he was even writing a][1] novel!, and speaking vaguely of a telephone call "from New York" which caused him to cancel his reservation. Frankly, this answer puts me in somewhat of a spot since I had wired Wilk and Warner that Faulkner was on a six-month leave to write a novel which would be shown to us for first motion picture refusal, and our Legal Department is in a position to point out that the agreement to that effect is still, unsigned, in Faulkner's possession.

I would, therefore, appreciate your assistance in making Bill see the advisability of signing the letter and also learning from you more specific details about Bill's writing plans. You may rest assured that I have Bill's welfare in mind and will do whatever I can to make his Warner contract as small a burden as possible. If he'll only co-operate!

Sincerely,
Finlay McDermid

[1]The bracketed material does not appear in the Brodsky copy but has been taken from the ribbon typescript of this same letter which is a part of the Faulkner Collections at the University of Virginia (Faulkner-Ober Papers, #8969). McDermid noticed the omission and retyped the letter before mailing it to Ober.

The editors are grateful to Michael Plunkett, Assistant Curator of Manuscripts, Alderman Library, for providing a xerox copy of the Virginia letter and thus making possible a collation of the two documents.

S-22 Warner Bros. Inter-Office Communication from Finlay McDermid to Jacob Wilk, April 13, 1946, carbon typescript with typed signature, 1 page.

Dear Jake:

The legal Department has just mailed to Faulkner a letter restating our position with regard to his writing a novel. In effect, this letter grants Faulkner the right to complete his novel before returning to the studio and waives any claims we might have upon such novel.

For your information, I have periodically tried to get approval for a complete rewriting—or even abandoning—the Faulkner contract. So far, however, I have had no success, hence the studio position is that we do not wish to default the contract on our part, even though we have been, in the past, extremely cooperative in granting Faulkner extended leaves of absence.

The Legal Department did not think it advisable to send Ober the Faulkner letter since our deal with Faulkner does not specify that Ober is his agent,[1] and any information given Ober as to the status of the contract should be given by Faulkner rather than by us.

Finlay McDermid

[1]William Herndon was the agent who had negotiated the Warner Bros. contract for Faulkner.

S-23 Warner Bros. Inter-Office Communication from Jacob Wilk to Finlay McDermid, April 15, 1946, signed ribbon typescript, 1 page.

Note your letter of April 13th. Have discussed this situation with Mr. Ober. He agrees that official communications should be sent to Mr. Faulkner. He is communicating with Mr. Faulkner, and will advise me as soon as he receives a definite message from him. He feels positive that everything will be worked out satisfactorily.

It might be helpful if you could send me a copy of the last letter that Roy Obringer wrote to Mr. Faulkner on this subject.

/s/ J. Wilk

S-24 Warner Bros. Inter-Office Communication from Finlay McDermid to Jacob Wilk, April 17, 1946, carbon typescript with typed signature, 1 page.

Dear Jake:

I am inclosing herewith a copy of the last letter sent to Faulkner from Obringer's office as requested in your April 15th memo. This letter was first misaddressed and was only mailed again yesterday, and as a consequence Faulkner may be a little late in receiving it.

Greatly appreciate your assistance in this matter.

Finlay McDermid

S-25 Warner Bros. Inter-Office Communication from Finlay McDermid to Jacob Wilk, June 18, 1946, carbon typescript with typed signature, 1 page.

Dear Jake:

I noted your memo of the 12th concerning Harold Ober and William Faulkner. I believe that the Legal Department has sent further letters to Faulkner since our last correspondence.

Finlay McDermid

S-26 Letter from Harold Ober to Finlay McDermid, June 21, 1946, signed ribbon typescript, 1 page.

Dear Mr. McDermid:

I haven't answered your letter regarding William Faulkner because the matter is very complicated. Mr. Howard Reinheimer[1] is leaving for the Coast today, and he is going to talk to Mr. Obringer about the whole matter.

Sincerely,
/s/ Harold Ober

[1] An Ober associate.

S-27 Letter from Finlay McDermid to Harold Ober, June 25, 1946, carbon typescript with typed signature, 1 page.

Dear Mr. Ober:

I have received your June 21st letter and will be glad to hear Howard Reinheimer's report on the William Faulkner situation.

Sincerely,
Finlay McDermid

1947

S-28 Warner Bros. Inter-Office Communication from Roy J. Obringer to Finlay McDermid, May 24, 1947, signed ribbon typescript, 1 page.

The following writer's option comes up in June:

WILLIAM FAULKNER

Date to exercise option:	June 14
Term of next option:	52 wks
Weeks vacation:	12
Present salary:	$500
Salary next option:	$600

NOTE: Contract has been suspended since Sept. 20, 1945; above option date reflects the maximum extension of 12 months.

Please let me know if you desire this option taken up.

/s/ RJO
/t/ R. J. Obringer

S-29 Warner Bros. Inter-Office Communication from Finlay McDermid to Steve Trilling, June 2, 1947, signed ribbon typescript, 1 page.

Dear Steve:

Our WILLIAM FAULKNER contract has been suspended since September 20, 1945. Maximum extension date on taking up his option will be 12 months. This means if we wish to retain the FAULKNER contract we would have to take up the option on June 14 for a 52-week period at $600.00 weekly (present salary $500).

My personal inclination would be to let the option lapse, since I would be extremely surprised if FAULKNER showed up on the scene again.[1]

/s/ F
/t/ Finlay McDermid

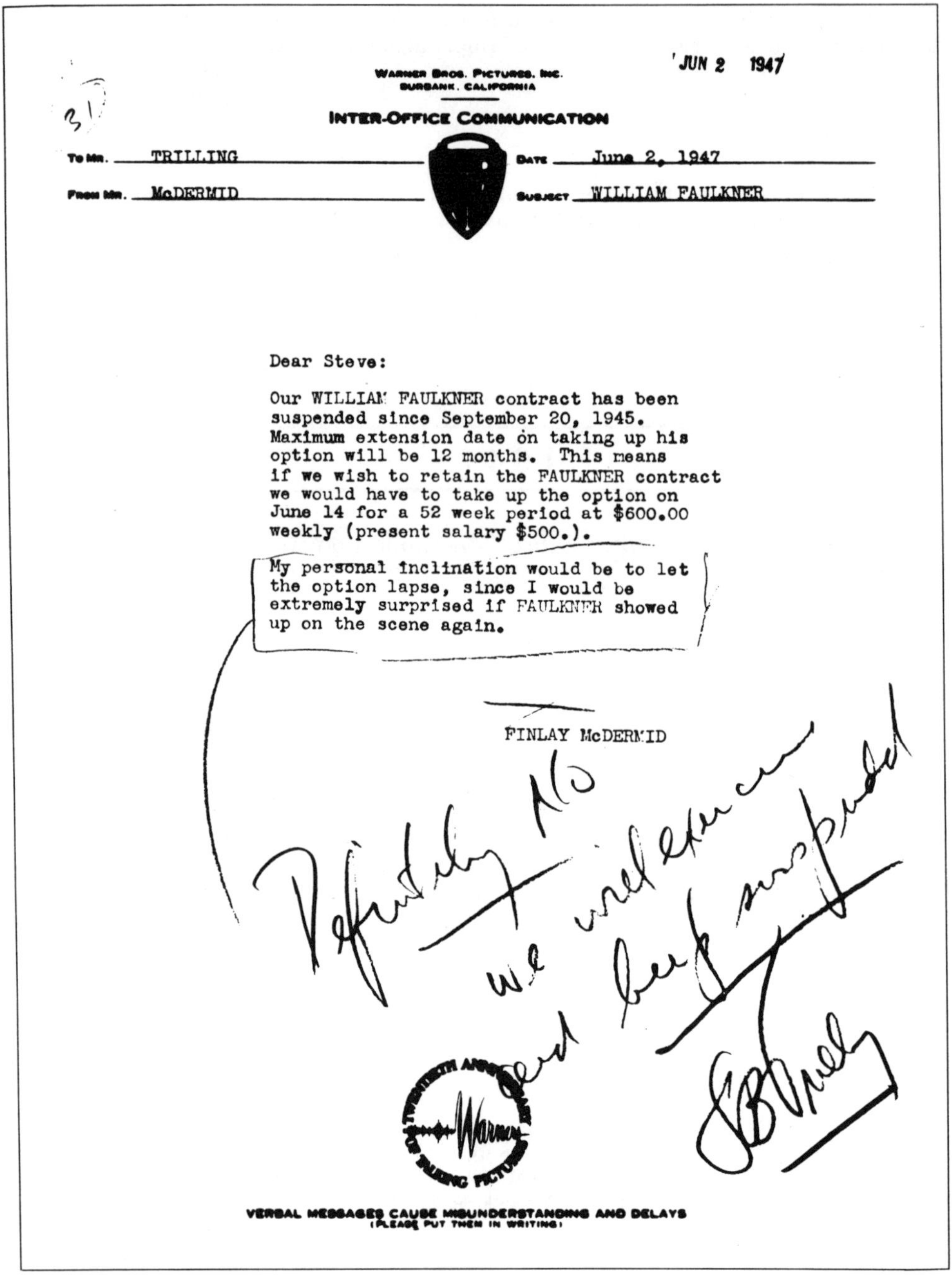

'JUN 2 1947

31

WARNER BROS. PICTURES, INC.
BURBANK, CALIFORNIA

INTER-OFFICE COMMUNICATION

To Mr. TRILLING Date June 2, 1947

From Mr. McDERMID Subject WILLIAM FAULKNER

Dear Steve:

Our WILLIAM FAULKNER contract has been suspended since September 20, 1945. Maximum extension date on taking up his option will be 12 months. This means if we wish to retain the FAULKNER contract we would have to take up the option on June 14 for a 52 week period at $600.00 weekly (present salary $500.).

My personal inclination would be to let the option lapse, since I would be extremely surprised if FAULKNER showed up on the scene again.

FINLAY McDERMID

Definitely No

VERBAL MESSAGES CAUSE MISUNDERSTANDING AND DELAYS
(PLEASE PUT THEM IN WRITING)

13. Memo regarding Faulkner's contract with Warner Bros. (item S-29)

[1]Trilling drew a box around this paragraph and penciled the following note at the bottom of the memo: "Definitely No. We will exercise and keep suspended. S B Trilling."

S-30 Warner Bros. Inter-Office Communication from Finlay McDermid to Roy J. Obringer, June 4, 1947, carbon typescript with typed signature, 1 page.

Dear Roy:
We will take up WILLIAM FAULKNER'S option and continue the contract under suspension.

Finlay McDermid

1949

668 Letter from Faulkner to Saxe Commins, "Wednesday" [January 19, 1949], signed ribbon typescript, 1 page.

Dear Saxe:
I am working at the Gavin Stevens volume.[1]
I dont have copies of these stories. I can recall only 4, though there seems to me to have been 5. But for my life, I cant recall another title nor even what it was about.[2]
SMOKE—In Dr Martino.
HAND UPON THE WATERS—SAT EVE POST. can you get a copy? some time about 1940[3]
TOMORROW ['AND TOMORROW' *del.*] (I think; am not even sure about title; Ober sold it) Sat Eve Post, about 1940[4]
AN ERROR IN CHEMISTRY (Ober sold it)—Ellery Queen mystery mag. 1945[5]
Ask Ober if he has record of any other.
KNIGHT'S GAMBIT—unpublished. Am rewriting, will be about 100 or 150 page novella.

/s/ Bill

[1]*Knight's Gambit.*
[2]The other story was "Monk," which had been published in the May 1937 issue of *Scribner's Magazine.*
[3]November 4, 1939.
[4]November 23, 1940.
[5]Actually the June 1946 issue.

669 Letter from Faulkner to Robert Haas, "7 Feb. 1949," unsigned ribbon typescript, 2 pages.

Dear Bob:
Here is the insert for INTRUDER re our recent correspondence.
Page 156 as set down through end of the paragraph, Stevens' speech ending: '. . . hide from one another behind a loud lipservice to a flag.'

(INSERT—NEW MATTER)[1]

'But what will happen?' he said. 'What will we do and he do, both of us, all of us. What will become of him—Sambo?'

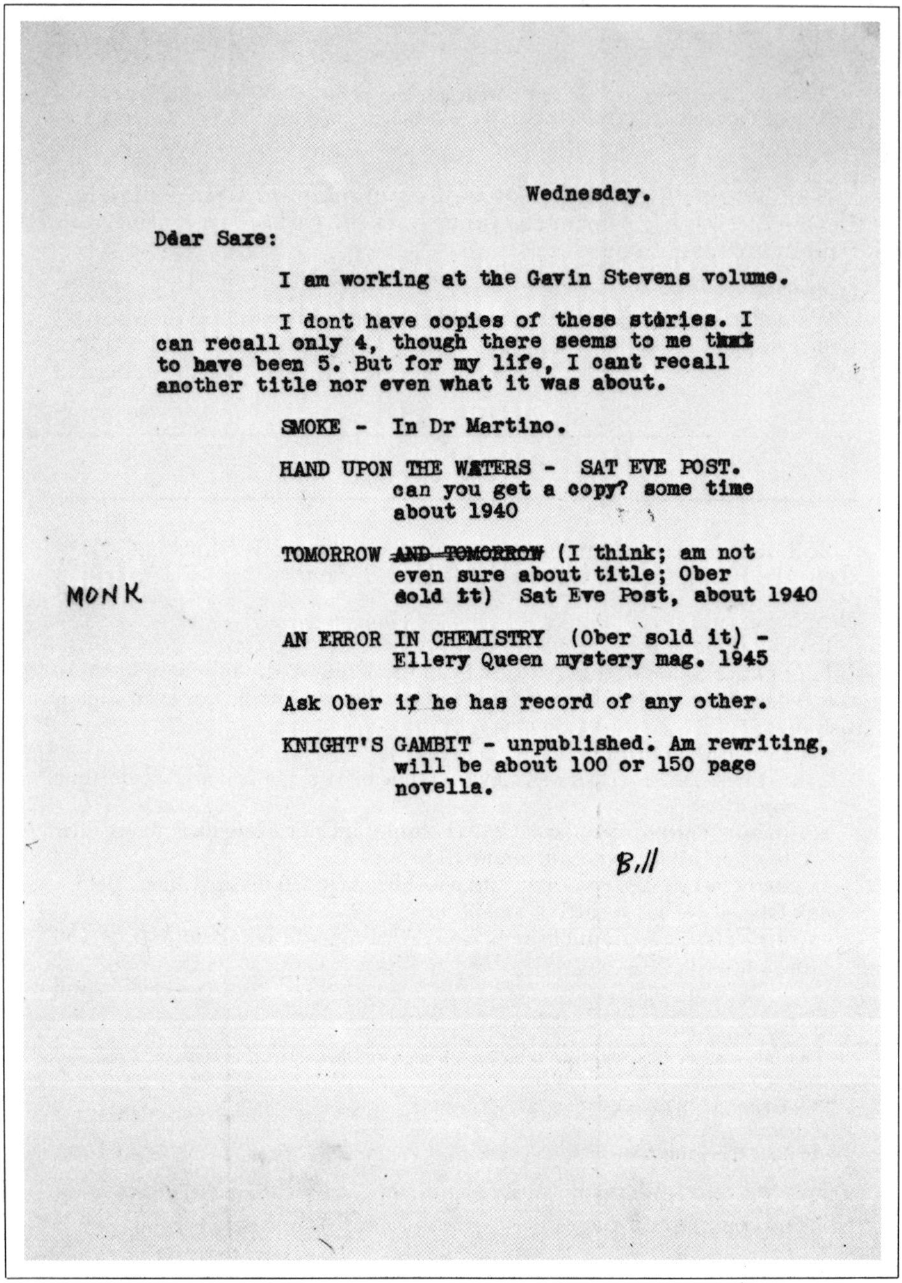

Wednesday.

Dear Saxe:

I am working at the Gavin Stevens volume.

I dont have copies of these stories. I can recall only 4, though there seems to me ~~that~~ to have been 5. But for my life, I cant recall another title nor even what it was about.

SMOKE - In Dr Martino.

HAND UPON THE WATERS - SAT EVE POST.
can you get a copy? some time
about 1940

MONK

TOMORROW ~~AND TOMORROW~~ (I think; am not
even sure about title; Ober
sold it) Sat Eve Post, about 1940

AN ERROR IN CHEMISTRY (Ober sold it) -
Ellery Queen mystery mag. 1945

Ask Ober if he has record of any other.

KNIGHT'S GAMBIT - unpublished. Am rewriting,
will be about 100 or 150 page
novella.

Bill

14. Letter from Faulkner to Saxe Commins regarding *Knight's Gambit* (item 668)

'I just told you,' his uncle said. 'He will disappear. There are not enough of him to resist, to repel, to hold intact his integrity even if he wished to remain a Negro. In time he would have got equity and justice without even asking for it. But by insisting on social equality, what he is actually demanding is racial extinction. Three hundred years ago he didn't exist in America; five hundred years from now he will have vanished and will be no more. Oh, he will still exist now and then as isolate and insulate phenomena, incorrigible, tieless, anachronic and paradox; archaeological and geological expeditions will stumble on him occasionally by individuals and even intact nests in caves in remote Tennessee and Carolina mountain fastnesses or Mississippi and Alabama and Louisiana swamps or, generations ago lost and unrecorded, in the mapless back areas of Detroit or Los Angeles tenement districts; travellers passing through the rotundas of the Croydon or Le Bourget or La Guardia airports or the supra transfer stations of space ships will gape at him intact with banjo and hound and screenless mudchinked cabin and naked pickaninnies playing with empty snuff-bottles in the dust, even to the washpot in the backyard and his bandana-turbaned mate bending over it, as the Union Pacific Railroad used to establish tepees of authentically costumed Blackfoot and Shoshone Indians in the lobby of the Commodore Hotel. But as a race he will be no more; his blood will obtain only in the dusty files of genealogical societies for the members of what will then be the Daughters of Founding Fathers or Lost Causes to wrangle and brag over as the Briton does over his mystic trace of Norman, so that in five hundred years or perhaps even less than that, all America can paraphrase the tag line of a book a novel of about twenty years ago by another Mississippian, the successfully mild little bloke over yonder at Oxford, in which a fictitious Canadian said to a fictitious self-lacerated Southerner in a dormitory room in a not too authentic Harvard: "I who regard you will have also sprung from the loins of African kings".'

(RESUME: p156)

Now they were there and not too long behind the sheriff. For though the car etc etc CONTINUE

[no signature]

[1] For a collation of this version of Faulkner's insert with the slightly different version published by Patrick H. Samway, see Brodsky and Hamblin, *Faulkner: A Comprehensive Guide to the Brodsky Collection,* I, p. 147.

670 Letter from Faulkner to Norman Unger, dated "Oxford, Miss. / 9 Feb. 1949," signed ribbon typescript, 1 page, with air mail envelope postmarked February 10, 1949, and bearing return address, Box 124, Oxford, Miss.

Dear Mr Unger[1]:

While cleaning out a desk today, I found the enclosed, which is obviously your missing letter. I ask your pardon again for having mislaid it, and anew for the long delay before I found it.

/s/ William Faulkner

[1] Unger was a book collector who lived in New York. The letter mentioned in Faulkner's reply has not been identified.

671 Letter from Faulkner to Saxe Commins, "Saturday" [March 5, 1949], signed ribbon typescript, 1 page.

Dear Saxe:

The pipe came today, the glass a few days ago, both in excellent shape, for which I thank you; I am sorry you dont need a pipe yourself, though I shant hold it against you.

I am at work on the long Stevens story. The volume will be: MONK, SMOKE, HAND UPON THE WATERS, AN ERROR IN CHEMISTRY, TOMORROW, and the new unpublished one, KNIGHT'S GAMBIT—that's correct, isn't it?

I dont remember MONK too well, though I think it is told from the outside, isn't it? in the 3rd person? Or does the nephew-protagonist tell it? In either case, I say, lead off with SMOKE, which is 3rd person, the boy not in it at all; also SMOKE is the first one I wrote. Then MONK, then HAND UPON THE WATERS, which is in its chronological order, also contains a murder, then TOMORROW, still in chronology but only incidentally concerned with a death, then ERROR in CHEMISTRY, which is a murder, then KNIGHT'S GAMBIT, the long one, not published yet, in chronology, a long, the longest, piece, also marking the end of a phase of Stevens' life, since he gets married; that is, he prevents a murder not for the sake of justice, etc., but to gain his childhood sweetheart whom he had lost.

If you will get the first 5 into shape, I will work at the last one. I see no reason why you shant have it by May 15th, perhaps earlier.

I haven't got a title yet. I think of something legal, perhaps in workaday legal Latin, some play on the word *res,* like *res in justicii* or *Ad Justicii.*

/s/ Bill

672 Letter from Saxe Commins to Faulkner, March 8, 1949, carbon typescript with typed signature, 1 page.

Dear Bill:

I am pleased that you like the pipe and that the binoculars are in pefect order again.

I'll follow the instructions in your letter to the letter. As I understand chess, the knight's gambit is an opening which involves the knight's pawn one or two squares forward in the first movement. It's an unorthodox opening. Usually, and for atrocious chess players like myself, reliance is on an opening of the king's or queen's pawn. But I do like the title KNIGHT'S GAMBIT for itself. I wish I could say as much for a generic Latin title for the book. It would be a little forbidding, it seems to me, to a non-legalistic reader. Anyhow, we have lots of time to think about that.

Best in the world to you, Bill,
Saxe Commins

673 Letter from Faulkner to Saxe Commins, "Sunday" [May 1, 1949], signed ribbon typescript, 1 page.

Dear Saxe:

I am near the end of the rewritten piece,[1] will send it in as soon as finished. It is running around 150 pages mss.

I cant remember if I wrote or not about a title and make-up. What do you think about

KNIGHT'S GAMBIT (title for book)

Then the stories in this order, each with its own title as you did Go Down, Moses, but if you like, set these titles in smaller type, more like chapter headings, except for chapter numbers, which we don't need.

Smoke
Monk
Hand Upon The Waters
Tomorrow
Error In Chemistry
Knight's Gambit

/s/ Bill

[1]Presumably "Knight's Gambit."

702b Letter from Phil Stone to Glenn O. Carey, December 30, 1949, carbon typescript with typed signature, 2 pages.

Dear Mr. Carey[1]:

I must apologize to you for not having answered sooner your letter of December 21, but I got it mixed up in some Christmas mail and have just now come across it.

I am glad that someone has finally decided to write on the humor in Faulkner's work. I have tried to get a dozen people to do it but without success. For a number of years I have had the opinion that Faulkner's future as a writer lay in the possibility of him becoming the great American Humorist.

I should like very much to have a copy of your thesis to read and I don't believe I could give you any intelligent information until I have read it. If you can send me a copy I shall take the best of care of it and return it to you but, on account of the press of my own business, I may have to keep it a month or two before I can get to read it.

With reference to the casual comments which I made to Peggy Parker[2] and which Harry Campbell[3] used, if you want them I expect you will have to get them from Harry. They were just casual remarks that Peggy took down and I have no record of them.

When it comes to further information about Faulkner, there are two difficulties. In the first place your request is so general that I would not know where to start. As Stark Young[4] tells his Yankee friends about the race situation in the South, it is something that would take three days to explain. Subject to the second objection which I shall state later, if you have any definite specific questions that you would like for me to answer, I shall do my best to do so.

The second objection is that Faulkner does not mind what is said about his work but does not want anything written about him personally. Since I am his literary executor in his will, he has gone so far as to request me not to furnish such information after his death. Of course, outsiders can do as they like about personal items, but since I am his closest personal friend I am sure that he would feel very much hurt if I should disregard his request and furnish personal items for publication.

Yours truly,
Phil Stone

[1]Carey, an English instructor at the University of Illinois, had recently completed a master's thesis entitled "The Humor in the Fiction of William Faulkner." He wrote Stone seeking information about Faulkner's early career.

[2] A University of Mississippi English instructor whose class Faulkner visited in 1946.
[3] English professor at the University of Mississippi and co-author, with Ruel E. Foster, of *William Faulkner: A Critical Appraisal* (Norman: University of Oklahoma Press, 1951), the first book-length study of Faulkner's work.
[4] Mississippi-born novelist, playwright, poet, drama critic, and painter, best known for his popular Civil War novel, *So Red the Rose* (1934). Young was a good friend of both Stone and Faulkner.

c. 1949

703 Note from Faulkner to Saxe Commins, undated [possibly 1949], signed autograph manuscript, 1 page, on Random House letterhead stationery.

Saxe—Please excuse me to Dorothy. Had accepted with Joel & Mrs. Sayre for Friday, too late now to re-arrange, as I want to see them.[1] So I cant go to hear the music Friday p m. Please thank Dorothy, and excuse me.

Bill

[1] Joel Sayre and Faulkner had been good friends since the early 1930s. They co-authored the movie script for *The Road to Glory* in 1935–1936.

1950

702d Letter from Phil Stone to Glenn O. Carey, January 21, 1950, carbon typescript with typed signature, 2 pages.

Dear Mr. Carey:

I have your letter of January 18.

First, with reference to the humor of Faulkner, the book which most typifies this humor is THE HAMLET.

As to writing Faulkner himself, I must defend his failure to answer your letter. If he answered all the letters he receives and all of the people who want to see him he would never have time to do anything else and would have to employ about two secretaries. As it is, my relationship with him causes me to have a great deal of my time taken up by people who can't get in touch with him.

As for the biographical matter which you asked about, I shall be glad to give it to you but give it with the understanding that you use it without quoting me.

In April, 1918, when I was in Yale Law School, Faulkner came to New Haven and stayed in my apartment until June of that year. Through some friends, I got him a job at Winchester Arms Company. We were both trying to get into the British Army but we failed at trying to be Canadians because we could not learn to roll our "r's." This situation was saved for us by an English friend by the name of Reed who ate at our table in Commons and who taught us to talk like Englishmen. In June, 1918, Faulkner went down to New York and enlisted in the Royal Air Force. Lord Wellesley was in charge of the Royal Air Force recruiting station in New York at that time. This was the latter part of June. Faulkner came on home on three weeks' leave and then went back to Toronto. He was there the whole time until he was discharged in the latter part of November or, as I remember now, early in December. He was never in the Royal Canadian Air Force and did not receive his commission until Christmas.

You should be able to get considerable information about his stay in New Orleans from George Healy and John McClure. I took Faulkner down there and got George and John to let him write stuff for the Times-Picayune so that he could make a living and got him in with a crowd that was then publishing The Double Dealer.[1]

. . . .

With reference to Faulkner's education, he never took any courses at Oxford, England. He was never in Europe until he went over there in the Summer of 1925 and came back home just before Christmas of that year.

Here, he quit school about the eighth grade of High School.[2] His next and only scholastic experience consisted of some special courses that he took at the University of Mississippi here. I don't remember exactly when this was except that it was early in the 1920's, I think, about 1921.[3] You can get this exact date and the courses he took, I should think, by writing to the Registrar, University, Mississippi. They have a separate post office.

I know that Faulkner never took any degree of any kind. You have probably surmised this by such things as appear all through his work, especially, the "one monogamus marriage" that appears in KNIGHT'S GAMBIT. Since [*monos*] is itself the Greek word that means "one," I don't see how a monogamus marriage could be more than one or how you could have two monogamus marriages.

I would like to see a copy of your thesis when you can send it and shall be glad to help all that I can. Please remember that any biographical data I give you may be used but there must be no reference to the fact that you have obtained it from me.

Yours truly,
Phil Stone

[1]George W. Healy, Jr., who had known Faulkner at Ole Miss, was Managing Editor of the New Orleans *Times-Picayune*. John McClure was associate editor of *The Double Dealer* and book reviewer for the *Times-Picayune*.

Healy has written that Faulkner preceded him to New Orleans and got the assignment for the *Times-Picayune* through the influence of Roark Bradford. See *William Faulkner of Oxford*, ed. James W. Webb and A. Wigfall Green (Baton Rouge: Louisiana State University Press, 1965), p. 59.

[2]Faulkner actually completed the eleventh grade.

[3]Records show that Faulkner was a special student at the University of Mississippi during the years 1919–1920.

702f Letter from Phil Stone to Glenn O. Carey, February 9, 1950, carbon typescript with typed signature, 2 pages.

Dear Mr. Carey:

I have your letter of February 7.

I shall be glad to go over the thesis when Harry Campbell gives it to me and I assure you that I shall not delay just through indolence.

Possibly I could help you with the humor. I am sure I can help you with this more than I can with anything else. I get credit for a lot that Faulkner has accomplished but as far as his actual writing is concerned I helped him very little except with the humor, but I actually made his humor for him. At the beginning he was a very humorless person.

I think you are right about such material needing to be published but I don't know that I can help you much there, probably not, as I know no publishers personally. With all the efforts we made, I was not able to get Faulkner published and Sherwood Anderson was the one who got him started so far as publication goes.

I feel sorry for you if you have to read MOSQUITOES because it is a very poor book. My recollection is that it only sold about 1200 copies and that was all it deserved to sell.

If you are looking for humor, don't overlook SOLDIERS' PAY. There is a good deal in there of the broad type.

My wife and I were disappointed with the final production of INTRUDER IN THE DUST. We thought the movie lacked tension and the movie people did not make near as much out of the photographic possibilities of Oxford as was possible.

If you ever get down this way come by to see us.

Yours truly,
Phil Stone

702h Letter from Phil Stone to Glenn O. Carey, April 5, 1950, carbon typescript with typed signature, 3 pages.

Dear Mr. Carey:

I was hoping that I was going to be able to take time and write you fully about your thesis but I see now that I am not going to be able to do it. So I am returning your thesis to you by parcel post and want you to write me when you get it.

However, there are a few things to which I feel I must call your attention in this letter. The story about General Longstreet on Page 5 of your thesis is amusing indeed. Bill never in his life saw a Confederate General and most of what he knows about the War between the States came from what I told him and from books I give him to read instead of what he heard around the family fireside. In fact, almost all of his relations who had served in the Confederate Army were dead before Bill got old enough to take notice.

It does not matter to me but I shall give you the true facts about the General Longstreet story. The first ten years of my life I was practically an invalid and was in bed at least a third of that time. L. Q. C. Lamar, who had served in the Confederate Army, had formerly lived in the old house where we lived. He had left behind a number of his books, many of which dealt with the War between the States. Not being able to play, I read all these books avidly and frequently. People like Lee, Jackson, Longstreet and Stuart were just demigods to me. I was saturated with this stuff but could not really take in the fact that such heroes actually existed in the flesh.

Because of my health, every summer that I was able to travel my mother took me to a cooler climate, frequently to Michigan. After the summer places closed in Michigan we would come back to Chicago and usually stay there on the South Side until the hot weather was over in Mississippi. During the year when I was eight years old, as I remember the year accurately, we were spending that September at the Hyde Park Hotel. General Longstreet was there with his flowing white beard, his second wife and a daughter by his former marriage. I was entranced and the old man took a liking to me. He began to take me on walks with him in the afternoon and when we were alone he would answer all of my questions about the War and would tell me many things about the details of various campaigns. After about ten days of that I finally got up courage to tell him that I wanted to ask him a question if it would not make him angry. He smiled indulgently and said that of course it would not make him angry. Then I asked him if it were true that we lost the Battle of Gettysburg because he disobeyed Lee's orders and failed to support Pickett's charge on the third day of the battle. (You may not know, as Yankees seldom do, that Pickett's charge did not fail. It actually broke through the Federal lines back to the artillery.) The old General's face turned purple, he threw down my hand he was holding, shouted a thunderous No! and strode angrily away. After that he ignored me and would have nothing to do with me. I don't mind Bill having the story if he likes it but these are the true facts.

I shall have to comment again on the letter from Bill Green which appears on Page 115. It must be that I, the closest friend that Faulkner has or ever had, am the "acquaintance" to whom Bill Green refers. I don't know where Bill Green would place himself as he never came to Mississippi until 1930, knows Faulkner only slightly and sees him only seldom.

I also do not know how Peggy Parker could get to be such an authority on the early life of Faulkner. Peggy is a good girl but she is another hero-worshiper of Faulkner. . . . In addition to that, Peggy never came to Mississippi until 1940 and she wasn't born until Bill was about ten years old. When she talked with me she certainly was no authority about Faulkner's early life because practically all she knows about it is what I told her or what she got from sources to which I directed her.

In conclusion, the idea that Faulkner served in World War I in active combat is laughable. Bill was never in either France or England until the summer of 1925. He could not have flown a plane because at that time in the R.A.F. only a commissioned officer could be a combat pilot and I was with Bill at the postoffice here after Bill had been discharged a few days before Christmas in 1918 when the letter containing his pip, his wings and his commission came. I saw him open the letter and I read the commission myself and he was not a commissioned officer until over one month after the War had ended. He went to Canada in July, 1918, came back in December, 1918, and was never out of Canada the whole time. Carvel Collins, who is an Assistant Professor in the English Department of Harvard, is here now getting background for a graduate course on Faulkner which he is giving at Harvard next year. At my suggestion he went to see Johncy Falkner (Bill's brother, who wrote MEN WORKING and DOLLAR COTTON) and Johncy laughed and told him the same thing about Bill's supposed war service. Then Johncy took Collins down to see Bill's mother and she told him the same thing.

You must beware of these people, especially people in the English Department of the University of Mississippi here, who tend to romanticize Faulkner. I am very friendly with almost all of these people, especially Bill Green, but when they go to talking about Faulkner personally they just don't know what they are talking about.

Yours truly,
Phil Stone

708a Letter from Phil Stone to Carvel Collins, April 20, 1950, carbon typescript with typed signature, 2 pages.

Dear Carvel:

I herewith enclose the work that Mr. Lang did.[1] I checked it over casually and it seems all right to me.

From the time he took and what he did I should say that you should pay him at least $10.00. I know I wouldn't have done it for that. You can just send the check to Mr. Eaton Lang, University, Mississippi.

Don't forget that any biographical information which you got from me alone and which you intend to submit is to be submitted to me before being submitted to a publisher. In fact, from your standpoint, I believe it would be a good thing to submit all of this biographical material to me so that I can check it for you.

Also, if you get photostatic copies of the articles that I wrote for the Saturday Review of Literature after 1940[2] and the article that Mr. Stark Young wrote about Bill and me in the New Republic,[3] I should like to have those copies. If it is not asking too much I should like to have two copies of each so that I can put one in Araminta's file and one in Philip's file.[4]

I saw Bill at the postoffice a few minutes ago and he says he is not feeling well again. He has not been feeling well for almost a year, off and on, and I am gently needling him now to get him to go through the Clinic but he probably won't do it. As I told you before, the Faulkners think they can even defy the laws of Nature.

It is beautiful spring weather down here now and we are all doing fine. If no one gets sick at home today Emily and I are taking off for the Southern Literary Festival to be held at State College tomorrow. Donald Davidson[5] is going to be there and so is David Cohn,[6] whom I am going to introduce tomorrow night.

I hope you got to see Mr. Stark Young and gave him our love.

Come to see us again as soon as you can.

Your friend,
Phil Stone

[1] Lang had supplied Collins with materials related to Faulkner's university days at Ole Miss.

[2] Only one article by Stone had appeared in the *Saturday Review of Literature:* "William Faulkner and His Neighbors," 25 (September 19, 1942), 12.

[3] "New Year's Craw," *New Republic,* 93 (January 12, 1938), 283–284.

[4] Stone maintained souvenir Faulkner files for his daughter Araminta and his son Philip.

[5] Poet, critic, and teacher, best known for his involvement with the "Fugitive group" of poets at Vanderbilt University in the 1920s.

[6] A native of Greenville, Mississippi, and author of various books, including *The Good Old Days, God Shakes Creation, Love in America,* and *The Fabulous Democrats.*

709b Letter from Phil Stone to Carvel Collins, April 28, 1950, carbon typescript with typed signature, 2 pages.

Dear Carvel:

I have your very nice letter of April 28 and I am glad that you saw Mr. Stark [Young] and got to talk with him. Emily and I both are so fond of him.

I am also glad that you got the contract for the critical book.

With reference to the article,[1] I still don't know and I shall have to think about it a few days or a week before writing you. If there is anything in the world I do not want to do it is to commercialize on my friendship with Bill, one of the finest things in my whole life. I certainly do not want to take any money out of this thing without Bill first knowing all about it. I shall talk with him at the first opportunity and write you. Just now, my tentative opinion is, if there is no doubt about you having complete control over the final verdict, that you should go ahead and take all the money.

Of course I want to see and pass upon even the final verdict before it is printed.

With reference to Bill's remarks on life and writing, ancedotes, my connection with him and all those things, I see no objection to that providing I am not put in a position of sponsoring the thing. What I mean is that you can use anything I have told you without quoting me as authority. Of course I shall not leave you out on a limb; if anyone should challenge your fact I shall write you a letter backing you up.

Going back to the projected book for a moment, you know more about writing than I do but about two chapters of biography in your book would be too much. It seems to me that one chapter of 7500 or 10,000 words should cover what you want.

I shall try to talk to Bill within the next few days although I have a term of court starting Monday and shall write you just as soon as I can.

We were so glad to see you because we like you and we do hope you will come again soon and bring your wife with you. We have all been well now for over three weeks although mother had a little bilious attack yesterday. Today is Emily's birthday and Philip and I have conspired to produce several surprises for her. Anna is over there cooking Emily's favorite dinner and tonight I am going to take her out to the "Mansion"[2] although she does not know it yet.

We went over to the Southern Literary Festival at State College last week and were very much disappointed with Donald Davidson whom we met for the first time. Dave Cohn was down there and made a speech and I introduced him. It was about world conditions and was the best talk I ever heard Dave make.

By the way, they have there in their English Department a young man by the name of Bob Holland who was here a year before the war, who writes verse and who, we think, has some ability and whom we like very much. He needs seasoning yet but I think Harvard would do well to keep its eye upon him for the future. He wrote a good sonnet on Will Percy and I am enclosing a copy of it which you may keep.

Your friend,
Phil Stone

P. S.: Over at State College I was very pleased to notice that Bill dominated the whole proceedings. Every speaker referred to him and his work and the consensus of opinion was that he is the best so far in the history of American fiction. Of course I was also vastly amused as I sat there and listened and thought of the situation twenty-five years ago.

P. S.

[1]The feature article on Faulkner which Collins had been invited to write for *Life* magazine. Collins had sought Stone's advice and assistance.

[2]An Oxford restaurant.

709c Letter from Carvel Collins to Phil Stone, May 1, 1950, signed ribbon typescript, 1 page.

Dear Phil,

Thank you very much for your letter. This possibility of doing an article for *Life* is certainly a moral problem. I respect Mr. Faulkner and his integrity about publicity. But I am an admirer of his works (did I tell you gushingly about my reading ABSALOM, ABSALOM straight through in one sitting the day it came out in 1936?—a rented copy; I was broke) and I think that a sympathetic, respectful, non-tabloid *Life* account of his works and their background would serve some good purposes.

I forgot one point in my other letter: I would not do the piece unless *Life* agreed not to invade Mr. Faulkner's life in any way—no interviews, no requests for the name of his breakfast food, and by all means no photographers taking pictures in his home. I thought the pictures in the *Life* article on Ernest Hemingway were bad in every way; so I would write "none of that" into the contract if I decided to agree to a contract.

In short, the thing would be written without anyone's hounding him and would deal with his fiction primarily and with Mr. Faulkner as a writer, not as a celebrity.

I am sorry that Davidson was a disappointment to you. I have never met him, and I have felt that some of his political ideas are odd but I have always respected the literary judgment he has shown in his writings about books—so I am sorry he let you down at the conference.

Tomorrow I am supposed to talk about two of Mr. Faulkner's books before a class my boss teaches; last week I was a silent (for a wonder) visitor at an evening class devoted to "The Bear"; this Thursday I talk with a club of young teachers who want to discuss THE SOUND AND THE FURY and AS I LAY DYING. One senior member of the department here says that the students have become so interested in Mr. Faulkner's works that Harvard needs seven men full time to teach classes devoted to them. All to the good, I say.

You will be amused to know that I have just been asked by the Finns to go to Finland next year to take a newly established chair of American literature to be filled each year by a different visiting American. There are many reasons why I may refuse, one of them being that, though the establishment of the chair is a gesture against Russia and I am all for that, I fear that the chair might turn into a "hot seat" for me and my family, who are expected to go along. The experience might be altogether too electrifying.

I hope that all of you are well, and that the birthday plans went off smoothly.

Sincerely,
/s/ Carvel

P.S. You are quite right: in a critical book I should only have one introductory chapter of a biographical sort, that almost entirely a kind of calendar.
/t/ —C.

709d Letter from Phil Stone to Carvel Collins, May 3, 1950, carbon typescript with typed signature, 2 pages.

Dear Carvel:

I have your letter of May 1 and we were very glad to hear from you again.

I have not yet seen Bill since Chancery Court is still in session but if I do not see him soon I shall drive down to his home next Sunday morning, talk with him and then write you Monday.

You told us about reading ABSALOM, ABSALOM. You are a better man than I am. The neglect of the great possibilities annoyed me so that I could not finish reading the manuscript. Perhaps I have already told you that. I told you so many things that I can't remember what I did tell you and what I did not.

I am very glad that you added the additional information that the proposed article will not cause Bill to be annoyed about his personal life.

We hope that we can make it next Fall and if we can it will probably be about the middle of October. If we can't come then I doubt if we can come until about the middle of January.

I got a letter from Mr. Stark Young saying that you were a very intelligent young man and that he liked you very much but that he was afraid that he was not entirely sober when talking to you. I wrote him immediately and pacified him by telling him that I was sure that this made no difference to you, that possibly you were not entirely sober.

I don't blame you for not wanting to take your family to Finland but I was not amused at that. I think the offer is a compliment. I also think the Finns are just about the greatest people in the world. You ought to talk to Dave Cohn about them. He was over there last summer and he says that the Finns and their courage and calm poise filled him with exaltation.

By the way, Ernest Trueblood[1] is a name that Bill uses when he wants to pop off. I don't know why he has kept this from me but I shall try to find out more about it when I talk to him and then write you about it.

We are all getting along fine now and the Birthday was quite a success.

My suggestion about the biographical chapter of the book was just a suggestion. You know more about it than I do. For God's sake don't always take my suggestions at face value. My tragedy seems to be that people either ignore my suggestions completely or take a casual suggestion as gospel. Almost never do they take the middle ground.

Your friend,
Phil Stone

[1]The pseudonym under which Faulkner published "L'Aprés-Midi d'une Vache" ("Afternoon of a Cow").

709e Letter from Phil Stone to Carvel Collins, May 8, 1950, carbon typescript with typed signature, 2 pages.

Dear Carvel:

I had a talk with Bill yesterday morning and he was very positive that he did not want any such article about him to appear in Life Magazine. He was quite disturbed about it and came out to my house later in the morning to be sure to see if he could prevent it being done.

He wanted his position explained. He says that, in the first place, he does not think a writer is a public figure and thinks that his personal life is his own and that it is the business of nobody else. I do not agree with this point of view but it is his point of view.

In the second place, he says that Malcolm Cowley wanted to do a similar article and he, Bill, requested Cowley not to do it and Cowley graciously complied. He says that Cowley had done him quite a big favor and if ever such an article is written for Life Magazine he, Bill, feels that Cowley should be allowed to write it. I can understand this point of view and confess that I think he is right about this since he and Cowley are such good friends.

Furthermore, from my own point of view, I simply do not feel that I can commercialize my friendship with Bill. After Emily, Philip and Araminta, I am fonder of Bill than I am of anybody in the world. In addition to that, if I did do such a thing I think it would be a very saddening shock to Bill, even more than he realizes, because I think that, of all the people in the world that he knows, he has a profound faith in my integrity and in my personal loyalty to him. If I should destroy this (although maybe I am now being vain) I don't know just how severe a shock it would be to him.

So please let the Life Magazine article go. Certainly I shall have no part of it and shall take none of the money. You will lose some immediate money but I think you will find that you will profit by it much more in the long run. I know Bill well enough to know that he will appreciate such action very much and it may even turn out that he will appreciate it so much that he might some day help you in some other way that will mean much more to you.

As soon as you get this letter please write me that the Life Magazine incident is closed. If it will make it easier for you, you are at liberty to show this letter to the Editors of the Magazine.

We are all doing fine and send you regards.

Your friend,
Phil Stone

709f Western Union telegram from Carvel Collins to Phil Stone, May 15, 1950.

IF MR FAULKNER WANTS KNOW [*sic*] LIFE MAGAZINE ARTICLE THERE SHOULD BE NONE.[1] I HAVE WRITTEN LIFE SO BEST WISHES

CARVEL

[1]Robert Coughlan subsequently wrote a two-part feature on Faulkner which was published in the September 28 and October 5, 1953 issues of *Life*.

710 Letter from Faulkner to Saxe Commins, "Saturday" [probably mid-May 1950], signed ribbon typescript, 1 page.

Dear Saxe:

You and Don[1] were both right about the collection and I was wrong; I mean, about the time and the place for it. I was worse than wrong: stupid; I didn't seem to understand what 'collection' meant. It's all right; the stuff stands up amazingly well after a few years, 10 and 20. I had forgotten a lot of it; I spent a whole evening laughing to myself about the mules and the shingles.

I have a Peterson pipe, old, it has developed a lateral crack, about ½ in. across one side of the bowl. I dont have Peterson agent's NY address. Will you contact them or any repairer, and see if anything can be done about such. So far, the crack is only a hairline; just found it tonight, though the bowl has been sweating at the place for a long time. Maybe bro. Erskine[2] will attend to it; you are the busiest of the two. Maybe Dunhill will repair it, if no Peterson shop available.

My best to all. Hope I can come up this winter.

/s/ Bill

[1] Donald Klopfer, a Random House executive, who had joined Commins in suggesting that a collection of Faulkner's short stories be published.
[2] Albert Erskine, an editor at Random House.

729 Letter from Faulkner to Saxe Commins, "Friday" [possibly October 16, 1950], signed ribbon typescript, 1 page.

Dear Saxe:
I sent the pipe to you Tuesday. I am afraid that a break like that, across grain in the bowl, cant be patched anyway. In case it cannot, will you see if Peterson shop can send me a duplicate of the pipe.

I have seen a brochure from some pipe shop somewhere, claims that they can repair any injury regardless. But I cant remember what shop now.

Thank you for attending to this. Weather fine here, getting in hay and corn, saw six deer in my oat field the other morning, already hunting coon, deer season next month, then quail shooting and duck, nice time of year here.

Will come up some time this late fall or winter if possible. Where might I find Parkman's History of France in the New World, and what will it cost me?

Read [Budd] Schulberg's new book today.[1] Good writing, but not about anything. Topical. Sad tragic thought: the capable ones of or since '30 have nothing to write about; the machine age has not destroyed the writers themselves, it has destroyed their material; human beings no longer exist. They are types, categorised, struggling not against the old tried true dramatic verities of the heart: honor and pride and cowardice and duty, because they dont even know what they are, remember them, but against the categories this free democratic world had forced individuals into whether they would or not, simply to make room for everybody. Same of O'Hara and all the others I have read since my lot—Hemingway, Dos P., Wolfe, and the real ones before us who have not yet got the recog. they deserve: Anderson, and the clumsy giant Dreiser for instance, and Cather

/s/ Bill

[1] *The Disenchanted.*

730 Letter from Faulkner to Saxe Commins, dated "Oxford, Wednesday" [probably late October 1950], signed ribbon typescript, 1 page.

Dear Saxe:
The parcel came yesterday. I dont know what to say about the two books.[1] To give away a book (I mean of your own, that you wanted and went to some trouble to get) is like giving away one of your children. So, if you have taken these out of a set on your library shelf, I will consider them the same as the physical transference of a child: mine as long as I treat them right, but true ownership to vest still in the books, to be returned to you whenever they (it:the child) wills.

That is, have no fear about their wellbeing. I will hold them; if or when (without trouble) you find or hear of other copies, send them to me and I will return yours.

The pipes are all right. Thank you for attending to them. When the old one burns, cracks on out, I will send it in to Peterson and re duplicate it. That address is 418 Madison, isn't it? or 417?

/s/ Bill

15. Faulkner and Jill during the Nobel Prize ceremonies

[1]Presumably the two-volume *Pioneers of France in the New World* by Francis Parkman, which Faulkner had mentioned in the previous letter.

742 Letter from Phil Stone to Editor, Memphis *Commercial Appeal,* November 13, 1950, carbon typescript with typed signature, 1 page.

Dear Sir:

In your leading editorial on William Faulkner in your issue of November 10, you refer to him as "a photographic realist."[1] How anybody can think that Faulkner is a realist, much less a photographic realist, is far beyond me. He is obviously a romanticist, sometimes almost Gothic. It is a civilization that is gone for which he mourns.

Yours truly,
Phil Stone

[1]The author of the editorial was Paul Flowers, the literary editor of the *Commercial Appeal.*

745 Postcard from Paul Flowers to Phil Stone, postmarked Memphis, Tennessee, November 20, 1950, signed autograph manuscript.

Phil: Can a confirmed romanticist portray scenes with photographic realism? Let's define terms over a decanter of Caledonian elixir.

P

750 Postcard from 'Bama McLean to Vance Broach, undated [possibly December 1950], signed autograph manuscript.

Vance dear—Thought you would like to have this picture & clipping.[1] Billie is so handsome. Iron grey hair & the years are so becoming to him. At air port so many recognized him & came up to say "Isnt this Mr Wm Faulkner" & he would smile graciously & say "Yes." With fond care. Bama

[1]Probably one of the feature stories in the Memphis papers on Faulkner's winning the Nobel Prize.

755 Printed Christmas card, made in Sweden, from Jill Faulkner to 'Bama McLean, December 1950, with signed autograph note.

Dear Aunt Bama,

We had a wonderful time in Stockholm[1] and then went on to Paris and London. Pappy looked so very nice at the presentation ceremony and I was so proud of him and all the ambassadors said what a fine stroke he had made for America in Sweden.

I wont try to tell you how much I appreciated my "mad money" but just say thank you.

Love,
Jill

[1]Jill accompanied Faulkner to Stockholm for the Nobel Prize presentation ceremony.

1951

765 Letter from Faulkner to Saxe Commins, "Friday" [possibly January 31, 1951], signed ribbon typescript, 1 page.

Dear Saxe:

Here is the first section of the new mss.[1] I am sending it in for you to keep, since I am going out to the coast tomorrow to do a movie job for Howard Hawks.[2] I dont know whether I shall be able to work further on this mss. while there. But in any case, I will be in New York in April, with more of it ready.

If Elliot Paul[3] is in New York now, will you please send me his address? That is, locate him, and I will write you from California; maybe I can send you a letter to be forwarded to him. Dont send any mail to me here, until you hear from me again.

/s/ Bill

[1] *Requiem for a Nun.*

[2] Noted Hollywood film director, who had enlisted Faulkner to work on a script based on a novel by William E. Barrett entitled *The Left Hand of God.*

[3] Journalist, author, and scenarist, best known for his nostalgic memoir, *The Last Time I Saw Paris* (1942).

769 Letter from Phil Stone to Faulkner, February 12, 1951, carbon typescript with typed signature, 2 pages.

Dear Bill:

I have not forgotten about redrawing those paragraphs of the Will, the phrasing of which I do not like. I did not get a chance to do it the week-end after you left[1] because I had to look after Araminta more than usual. When Emily got home she was worsely cut up than I expected, almost a nervous wreck. Yesterday she began to feel better and is more her natural self. I shall try to attend to the business of the Will this week or not later than the coming week-end.

Meanwhile, if you have time, it would not hurt for you to take up with a tax expert the question of the tax effect of your Will and of your Trust Agreement[2] and to have him write me about this so that if you think it advisable to change your Will when you come home I shall already have this information and shall have studied it.

I did not ask you anything about your trust or how you are going to handle it because I did not consider that any of my business. Since you left I have been thinking of it and wondering if it is possible that you intend to keep the principal fund intact and to use only the interest. If this is what you intend to do I can get you some real estate loans around here that will be entirely safe, will pay five per cent (5%) interest and on which I shall check the title and draw all the papers and I can make a little money out of it. Abe Linker and I have lent about $30,000 he had to lend for other people. If you want to do anything like this let me know and at the same time let me know the maximum amount that you would want to put into any one loan.

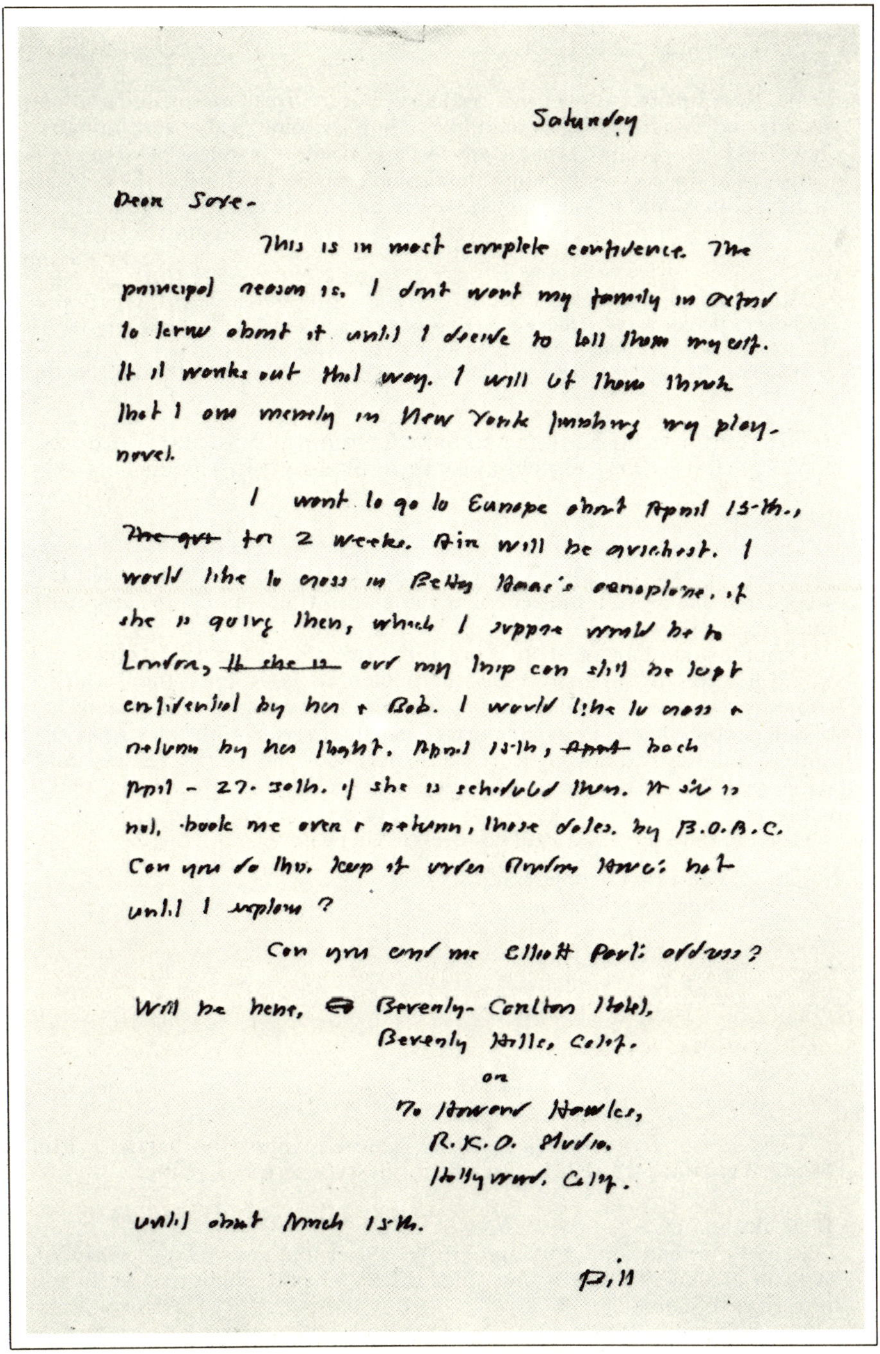

Saturday

Dear Saxe-

This is in most complete confidence. The principal reason is, I dont want my family in Oxford to learn about it until I decide to tell them myself. If it works out that way, I will let them think that I am merely in New York finishing my play-novel.

I want to go to Europe about April 15-th., ~~The first~~ for 2 weeks. Air will be quickest. I would like to cross in Betty Hoare's aeroplane, if she is going then, which I suppose would be to London, ~~If she is~~ and my trip can still be kept confidential by her & Bob. I would like to cross & return by her flight. April 15th, ~~April~~ back April - 27-30th. if she is scheduled then. If she is not, book me over & return, those dates, by B.O.A.C. Can you do this, keep it under Random House' hat until I explain?

Can you send me Elliott Paul's address?

Will be here, ~~@~~ Beverly-Carlton Hotel,
Beverly Hills, Calif.
or
c/o Howard Hawks,
R.K.O. Studio,
Hollywood, Calif.

until about March 15th.

Bill

16. Letter from Faulkner to Saxe Commins (item 770)

We have finally got over our cold spell but the weather is still damp and cloudy and disagreeable. I would like to borrow some of that sunshine for a few weeks. The ground is just soggy wet and I believe it will take two weeks of sunshine at the very least before the farmers can do anything in the fields.

Best of luck, and let me know if there is anything I can do for you.

Your friend,
Phil Stone

[1]Stone had redrawn Faulkner's will (signed and dated February 1, 1951) just prior to Faulkner's departure for Hollywood. This letter is addressed to Faulkner c/o Charles Feldman, California Bank Building, Beverly Hills, California.

[2]Faulkner had created a trust fund with $25,000 taken from the Nobel Prize award.

770 Letter from Faulkner to Saxe Commins, "Saturday" [probably mid-February 1951], signed autograph manuscript, 1 page.

Dear Saxe—

This is in most complete confidence. The principal reason is, I dont want my family in Oxford to learn about it until I decide to tell them myself. If it works out that way, I will let them think that I am merely in New York finishing my play-novel.

I want to go to Europe about April 15th, for 2 weeks. Air will be quickest. I would like to cross in Betty Haas's aeroplane, if she is going then, which I suppose would be to London, and my trip can still be kept confidential by her & Bob. I would like to cross & return by her flight, April 15th, back April 27–30th, if she is scheduled then. If she is not, book me over & return, those dates, by B.O.A.C. Can you do this, keep it under Random House's hat until I explain?

Can you send me Elliot Paul's address? Will be here,

Beverly-Carlton Hotel,
Beverly Hills, Calif.
or
c/o Howard Hawks,
R.K.O. Studio,
Hollywood, Calif.

until about March 15th.

Bill

771a Letter from James T. Babb, Yale University librarian, to Phil Stone, February 22, 1951, signed ribbon typescript, 1 page.

Dear Mr. Stone:

In 1947 we had some correspondence concerning your fellow townsman, William Faulkner. There is one other matter which I might pass on to you with regard to him.

Mr. William B. Wisdom of New Orleans has, I understand, a very fine Faulkner collection. Mr. Wisdom, although not an alumnus of Yale, is chairman of our local Alumni Library Committee. If you know him or can make the opportunity to meet him, I should appreciate your putting in a good word for us at any time. Mr. Wisdom gave his magnificent Thomas Wolfe collection to Harvard, and someday, I imagine, he may be giving away his Faulkner collection. Of course, we should be delighted to have it.

Sincerely yours,
/s/ James T. Babb

774 Letter from Faulkner to Saxe Commins, "Tuesday" [probably late February 1951], signed autograph manuscript, 1 page. From Beverly Hills, California.

Dear Saxe—

I am ashamed for having neglected to acknowledge your letters. I did not ignore them—I was just waiting until I could be definite—more so about whether I could afford the trip,[1] also some good covering reason because of Oxford, and my present notoriety. Also, since the tickets do not have to be picked up until April 1, I did not hurry.

Saw Bob[2] today (he sends his best, looks rested and content) who has given me an official reason to go. But if possible, please wait a little longer about taking up the tickets. I am returning home Monday, 12th. Will try to complete all plans by Thurs. and will wire you to pick up tickets.

My best to you, as always, bless your kind heart.

Bill

[1]The two-week trip to Europe which Faulkner had proposed in an earlier letter to Commins.

[2]Robert Haas, who suggested that Faulkner take advantage of the European trip to tour World War I battlefields in France and thus refresh his memory for the writing of particular scenes in *A Fable.*

773a Letter from Perrin H. Lowrey, Jr., to Phil Stone, February 28, 1951, signed ribbon typescript, 1 page.

Dear Mr. Stone:

I have taken the liberty of writing you because my father has told me a good deal about you, and because I know that Mr. Faulkner, very rightly, does not like to bother with letters that are really only praise.

But as a young writer, I wanted to tell someone close to him how much his speech of acceptance in Stockholm meant to those of us who are trying to turn out something good. The dignity and selflessness and awareness of that speech must have been particularly meaningful and encouraging to all the young writers of my generation. And to me, who in forming have realized ever since I could read intelligently—which wasn't long ago—just how good an artist Mr. Faulkner is, it meant even more.

So I wanted him to know, if you think it would give him pleasure, that it and his books are things that strengthen us for what we are writing and for what we hope to write. I simply wanted to thank him for doing so generous and so fine a thing.

Sincerely,
/s/ P. H. Lowrey Jr.

773b Letter from Phil Stone to Perrin H. Lowrey, Jr., March 3, 1951, carbon typescript with typed signature, 1 page.

Dear Mr. Lowrey:

I have your letter of February 28 and appreciate it very much.

I agree with you that Faulkner's speech was the best thing that he has ever written, although it did amuse me a little because I think he has written more of the gland than of the heart. Still, I think he is the best of the present group and when he returns from California I shall let him read your letter.

Thank you for writing me.

Yours truly,
Phil Stone

771d Letter from James T. Babb to Phil Stone, March 6, 1951, signed ribbon typescript, 1 page.

Dear Mr. Stone:

Thank you for your prompt reply to my letter of February 22. Mr. William B. Wisdom's address is 715 American Bank Building, New Orleans, Louisiana. I have had correspondence with Mr. Wisdom in recent years.

I had never specifically asked Mr. Wisdom to give us his Faulkner collection; in fact, I think it would better if the idea originated in his own mind. That is why I wrote you, as I felt a good word from you would help.

Sincerely yours,
/s/ James T. Babb

778 Letter from Robert K. Haas to Faulkner, March 8, 1951, carbon typescript with typed signature, 1 page.

Dear Bill:

Since you take kindly to the notion, I agree to the plan that you take Random House's blessing and go and look at these places[1] yourself, and get whatever information and atmosphere you will need at first hand.

Saxe informs that your passage is booked B.O.A.C. for April 15th to London return April 29th.

Yours,
Robert K. Haas

[1] In France.

771e Letter from Phil Stone to William B. Wisdom, March 13, 1951, carbon typescript with typed signature, 1 page.

Dear Mr. Wisdom:

I heard somewhere some time ago that you had given to someone your extensive collection of Wolfe, and that you also had made a similar collection of Faulkner. Would there be any chance to get you to give your Faulkner collection to the Library at my old college, Yale?

We both remember very delightfully the conversation we had in our back yard several years ago and we think and talk of you often and wish that you would come to see us again. If and when I see you I shall tell you about the trouble we had about getting Faulkner off to Sweden but I would not want to write it. It is quite a saga, sounds like one of his Snopes tales, and I think it will amuse you.

Yours truly,
Phil Stone

771g Letter from James T. Babb to Phil Stone, March 16, 1951, signed ribbon typescript, 1 page.

Dear Mr. Stone:

I have your note of March 13 and the copy of the letter you wrote to Mr. Wisdom. It is perfect and I do thank you for it. Such a suggestion comes much better from a neighbor and friend of Faulkner's than from the Librarian, and I hope it will bear fruit.

Sincerely yours,
/s/ Jim Babb

789 Letter from Faulkner to Saxe Commins, "Wednesday" [late March 1951], signed ribbon typescript, 1 page.

Dear Saxe:

Here is the second of the three sections.[1]

I had hoped to have an answer by now to mine of last week, asking you to take up the tickets. As far as I can tell now, I will use them on 15th April, will be in New York about April 12th. Am waiting now for final ratification from Europe, but I think it will come through and that I will go on that date. Can always cancel if something happens, which I dont anticipate.

Have discussed the trip somewhat with Bob in Cal. and plan to use some of the two weeks in looking again at old 1918 battle fields, etc., to freshen up and get at the big book[2] again. I imagine that Gallimard[3] will help me about this, getting a car, driver, an expert guide, etc.

I think you can expect me in town by airline April 12th, which is Thursday, isn't it? Have notice of an award of some kind called Page One, for April 13th.[4] They want me to designate someone to attend a ball and accept for me. Who can—will—do this? It sounds more like Erskine, if he will, doesn't it? They sent two ball room tickets, which I enclose.

Am wiring you today, if I dont hear from you, to take up the tickets for Europe. If you have not written, please take up the tickets and then write me an acknowledgement which I can use at home here to make the business look businesslike.

/s/ Bill

[1] *Requiem for a Nun.*
[2] *A Fable.*
[3] Pierre Gallimard, publisher of the French editions of Faulkner's works.
[4] The Page One Award of the Newspaper Guild of New York, which Commins accepted on Faulkner's behalf.

791 Western Union telegram from Faulkner to Saxe Commins, March 29 [1951].

PLEASE TAKE UP TICKETS BEFORE DEADLINE NOTIFY ME BY LETTER

BILL

790 Faulkner's instructions to his editor, Saxe Commins, concerning the title of Act II of *Requiem for a Nun,* undated [late March 1951], unsigned autograph manuscript, 1 page.

Re Title—Act II—The Golden Dome
(Beginning Was——)
What I wanted here was to paraphrase Eliot:
'In the beginning was the Word,
Superfetation of τὸ ἕν.'[1]
I dont know Greek.
Can we use
(Beginning Was τὸ ἕν)?
If not,
(Beginning Was The Word)

[no signature]

[1]Faulkner was quoting T. S. Eliot's "Mr. Eliot's Sunday Morning Service."

793 Letter from Faulkner to Saxe Commins, dated "Oxford, Friday" [early April 1951], signed ribbon typescript, 1 page.

Dear Saxe:

Please forgive this delay and trouble. I will explain it to you when I reach New York, which will be about the 13th.

Can you engage a room for me at Hotel Leutetia, Boulevard Raspail, Paris, for April 17th, one at Brown's Hotel, Dover St., London, for April 16th? Can you wait as long as possible before taking up the air tickets, in case something goes wrong? If at any time they must be taken up or cancelled, take them up of course.

One more thing. Can you get in touch with Elliot Paul, and get the name of another Paris hotel reasonably near the Leutetia, more obscure if anything, so I wont be too well known?

You can see by now what all this is leading to[1]; of course, I will tell you as much more as you want to know.

Or do this. What connection can I make from London for Paris, without staying in London overnight, which will give me plenty of time in London to go into town and buy a Burberry coat? I could leave my bags at customs, go in to Burberry's and return and go on to Paris night of 16th, if I have a hotel reservation. If the time figures too close, try for Brown's Hotel night of 16th, then book me on to Paris the 17th.

If Paul cant help on another hotel, or this is too troublesome, reserve me two rooms at Leutetia.

Will see you about 13th.

/s/ Bill

[1]Faulkner had arranged a rendezvous with Else Jonsson, whom he had first met in Stockholm the previous November. The widow of newspaperman Thorsten Jonsson, and an editor for Bonniers, Faulkner's Swedish publisher, Mrs. Jonsson had served as Faulkner's guide during the Nobel Prize festivities.

794 Letter from Faulkner to Saxe Commins, dated "Oxford, Monday" [early April 1951], signed ribbon typescript, 1 page.

Dear Saxe:

I haven't heard from you since mine of week before last, asking if you could reserve Paris rooms.

Will you cable Hotel Leutetia, Paris, right away, make sure one room anyway is ready for guest who will arrive early on 17th April?

Am planning to reach New York 12th; assume you have taken up BOAC ticket.

Had wire from French Ambassador Friday that France has given me Legion of Honor. Have heard no more since I acknowledged it, am standing by in case I am supposed to go anywhere to be conferred, etc.[1]

As soon as I hear from you, I will complete plans to come up.

Am sorry to put this all on you, but cant do much myself from here, since I hope to keep down fanfare about the trip.

Yours,

/s/ Bill

[1] Faulkner was presented the Legion of Honor award in New Orleans on October 26, 1951.

796 Letter from Faulkner to Ben Wasson and Hodding Carter, The Levee Press, Greenville, Mississippi, dated "Oxford, Mississippi / April 13, 1951," unsigned carbon typescript, 1 page.

Dear Ben and Hodding,

I don't think this question came up when we discussed the "Notes on a Horse Thief" manuscript. At the time my understanding was—and still is—that this was to be an exclusive edition.[1] Therefore, I am assuming that you, too, understand that there can be no reprints or other use of it without my permission.

This is correct, isn't it? As you know, this is a part of my unfinished book, and so I don't want another printing of it for that reason.

Yours,

[no signature]

[1] The Levee Press edition of *Notes on a Horsethief* had appeared in January 1951 in a signed, limited edition of 975 copies. The story eventually became a part of *A Fable.*

771h Letter from William B. Wisdom to Phil Stone, April 18, 1951, signed ribbon typescript, 1 page.

Dear Phil Stone:

I am finally getting around to answering some of my correspondence, which is more than I can say for Bill Faulkner. I wrote him several months ago, commenting very favorably on INTRUDER IN THE DUST, and telling him of my Wolfe collection, of my "Faulkner Collection" (I have all of his first editions, some manuscripts and some letters), of my interest in him, his work, and of my desire to form as complete a collection of him as possible.

The letter was not too effusive. He may have considered it gratuitously officious, but it was not so intended. I don't suppose I really expected an answer. I just hoped for one.

If you see him you may tell him that I think his Nobel Prize acceptance speech the finest utterance since Lincoln's Gettysburg Address. If that be hyperbole, let someone make the most of it.

Now tell me if I am wrong about this. I have the clear conviction in my mind that someone has only recently given a complete Faulkner Collection to Yale. I may have seen this in the Yale Library Gazette. By the way, I happen to be the Chairman of Yale's Library Committee for Louisiana. It doesn't mean anything except that Yale or rather Mr. Babb, the librarian, is not overlooking any bets.

I, too, remember with distinct pleasure our conversation in your backyard, when I was in the Marine Corps. It was a delighful oasis in more ways than one. Afterwards, I met and saw a good deal of John Faulkner and his family in Memphis when he was in the Navy. This came about from my reviewing his book "Men Working" or "Dollar Cotton" for the Commercial Appeal. I still think MEN WORKING is the best picture of the depression we have. It is far superior to THE GRAPES OF WRATH. Its splendid objectivity and detachment is just the opposite of Steinbeck's maudlin sentimentality for his characters.

I certainly do hope that we can see each other again. Don't you ever come to New Orleans?

Sincerely,
/s/ Bill Wisdom
/t/ William B. Wisdom

771i Letter from Phil Stone to William B. Wisdom, April 23, 1951, carbon typescript with typed signature, 2 pages.

Dear Bill:

Your letter of April 18 came while I was in Jackson at the Southern Literary Festival.

First, with regard to your letter to Bill Faulkner, I am not going to tell Bill anything. Sometimes he makes me so damn tired I would like to kick the seat of his pants clean off. Back in 1924 when we were trying so hard to get started and met with nothing but defeat, I got my friend, Stark Young, to put Bill up in New York at his own apartment and to get him a job there in New York. Mr. Stark has written Bill a letter and Bill, the last I heard, had not even answered that letter.

Please don't get the idea, as some people do, that this is just one of the peculiarities of genius. It is nothing but that damn Faulkner in him. If you had known four generations of them as I have you would understand.

I agree with you that his Nobel Prize speech is the best thing that he has ever written and your opinion of it is no higher than mine.

I don't know about what the Yale Library has but I shall write Mr. Babb and find out and let you know.

I do wish you would come to see us sometime because, with our two children, it is so hard for us to get anywhere on a pleasure trip. I am hoping to be in New Orleans May 24 and 25 but I shall be there as a delegate to the Judicial Conference of the Fifth Circuit and I shall probably be tied up with that all the time. However, I am going to call you and I hope that I can bring Emily with me and if I do you will have more fun talking with her than you would with me although I would miss much.

I confess that we were shocked at what you said about John Faulkner's book.[1] We think John can't write at all and it amuses us that he can get the stuff published at all. Don't repeat this because we are very fond of both John and Lucille and John's success just pleases us beyond words. I think he is really the nicest one of all the Falkners, personally.

It may be that you will have other callers this year and that will be due to our propaganda about you. We told Hudson Strode,[2] the other day at Jackson, that it would be well worth the trip for him to go to New Orleans just to talk with you, that you were the most intelligent and the most stimulating person intellectually that we had met in about fifteen years.

If you ever come up this way be sure to come to see us.

Your friend,
Phil Stone

[1]*Men Working,* which Wisdom had described as "the best picture of the depression we have."

[2]Author of books on various foreign countries, biographer of Jefferson Davis, and popular creative writing professor at the University of Alabama.

797 Letter from Phil Stone to Hudson Strode, April 23, 1951, carbon typescript with typed signature, 1 page.

Dear Hudson:

Bill's mother says that Bill was born about 11:00 o'clock on a Saturday night. When you have time write us what his horoscope indicates.

It certainly was a pleasure to see you and we do hope that you will come to see us sometime when you can.

Your friend,
Phil Stone

803 Letter from Saxe Commins to "Printer," July 10, 1951, carbon typescript with typed signature "SC," 1 page.

PRINTER:

Herewith new insert copy for the end of Act Two, Scene III, REQUIEM FOR A NUN. You will find old copy attached to galleys at this point. Please remove that copy and replace it by pages 2-3-48 to 2-3-52 herewith.

On page 2-3-47, please find speech

GOWAN

Stop it, Boots. Quit it now.

Please delete this speech and substitute for it the speech at top of new page 2-3-48.

STEVENS

(To Temple)

Stop it.

and continue with new copy attached herewith to the end of Act Two.

SC

PS. Attached herewith is also new copy for the end of the play, Galley 93—Act Three, Scene I. It replaces the portioned [*sic*] deleted in pen on that galley.

805 Letter from Faulkner to Saxe Commins, "Thursday" [probably September 6, 1951], signed ribbon typescript, 1 page.

Dear Saxe:

Yours at hand. We will drive up, leaving here Wednesday, will reach New York Sunday afternoon I think, though please have them hold the rooms if we should be late. A good plan for a country driver might be to have a pro chauffeur meet us somewhere about Jersey or maybe Philadelphia and drive me in to the hotel and put the car away until I start up to Boston the 19th.[1] Can this be done? If you could arrange with the driver and give me a telephone number which I could call say, Saturday, and arrange then where to meet the driver Sunday morning? Will try to bypass big towns, Washington, Philadelphia etc, some place in New Jersey Sunday morning would do, then the driver could deliver us to the New Weston[2] and store the car. Choose some Jersey town, maybe Princeton would be a good one to pick him up in, and I will fix my course to coincide there Sunday morning.

There will be Jill, her mother, and me. You wont need to meet us at airport, but will you meet us for dinner Sunday night, I mean you and Dorothy both of course.

The book[3] is very fine, handsome.

/s/ Bill

[1]To enroll Jill in Pine Manor Junior College, Wellesley, Massachusetts.
[2]A New York hotel.
[3]*Requiem for a Nun.*

807 Typescript draft of Western Union telegraph message from Faulkner to Estelle Faulkner, undated [probably 1951].

Decided do rewrite here.[1] May remain week more. Will telephone this week-end.

Pappy

[1]Presumably New York, though possibly Cambridge, Massachusetts. The draft of the message appears on the same page as an autograph manuscript section of *Requiem for a Nun.* Faulkner apparently interrupted his work in transcribing manuscript to type out the message which someone else may have mailed for him.

833 Letter from Estelle Faulkner to Dorothy and Saxe Commins, dated "Rowan oak [*sic*]/Sunday," signed autograph manuscript, 2 pages with envelope addressed in Mrs. Faulkner's hand and postmarked Oxford, October 7, 1951.

Dear Dorothy and Saxe—

Please don't believe me always this rude and seemingly ungrateful—You both (and dear little Frances too) were so very kind, attentive and good to Jill, Billy and me[1] that I am utterly at loss for words to express my appreciation—I shan't even try—just wait, and let the rest of my life attest my sincerity!

Physically, I was rather worn when we at last got Home—There was so much to do—see about in the house and grounds—and decisions to make during the brief week that Billy spent here before rushing back East again[2]—Somehow—letter writing and I played hide-and-seek until now—

I think that I'm on a good hot trail for your hanging lamp, Dorothy—Will know definitely in a few days—

When Saxe comes down, (and I *do* wish you *both* would come) we will attend to the chairs—

Dorothy and I could scour the country-side for pretties for our houses, while Saxe and Billy work—Do think seriously of this and write me—so that I'll have that pleasure and privilege to look forward to—

With a heart *full* of love
Estelle

[1]During the Faulkners' trip East to enroll Jill in Pine Manor Junior College.
[2]To Cambridge, Massachusetts, to work on the play version of *Requiem for a Nun.*

837 Letter from Faulkner to Saxe Commins, "Tuesday" [possibly December 4 or 11, 1951], unsigned ribbon typescript, 1 page.

Dear Saxe:

I have changed Missy's[1] plane ticket to Flight 347, which leaves Boston 11 a.m. the 19th, and goes straight through to Memphis without change. I am insisting that she stick to this one, so she will not need to get off it at La Guardia at all, and you will not need to meet her and help her change. This will obviate her and her baggage getting separated; she will arrive Memphis 5:30 pm. when I will meet her.

Will you please send me $2500.00. I will try to finish the year on this. Luckily, I have already paid income tax on $14,000.00 earned in Cal. this year,[2] which will ease the burden a little.

All well here; no news. My best to everyone.

[no signature]

[1] Jill. Her father had asked Commins to assist her in changing planes in New York, en route to Oxford from Pine Manor Junior College.

[2] In February and early March, when Faulkner had produced a film script based on *The Left Hand of God,* a novel by William E. Barrett.

838 Letter from Faulkner to Saxe Commins, "Monday" [late December 1951], signed ribbon typescript, 1 page.

Dear Saxe:

Jill and a schoolmate, Victoria Lilly, will reach LaGuardia Monday, Jan. 7th, American Airlines Flight 262, between 8 and 9 P.M., nearer nine as I remember. They must report in at school in Wellesley before 6 P.M. Jan 8th. If they stop at a New York hotel, the school requires that it be the Biltmore. So will you please make reservations at the Biltmore for them for Jan 7th, evening and night, and put them on a Boston train which will give them plenty of time from Back Bay to Wellesley, they had better reach Boston not much later than 3 P.M.

Will you please have Manny[1] send me $15,000.00 immediately after Jan 1st, 52.

All well here, a good Xmas. I am getting bored, and shall get to work at something soon now.

Best seasonal greetings to everybody, not to mention eternal devotion etc &c ad f. rsvp.

/s/ Bill

[1] Emmanuel Harper, Random House accountant.

1952

---

853 Letter from Faulkner to Saxe Commins, "Sunday" [probably mid-January 1952], signed ribbon typescript, 2 pages.

Dear Saxe:

Will you consult with Bob, Bennett,[1] etc. on this, and give me your advice and information as soon as possible?

I had heard nothing about the play from Ayers or Marre either, since November, when I did the last rewriting.[2] I heard rumors from time to time: that it was to open Jan. 10th, to open Feb. 20th, that it had already opened in fact in Cambridge.

Then Marre telephoned me last week, the play was to open in Paris May 30th. and that he would come down to see me. He is here now. He tells me that the situation is this:

Ayers was unable to raise enough money from his backers, due to the fact that the publication of the book had taken the original 'shine' off the thing. Ayers then planned to open it in Sept. this year.

Ruth,[3] Marre, Ayers and I had talked about taking it to Europe first, last November. All favored Europe except Ayers. Ruth, who because of her known commitment to the part, had had a pretty hard winter, missing radio and t.v. jobs because her known commitment to the play had removed her from availability in people's minds, went to Ayers recently and asked, first, if he wanted any part of taking it to Europe in order to open this spring. Ayers said he didn't. Ruth then said, will you let us do it? Ayers said, yes, only to leave him out.

Marre then contacted the people in charge of the Paris festival[4] for this spring. They will accept the play into their official auspices, to open June 1st. They will put up the equivalent of $7,000.00. We will have to put up the remaining $15,000.00 which Marre estimates as top to run the play for one week, rehearsal, salaries, etc. The old-Russian painter, [Pavel Tchelitchew],[5] will design the sets, getting back to my original version of the script. If the play runs a week, Marre believes (the French people will give us all the gate receipts) it will earn 10 or 12 thousand dollars in francs. If it is that successful, Marre has promise of 'second money' to carry it on, perhaps to London. If it is that successful, we will own the whole job, sets, tried play and all, to sell to an American producer.

The problem is this. I will have to put up the $15,000.00. Under the auspices of the festival, it will run at least a week, earn the estimated $10,000.00 back, but in francs, which I cant take out of France. That is, if it fails, I will have swapped $15,000.00 dollars for its equivalent in francs, which I cant use except in France. If it is a success, of course that wont matter.

I am inclined to risk it, since the Russian's idea sounds like me, but mainly on Miss Ford's account, who to an extent has suffered because of the delay. That is, she is shooting the works on this, her last-best-chance to make tops as an actress.

I dont mind risking the money, and even losing it, since this idea of the staging of the play sounds like me, instead of a conventional run-of-the-mill American play. But to draw this much, will run my income tax out of sight. I would risk and even lose the money, but I dont want to have to pay Uncle Sam about half of it again for the privilege.

Is there any way this can be avoided? that I could take it as a loan, to be amortised at an increase on my income of a thousand a year for fifteen years, instead of 15 thousand in one year?

The French people will have to have an answer pretty quick from me, to make their own schedule. All we need to do is, pay for the transportation, the salaries, the sets of the American troupe, the sets, living expenses in France. The festival does the rest: rents the theatre, pays the French hands, etc., will give us all the gate.

Perhaps you had better telephone me, wire me what hour, etc. Marre will leave here about Monday, he says, but you can telephone me here, I imagine it will be about Wednesday. Think it over well.

/s/ Bill

[1]Robert Haas and Bennett Cerf, who joined with Commins in advising Faulkner not to pursue the course of action outlined in this letter.
[2]Faulkner's play version of *Requiem for a Nun,* which Lemuel Ayers was planning to produce and Albert Marre was hoping to direct, had failed to receive the necessary financial backing.
[3]Ruth Ford, the actress for whom Faulkner wrote *Requiem for a Nun.*
[4]The *Œuvres du XXe Siècle* festival. Faulkner attended as a delegate, but his play was not a part of the program.
[5]Faulkner left this space blank.

854 Western Union telegram from Faulkner to Saxe Commins, January 28 [1952].

FORGOT THIS ON TELEPHONE PLEASE GET AT LEAST THREE TICKETS FOR THE KING AND I. EITHER FRIDAY OR SATURDAY FEBRUARY FIRST OR SECOND

BILL

855 Western Union telegram from Faulkner to Saxe Commins, January 30 [1952].

IF JILL AND ESTELLE ARRIVAL CONFLICT PLEASE MEET JILL GRAND CENTRAL I THINK 5PM. ESTELLE AND MISS SOMERVILLE[1] WILL BE ALL RIGHT UNASSISTED. WOULD YOU CARE TO ASK LINSCOTT[2] FOR DINNER TOO

BILL

[1]Probably Ella Somerville, an Oxford friend of the Faulkners.
[2]Robert Linscott, a Random House editor.

856 Western Union telegram from Jill Faulkner to Saxe Commins, dated Wellesley, Massachusetts, January 30 [1952].

DEAR MR SAXE. WILL ARRIVE THURSDAY 5:00 PM TAKE TAXI TO NEW WESTON PLEASE MEET MAMA INSTEAD DONT WORRY

JILL

858b Letter from Phil Stone to Jerrold Nedwick, a Chicago bookseller, March 17, 1952, carbon typescript with typed signature, 1 page.

Dear Sir:

I have your letter of March 14.

The copies of THE MARBLE FAUN are not in such good condition, especially with reference to the dust jackets. The books themselves do pretty good. They are both autographed presentation copies of the first run of the book and have also been autographed by me.

I am not very anxious to sell either copy and at this time I would not care to sell but one. My price for the one is $150.00 and if you are interested I will send you the best of the two copies by registered mail for your inspection.

Yours truly,
Phil Stone

860 Letter from Faulkner to Saxe Commins, undated [April 1952], signed ribbon typescript, 1 page.

Dear Saxe:

Among the letters I mailed you Friday, did you find one page completely out of context? a single, unfinished typed page, which is part of a speech I am making next month,[1] beginning something about being invited to speak, have chosen to talk about responsibility, I think. It is unmistakable, if it is among them. If so, will you please send it back to me airmail? I cant find it here, and my only hope is that I bundled it up with the France letters[2] and sent it to you.

/s/ Bill

[1] To the Delta Council, at its meeting on the campus of Delta State College, Cleveland, Mississippi, May 15, 1952.

[2] Probably relating to the *Œuvres du XXe Siècle* festival.

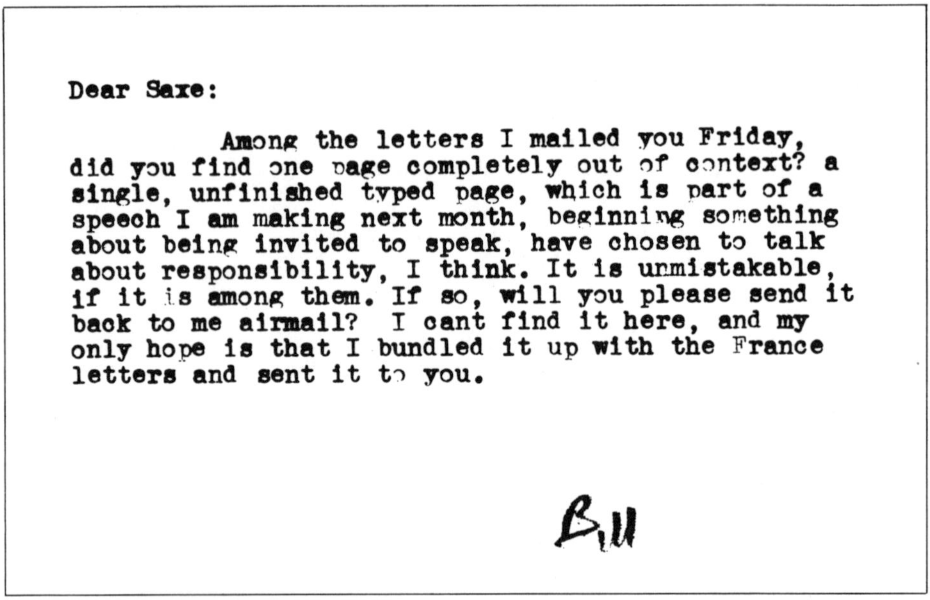

Dear Saxe:

Among the letters I mailed you Friday, did you find one page completely out of context? a single, unfinished typed page, which is part of a speech I am making next month, beginning something about being invited to speak, have chosen to talk about responsibility, I think. It is unmistakable, if it is among them. If so, will you please send it back to me airmail? I cant find it here, and my only hope is that I bundled it up with the France letters and sent it to you.

Bill

17. Letter from Faulkner to Saxe Commins (item 860)

861 Letter from Faulkner to Saxe Commins, undated [April 1952], signed ribbon typescript, 1 page.

Dear Saxe:

The enclosed explain themselves. I would like the trip to Paris, especially on the cuff like this.[1] But I cannot quite reconcile the words 'delegate' and 'freedom' in the same sentence; it's a little amusing, not to mention terrifying.

In fact, I dont want to be an official delegate anywhere to or from or for anything, though dont tell these people that.

But I would still like the two or three weeks in Europe, and this will be a fine excuse to leave here with, since mine is the sort of family which, if I refused to take it to Europe with me, on my return I would find had bought itself a new fur coat, just to keep the books balanced, you might say.

So will you see if B.O.A.C. will book me to Paris via London and return, May 18th—June 7th, with privilege of cancelling at latest date possible before departure, and I will see what I can do here about escaping.

Yours,
/s/ Bill

[1] Faulkner had been invited by the French government to participate in the *Œuvres du XXe Siècle* festival in Paris.

862 Letter from Faulkner to Saxe Commins, "Wednesday" [early May 1952], signed ribbon typescript, 1 page.

Dear Saxe:

Thank you for kindness. I will be in about 5 or 6 pm the 16th. Will you get me a room at New Weston, will see you at the office that afternoon. No need to meet me at airport.

A certain straw in the wind has indicated it is about time to warn you about this matter. You dont know Estelle too well yet. In ten minutes, she can have you believing that black is white. Of course, in eleven minutes you know better, but sometimes it is too late by then. So dont ever send her any money, no matter what tale she tells you, no matter how plausible. She will be very plausible, and will go to any length. If such a request or plea ever comes to you, you can say you cannot do it without authority from me, your auditors will not accept it otherwise, or if you like, just send her this letter. It may never happen, I hope it wont.

Am making a speech at the State Cotton Council meeting 15th,[1] may, will take Flight 8 to NY 16th.

/s/ Bill

[1] The Delta Council Address, Cleveland, Mississippi, May 15, 1952.

863 Letter from Faulkner to Saxe Commins, "Friday" [May 1952], signed ribbon typescript, 1 page.

Dear Saxe:

I think now I shall go straight to Paris, find just how much I shall have to commit myself in order to accept—if I do accept—their offer to pay some or part of the cost, and get that over with and then visit England or other parts.

It is too late, even if worth the bother, to change to a direct Paris line or flight, so will you call BOAC and see if I can be routed straight on from London to Paris the 19th, maybe I shant have to go through English customs, though probably I will have to. I am sure I shall have to change airports, from London airport to Northolt. If Paris flights are not crowded, maybe I can do this myself in New York the 17th. I suppose the 17th will be soon enough to cancel the Brown's Hotel res. for the 19th, wont it? That is, if nothing has to be done right away about rerouting direct to Paris, I can wait until I am in NY and decide whether to go straight on or not. But if better to reroute right away, please do so and cancel the London Hotel.

Just in case BOAC suggest or offer to swap me to a direct line to Paris for the 19th, I will accept at once, but if foreign lines do not like to scratch each other's backs like domestic lines do, it is all right, we will keep the BOAC flight and change at London and go on to Paris the same day by British.

Will see you 16th.

/s/ Bill

864 BOAC note of confirmation for Faulkner's flight from New York to Paris via London, May 17–18, 1952, autograph manuscript, 1 page.

British European
Flight BE 333
London/Paris—May 18th
Leave London 1:00 PM
Arrive Paris 2:20 PM
Confirmed
BA-510
Leaves New York 5:00 PM
Arrives London 10:30 AM

870a Letter from Harold Ober to Saxe Commins, June 6, 1952, signed ribbon typescript, 1 page.

Dear Saxe:

I enclose a memo[1] of my talk with Lemuel Ayers regarding the William Faulkner play, REQUIEM FOR A NUN. Will you talk this over with Bill when he gets back?

Sincerely,
/s/ Harold

[1] See next item.

870a Memo of conversation between Harold Ober and Lemuel Ayers, June 6, 1952, unsigned ribbon typescript (with carbon copy), 1 page.

Lemuel Ayers had a long talk with me about REQUIEM FOR A NUN. He says the play in its present form is too static—there is too much talk and not enough action—that Mr. Faulkner realizes this but doesn't want to do any more work on it himself. Ayers has talked to Whitfield Cook, who is a great admirer of Faulkner and of the play. He has worked with Hitchcock on most of his pictures and is now doing an Anne Parrish[1] play. He is very good on construction. He thinks the play should be handled in something the way DEATH OF A SALESMAN was done. His idea would be to go back to SANCTUARY for some scenes. He would go through the whole play and do it in dummy scenes and if Bill approved the scheme and wanted to he could do the actual writing of the scenes. Cook would do all this on speculation and if Bill didn't like it that would be the end of it.

If Bill approves, Ayers suggests Cook get 3% of the royalties and earnings of the play and Ayers would, in that case, make the royalty on the play 10% from the start so that Bill would be getting 7% from the start.

Cook is willing to do this without credit but would appreciate some such line in small print as "adaptation by Whitfield Cook."

Ayers is still very enthusiastic about the play and wants to do it and make it a great success.

[1]Novelist whose works include *The Perennial Bachelor* (1935), *Mr. Despondency's Daughter* (1938), *Pray for Tomorrow* (1941), and *A Clouded Star* (1948).

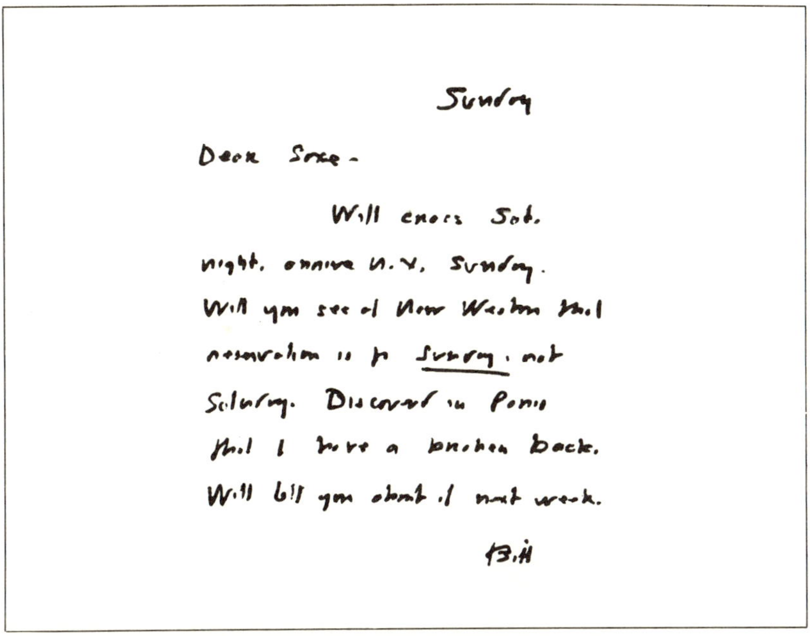
Sunday

Dear Saxe-

Will cross Sat. night, arrive N.Y. Sunday. Will you see at New Weston that reservation is for Sunday, not Saturday. Discovered in Paris that I have a broken back. Will tell you about it next week.

Bill

18. Letter from Faulkner to Saxe Commins (item 871)

871 Letter from Faulkner to Saxe Commins, "Sunday" [June 8, 1952], signed autograph manuscript, 1 page.

Dear Saxe—

Will cross[1] Sat. night, arrive N. Y. Sunday. Will you see at New Weston that reservation is for *Sunday,* not Saturday. Discovered in Paris that I have a broken back. Will tell you about it next week.

Bill

[1]On return flight from the Paris trip. Faulkner wrote this brief note from near Oslo, Norway, where he had gone to rest and recuperate from a siege of back pain and alcoholism.

872a Letter from Carvel Collins to Phil Stone, June 9, 1952, signed ribbon typescript, 1 page.

Dear Phil,

. . . .

I am very grateful to you for sending me the issue of *The Commercial Appeal* reporting William Faulkner's speech to the Delta Council. In sending it you were, as always, very kind and perceptive.

Three weeks ago or so Mary and I had the pleasure of taking Jill and Malcolm Franklin and his wife to Martha's Vineyard for a weekend. Malcolm, as you probably know, is at Woods Hole, Massachusetts, for the summer doing some work at the Marine Biological Laboratory. He and Jill had not seen each other for some time and the weekend made for a pleasant reunion. Mary and I enjoyed seeing them and showing them about this part of the country. Malcolm wrote that a week or so later he was in New York walking along the street with his father when entirely by accident they bumped into "Pappy" who was in New York on his way to Paris for the current Cultural Congress. It is a small world after all.

. . . .

As ever,
/s/ Carvel

872b Letter from Phil Stone to Carvel Collins, June 11, 1952, carbon typescript with typed signature, 1 page.

Dear Carvel:

. . . .

Also what has become of Bill's play?[1] We should like to know about this because we think it is a very poor play.

Have you received the bulletin FAULKNER STUDIES, 1611 Adams Street, Denver 6, Colorado? I am afraid that these people are doing what Mr. Archibald told Charlie Watts, taking the thing too seriously.

We would love to see you and Mary again.

Your friend,
Phil Stone

[1] *Requiem for a Nun*, the production of which had been delayed.

870b Letter from Harold Ober to Saxe Commins, June 13, 1952, signed ribbon typescript, 1 page.

Dear Saxe:

You might add to your memo for William Faulkner the following note from Lemuel Ayers:

"As per our understanding during my visit to your office on May 27th (please correct me if I am wrong) you are going to speak to Faulkner upon his return from Paris concerning the possibility of Whitfield Cook doing work on REQUIEM and that also while this work is being done any further advances to Mr. Faulkner will be waived until Mr. Cook submits his treatment for Mr. Faulkner's approval or rejection. Thanking you very much for your interest and consideration."

Ayers says he has spent around $3500 on the play and I should think that suspension of payments while Mr. Cook works on the play would be fair.

Sincerely,
/s/ Harold

Tuesday

Dear Saxe:

Thank you for your note. No, I dont feel too well. My back gives me a little trouble, but not much; mainly, for the first time in my life, I am completely bored, fed up, my days are being wasted. It is just possible that I shall do something quite drastic about the matter before long. I have done no work in a year, do not want to, yet I have work which I must do. We talked some of my giving myself six months of absence, getting completely away from here and all my familiar life. I think now it will take more than that. I think now I may, to save my soul, something of peace, contentment, save the work at least, quit the whole thing, give it all to them, leave and be done with it. I can earn enough to live on, I think. I am really sick, I think. Cant sleep too well, nervous, idle, have to make an effort not to let the farm go to pot, look forward only with boredom to the next sunrise. I dont like it. Maybe I will have to get away, for at least a year, almost vanish. Then maybe I will get to work again, and get well again. But I dont have enough time left to spend it like this. That is, I still want what I have always wanted: to be free; probably until now I have still believed that somehow, in some way, someday I would be free again; now at last I have begun to realise that perhaps I will not, I have waited, hoped too long, done nothing about it; and so now I must, or -- in spirit -- die.

I haven't quite reached the point yet, but I dont think I shall be much longer. There will be scorn and opprobrium of course, but perhaps I have already sacrificed too much already to try to be a good artist, to boggle at a little more in order to still try to be one.

Yours,

Bill

19. Letter from Faulkner to Saxe Commins (item 877)

874 Letter from Faulkner to Saxe Commins, "Sunday" [June 22, 1952], signed ribbon typescript, 1 page.

Dear Saxe:

I send the enclosed[1] to you, since I dont know whether Harvey Brite [*sic*] has left the Times yet or not. Please send it to him, or if he is gone, maybe to send it to Hemingway's publisher would do.

Here is a list of Jill's summer required reading. Will you please locate them for us and have them sent down?

Hot as hell here. I can ride, but Jill is working the horses in good shape while I sit on the rail and supervise. All are well and send love.

/s/ Bill

[1]The enclosure was a statement on the work of Ernest Hemingway, prepared at the request of Harvey Breit, of the *New York Times Book Review*. See *Selected Letters of William Faulkner,* pp. 333–334, for the text of the statement, which Faulkner intended as a compliment but which Hemingway interpreted as an insult.

877 Letter from Faulkner to Saxe Commins, "Tuesday," signed ribbon typescript, 1 page, with envelope postmarked Oxford, July 30, 1952.

Dear Saxe:

Thank you for your note. No, I dont feel too well. My back gives me a little trouble, but not much; mainly, for the first time in my life, I am completely bored, fed up, my days are being wasted. It is just possible that I shall do something quite drastic about the matter before long. I have done no work in a year, do not want to, yet I have work which I must do. We talked some of my giving myself six months of absence, getting completely away from here and all my familiar life. I think now it will take more than that. I think now I may, to save my soul, something of peace, contentment, save the work at least, quit the whole thing, give it all to them, leave and be done with it. I can earn enough to live on, I think. I am really sick, I think. Cant sleep too well, nervous, idle, have to make an effort not to let the farm go to pot, look forward only with boredom to the next sunrise. I dont like it. Maybe I will have to get away, for at least a year, almost vanish. Then maybe I will get to work again, and get well again. But I dont have enough time left to spend it like this. That is, I still want what I have always wanted: to be free; probably until now I have still believed that somehow, in some way, someday I would be free again; now at last I have begun to realise that perhaps I will not, I have waited, hoped too long, done nothing about it; and so now I must, or—in spirit—die.

I haven't quite reached the point yet, but I dont think I shall be much longer. There will be scorn and opprobrium of course, but perhaps I have already sacrificed too much already to try to be a good artist, to boggle at a little more in order to still try to be one.

Yours,
/s/ Bill

S-31 Letter from Faulkner to Joan Williams, undated [probably mid-August 1952], unsigned ribbon typescript, 1 page.

It's still all right.[1] I cant find anything you could leave out. If you could break up the idiot section into shorter paragraphs, even at times a single sentence to a paragraph, it would help the effect: of his simple mental processes, his mental fumbling, innocence.

Let him be one section. Let the proprietor be one section, with a break, a gap to page four, when Jake himself takes over where the change from the pro. to Jake occurs, as though the story itself began with 'Jake straightened up' etc.

I dont like the title. You are writing about a human being, true. But I think the title should refer to a *condition,* some applicable quotation, like a little child shall lead them, though that is not quite right. Some word maybe, like Twilight, some tender word, or, for emphasis, some savage word or phrase out of Hollywood motion picture slogans, about the educational or artistic value or the importance of motion pictures.

Let the first section, the proprietor's begin: The owner-manager (and ticket-seller and -taker and everything else too, with the exception of the licensed projectionist whom labor union regulations compelled him to hire) did not take the first customer in the line beyond the window, for a looney, and tried to charge him full admission.

Then continue, call the owner by that title throughout his section and the story.

Had a flat tire on way back yesterday, changing tires did my back no good, still painful this morning, though probably that is not the reason, but the unhappiness from yesterday, very unhappy, but after all they are your mouth and your bottom and yours the right to say no about them and anyone that dont like it should better go back where he came from and maybe stay there, hadn't he?

The story is laid in Miss. and a mag. editor may find a little Faulkner in it (idiot and cow), so I think better not to enclose my letter with the story, but for me to send the letter in from here, as if you knew nothing about the letter. When you have a clean copy ready to send in, I will wait a day or so, then write the letter.

It's all right, this time. I think you can stop worrying, and just write. The next one may not be this good, but dont let that trouble you either.

[no signature]

[1]The suggestions which follow relate to the manuscript of Miss Williams' short story, "The Morning and the Evening."

879 Letter from Faulkner to Saxe Commins, "Sunday" [possibly August 1952], signed ribbon typescript, 1 page.

Dear Saxe:

Am returning the papers[1] intact. I am not able to do this sort of thing. I am no propagandist, polemicist; I am a fictionist. I have never been able to write fiction even on demand or to pattern; I could never write propaganda on demand when I cant even do it by volition. Sorry.

Enclosed is Abercrombie[2] bill. You kindly agreed to pay such and chg. to me, in case it will help income. I still feel rotten, no life much. For a while I kidded myself I was feeling better day by day. Now, I dont know.

Love to all.

/s/ Bill

[1]Unidentified.

[2]Abercrombie & Fitch, an exclusive New York store which specializes in sporting goods.

880 Letter from Faulkner to Saxe Commins, "Saturday" [early September] and "28 Sept." [1952], signed ribbon typescript, 1 page.

Dear Saxe:

I am working at the big book[1] again. I think that I may go on through and finish it, this time. We talked last spring, I think I shall take six months, maybe a year, cut completely away from here, all this responsibility, maybe Mexico. I will need money. That is, this establishment here takes all my income. It will continue to do so. I will need extra money for myself. Can I have it? I can earn extra money I believe, if I am free of all this, happy a little, at something resembling peace.

I think I will come up about first Oct. and talk to you. This letter does not even make sense; you can see that I am in a bad condition.

Please send me $5000.00.

Miss Joan Williams, whom you will remember from two years ago, is coming to New York. She will bring to you 3 sections of the rewritten mss. which is right. I will bring more of it when I come up.

28 Sept.

I should have got this letter off to you almost a month ago. I have been sick again, with my back; it begins to hurt, and I make the mistake of trying at first to treat it here at home with alcohol, before I give up and go to hosptl. where I have been for the last 9 days, am now having a brace built to wear. I go for a fitting Thursday a fortnight. When I have the brace, I will come up for a week or so.

Here are Miss Williams' address and telephone:

288 West 4 St.
Chelsea 34017

If there is anything she needs that you can do, do it for me. I have made a writer out of her, showed her how to do one TV script which she sold,[2] and a story which Ober has just sold to the Atlantic.[3] Now I am going to make her write a novel for Random House.[4] She is shy and independent and will probably ask nothing of you. Will you write her a note and tell her to call on you at need, for my sake? I will see you about middle of Oct. I feel like hell now, should be better with the brace.

/s/ Bill

[1] *A Fable.*

[2] "The Graduation Dress."

[3] "The Morning and the Evening," which appeared in the January 1953 issue.

[4] Joan Williams' first novel, *The Morning and the Evening,* was published in 1961 by Atheneum Press.

881b Letter from Phil Stone to Fred Wieck, The Newberry Library, Chicago, September 19, 1952, carbon typescript with typed signature, 1 page.

Dear Mr. Wieck:

I have your letter of September 17th with inclosures and thank you very much.

I am sorry that I cannot help you with this.[1] Several years ago I did give a few things to the Yale Library. Since that time twelve large folders which I had containing a number of letters from Faulkner and many original manuscripts were burned when my old house burned in 1942.

Nor do I know of any people to whom Faulkner might have written because he won't write letters unless he has to do it. Just now I can't think of anyone. Perhaps Mr. Cerf of Random House, Faulkner's publisher, might be able to help you.

It would not hurt to write Faulkner direct, although you probably will not get an answer.

Yours truly,
Phil Stone

P. S.: Since dictating the above I find that I did not tell you anything about the articles of which you speak. I did do one or two short, and very poor articles for the little magazine which they started here,[2] but my copies were all burned. I suggest that you write Mr. Phillip Mullen, Paris, Tennessee, and tell him what you want.

The only other things I remember writing about Faulkner were the Foreword to THE MARBLE FAUN and an article which appeared in The Saturday Review of Literature five or six years ago or more,[3] and I do not have copies of these.

[1] Wieck had sought Stone's assistance in developing a collection of Faulkner papers for the Newberry Library.

[2] *The Oxford Magazine* (numbers 1, 2, and 3, 1934). The three-part series ("William Faulkner, the Man and His Work") which Stone produced for this short-lived magazine has been reprinted in James Meriwether, "Early Notices of Faulkner by Phil Stone and Louis B. Cochran," *Mississippi Quarterly*, 17 (Summer 1964), 136–164.

[3] "William Faulkner and His Neighbors," *Saturday Review of Literature*, 25 (September 19, 1942), 12.

882a Letter from Robert Coughlan to Phil Stone, September 26, 1952, signed ribbon typescript, 1 page.

Dear Phil:

Probably you have given me up for dead by now; but I had several European subjects to get out of the way, and then a five weeks' vacation, and then at last was able to take up the Faulkner article[1] again, almost a year to the day from the time I was snatched off to Yugoslavia. The result is enclosed here. I think that this time it comes fairly close, within shooting distance, of what I had wanted to do with it. But I am by no means entirely satisfied with it, and I will be deeply appreciative for your comments and suggestions.

There are a lot of errors in it, I know. The small ones I will ask Phil Mullen to check (he has had a fee for checking the whole manuscript, paid in advance). I'll send him a mss. later on, perhaps not until I have had your reply and have done a revised draft. But there may be some big errors, either of commission or omission, and if there are, I hope that you will straighten me out on them.

My immediate superior at the magazine has read the piece and likes it in general, but feels that it doesn't really "come to grips" with Faulkner: doesn't portray him vividly enough as a person, and doesn't sufficiently explain either his peculiarities or his talents as a writer. Maybe so. If you have any thoughts as to how these faults can be corrected, let me know.

My best regards to Miss Emily and to young Philip, whose letter to me I enjoyed a great deal.

Sincerely,
/s/ Bob Coughlan

[1] The *Life* magazine feature. Stone had agreed to assist with the project, provided he would be allowed to review the manuscript.

883a Letter from Phil Stone to Ward L. Miner, September 29, 1952, carbon typescript with typed signature, 1 page.

Dear Mr. Miner:

Thank you very much for your thoughtfulness in sending me the autographed copy of THE WORLD OF WILLIAM FAULKNER.

If I don't read it and write you about it soon please don't think that I don't appreciate it. I have a heavy load of work for the rest of this year and it is seldom that I get to read a whole book.

Also, there are so many persistent repetitions of Faulkner myths which I personally know not to be true and the critics read into his work so many things that are not there and so many things that may be there but which were entirely unintentional on Faulkner's part, that it is hard for me to read criticism about his work. Perhaps I know too much about the author and the subject.

Another thing is that such critiques make me a little sad because they seem to be in the nature of literary obituaries. After all, the Nobel Prize was for work he did between 1928 and 1940 and he has done very little since then of the same stature as the work of that period. I think now that he never will and I think that his great success and the adulation that has followed it has really been a misfortune.

The people who write about him are too much in awe of him and I think that you remember that I am of the opinion that his merits as a writer are overestimated by contemporary critics just as they were underestimated for fifteen long years.

He is good, probably the best of the lot in contemporary American fiction, but he is just not as good as his present worshippers think he is.

We hope you will come back again to see us.

Yours truly,
Phil Stone

882c Letter from Phil Stone to Robert Coughlan, September 30, 1952, carbon typescript with typed signature, 8 pages.

Dear Bob:

I herewith return your manuscript.

I took it home at noon and Emily read it yesterday afternoon and I took off a while and read it last night. I read it twice, once for the various suggestions and criticisms and once to read it through as a whole in order to get the effect.

First, we both think the article is extremely good and has in it some splendid phrasing. Your editor is all wet about thinking that you didn't cover Bill sufficiently personally and his talents as a writer. It would be impossible for you to do both of these things well in one article. If you tried to write the personal sketch and the literary criticism in one article, the article would be too long and would not have a unified effect.

There are two things in general in which I think you give an incorrect impression. The first thing is that you emphasize too much the fact that Bill occasionally, very occasionally, throws a drunk. I think you should re-work this part and avoid so much reference to his drinking. On the whole he drinks very little. Apparently you have still not quite got away from your previous mind-set of explaining Bill on a Freudian basis and still remain unconvinced that Bill's is not at all a complex personality.

The second thing is that you say nothing at all about his patience, kindness and tolerance toward young children and old people and his very sincere liking for them. When you leave this out you leave out one entire side of the man and one of his few attractive sides as an individual.

I am now going to give you a list of the things which Emily and I noticed and which need to be corrected, and first I shall give you Emily's, referring to the numbers of the manuscript pages.

Page 1: It was General A. J. Smith who burned Oxford and not Sherman. Sherman never operated up this far in Mississippi.

Page 2: Jill is not going to school at Holyoke. She is going to some girls' school near Bryn Mawr and I think it is Pine Manor Junior College. (Reported in the Alumni column of the local high school paper).

Bill did not put the "u" in his name. A type-setter for The Four Seas [Company] did this when THE MARBLE FAUN was published.[1]

Miss Maud is not an Episcopalian although Jill is. Certainly Miss Maud is not a devout one and she doesn't do much of anything in connection with any church. We know because this is our church.

Miss Maud lives on South Lamar, which street was named for L. Q. C. Lamar, a member of Congress, officer in the Confederate Army, a United States Senator, Secretary of the Interior under Cleveland, and finally an Associate Justice of the Supreme Court of the United States.

I don't think Bill gave Miss Maud that house. I know that Mr. Murry built it during his lifetime.

Page 3: J. W. T. Falkner is not sheriff and never has been. He is United States Marshall for the Northern District of Mississippi. He has never been called Jack. "Jack" is the nickname of Murry C., Bill's second brother who is now with the F. B. I.

It is not at all difficult for the Falkners to keep up with their family relationship.

Page 4: Emily thinks the comment on Bill's inconsistencies is good and well written.

Page 5: Regarding "SPOTTED HORSES," she thinks the crucial point is that the man from Texas and the local scoundrel outsmarted the experts. That is the basic characteristic of the Snopeses who are the epitome of the poor white trash: cunning, unrelenting chicanery, completely unprincipled, grasping, and God help the helpless.

Page 8: If you read Bill's books carefully you will see that Jefferson is not the home of the University of Mississippi. It is located at Oxford, 40 or 60 miles away from Jefferson according to the books.

Page 14: It is Van Buren Avenue and not "Street."

Page 16: The proper spelling of the current affectionate title of the University of Mississippi is not as you have it but is "Ole Miss," as a negro would say it. For God's sake correct this if you want your article to have the local flavor.

Page 17: The name, my dear sir, is Phil Stone and not Philip Stone. Philip Stone is my son. Be sure to correct this all the way through; otherwise I may sue.

Page 21: All we know about the lucky gold piece we learned from "Moon" Mullen. It was Mack Reed's gold piece and it had a sentimental value.[2]

Page 22: Mr. Stark Young is not actually a native of Oxford, but a native of near Como in Panola County. He grew up in Oxford and lived here a long time and taught at the University.

Page 23: Estelle first married Cornell Franklin, who was a lawyer in Honolulu, a Federal Judge there, later a lawyer in Shanghai and is now, I understand, a lawyer in New York. I never heard of him having anything to do with the jewelry trade.

It is South Lamar Street. Get this right all the way through.

It is the Episcopal Church, not Episcopalian. The members are Episcopalians.

Page 26: As said above, this was not Bill's gold piece. Mullen can put you right on that story.

Page 27: Stone Stop was a railroad stop on the Batesville & Southwestern Railroad. It was on some land my Daddy owned and on which his late friend Paul J. Rainey built a club house so he and Dad could go bear hunting there. It is southwest of Oxford, but it is actually in the Mississippi Delta in the corner of Panola and Quitman Counties. The fact that it is in the Delta and not in the hills is important.

Page 28: I married Emily Whitehurst, who was a teacher in the University High School here and who was originally from Dublin, Georgia.

Page 28: My dear sir, The American Bar Association does not have directors. I have been president of the Mississippi State Bar and am now a member, and have been for several years, of the House of Delegates of The American Bar Association.

Page 32: The name of the Chevrolet dealer is Sykes Haney. . . . The name of the Ford dealer is Henry Mansell.

These are the comments that Emily made, although not exactly in her exact language. Mine follow. It may be that they will duplicate those of Emily to some extent but I don't have time to check through these now.

Page 1: There is no hatred in Bill's eyes nor in Bill. If anything, he is far too indifferent and too cold for hatred.

Neither is Bill given to rages, sudden or otherwise. You got that impression from your first meeting with him. I am sure he would resent your coming but that was partly for effect and to bluff you off.

The house was built by old Colonel Bailey.[3]

Page 2: Not *cypresses* in the yard! They are cedars. My dear friend, a boy from Kokomo, Indiana, should know that cypresses don't grow on hillsides.

Page 3: "Third brother." This is confusing. I know you are referring to Bill's second brother, Jack, but it is not clear.

Page 7: Isn't the name "Millard"? That is my recollection.

Page 9: Lafayette is one word and is pronounced here with the accent on the second syllable (long "a").

Page 10: When you spell reconstruction with a capital "R" you have made a terrible mistake. "Reconstruction" with a capital "R" down here refers only to the terrible period of negro and carpetbagger domination that followed the Civil War and to indicate that old Colonel Falkner was taking part in that would subject your magazine to a very well-founded libel suit.

Page 22: He was not fired from the Post Office. They wanted to fire him but I was determined that they should not do so and put on lots of political pressure to prevent it, mainly through Pat Harrison.[4] When they had failed to fire him we later had him resign.

Page 24: We had sold a little poem to THE NEW REPUBLIC for $15.00 and that was before the time you speak of.[5]

Page 25: SARTORIS was the third novel and SOUND AND FURY the fourth. SARTORIS was deliberately written to sell and was the book that we thought would sell but it did not. I invented a great number of the incidents in SARTORIS and several of the characters. It is the one novel of Bill with which I had anything to do.

Bill and Estelle were married in the old Presbyterian Church at College Hill by the revered late Dr. W. D. Heddleston, and were not married in the Episcopal Church in Oxford. They ran off to get married like two children.

. . . .

Thank you for what you said about me. You certainly did me justice, if not more.

Your friend,
Phil Stone

[P.S.] Since the above was typed I have thought of two other things which perhaps I should tell you.

The first thing is about your bearing down so hard on Bill's father. What you say about him is true but you are going to offend needlessly a lot of people here and will hurt Miss Maud, a grand old lady, very deeply. I think you could tone this down by giving a mere statement of Mr. Murry's business activities and a more or less general statement showing that he had no interest in literature nor in Bill's hopes of success. As a matter of fact, I think he was very generous in giving Bill board and lodging because no one knew then what Bill's future held. Although I knew it was absolutely obvious that Bill would be a success from a literary standpoint I did not think he would make much money ever, and I never dreamed that he would receive the Nobel Prize. It is very easy to be wise after the event, but to judge Bill's father fairly we must go back to the situation as I know it existed in the 20's.

There is another thing I feel that I should tell you, but it is in the strictest confidence because I like Moon Mullen personally. It is, not to rely too much on Moon's ideas about Bill. I don't mean by this that Moon would deliberately misstate anything to you. What I do mean is that Moon seems to think that he is much better informed on the subject of Bill than he really is. Really all he knows about Bill is just surface. Since I know more about Bill than anybody in the world does, I realize how little Moon really knows probably much more clearly than you or any other outsider would suspect. Moon can give you many little anecdotes he has picked up.

Another reason is that Moon is not equipped to really sense the full flavor of Bill's background. Being a Southerner is in one's blood or it is not and, after all, Moon is a Yankee who only came here in 1933 and, as I remember, had never lived in the South before. He had no forebears in the Confederate Army; neither of his grandfathers or grandmothers lived through Reconstruction days. My experience is that it takes a second generation of Yankees to really become authentic Southerners. Being a Southerner is not only a way of life (admirable or not, as one may choose to think) but it is something one has to have in his blood, something as natural and unthinking as the way one's heart beats or the way one breathes, and, I believe it is something that may never be acquired consciously.

If you failed to realize that Bill is truly a Southerner with both the shortcomings and the admirable qualities of such, it is impossible to understand either him or his work. I am sure that Moon thinks he does realize these things but I can state positively that he does not and cannot and never will. Even yet, Moon does not seem to understand that the situation in the South about negroes voting is not just a matter of denying equal rights to negroes, but that it is a natural attempt to prevent happening what has happened once before and what we have reason to think will happen again, complete negro domination. When you Yankees get your negro population up to 50% and we get ours down to 10%, we shall be glad to join you in helping the negroes get equality.

Your friend,
Phil Stone

[1]As Carvel Collins has proved, it was Faulkner who put the "u" in his name (see *William Faulkner: Early Prose and Poetry* [Boston: Little, Brown and Company, 1962], pp. 10–13). Faulkner may have been reverting to an earlier spelling of his family name, one which recent generations (possibly beginning with his great-grandfather, W. C. Falkner) had abandoned.

[2]During a period of financial difficulty Faulkner had exchanged a ten-dollar gold piece for cash at Mac Reed's drug store. See Blotner, *Faulkner,* p. 679.

[3]Rowan Oak was built by William Turner, an English architect, for "Colonel" Robert B. Shegog about 1848.

[4]U.S. Senator from Mississippi who was a friend of Stone.

[5]"L'Apres-Midi d'un Faune," *New Republic,* 20 (August 6, 1919), 24.

882d Letter from Robert Coughlan to Phil and Emily Stone, October 7 [1952], signed ribbon typescript, 2 pages.

Dear Phil and Emily,

I was delighted to have your letter and comments and to know that you like the article in general. He is a difficult journalistic subject and I have never felt sure that I understood him well enough to present him to the public, but if you say the picture is accurate then I know it is, and am much relieved. I am really very grateful to both of you.

Incidentally, Phil, I engaged Mullen not because I regard him as an expert on the subject, but simply because in the process of factual checking we need a leg man on the scene, and I didn't want to bother you with the dozens of small details that our checker will be worrying about at the time the article goes to press. He is, I think, capable of names and dates and spellings and of gathering material for picture captions, but I do not intend to rely on him for any basic material.

There are two points I would like to ask you about just now. I had thought that the resolution to write "for the ages"—"If people aren't going to buy them, let's write them to please ourselves," you had said—came after the failure of Soldiers' Pay and Mosquitoes, and that this led to Sound and Fury; but you point out that Sartoris intervened. Does that mean that Sartoris had been written and published and had failed financially before he began to write Sound and Fury, and that this—the third strike—resulted in the above decision? Or was it during the period when Sartoris was being shopped around among the publishers and finding no takers?

The other point: one of our people here heard that when the first child[1] was born it was premature, or sickly at any rate, and had to be kept for several weeks at the hospital; that Bill, becoming impatient, demanded that it be brought home; that the doctor told him he could take her against his advice and would have to bear the responsibility; that the child was taken home and soon died; that Bill then got his gun and went out to shoot the doctor, who had to stay in hiding for several weeks until friends had brought Bill back to reason. Is there any truth in this? I'm not at all sure I would want to use the incident—and if I did, it would be put briefly and softly—but I need to know whether it is true or not in order to deal with this particular editor.

Probably there will be other points I will want to ask about later, but I will try to keep them in the realm of the important, because I understand how busy you must be and I don't want to impose on your generosity more than I can help—more than I have already done.

Miss Emily, excuse me for not remembering your maiden name. . . .

I've told my wife so much about you both that she feels she knows you and she hopes, as I do, that soon we can get together either in Oxford or New York.

Hello to Philip and Araminta.

Sincerely,
/s/ Bob

[1] Alabama, who died on January 20, 1931, after living only nine days.

888 Letter from Saxe Commins to his wife Dorothy, October 8, 1952, signed autograph manuscript, 2 pages (1 leaf), with envelope addressed in Commins' hand and postmarked Oxford, the same day.

Dearest Do,

Well, here I am. It is after seven and I have just had breakfast after a night of strange and pathetic happenings. It is impossible to give you details, but I started a journal last night which will, in time, complete the picture, and a ghastly one it is.[1]

The flight was smooth and uneventful. I arrived in Memphis at 6 o clock, Central Time, and was met by Estelle, Malcolm, her son, and his wife, Gloria. We had dinner at the airport and there I heard what has happened here during the last six weeks. The tale continued for the 75 miles we drove from the corner of Tennessee to Oxford, where we arrived at about 10.

I found Bill completely deteriorated in mind and body. He mumbles incoherently and is totally incapable of controlling his bodily functions. He pleads piteously for beer all the time and mumbles deliriously. Every twenty minutes or so through the night I had to carry him virtually to the bathroom. His body is bloated and bruised from his many falls and bears even worse marks.

Of course I do what I can but this is a case for commitment and professional care. The disintegration of a man is tragic to witness. I try to be stern and gentle and placating, but I doubt whether anything registers. Right now he is asleep and will probably slumber most of the day.

I'll take advantage of that respite to talk to his local doctor. It is unthinkable to move him from here, even as far as Memphis, where he could get hospital care. Perhaps the doctor can give him enough sedation to keep him under for long enough to get his bodily functions going. I don't know.

How long I shall stay depends on what the doctor advises. In no case will I bring him back.[2] That is out of the question. He cannot take a step unaided. This is more than a case of acute alcoholism. It is a complete disintegration of a man.

It was pitch dark when I arrived in Memphis and now I am getting my first glimpse of Southern daylight. So I have no impression whatever of the country. The house, however, has left a strong and rather distasteful impression on me. It is a rambling Southern mansion, deteriorated like its owner, built in 1838 and not much improved since. Ours is a heavenly mansion in comparison, if very much smaller. The rooms are bare and what they do contain is rickety, tasteless, ordinary. There is none of the charm and orderliness and comfort that you give to a home.

But I am seeing it under difficult circumstances. Maybe the shock of what I found on my arrival colors my view.

I'll have to stay here until the end of the week at least.[3] Not until I know what can be done for Bill will I be able to think of leaving. That means I shall miss seeing Frannie and Gene this week-end and I'm sick about it.

Please try to keep things going without me. I know I can count on it. One needs an experience like this to appreciate you and the amenity you bring to our home. I tell you this is a ghastly business and I don't let myself think how it can be straightened out. I'll try to do what I can and not worry too much about it. If I succeed, all right, and if not I wont be sorry I tried.

I hope your visit with Frannie was all you wanted it to be. She is such a superior person and deserves everything good that we or life can offer her. I'm dying to know all that happened in New York.

Please explain everything to Eugene. He'll understand and tell him I'll go to Swarthmore to see him the first Saturday I can manage it.

Give them both my deep love and you too. Remember me to Franz and John. I hope Franz is well.

How did you find Laurie on her return from the kennels? A hug for her too.

Kiss my Frannie and all my heart to you, Do.

Dad

[1]Estelle Faulkner had asked Commins to come to Oxford to assist during one of Faulkner's severe bouts with alcoholism. Commins nursed Faulkner overnight and arranged for his hospitalization in Memphis.

[2]Commins had considered attempting to persuade Faulkner to travel to New York to secure medical help.

[3]As it turned out, Commins returned home later this same day.

889 Letter from Saxe Commins to Robert K. Haas and Bennett Cerf, October 8, 1952, signed autograph manuscript, 2 pages (1 leaf).

Dear Bob & Bennett,

Well, here I am! What I have to report is very discouraging.

It is now 8 in the morning and I am a little shaky after a harrowing night. When I arrived at 10 last night after a smooth flight and dinner at the Memphis airport with Estelle, Malcolm, her son, and Gloria, his wife, we drove the 75 miles to Oxford. On the way I was given a history of the last six weeks, and it was disheartening.

At first I thought their dismal account was slightly exaggerated but my first glimpse of Bill made me realize how accurately they had reported on his condition. He was lying on the couch in the drawing room in a stupor. His face is covered with bruises and contusions. His pajamas had slipped down and I could see how battered his body is. He greeted me mumblingly and incoherently, saying, "I need you. Get me beer!"

We carried him to the bathroom and up to bed. Then began a long vigil.

Every few minutes he had to be carried to the bathroom and since he has little control of his functions, it was a disagreeable as well as a pathetic office we had to perform. All the while he pleaded for drink. I tried to be stern, threatening, cajoling, with no success. We placated him with a few tins of beer and then the moaning and pleading began again.

The fact is that Bill has deteriorated shockingly both in body and mind. He can neither take care of himself in the most elementary way or think with any coherence at all. This may be only evidence of his condition in a state of acute alcoholism. But I believe it goes much deeper and is real disintegration.

What to do? I realized at once that this is a case for professional care. No good intentions or friendship or understanding of the psychological causes are of any help at this stage. He needs a hospital, nurses, discipline.

To move him even as far as Memphis is unthinkable. New York or Princeton is totally out of the question. So this morning I'm going into town to talk to his local doctor and try to find out what can be done medically. I'll know better what to do after I get his advice.

Estelle is really desperate and doesn't know where to turn. Malcolm, her son and a very fine fellow, is doing all he can but he too is helpless.

We cannot take Bill to the local hospital for the simple reason that they are not equipped to handle so difficult a case. We can't take him to Memphis because he is in no condition to bear the 75-mile drive. Perhaps we can get the local doctor to put him under heavy sedation, so that he can rid himself of the accumulated alcoholic poisoning in his body. I don't know.

I shall have to stay here until something effective can be decided upon. The decisions, God help me, will have to be mine. Please rely on my judgment. Actually there is little that I can do besides helping him move about and guarding him from injury. If he regains enough consciousness to take care of himself I'll beat a hasty retreat to New York and the amenities of publishing.

Under the circumstances, particularly the one that would make me terribly sorry if anything happened and I did not make the trip, I am glad I came down here. It may turn out that I will be of some use. It's the least one does for a friend.

I'm really sorry my report has to be so dismal. But I count on your understanding. Haven't I had it in perfect trust for twenty years?

As soon as there is any development whatever, I'll write in all detail.

My love and devotion to both of you.

Saxe

891 Western Union telegram from Estelle Faulkner to Saxe Commins, October 10, 1952.

PLEASE, IF YOU WILL, KEEP BILLS WHEREABOUTS CONFIDENTIAL. THANK YOU

ESTELLE

890 Letter from Estelle Faulkner to Saxe and Dorothy Commins, "Friday," signed autograph manuscript, 2 pages, with envelope addressed in Mrs. Faulkner's hand and postmarked Oxford, October 10, 1952.

Dearest Dorothy and Saxe—

Just a note with my love enclosed—and a word about Billy—His nurse reports this morning, that he had a good night, last night, ate a splendid breakfast, and was *very* co-operative—*That* means a lot—

We can never thank you enough, Saxe, for, in your gentle way, taking charge of the situation and getting our "Pappy" back to the hospital—I am optimistic about him for the first time in many fearful weeks—and *you* turned the tide!

The weather has cleared, and everything outside is quite lovely—all the dry summer's dust washed away—

Malcolm, Ria and I hope to go out and fish awhile this afternoon—Those two sweet children are ever mindful of me, and now, that we aren't frantic with worry any more—plan to stay outside some—fish, hunt and roam in the woods—

Thank you again, Dorothy (and thank Franny for me too), for being so sweet and unselfish, lending us Saxe—Someday, I *do* hope that we can welcome you *all,* in the happiest of circumstances—to our Home—

Saxe, I'm sure that you understood my somewhat cryptic wire this morning,[1] so I need not elaborate—but I want Dorothy to know too, everything that you know—

A heart *full* of love and
gratitude—
Always
Estelle

[1] See the previous item.

882e Letter from Phil Stone to Robert Coughlan, October 10, 1952, carbon typescript with typed signature, 2 pages.

Dear Bob:

We have your letter of October 7 and were very glad to hear from you.

We do think that your article was good, but we did not say it was accurate. A lot of it is not accurate. Refer to our comments.

I think that Mullen will make a very good man for what you want. It is the kind of thing which he does very well although he is not likely to be very imaginative. His tendency is to follow the usual groove, but you know enough about your business to correct for that.

SARTORIS was the third novel. We had no particular trouble getting a publisher to take it[1] but it just did not sell and nobody noticed it much. SOUND AND FURY was written and published after SARTORIS and my recollection is that none of it was written until a good while after SARTORIS was published, but I am not sure about that. The decision for Bill to write just as he wanted to came after we found that SARTORIS did not sell. I don't know whether or not I remembered to tell you that SOUND AND FURY was the title suggested by me.

As for your other point, this is another typical Faulkner myth. It sounds like some tale that Bill may have told to a bunch of credulous Yankees when he, Bill, was drunk. I am sure that there is not a word of fact in it except that the little girl was premature and that they did try to save her by putting her in an incubator. Bill never took her home against the doctor's advice, he never got a gun and looked for the doctor and the doctor never hid out. This is just a tall tale. As far as I know, Bill never got a gun and went looking for anybody at any time. The doctor was John Culley at the Oxford Hospital and he was there every day both before and after the death of the little girl. The little girl was named Alabama after Bill's great-aunt Mrs. McLain [*sic*], who is still living in Memphis, and whom Bill escorted to the premiere of "Intruder in the Dust" here.

Please don't hesitate to call on me for anything in the world I can tell you. That sort of thing is no trouble to me and I would like for your article to be as accurate as possible, to not give any false impression of Bill, and to not spread any more of the wild-eyed Faulkner myths.

. . . .

Your friend,
Phil Stone

[1]Stone is incorrect here. *Flags in the Dust* was rejected by eleven publishers before being published as *Sartoris*. See Douglas Day, "Introduction," *Flags in the Dust* (New York: Random House, 1973).

892 Letter from Estelle Faulkner to Saxe Commins, "Wednesday" [possibly October 15, 1952], signed autograph manuscript, 2 pages.

Dear Saxe—

Have just talked to Dr. Adler—He says that Billy is doing wonderfully well—nerves steadier, and appetite—good. Still has beer three times a day, but the doctor, being a good German gentleman—evidently thinks it's good for Bill, and no doubt is—

Adler said that I might go up to see him on Friday—he thought maybe I should—but intends keeping Bill for a[t] least a week longer to get *everything* straightened out—So far, they've done nothing about his back—

Am sure that Bob showed you my letter—I'm sorry that I haven't sent in a daily report—but really there's been so little to tell you—Improving—but slowly—is the nurse's song when I call—

I was a little startled when I saw your letter addressed to Mrs. *Estelle* Faulkner—Aren't you a bit premature—or has something happened that I'm in the dark about?

Right now, though, I know that I'm super-sensitive—Excuse me, if that unusual (to me) form of address worried me without cause—

Saxe, I am worried—almost to the point of desperation—but mostly about Jill and her future—Unless it's the *only* way to save Billy—I *must* put Jill and her happiness, first—

Can't you and Dorothy advise me? Please believe that I'm not thinking of myself—only Bill, Jill and Malcolm—

Thank you for the nice letter—

Love to the Four of You
D. F. E. S.[1]—
Fondly
Estelle

[1]The Comminses: Dorothy, Franny, Eugene, and Saxe.

882f Letter from Robert Coughlan to Phil Stone, October 20, 1952, signed ribbon typescript, 1 page.

Dear Phil,

. . . .

By the way, I didn't mean to imply that you had given carte blanche to the Faulkner article, just that you had thought the tone and characterization right in a general way. Yours and Miss Emily's corrections will of course be taken account of fully in a revised and shortened mss.

Best regards,
/s/ Bob

893 Western Union telegram from Estelle Faulkner to Saxe Commins, October 21, 1952.

BILL HOME TODAY. GREATLY IMPROVED. WILL WRITE LATER LOVE

ESTELLE

894 Letter from Faulkner to Saxe Commins, "Saturday," signed ribbon typescript, 1 page, with envelope addressed in typescript and postmarked Oxford, October 25, 1952.

Dear Saxe:

Hell's to pay here now. While I was hors de combat, E. opened and read Joan Williams' letters to me. Now E. is drunk, and I am trying to nurse her before Malcolm sends her to a hospital, which costs like fury and does no good unless you make an effort yourself. I cant really blame her, certainly I cant criticise her, I am even sorry for her, even if people who will open and read another's private and personal letters, do deserve exactly what they get.

But this is a terrible situation; never can I remember ever being so unhappy and downhearted and despaired. I have done no work in a year, am living on my fat, will begin soon to worry about money, and I do not believe I can work here. I must get away. I want to come up to Princeton, per your invitation, and finish the big book.[1] Yet I cant leave E. drunk here, and if I came anywhere in the neighborhood of N.Y. city, nothing would ever convince her that it was not only to be near Joan, since she (E.) has never had any regard or respect for my work, has always looked on it as a hobby, like collecting stamps.

But I still hope that somehow, somehow, it can be done: I can take the mss. and come up and finish it in peace. Of course, I could come anyway, regardless. But I am fearful about Jill. I mean, to disrupt her in the middle of her senior year at her school.[2] I am afraid that, if I came up, E. would insist on some public formal separation and so forth, so that every time Jill entered a class room or the dining room, she would think: *All these people know that my parents have separated,* and it would ruin her year, even if she herself did not do something in desperation. So I dont see much hope until after she graduates, though I dont see either how I can go on like this; particularly have I got to get back to work, not only for the money, but to get the book finished. I am still weak and nervous, cant sleep much; maybe in another week my strength and common sense will have returned, and I can find some way to bring the mss. up and still not cause an explosion here that will ruin Jill's last year in her school. I will always believe that my first responsibility is to the artist, the work; it is terrible that my wife does not realise or at least accept that. But there is a responsibility too to the female child whose presence in the world I am accountable for. I used to be the cat who walked by himself, and wanted, needed nothing from anyone. But not any more. Let me have your advice, if you have any. I probably wont take it, but it should comfort me.

/s/ Bill

[1] *A Fable.*
[2] Pine Manor Junior College.

883b Letter from Phil Stone to Ward Miner, October 27, 1952, carbon typescript with typed signature, 2 pages.

Dear Mr. Miner:

I finally succeeded in finding time to read the pamphlet[1] which you sent me. I enjoyed and I think it is a very good job. My wife has not yet had time to read it.

However, there are some inaccuracies in it to which I wish to call your attention:

Page 12. It is true that Oxford has no town library but it is also true that right across the bridge it has the library of the University of Mississippi, so it doesn't need a town library.

Page 37. The law did not set aside 1/16 of each township for the schools. It set aside the 16th Section of each Township.

Page 45. The University of Mississippi is State-owned property and it is not a town and it is not incorporated. It does have a separate post office, and Bill was, from 1920 to 1925, the worst postmaster that post office ever had.

Page 78. You are wrong about Tennessee. There are three unofficial divisions of Tennessee: East Tennessee, Middle Tennessee, and West Tennessee. East Tennessee includes mainly the First and Second Congressional Districts. They do not vote Republican as often as they vote Democratic. These two districts vote Republican all the time and now have two Republican Congressmen.

Page 83. Here again I think you make the mistake of attributing to Bill much more profundity than he has, and are reading into his book something which is not there, or, if it is there, is there accidentally.[2]

Page 97. The name here is John M. Stone and not John W. Stone. He was from Iuka, Tishomingo County, the northeast county of Mississippi, and made a splendid Governor. He was no relation of ours.

Page 103. Bill's father was never a banker. His grandfather, J. W. T. Falkner, son of W. C. Falkner, was the banker and was also a lawyer.

Page 108. The name here is wrong. David's last name is spelled Cohn and not Kohn.

Come to see us sometime and thank you again for the book.

Yours truly,
Phil Stone

[1] *The World of William Faulkner.*

[2] In the passage in question Miner relates *Pylon* and *Sanctuary* to "the standards of materialism within our modern, mechanized society" and describes Percy Grimm of *Light in August* as "a kind of prototype of native American fascism." Miner goes on to contrast this decadent, violent world with the "patience, kindness, and durability" exhibited by Faulkner's black characters.

895 Letter from Estelle Faulkner to Saxe Commins, "Wednesday," signed autograph manuscript, 3 pages, with envelope addressed in Mrs. Faulkner's hand and postmarked Oxford, October 29, 1952.

Dear Saxe—

Billy is getting stronger and better every day—is trying to unravel snarls—such as unanswered correspondence—*undone* farm duties—

Truly, he has too much to do here—It is bad, I know, for an artist to undertake all Bill does—but how to circumvent it? I am at loss—

The Ford Foundation people are coming Saturday—at last[1]—but even that is a bother to him—He is afraid his voice is bad, and that perhaps it is the wrong time of year—Ordinarily—all this would have been done with Billy's usual detachment and ease—but now, he seems actually to worry what people might ['seem to' *del.*] think—Something so foreign to his nature—

I write halteringly [*sic*], and perhaps, stupidly—but as you know—*earnestly*—

So far, the brace for his back hasn't been made—or at least I haven't heard from the clinic about it—nor has he—Sometime next week, I intend going to Memphis and having a talk with both doctors—I must—

In the meantime, I can only do what I may for Billy's comfort and well-being—Keeping an even keel mostly!—

You have no idea how ashamed I am of my childish outburst toward you,[2] and how grateful I am for your beautiful letter—Still, Estelle Faulkner, without Bill & Jill, *would* be a total nonentity—

Malcolm has impressed Billy with his faith in you and what you did for us—Gloria too, added her paeans—

Jill was so happy to have her little time with you in New York—Your infinite understanding made us both much happier—

Sometime soon, I'll write both Bob and Bennett a note—anyhow, tell them again, please, what your coming down meant to us *all*—

My dearest love to Dorothy, Franny, Eugene—and—Professor Einstein—How are they?

Kindest regards to Random House—how fine you all are!

Always, Love to you

Estelle—

[1] To film the television documentary on Faulkner.

[2] Probably a reference to her letter of [October 15]. See item 892, printed above.

900 Letter from Faulkner to Saxe Commins, "Saturday," signed ribbon typescript, 1 page, with envelope addressed in typescript and postmarked Oxford, November 1, 1952.

Dear Saxe:

Your letter was comforting. I believe now that conditions are such that I shall be able to come up about Nov. 12–15; the Ford people are coming next week, they say the job will take about a week to do.

I will be frank: I would like to stay in Princeton with Dorothy and you, not only because it will be good to work in the quiet, and you and I can unravel the mss.,[1] but because of money. I am worrying a little about money again; with the drouth we had this year, my crop was a failure and I shall have to buy feed, etc.

I am trying to work on the mss. here. My judgment is still good; what I have done is all right, but very slow, difficult. I must have peace again; I have almost got to teach myself again to believe in it. I seem to have reached a point I never believed I ever would: where I need to have someone read it and tell me, Yes, it's all right. You must go ahead with it.

If I come up in the middle of the week about the 12th, I will let you know in time to get a hotel room for me to stay in town that night, and go down to Princeton with you the next day; you will not need to meet me at airport, just engage the room. If I come up Friday, do the same: engage the hotel room, I will stay in town over the week-end and go down to P. with you Monday.

From what I know of motion picture cameras and their work, it will probably be Friday before I can get away.

I have not heard from Joan Williams since I wrote her, which I felt I had to do, that Estelle had opened her innocent letters and misconstrued them. Joan knows E. a little too, and the poor child is probably afraid to write. Will you telephone her at LOOK[2] and see if she is all right, if she needs anything? Tell her I asked you to, if you prefer.

Yours,
/s/ Bill

[1]*A Fable.*
[2]*Look* magazine, with which Joan Williams had recently secured a position.

901 Letter from Faulkner to Dorothy Commins, dated "Oxford, Miss. / Saturday" [November 1, 1952], signed ribbon typescript, 1 page.

Dear Dorothy:

I hope to be able to accept the kind Commins' kind invitation to come to Princeton and work on my book, about the middle of this month.

I thank you, I know I will have peace to work in, and pleasure too.

Sincerely,
/s/ William Faulkner

872d Letter from Carvel Collins to Phil Stone, November 9, 1952, signed ribbon typescript, 2 pages.

Dear Phil,

. . . .

Your Faulkner manuscripts[1] are in a fire-proof office at M. I. T., and a scientist full of repute in national experimental photography circles is in the process of trying to bring out more words from the burned portions of the papers. He has temporarily shelved the project, thinking there was no especial rush and having to take over another piece of experimentation this month. If you are willing to trust the safety of the papers to me for a little longer, I should be very grateful; for I am hopeful that by some adaptations of infra-red photography he will be able to recover parts which are at present lost. But if you want the papers back right away, do not hesitate to let me know so that I can send them to you at once. You have already—in this matter as in all others—been most generous and helpful.

. . . .

Last evening Mary and I went to the Harry Campbells for dinner—he is in Cambridge on a Ford Foundation grant for study at Harvard. The other guests were Professor and Mrs. Willis of the Department of Classics at the University of Mississippi. It was a pleasant enough evening despite the fact that I had had to review Harry's Faulkner book in the New York HERALD-TRIBUNE without giving it much praise. Harry seems to be enjoying himself in the classes he is attending.

As I told you in my last letter, Mary and I took Jill Faulkner and the Malcolm Franklins to our summer house on Martha's Vineyard last spring. But so far this autumn we have been so unbelievably snowed under that we have not seen Jill. The other day someone at her college asked me whether or not William Faulkner could be persuaded to give the commencement address when Jill is graduated this spring. I told them they should ask him through Jill. I hope that was right; was it?

I have been here so steadily for the past year and so stupidly overworked and driven by basically irrelevant details that I have been looking forward to spending the two weeks of our Christmas holiday in the Colonial Hotel in Oxford. But I have just been asked to give a speech at the national meeting of The Modern Language Association (here in Boston this year!) three days after Christmas; so that vacation and pleasant change have become impossible. The days and months and years have come to seem so damned short! Like everyone else, I don't know where they go. And this situation has been aggravated during the recent months of drastic change in our way of life here.

There now seems to be a very good chance that I can drop in on you and yours next summer. Of late I have been asked to give a good many talks one place and another, and have just been invited to give a lecture at a college in Nashville next summer. I hope to be able to accept and to drive on to Oxford and see you. The only probable barrier is that Harvard has invited me to be chairman and moderator of a fairly fancy three-day session of novelists and critics to be held here this summer to discuss "The Contemporary Novel." If the dates of this conference conflict with the date Nashville eventually selects, I'll have to call off Nashville. But I am also on the point of being asked to give a speech at Randolph-Macon College, and failing that I shall just do what I want to do—which is to drop in on you under my own power and apart from all these commitments.

Mary joins me in best to all of you. She often speaks of the fine time you showed her on her visit. And the other evening at a party I heard her basing some large, favorable judgment about Mississippi on the high regard she has for the Stone family. She looks forward to coming with me next summer—I hope we can arrange it for her to get away.

As ever,
/s/ Carvel

[1] That is, the burned fragments which Collins had recently salvaged from the ruins of Stone's house, destroyed by fire in 1942. Some of these materials are now in the Brodsky Collection. See *Faulkner: A Comprehensive Guide to the Brodsky Collection,* I, pp. 23–29.

902 Western Union telegram from Faulkner to Saxe Commins, November 10 [possibly 1952].

PLEASE RESERVE ROOM ALGONQUIN FOR FRIDAY. SHOULD REACH TOWN IN TIME TO SEE YOU. OTHERWISE, MONDAY

BILL

872e Letter from Phil Stone to Carvel Collins, November 13, 1952, carbon typescript with typed signature, 2 pages.

Dear Carvel:

We were so glad to get your nice long letter of November 9th.

. . . .

It is all right about the Faulkner manuscripts. Keep them longer if you wish.

. . . .

You are exactly right about how to get Bill to deliver the Commencement address at Jill's college, but the request should come because Jill wants him to. If Bill thinks they are trying to exploit him through Jill he will not do it.

. . . .

Bob Coughlan is coming out in Life with an article about Bill. I think it emphasizes too much Bill's drinking and that it is unnecessarily unkind to Bill's father, but he didn't get that information from me and all I could do was protest. It sounds to me as though he got most of the personal information either from Bill's brother John or from Bill's Uncle John. I told him that he could not use anything I gave him except my part in the production of the books and I checked the proofs. He does give me my full due.

In addition to that, the Ford Foundation has been here making a TV movie for their History of America series and they took shots of me and Bill all day long one day in the office. Bill was just as gracious and patient about this as possible, and I am quite alarmed about him. I want to get him to a doctor soon to be sure that he is not developing a split personality. . . .

Your friend,
Phil Stone

907 Letter from Robert K. Haas to Dorothy Commins, November 28, 1952, signed autograph manuscript, 1 page.

Dear Dorothy—

This is just to say that while—as you know—Saxe has been wonderful, you (and I have an idea that this may not have occurred to you) have been and are nothing short of miraculous.[1] A thousand thanks to you—and a great deal of love!

Faithfully,
Bob

[1] Haas is referring here to the kindness of the Commínses in opening their home to Faulkner during his serious illness.

883c Letter from Ward L. Miner to Phil Stone, November 29, 1952, signed ribbon typescript, 1 page. From Paris.

Dear Mr. Stone:

Thank you very much for your recent kind letter regarding my book on Faulkner. What I so very much appreciate are your listing of various errors that I committed. That they should be there does not surprise me in the least since the book was finally put together here in Paris and I had on hands only my own manuscript—no notes, reference works or any thing like that. I had a thousand copies printed here, and there does exist the possibility, remote at the moment, that it will have to be reprinted. If it is, it will have to be done from new plates in America, making possible a revised copy in details. Even if I had the facilities available for checking myself, I don't know whether I could or not since I've gotten rather bored with the constant need in printing here in France in English to go through and through the text. Actually I wonder

20. Faulkner with Dorothy and Saxe Commins, Princeton, Thanksgiving 1952

how anybody could even possibly like the pesky thing. Anyway, if there is a new printing, I'll try to get the errors you so kindly caught corrected. I only wish I had other friends reading this thing who are as observant as you are. Thank you again.

You might be interested in the reception that Faulkner got last spring when he was presented to a French audience on the occasion of the 20th Century Masterpieces festival in Paris. The hall was packed and it was quite evident that they were there for one person—Faulkner—even though people such as Malraux, Auden, etc. were also on the platform. When Faulkner stood up, there was a tremendous ovation for several minutes. Unfortunately his talk was rather feeble, and so the applause was not nearly as great at the conclusion. But it was apparent to anybody that Faulkner the novelist was looked up to with awe even though Faulkner the speaker was not. What is amusing to an American is to find French novelists trying to imitate Faulkner's mannerisms of writing, and the result is usually so bad as to be really funny. The prestige of Faulkner is still greater in France than in the States. The three books they like the best are *Sanctuary, Light in August,* and *The Sound and the Fury. Hamlet* and *Absalom* they have not read, since they have not as yet been translated. One could go on forever about the oddities of French criticism. It looks as though my wife and I will go on for at least a book, though Faulkner will only be just one chapter in the picture of what the French have made of the contemporary American novel.[1]

Sincerely yours,
/s/ Ward L. Miner

[1]See Thelma M. Smith and Ward L. Miner, *Transatlantic Migration: The Contemporary American Novel in France* (Durham, N.C.: Duke University Press, 1955).

906 Letter from Faulkner to Dorothy Commins, undated [probably late November 1952], signed autograph manuscript, 1 page.

Dear Dorothy—

I can never bear to say goodbye to you, even when I know I will not be gone very long.[1] So, au bon retour, until December or maybe New Year's.

Bill

[1]Faulkner spent several days in the Comminses' home during November 1952, working on *A Fable.*

908 Letter from Faulkner to Saxe Commins, "9 December, 1952," signed carbon typescript, 1 page. Probably written in New York.

Dear Saxe:

The manuscript of THE SOUND AND THE FURY, in my handwriting, now in your custody, is the property of Joan Williams, whose present address is: 288 West 4th St., New York, N.Y.

Her right to it is not to be challenged. It is my request to you, as my literary executor, that the manuscript be surrendered to her on demand at any time.

It is my request to you that her right to the manuscript be defended and protected in any situation that may ever arise.[1]

Yours sincerely,
/s/ William Faulkner
/t/ William Faulkner

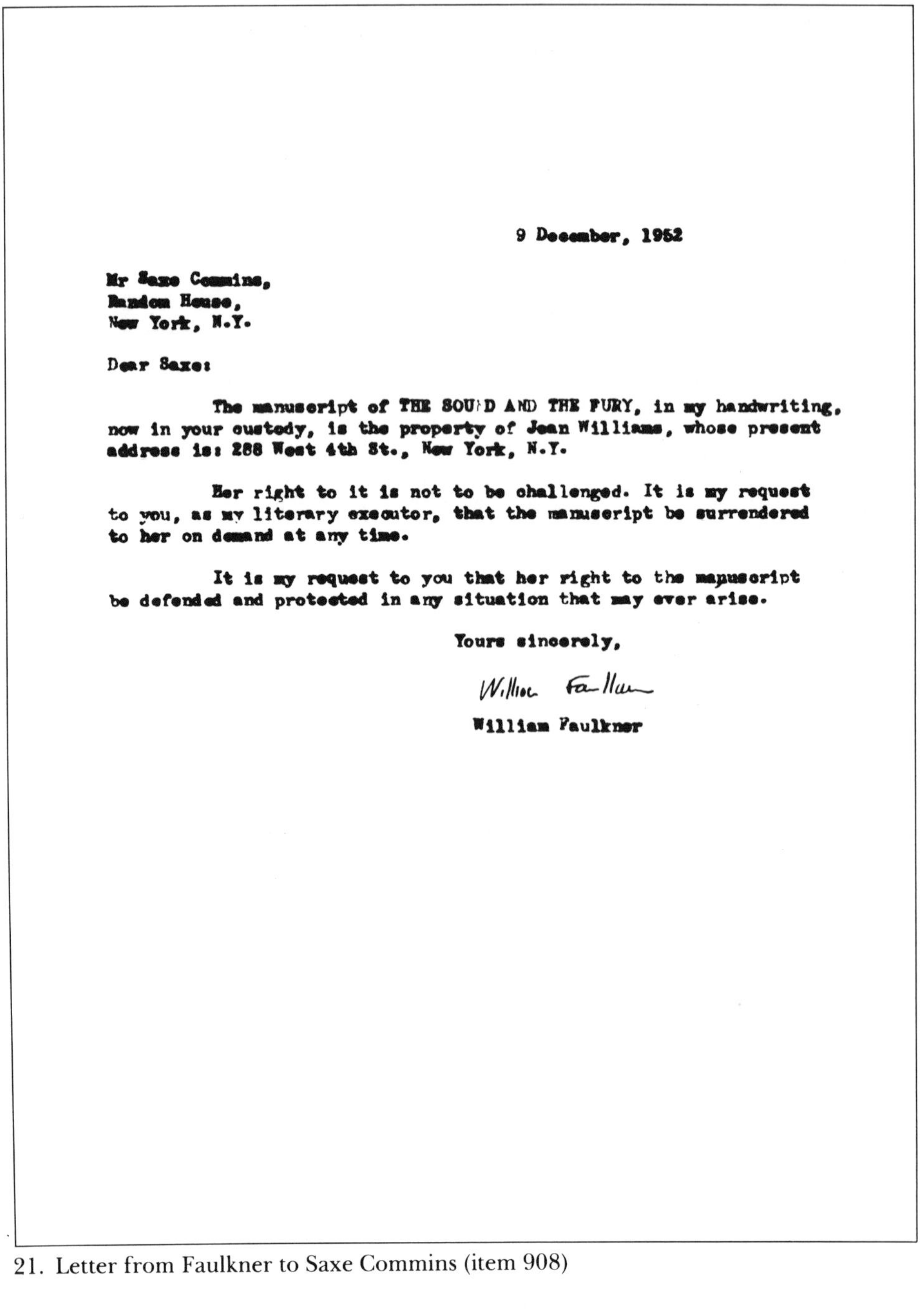

9 December, 1952

Mr Saxe Commins,
Random House,
New York, N.Y.

Dear Saxe:

The manuscript of THE SOUND AND THE FURY, in my handwriting, now in your custody, is the property of Jean Williams, whose present address is: 288 West 4th St., New York, N.Y.

Her right to it is not to be challenged. It is my request to you, as my literary executor, that the manuscript be surrendered to her on demand at any time.

It is my request to you that her right to the manuscript be defended and protected in any situation that may ever arise.

Yours sincerely,

William Faulkner

William Faulkner

21. Letter from Faulkner to Saxe Commins (item 908)

[1]On December 28, 1960, Faulkner executed a codicil to his last will and testament bequeathing his manuscripts and other personal property to the William Faulkner Foundation, Charlottesville, Virginia.

870c Letter from Harold Ober to Faulkner, December 18, 1952, unsigned carbon typescript 2 pages (1 leaf).

Dear Bill:

Lemuel Ayers came in to see me yesterday afternoon and I had a long talk with him about your play. He is as enthusiastic about it as ever (he says) but is convinced that he can never raise the money to produce it if he has to promise to give Ruth Ford the lead. He says he likes Miss Ford and doesn't want to hurt her feelings but the lead part is a very difficult one and he feels that the play could be a success only with a really great actress. He has just had a bad flop with SEE THE JAGUAR and this may have something to do with his present feeling about your play.

Anyway, he feels that he must bow out and he wants me to tell you that if, later on, the play is available without the stipulation that Miss Ford shall have the lead he would like to have another chance to produce it.

He says Miss Ford has asked him to give the play (I suppose she means the script) to her, but he feels they should be returned to me and I think that would be the more businesslike precedure.

I wish you would let me know your present ideas about the play. I am quite sure that it will be very difficult to sell the play—or any play—to a really good producer with the condition that a certain actress is to have the leading part. I know, however, that Miss Ford feels that the play was written for her and if you wish I could tell her that she could try to sell herself with the play with the understanding that if she gets a producer interested she would leave terms and contract to me. It seems to me we should give her a reasonable time to do this and if she doesn't succeed you should be free to offer the play without making her part of the deal.

Let me know what you want to do about this. If you have other ideas about the play, I'll be glad to do anything you want me to.

Sincerely,
[no signature]

909 Letter from Faulkner to Saxe Commins, "24 Dec." [probably 1952], signed ribbon typescript, 1 page.

Dear Saxe:

Yours at hand. The piece was dashed off for money.[1] Though I think it is (mildly) amusing, honest as regards the people. That is, as you know, if I had felt otherwise, that it was false, I would not have put my name on it. I doubt if it could hurt my reputation, though I agree that you and Ober know more about this than I do.

Could he sell it under a pseudonym, or is what we might get for it worth this either?

The matter is not too important, except that if we could make some money out of it, or similar ones, without doing any harm to ourselves or you or Ober, money is what I am going to need to extricate myself and still live in the state of creature comfort that I have let myself get used to. I should have stayed the tramp, with one shirt, which I was born to be.

I may be obtuse, but I doubt if what a tv screen shows is going to hurt what Random House prints in books, any more that what movie screens have shown that I did.

But we will leave the final decision to you and Ober.

My best love to Dorothy and all of you. I would have written sooner, but am busy, trying to keep up a decent daily stint on the mss.,[2] and am gradually settling the farm problem. Things are calm here yet, due to Jill's presence.[3] But it will probably blow up as soon as she is gone; already, after a few drinks in her,[4] the lightning flicks a little. Hope to God I can keep J out of it, but dont know of course.

My love to Dorothy again. I cant say that often enough.

/s/ Bill

[P.S.] Please *type* your envelopes, never write Personal on one. She will be sure to open that one if she gets it.

[1] This work has not been identified. The reference may be to "Innocent's Return," a one-act play Faulkner had written in collaboration with Joan Williams.

[2] *A Fable.*

[3] Jill was home on Christmas vacation from Pine Manor Junior College.

[4] Estelle.

904b Letter from Phil Stone to Howard Magwood, December 27, 1952, carbon typescript with typed signature, 1 page.

Dear Howard:

Don't forget to send me that print with the sound track as soon as you can.[1]

Bill and I were talking about it the other day and we are anxious to get one and to let Ike Roberts see it at a private showing while Ike is still here. He is very frail and he might go out almost any time.

Also his youngest son Wilson Roberts died yesterday and I think it would be very nice and that Ike would appreciate it if you would write him a letter of sympathy. Just address it to W. I. Roberts, Oxford.

We hope that you and yours had a nice Christmas and will have a pleasant New Year.

Your friend,
Phil Stone

[1] The Ford Foundation documentary on Faulkner, which had been directed by Magwood. Ike Roberts, one of Faulkner's hunting companions, appears in the film.

910 Note from Faulkner to Saxe Commins, undated [possibly December 1952], signed autograph manuscript, 1 page.

Gone home[1] to change clothes. See you.

Bill

[P.S.] Love to Dorothy.

[1] According to Dorothy Commins, Faulkner left this note for Commins just prior to leaving New York for Oxford.

1953

904c Letter from E. Melville Price to Phil Stone, January 5, 1953, signed ribbon typescript, 1 page.

Dear Phil:

Two Sundays ago, I had the good fortune to watch the "Omnibus" show on TV,[1] and was delighted to see my old classmate,[2] and very proud to learn of the part you have played in the ultimate recognition of William Faulkner. What a satisfying accomplishment that must be, and how fortunate Faulkner was to have a staunch friend at his side during all those years of discouragement.

Congratulations, Phil, and every good wish.

Sincerely,
/s/ Mel
/t/ E. Melville Price

[1] The Ford Foundation documentary on Faulkner, televised by CBS on December 28, 1952.

[2] Price, the advertising manager for the *New Yorker,* had been a classmate of Stone at Yale.

922 Letter from Faulkner to Saxe Commins, "5 Jan. 1953," signed ribbon typescript, 1 page.

Dear Saxe:

Please send me $5000.00. I will begin to pay up all small current debts here at once.

Am working at the mss.[1] daily. The initial momentum ran out, and it is getting more and more difficult, a matter of deliberate will power, concentration, which can be deadly after a while. I must get away as soon as I can.

Have made a tentative arrangement about my registered cattle, to let my nephew,[2] who owns a small farm, have them, to pay me on demand in calves. Will probably rent the farm itself to the people who live on it, to take care of it, pay the taxes, etc. for a year or until I decide what to do. I hope to be able to come up between 15–30 Jan. Who would be a good agent to write to re an apartment in Princeton?

This is a very incoherent letter; forgive it. Please send the money, and any suggestion about how to locate an apt. Princeton, about Feb 1st.

Love to Dorothy. Had a charming note from Frannie,[3] bless her.

/s/ Bill

[1] *A Fable.*

[2] James M. Faulkner.

[3] Saxe and Dorothy Commins' daughter, Frances.

904e Letter from Phil Stone to E. Melville Price, January 8, 1953, carbon typescript with typed signature, 2 pages.

Dear Mel:

I was very glad to get your letter of January 5 and am also glad that you got to see the film. All of our television in this area is on NBC and we have not yet seen it.

I have thought of you many times since we were at New Haven together, and I still tell your story about the Hartford fire and the little man who "saved the books." I think it is one of the best stories I ever heard.

. . . .

I might add that my movie career is now over. When they filmed INTRUDER IN THE DUST here they got a bunch of us down in our little Episcopal Church and told us we would be there just a little while, and kept us there all the morning.

When they made this TV film Howard Magwood, the director, promised me we would start at 8:30 a.m. and be through in two hours, then kept myself and my secretary all day until 6:20 p.m. I told Bill I would be glad when he got through being famous.

By the way, I am a member of the vestry in our church. I wonder if you and Boz Hawley have yet approached such a degree of sanctification?

Your friend,
Phil Stone

923 Letter from Estelle Faulkner to Dorothy Commins, January 8, 1953, signed autograph manuscript, 2 pages, with envelope addressed in Mrs. Faulkner's hand and postmarked Oxford, January 9, 1953.

Dear Dorothy—

Do forgive an erring mortal! For weeks, I have intended writing to you and Saxe, but the Holidays—Jill being at home—my mother's serious illness—*all*, have contributed to my procrastination—

First, let *me* thank you both for what you've done for Bill—He came back to Oxford a new man[1]— No two people on earth, but you, could have done that for him, and I'm sure that Bill feels as grateful as the rest of us do—Jill, Malcolm, Gloria and I thank you from the bottom of our hearts—

We are so happy, and interested, in Franny's new happiness—*Do* sometime, write and tell me about her—where she is living—keeping-house?—just please, let me know—

Bill tells me that your new house is perfect, and I know it must be—Perhaps when I get back East this summer, for Jill's graduation, we may have the joy of running in to see you—and the House—

This is just a note, Dorothy, but a heartfelt one—My eyes are growing steadily worse, and until they can operate, am afraid I'm doomed to a hazy world—too blurred, anyway, for very legible writing—

Am sure that Bill has written—but wanted to add my confidential bit—You did *amazing* things for him—

Love to you *All*
Devotedly
Estelle

[1]Faulkner had recently spent a month in Princeton and New York, recuperating from illness and working on *A Fable*.

904f Letter from Carvel Collins to Phil Stone, January 9, 1953, signed ribbon typescript, 1 page.

Dear Phil:

We do not have a television set and I do not follow the program announcements for television; so I was very disappointed the other Sunday when I learned, too late, that you were appearing on the Omnibus program dealing with Faulkner. Friends of mine who did see it liked it very much and I should like to pass on to you their pleasant responses. I hope one of these days to talk the Ford Foundation into letting me see the film so that I will not have lost the thing forever.

Mary and I are delighted with the possibility that you and yours may be driving here for the meeting of the American Bar Association the latter part of August. Now that we have a house with many rooms instead of our tiny Cambridge apartment, we hope very much that you will make your headquarters with us, or if the meeting, as I should imagine it might, requires your living at a hotel at least the family might stay with us. Let's try to work it out. And in connection with your trip here, if I do get to Mississippi—which I very much hope to do—I shall try to come in July as you suggest.

The three-day session of novelists and critics at Harvard is at present scheduled to be held early next August. So far we are having some difficulty in getting just the writers and critics we want, but I hope we will eventually have arranged an attractive program. If there was the slightest chance that William Faulkner would come to this conference for the rather modest fee we are at the moment able to pay, all of us here would fall over each other in our eagerness and delight. But so far I have not got up nerve to ask him.

Before Christmas Jill Faulkner came out to us here in the country for a Sunday. We like her very much and certainly hope that her engagement and coming marriage are extremely happy. She deserves the best.

. . . .

Mary and I talk of you often and look forward to seeing you during this new year either in Oxford or here or both.

As ever,
/s/ Carvel

924 Letter from Faulkner to Saxe Commins, "Saturday" [probably January 10, 1953], unsigned ribbon typescript, 1 page.

Dear Saxe:

Yours at hand. I did not want to impose on you re the apt. But if you will, without committing me, ask about one for say Feb. 1st, for two months if possible, if not that, what is shortest lease, all information. If shortest lease is 6 mo. or a year, I will be able to have an answer by the time I come up, which will be before Jan 24th, maybe by Jan 17th.

Can I send baggage express to you in P.?[1] It can stay in the garage until I move it.

Will tell E.[2] tomorrow probably when I intend to leave; the subsequent explosion will determine just when and under what conditions. I said as soon as I got home that I was going back after New Year; the reaction was as I prophesied: Take me with you.

Will keep you posted. Work still going, but the effort is too much; I must get away again as soon as I can. Have things here in good enough shape to leave until June anyway, with possibly a week's return in the spring. Will know more when I see you.

[no signature]

[1] Princeton.
[2] Estelle.

904p Letter from Phil Stone to Boris Kaplan, Ford Foundation, February 3, 1953, carbon typescript with typed signature, 1 page.

Dear Mr. Kaplan:

When Mr. Howard Magwood was down here last fall making the Faulkner film for your Foundation, they used my office for part of the film and took the time of myself and my secretary for an entire day. I was extremely busy at the time but we were glad to cooperate with them and asked and expected no pay and received none.

I did tell Mr. Magwood that I wanted a print of the film and of the sound track for two reasons.

The first reason is that I wanted to save it for my 12-year-old son, whose god-father Mr. Faulkner is.

The second reason is that we have no CBS television in this area and I wanted Ike Roberts, former sheriff and the dean of Mr. Faulkner's deer-hunting crowd, to see this film before he dies. Mr. Roberts is about 75 years old, is not in good health, is very feeble and has recently had the shock of the sudden death of his youngest son. Mr. Roberts might go out any time and I have arranged to have a private, non-charge exhibition, using the projector of a friend, so that Mr. Roberts and his family could see the film. Mr. Magwood assured me that he would do his best to see that I got this and I am sure that he did, but he tells me that I shall have to write you direct about it.

Mr. Faulkner informed me that he was getting a print, but he left several days ago for Princeton and will not be back home until he brings his daughter Jill home for the Easter holidays. Mr. Roberts might be living then and he might not be, so I would appreciate very much if you would send me a print of this film and of the sound track.

I gave my time when I was very busy and it looks to me as if the Foundation might do this one little thing for me. I shall appreciate anything you can do.

Yours truly,
Phil Stone

933 Note from Faulkner to Dorothy Commins, "Wednesday" [February 1953], signed autograph manuscript, 1 page, with Random House envelope addressed in Faulkner's hand: "Mrs Saxe Commins / courtesy of Mr Commins."

Dear Dorothy—

I am well and working, most successfully I think. I saw Jill Saturday, who sends messages of love to you which I will deliver in person as soon as I see you, which must be soon indeed.

My sympathy went to you in your recent grief,[1] and my love always.

Bill

[1] Due to the death of her brother.

938 Letter from Phil Stone to Faulkner, April 10, 1953, carbon typescript with typed signature, 1 page.

Dear Bill:

Wes Sturges, Dean of the Yale Law School, and his wife are here now and both of them told me that Mr. Carl Rollins, who was the head of the Yale University Press when you were up at New Haven in the spring of 1918, especially asked to be remembered to me and asked about you.

He was the man with the closely cropped brown hair, the thick-lensed glasses and the brown goatee who used to come over to my rooms for bull sessions. You may remember that he, Herb Starr,[1] yourself, myself and Joe Biglin were over there one night and you and he were discussing Swinburne with Mr. Rollins, when, in a lull Joe stated that you and that black-headed fellow (meaning Arthur Head) would sit around Longley's and drink coffee and spout that stuff and pull one another's hair and hold one another's hands. You might remember that Mr. Rollins looked like somebody had shot him and Joe got up and swaggered out and said he believed he would go and shoot a little pool.

Wes and Mrs. Sturges tell me that Mr. Rollins is now retired, is almost completely blind and probably wont be here for long. I understand that he is living in New Haven and can be reached through the Yale University Press.

I feel sure that you wont do it, but it would be a very kindly deed if you would get off your caboose just one day and run up to New Haven[2] and go to see Mr. Rollins. It would not be much trouble to you and he would appreciate it deeply.

Your friend,
Phil Stone

[1]Hubert Starr, a native Mississippian, subsequently moved to California. Faulkner, during his early Hollywood scriptwriting days in the 1930s, was a frequent guest in Starr's home.

[2]From New York, where Faulkner was staying at this time. Stone's letter was addressed to Faulkner c/o Random House.

935c Letter from Phil Stone to Carvel Collins, April 20, 1953, carbon typescript with typed signature, 2 pages.

Dear Carvel:

I have your letter of April 17, and the reason I am answering it right away is because, as I have told you before, I seem to have so much to do that if I don't get letters answered right away I frequently don't get them answered at all.

. . . .

We are looking forward to seeing you in July but I want you to write me immediately and tell me just what day or days in July you expect to be here. If you were a lawyer you would know that "early in July" or "the latter part of November" don't mean a thing. Contrary to the belief of most laymen, matters of law are almost always very definite. A lawsuit is not set for some time in the second week of July. For instance, it is set for 9 o'clock A.M. on Wednesday, July 17. So write me a note at once and give me the exact date when you expect to leave Nashville and arrive here because I want to be here when you and Mary are here.

I did not see the TV show[1] either but the critics had just as well quit fuming at Bill about it. In the first place Bill did it, as he said, to make money. In the

22. Faulkner with Dan Duryea, host of Lux Video Theatre, April 2, 1953

second place, I think what is subconsciously ailing these critics is what I have been saying for some years and what I told you, that the critics have recently been overrating Bill as a writer. He is undoubtedly the best around but he is just not as good as they think he is and I think that uneasy doubt is now pervading the subconsciousness of the critics.

I just saw Bill a while ago and he tells me that he made a lot of money out of the TV. Surely it is not as bad as being a slave to the movies. He came home, and Jill is home too, because Estelle has been having internal hemorrhages and her condition may require surgery. We knew she was sick but we didn't pay any attention to it because we just took it for granted that she was probably getting off of a drunk.

I note what you say about Bill's productiveness and I shall watch for the article on Sherwood Anderson.[2]

Bill may be being productive, but I still have my doubts that he is being creative or is going to be again. If the novel[3] is the one of which we read a part of the manuscript several years ago, it will come out with some marvelous Faulkner prose, with some irrelevant material inserted in very bad aesthetic taste and will be a flop as a whole. That kind of book requires a great humility and in 60 years I have never known a Faulkner who was endowed with humility.

. . . .

Your friend,
Phil Stone

[1]The dramatization of Faulkner's short story, "The Brooch," telecast on the *Lux Video Theatre,* April 2, 1953.
[2]Faulkner's "Sherwood Anderson: An Appreciation," which would appear in the June 1953 issue of the *Atlantic.*
[3]*A Fable.*

940 Letter from Faulkner to Saxe Commins, "Wednesday" [April 22, 1953], signed ribbon typescript, 1 page.

Dear Saxe:

She[1] was almost gone Saturday, but rallied and has improved, soon they will be able to make tests and find what is wrong, to correct it, whether with surgery or not, they dont know yet. Still having blood transfusions.

I dont know yet if I can come back up before June 1st or not. If I can arrange to have someone drive the car up about June 5th. and pick me up in N.Y., and I can leave here in time to have May in N.Y., I will come up. Otherwise, I will wait here until time to fetch Jill home from Wellesley in June after graduation. This all depends on E's condition, whether she can be left.

Enclosed is my check for May rent. I am already committed for that, since 15 day notice is required to vacate the apt. Please send the check direct to the owners. One of them called to see me, her name and address are on a piece of paper in the second drawer of the small chest the telephone sits on. I think it is

Miss Deborah Frank,
20 West 16 St.

Though if you will telephone Linder, he can tell you the correct address and designation, then you can fill in the check and mail it direct to the owners, as I promised to do.

I'm sorry to leave this all on your shoulders. Maybe Linder could get a cleaning woman, clean the place, send bed linen, towels etc. to a laundry; give Linder notice I will vacate the apt. June 1st., tentatively, unless I communicate with him differently before May 15th.

I still hope to come up again, for that month, May; this business at the hospital here is going to cost like hell too, and another TV job will help.

I left the key with Joan, to deliver to you. She will help in this in any way she can.

Will keep you advised. Am working on big book, it goes well.

/s/ Bill

[1]Estelle had suffered a hemorrhage on April 18 and had been rushed to the Oxford Hospital.

941 Letter from Faulkner to Saxe Commins, "Friday" [April 24, 1953], signed ribbon typescript, 1 page.

Dear Saxe:

Things look much better here, bleeding stopped, she can take food now, will be allowed to come home tomorrow. My idea now is, since they are not equipped here to make a thorough examination, to keep her at home until her strength is built up (provided no more hemorrhage, of course,) take her to Memphis next week and see what the trouble is.

I have mislaid a pipe. It is a G.B.D. shaped as below.[1] I had it last fall, may have left it in the jar in Eugene's room in Princeton. Will you look, and let me know? Meanwhile, will you send me the light-blue-covered ledger, containing an envelope and some papers, which I left on the work-table in your office?

May still be able to come up in June. Please hold all else there until you hear from me. Malcolm and Rhea[2] send love.

/s/ Bill

[1] Faulkner drew a picture of the pipe at the bottom of the letter.
[2] That is, Ria—Gloria Franklin.

882j Letter from Robert Coughlan to Phil Stone, May 1, 1953, signed ribbon typescript, 2 pages.

Dear Phil,

I don't wonder at your curiosity about the Faulkner piece[1]—I often feel that way myself. But what has happened is this: ever since last spring, when the election news began to hot up, there has been so much interest in national and international political stories that it has been difficult to get anything else in the magazine. And, since the Faulkner mss. is too long to be run in one installment, that has counted against it even more, because the managing editor hasn't wanted to commit two successive issues to it and thus maybe have his text space tied up the week the world blows up.

However—so I am assured—the piece is very much liked and *will* run eventually.

. . . .

Incidentally, as you doubtless know, Bill went on one of his big, economy size toots here in New York not long ago and had to be hauled off to the hospital. But they fixed him up and he was out soon and is behaving himself now, so far as I know.

My best to Miss Emily and the kids.

All regards,
/s/ Bob

[1] The *Life* magazine feature on Faulkner.

944 Letter from Estelle Faulkner to Dorothy Commins, dated "Oxford—/June 18th," signed autograph manuscript, 2 pages, with envelope addressed in Mrs. Faulkner's hand and postmarked Oxford, June 18, 1953.

Dearest Dorothy—

What a lovely trip I had and how good it is to be Home once more! The very nicest and *best* part of my little vacation was the three days spent with you and Saxe—Surely your ears have burned—for I've done little but sing your praises to all and sundry—

Gloria and Jill (naturally) are quite fascinated with my descriptions of your very charming and unique home—and both hope sometime to be able to see it—

We are all thrilled over your promise of a visit to us this fall, and Malcolm, Gloria, Jill, Bill and I will do our utmost to make you love our South as we do—You and Saxe drive, or fly down to Memphis where we will meet you—stay awhile in Oxford, then we will drive down to New Orleans—Having you here will be wonderful for us *all,* but for Bill to have Saxe come for a visit would please Pappy no end!

Needless to tell you how proud and happy I was in Wellesley—Jill graduated with honors—in fact, had the highest scholastic record in her class—and Bill's address was perfect—He looked very handsome and distinguished in his cap and gown—and evidently he remembered Saxe's injunction—for every word was clearly and carefully spoken—hence the message was plainly understood—

Our motor trip home was pleasant and without incident or accident—though I don't think Bill could have lasted another day on account of his back—

We are rested again, and I, especially, am enjoying having my family at home once more—I was so long without them—

Had a delightful letter from Frannie today, bless her heart—

Please let me thank you and Saxe again and again for your marvelous hospitality to Bill and me—My stay with you was joyous!

Love to *All,* including "Bill
who belongs to Frannie"
Always devotedly
Estelle

945 Western Union telegram from Faulkner to Saxe Commins, June 22 [probably 1953].

PLEASE SEND 5000 ALL WELL HERE. TRYING TO WORK

BILL

947 Two thank you notes from Jill Faulkner to Mrs. Saxe Commins, dated "Friday" [probably June 19, 1953] and "Thursday" [June 25, 1953], with envelope addressed in Miss Faulkner's hand and postmarked Oxford, June 27, 1953.

Dear Miss Dorothy—

You have the most charming knack for choosing exactly the right gift—the lovely belts two years ago which I wear constantly, & now the address book.

Mama brought it just as I was saying good-bye's to my friends of these years at Pine Manor, therefore of course just at the time there were many many addresses I wanted to keep & remember. I can't thank you enough.

To these poor thanks let me add my deepest for all you did to make Mama's visit with you wonderful—& wonderful for her.

My very best to all the family.

Love—
Jill

Dear Miss Dorothy—

My brother Malcolm found the enclosed[1] in our drive this morning, rather the worse for wear. I enclose it only to prove my good intentions. My mistake was relying on Pappy, with so very many things on his mind, to mail it for me.

Please forgive us both, if you can find it in your heart even to read this after such a disgraceful length of time has lapsed.

Love—
Jill

[1]The previous note, which, as this second note explains, Faulkner had dropped on his way to the post office.

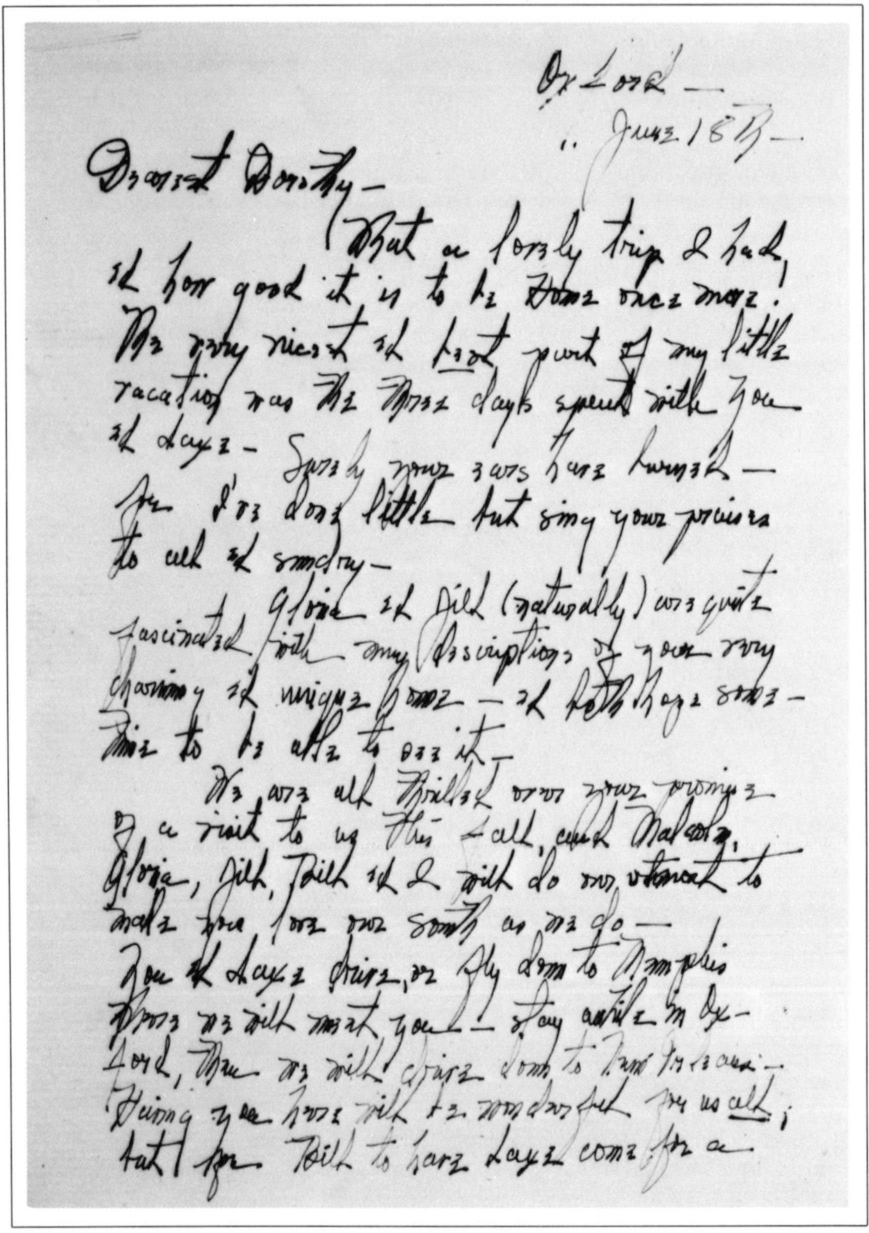

Oxford —
June 18th —

Dearest Dorothy —

What a lovely trip I had, and how good it is to be home once more! The very nicest and best part of my little vacation was the three days spent with you and Saxe — Surely your ears have burned — for I've done little but sing your praises to all and sundry —

Gloria and Jill (naturally) were quite fascinated with my descriptions of your very charming and unique home — and both hope some-time to be able to see it.

We were all thrilled over your promise of a visit to us this fall, and Malcolm, Gloria, Jill, Bill and I will do our utmost to make you love our South as we do — You and Saxe drive, or fly down to Memphis where we will meet you — stay awhile in Oxford, then we will drive down to New Orleans — Having you here will be wonderful for us all; but for Bill to have Saxe come for a

23. Letter from Estelle Faulkner to Dorothy Commins (item 944)

visit would please Pappy no end!

Needless to tell you how proud and happy I was in Wellesley — Jill graduated with honors — in fact, had the highest scholastic record in her class — and Bill's address was perfect — He looked very handsome and distinguished in his cap and gown — and evidently he remembered Dean's injunction — for every word was clearly and carefully spoken — hence the message was plainly understood —

Our motor trip home was pleasant and without incident or accident — though I don't think Bill would have lasted another day on account of his [illegible] —

We are rested again, and I, especially, am enjoying having my family at home once more — I was so long without them —

Had a delightful letter from Frannie today, bless her heart —

Please let me thank you and Dean again and again for your marvelous hospitality to Bill and me — Our stay with you was joyous!

Love to all, including Bill who belongs to "Frannie" Always devotedly

Estelle

948 Letter from Faulkner to Saxe Commins, "Monday" [July 13, 1953], signed ribbon typescript, 1 page.

Dear Saxe:

Howard Hawks, the movie director, telephoned me from Paris Friday. He and Gary Cooper, who are both in Europe, are cooking up a job, Hawks wants me to come over and write it for them.[1] He is to let me know definitely soon, wants me pretty quick. I sent in my passport for renewal, asked that it be returned to me care of you there, please hold it until you hear from me, it will be in an official state dept. cover I think, so you will recognise it.

As soon as I hear from Hawks, I will contact you, ask you to book for me, etc. Will spend a few days in NY first.

Big book[2] is going well now. Slow, very hard to work here, will have to get away regardless soon, whether the Paris thing comes through or not. But the mss. going all right, have cleaned it up through 288 pages, have shortened that part of it probably ⅓. I think that part is right now. I will probably bring it on to you for safety when I come up.

My best to everyone, love to D.[3]

/s/ Bill

[1] Apparently the film subsequently produced as *Land of the Pharaohs*. Faulkner, with the assistance of Harry Kurnitz and Harold Jack Bloom, would write the screenplay; but surgery would force Cooper to withdraw from the project.

[2] *A Fable*.

[3] Dorothy, Saxe Commins' wife.

949 Western Union telegram from Faulkner to Saxe Commins, July 27 [1953].

THANKS FOR LETTER. HAVE 500 PLUS PAGES. END OF BOOK POSSIBLE IN TWO MONTHS.[1] WILL ADVISE PLANS SOON. PLEASE SEND 25 HUNDRED. REGARDS

BILL

[1] *A Fable*, which was not actually completed until November 1953.

950 Letter from Estelle Faulkner to Dorothy and Saxe Commins, dated "Oxford—July 29th," signed autograph manuscript, 2 pages, with envelope addressed in Mrs. Faulkner's hand and postmarked Oxford, July 31, 1953.

Dear Dorothy and Saxe—

It really seems such a long time ago—my lovely three days spent in your home—and never a day passes here in Mississippi that I don't think of you and thank God for such friends!

The summer has been hot and most trying—however, I've persevered and restocked our pantry with jellies, jams, preserves etc—more to be busy I dare say than from necessity—

Bill has done a prodigious amount of work on his book, despite interruptions of all sorts that I've been unable to prevent—But even at *that*—he is frightfully unhappy here, and Jill and I will be relieved and glad when he decides to "take off" again—

Lately though, Joan has come South ['again' *del.*]—I've heard, so perhaps Jill and I will leave *first* after all—

Jill wants to go to the University of Mexico until Christmas—so I'll go down with her, take an apartment and play duenna! She decided against Europe this year because we had heard that *other people* were planning a stay in France—

Unfortunately, a man in Bill's position is an object of envy—and an awful lot of malice—A friend ? of mine from Shanghai days delights in sending me accounts that could be disturbing—

Luckily I have managed a stiff upper lip—and retained my dignity—

I asked Bill about the manuscripts, but got no answer—No doubt it was a foolish question, and Saxe has them stored safely—Bless him—The gloves, Dorothy, will be on their way after Friday—I had *not* forgotten, but have had no occasion other than exchanging the gloves, to go to Memphis—Forgive me for being so lazy!

Do write sometime when it won't be a chore—I love you *all* and am so interested in your wellbeing—

Jill, Gloria and Malcolm join in sending Love—Always devotedly

Estelle

952 Letter from Saxe Commins to Faulkner, August 3, 1953, signed ribbon typescript, 1 page, on Random House letterhead stationery.

Dear Bill:

This is a matter of business. We have had an offer from the New American Library for two paper-bound volumes of yours. The first would combine SANCTUARY and REQUIEM FOR A NUN and the other would include THE WILD PALMS and THE OLD MAN.

As you know, SANCTUARY and THE OLD MAN had been issued by them with great success. Now they feel as we do that the combination would in each instance meet with enormous popular response. They offer a generous advance.

I recommend this arrangement and all I need is your approval. Will you send it to me by return mail, please?

There is only one matter that you must settle if you want to go ahead with this plan. It concerns THE WILD PALMS and THE OLD MAN. Their suggestion is that instead of having the sections run alternately, they would make them consecutively; thus the first part would be THE WILD PALMS and the second THE OLD MAN. Is this all right with you?

Best always,

/s/ Saxe

952 Letter from Faulkner to Saxe Commins, undated [early August 1953], unsigned ribbon typescript, 2 pages (1 leaf). Appears at bottom and on verso of letter from Commins to Faulkner, August 3, 1953.

Of course I agree, appreciate the notice, which you never fail to give me anyhow. Dismembering THE WILD PALMS will in my opinion destroy the overall impact which I intended. But apparently my vanity (if it is vanity) regarding my work has at least reached that pitch where I consider it does not need petty defending. Am so near end of the big one[1] that I am frightened, that lightning might strike me before I can finish it. It is either nothing and I am blind in my dotage, or it is the best of my time. Damn it, I did have genius, Saxe. It just took me 55 years to find it out. I suppose I was too busy working to notice it before.

Jill is taking a 3 month languages, culture, humanities in Univ of Mexico City this fall, she and E leave here about Aug 25 to Xmas. Will let you know my own plans as soon as I know them. You and I will need about 2 weeks to go through this mss. and get everything out of it that it will spare. It will be about 700 typed pages.

[no signature]

[1] *A Fable.*

953 Western Union telegram from Faulkner to Saxe Commins, August 13 [1953].

YES TO FAULKNER READER.[1] ASSUME FOREWORD DEADLINE WONT HALT PRESENT WORK. WRITE OR PHONE ALL NECESSARY DATA IF ANY. THANK YOU TO ALL—BILL

[1] Commins had contacted Faulkner about Random House's plans to issue *The Faulkner Reader* and had requested that Faulkner write a foreword for the book.

954 Western Union telegram from Saxe Commins to Faulkner, August 14, 1953.

FOREWORD CAN BE WRITTEN AT YOUR CONVENIENCE AFTER YOUR RETURN TO NEW YORK. THANKS FOR PROMPT REPLY. LOVE,

SAXE

955 Letter from Faulkner to Saxe Commins, "Friday" [mid-August 1953], signed ribbon typescript, 1 page.

Dear Saxe:

One more chapter, and the mss. will be finished.[1] So now I feel that I can draw more money. I plan to invest $2500.00 in a business which I will explain when I see you. How much can I draw this year?

As soon as I finish the mss. I will get in touch with Ober and try to earn more outside as I did last spring, or the OLD MAN script[2] may materialise. The Europe job with Hawks is out until next year because of Cooper's operation.[3]

I will probably be up East about Sept 1st or so. Will let you know later.

Will fix finances for J & E in Mexico Sept to Dec.[4]

Please send $10,000.00 now.

/s/ Bill

[1] *A Fable.*

[2] The sale of the film rights to "Old Man" was concluded in October 1954. Horton Foote's adaptation of the story was first telecast on *Playhouse 90* in 1958.

[3] The film assignment Faulkner had mentioned in a previous letter to Commins. See item 948 above.

[4] Jill, accompanied by her mother, was enrolled during this period in the University of Mexico.

956 Letter from Faulkner to Saxe Commins, undated [possibly mid-August 1953], signed autograph manuscript, 1 page.

Dear Saxe—
Please let Estelle have what money she asks for, to my acct.
Am at the big book, I think in earnest. My best to Dorothy.

Bill

[P.S.] Charge hotel bill to me.

957 Western Union telegram from Faulkner to Saxe Commins, August 29, 1953.

GLAD TO HEAR IT.[1] BEGGED YOU LAST SPRING TO REST AND LET JOINT EXPLODE. MAYBE YOU WILL NOW. LOVE TO DOROTHY

BILL

[1] Commins had suffered a heart attack.

958 Letter from Phil Stone to William B. Wisdom, September 1, 1953, unsigned carbon typescript, 1 page.

Dear Bill:

This morning I got a letter from Carvel Collins telling me that you wanted to know whether or not I would sell the partially burned Faulkner manuscript which I have. I do not want to sell any of them because they are the few [remaining] of a stack of manuscripts. Anyway, I would not want to dispose of them at all without the permission of Bill Faulkner.

We do wish you would come to see us again. Often we think of you and talk about the pleasure we had from your visit. It is hard for us to get to New Orleans because of the children but if and when we do get there we shall certainly call you.

Your Friend,
[no signature]

959 Letter from Faulkner to Saxe Commins, undated [September 1953], unsigned ribbon typescript, 1 page.

Dear Saxe:

Here are a few more pages, 197–295.[1]

I haven't read proof[2] yet. When you read, please check or correct misprints and obscurities, then I can run through fast and clean up.

I will be in town about Sept 25–Oct 1st.

[no signature]

[1] Presumably *A Fable*.
[2] Probably *The Faulkner Reader*.

882m Letter from Phil Stone to Robert Coughlan, September 24, 1953, carbon typescript with typed signature, 1 page.

Dear Bob:

We got our advance copy of LIFE yesterday and read the first part of the article.[1] We think it is very good indeed. In fact, it looks better to us in print than it did before.

I suppose Bill is still on a drunk. I have not been to see him and I am not going because I have told him many times that any man over 30 years of age who gets drunk the second day is just a damn fool.

Ike Roberts told me yesterday he was going down to see how Bill was doing but I have not seen Ike since.

Last night I sat in the living room at home and read your article again carefully. Philip had washed the supper dishes for Emily and had sat down in the living room to look at the article while I went into the kitchen to dry the dishes. He called out to me: "Do you reckon he (meaning Bill) will read it?"

Before stopping to think, I answered immediately: "I think he will read it and will pretend that he has not."

. . . .

Your friend,
Phil Stone

[1]Coughlan's essay, "The Private World of William Faulkner," in the September 28, 1953 issue.

882n Letter from Phil Stone to Robert Coughlan, October 1, 1953, carbon typescript with typed signature, 1 page.

Dear Bob:

. . . .

We got our advance copy of LIFE last week but have not got the one for this week, and they are all sold out here.[1] I do want to keep one in the file we keep for Philip and one in the file we keep for Araminta, so if it is not too much trouble I will appreciate it if you will have them send it.

Your article, I think, has the town stewing. All of this I am telling you now is confidential and all I tell you about it in the future will be, but I look for a terrific feud in the Faulkner family because they surely can't blame those family photographs on me.

I am having two of my friends who have time to be around on the street (which time I don't have because I have to keep working) and who keep up with all the gossip, to quietly gather it for me and some time soon, possibly next week, I shall tell you all of it off the record.

Your friend,
Phil Stone

[1]The second installment of Coughlan's feature on Faulkner, entitled "The Man Behind the Faulkner Myth," appeared in the October 5, 1953 issue of *Life.*

882o Letter from Phil Stone to Editors, *Life* magazine, October 1, 1953, carbon typescript with typed signature, 1 page.

Gentlemen:

In your article regarding William Faulkner in issue of October 4,[1] you have the name of my grandfather who rode with General Forrest as "Major Philip Alston Stone." That was not his name. He was my maternal grandfather and his name was Philip Summerfield Alston.

Yours truly,
Phil Stone

[1]Actually October 5.

882p Letter from Phil Stone to Robert Coughlan, October 5, 1953, carbon typescript with typed signature, 1 page.

Dear Bob:

We thought your article was very good and I think you did well to end it where you did.

I have not forgotten that I shall gather the reactions of the Faulkner family and write you later, but I want to know if you are going to be in New York because that letter will be off the record, top secret, personal and confidential.

We thought you would also like to know that almost all the grand old ladies around Oxford think your article is very fair and very accurate.

I just took it for granted that the title on the last article, "The Man Behind the Myth," referred to Bill, but so many of the people around here seem to think you were referring to me. Which is correct?

. . . .

I don't know whether Bill is still drunk or not, but I haven't seen him for two weeks.

Your friend,
Phil Stone

S-32 Letter from Faulkner to Phillip E. Mullen, October 5, 1953, signed ribbon typescript, 1 page.

Dear Moon,

Thank you for your letter. No, I haven't seen the piece in LIFE[1] yet, but if you had anything to do with it, I know it is alright and I hope you make a nickle out of it.[2]

Yours,
/s/ Bill

[1] The two-part feature on Faulkner by Robert Coughlan.
[2] Mullen had assisted Coughlan with some of the research for the article.

964a Letter from Phil Stone to George A. Saucier, Mississippi Department of Public Safety, October 6, 1953, carbon typescript with typed signature, 1 page.

Dear Sir:

I represent Mr. William Faulkner of this place. I understand that his wife was involved in a slight accident here in Oxford on September 21, 1953, and that she failed to make a report of same.[1] I am informed that all damages were paid and that there is no contest about this.

Mrs. Faulkner is now in Mexico City and has been for some time and will not return for about thirty days. As soon as she returns, proper report will be made to your office. Mr. Faulkner is not sufficiently informed to be able to make this report himself.

If you will be so kind as to hold this matter in abeyance until Mrs. Faulkner returns we shall then make the report. Please advise me.

Yours truly,
Phil Stone

[1] Mrs. Faulkner's driver's license had been suspended because of her failure to report the accident. Stone arranged to have the license reinstated.

S-33 Letter from Faulkner to Phillip E. Mullen, "Wednesday" [early October 1953], signed ribbon typescript, 1 page.

Dear Phil:

I haven't seen the LIFE thing yet, and wont. I have found that my mother is furious over it, seems to consider it inferentially lies, cancelled her subscription.

I tried for years to prevent it, refused always, asked them to let me alone. It's too bad the individual in this country has no protection from journalism, I suppose they call it. But apparently he hasn't. There seems to be in this the same spirit which permits strangers to drive into my yard and pick up books or pipes I left in the chair where I had been sitting, as souvenirs.

What a commentary. Sweden gave me the Nobel Prize. France gave me the Legion d'Honneur. All my native land did for me was to invade my privacy over my protest and my plea. No wonder people in the rest of the world dont like us, since we seem to have neither taste nor courtesy, and know and believe in nothing but money and it doesn't much matter how you get it.

Yours,

/s/ Bill

[P. S.] This time I wasn't even consulted, didn't even know it was being done, nor did my mother. She knew she was being photographed and specifically asked the photographer not to print the picture anywhere.

This seems to me to be a pretty sorry return for a man who has only tried to be an artist and bring what honor that implies to the land of his birth.

965 Letter from Jill Faulkner to Saxe Commins, October 16, 1953, signed autograph manuscript, 1 page.

Dear Mr. Saxe—

As always I write to ask a favor of you. We've had no word from Pappy since hearing he was on his way to New York & perhaps from there on to Egypt.[1] If he is in the city would you please see that he gets the enclosed note. Thank you, sir.

You're in the midst of the nicest part of the year up your way now. Know Princeton is lovely. Someday, yet, I'm going to see your new home. Each time I mention building when I'm married, Mama insists that first I must see it. Miss Dorothy, you, & your house seem without comparison to Mama.

Please remember me to Miss Dorothy, Frannie & Eugene.

Love—

Jill

[1] To work on *Land of the Pharaohs.* Jill was writing from Mexico City.

S-34 Letter from Robert K. Haas to Saxe Commins, October 26, 1953, signed ribbon typescript, 1 page.

Dear Saxe:

I haven't written you since I saw you because your condition seemed so robust that I didn't feel you rated another letter. However, I do want to say that I think Bill's book[1] is simply tremendous. To my mind it's one of the greatest novels that I've ever read, and I use the word "greatest" advisedly. I may be wrong, but that's my perfectly honest opinion. I do find that some

Wednesday

Dear Phil:

I haven't seen the LIFE thing yet, and wont. I have found that my mother is furious over it, seems to consider it inferentially lies , cancelled her subscription.

I tried for years to prevent it, refused always, asked them to let me alone. It's too bad the individual in this country has no protection from journalism, I suppose they call it. But apparently he hasn't. There seems to be in this the same spirit which permits strangers to drive into my yard and pick up books or pipes I left in the chair where I had been sitting, as souvenirs.

What a commentary. Sweden gave me the Nobel Prize. France gave me the Legion d'Honneur. All my native land did fro me was to invade my privacy over my protest and my plea. No wonder people in the rest of the world dont like us, since we seem to have neither taste nor courtesy, and know and believe in nothing but money and it doesn't much matter how you get it.

Yours,

Bill

This time I wasn't even consulted, didn't even know it was being done. Nor did my mother. She knew she was being photographed and specifically asked the photographer not to print the picture anywhere.

This seems to me to be a pretty sorry return for a man who has only tried to be an artist and bring what honor that implies to the land of his birth.

24. Letter from Faulkner to Phil Mullen (item S-33)

parts of it are confusing, and that the structure and sequences are sometimes harder to follow than need be. I also think that the section about the horse is unduly long. It has, I think, the vices of its virtues—its virtue being that it is so absorbing in itself that it throws the reader off the main track of the story.

I'd like to know what you think of these things, which I of course tell you confidentially, and your slant on the whole opus. Let me know when you get a chance, won't you? In the meantime, I've been told that you've been a rather bad boy. Cut out that nonsense, and take it easy.

With love to you and Dorothy,

Faithfully,
/s/ Bob

[1] *A Fable,* which Commins had edited.

963u Letter from Phil Stone to Henry Dalton, October 27, 1953, carbon typescript with typed signature, 1 page.

Dear Mr. Dalton:

I have your letter of October 25.[1]

The writing racket is so tough that it always gives me a twinge of heart to refuse to do what little I can to help any beginning writer. I always say that I give to anybody who wants to write, first, the same advice I always give to a friend who wants to run for political office: Don't. However, if they really have the urge neither will be stopped by that admonition.

Personally, I have just all that I can handle. I am working now about five nights a week on my law business and have done so most of this year. When "Sanctuary" was published I told Bill Faulkner that he didn't need any more help and that I was through reading manuscripts and fooling with writers. Then I married a wife who is a writer and became the father of a boy who is now 13 years old and who is a writer. So what little spare time I have is taken up with manuscripts at home. I do well to get to read one book a month. I told my wife the other night just before we went to sleep that one of the smartest things I ever did was to see that our fox terrier never learned the alphabet.

There are just not enough hours in the day and I just don't have time. However, I wish you all sorts of luck. Why don't you talk to Hal Phillips[2] about writing some fiction and going down to study with Hudson Strode[3] at Tuscaloosa? I don't mean that you should give up your poetry entirely but it furnishes mighty scanty eating. I don't agree with Hudson about lots of things but he certainly does know how to sell the Yankees on the work of his students.

Yours truly,
Phil Stone

[1] Dalton, a poet from Corinth, Mississippi, having read in *Life* magazine about Stone's encouragement of Faulkner, wrote to ask for advice and support regarding his poetry.

[2] Thomas Hal Phillips, novelist from Kossuth, Mississippi, author of *The Bitterweed Path, The Golden Lie, The Loved and the Unloved,* and other works.

[3] Creative writing instructor at the University of Alabama.

963v Letter from Phil Stone to Edwin R. Holmes, United States Circuit Judge, Yazoo City, Mississippi, October 28, 1953, carbon typescript with typed signature, 1 page.

Dear Judge:

Thank you for your nice letter of October 27.[1]

While Mac Reed here was and still is Bill's loyal friend it is true that I was the only one who believed that he could be a successful writer and it took me ten years to convince anybody else.

An interesting and amusing situation has arisen about that. During that time most of the people in Oxford and at the University made fun of me about my claims for Bill but now that he has become famous the same type of people and some of the same people have become his ardent friends and those people take particular pains to discredit my association with Bill. This is natural because I am the only one who knows the details as to how none of them would lend a shoulder to push the bandwagon uphill.

It was in 1925 that I sent you the copy of THE MARBLE FAUN and I hope you still have it because the last I heard it is worth from $75.00 to $100.00 as a collector's item.

. . . .

Your friend,
Phil Stone

[1] Judge Holmes had written to congratulate Stone on his role in Faulkner's career, as reported in Coughlan's *Life* magazine feature. In his letter Holmes recalled "a copy of [Faulkner's] poems" which Stone had mailed him years before.

967 Letter from Donald S. Klopfer to Saxe Commins, October 30, 1953, signed ribbon typescript, 1 page.

Dear Saxe:

Mary[1] is bringing down the balance of the Faulkner. It's great. Bill has promised to do a couple of page summary, not for publication but for us, on what he is really trying to do in this book—the story line, the symbolism, what the characters stand for, etc. By all means encourage him to do so, because it will mean that a uniform story can go out of Random House.

I spoke to Behrman's[2] secretary. He is busy working with Korda on something now, I don't know what. I told Miss Bernstein that you'd like to work with him week after next and finish up the book. If he doesn't do it, I am going to take it off the Spring list.

As soon as you've finished the Faulkner, I will send you the Gilson.[3] That'll keep you home and quiet for a good, long time.

I do know, Saxe, that you think you're being obedient and relaxing, but I am sure you're doing too much, and you simply have to slow down and take things in their stride. By the letters you've received, you know how valuable you are to your friends and to Random House, and you've also discovered, to my great pleasure, how much more work you can do in Princeton than you can at 457. You're going to have to divide your time more evenly between the two places.

My deep love to you.

As always,
/s/ Donald

[1] Mary Randolph, secretary to Bennett Cerf and Donald Klopfer at Random House.

[2] S. N. Behrman, whose autobiographical work, *The Worcester Account,* was published by Random House in 1954.

[3] Probably a reference to Étienne Henry Gilson's *History of Christian Philosophy in the Middle Ages,* published by Random House in 1955.

S-35 Letter from Faulkner to Joan Williams, undated [possibly October 1953], unsigned ribbon typescript, 1 page.

I wont stop in. If this is the end, and I suppose, assume it is, I think the two people drawn together as we were and held together for four years by whatever it was we had, knew—love, sympathy, understanding, trust, belief—deserve a better period than a cup of coffee—not to end like two high school sweethearts breaking up over a coca cola in the corner drugstore.

Am leaving the car in Princeton, a garage there costs 10$ a month, against $45.00. Before I leave, I will write you a letter of authority to get it whenever you want it; right now I am not sure of the name of the manager, and the address on the place, which is on Nassau street, and Saxe knows it. I will find that out when I leave the car, and authorise them for you to use it; also I will write you a letter to present them for identification.

[no signature]

S-36 Letter from Saxe Commins to Donald Klopfer, November 5, 1953, unsigned ribbon typescript, 2 pages.

Dear Don,

With this letter Bill is bringing the final, complete, ready-for-the printer manuscript of *A Fable*. Both of us feel, in the excitement and lift of working so steadily and to such wonderful purpose, that the script is as near perfection as we can make it. With what cuts we have been able to make (and there isn't a word we can think of to take out any more), the entire book runs to approximately 175,000 words, give a few thousand either way.

I don't have to tell you how I feel about it as a work of art; what is important here is to set down a few suggestions for your guidance in handling the manuscript from now until we have final book, or galleys at least.

You will notice that all front matter is in place and ready for composition. On the copyright page, we have only to supply the Library of Congress Card Catalog Number. The 1950 date of copyright is to cover the copyright issued in Bill's name when *Notes on a Horse Thief* appeared as a Limited Edition under the imprint of the Levee Press in Greenville, Mississippi. The story itself is rewritten for the purposes of *A Fable*.

On the acknowledgment page (which is VI in our front matter) you will see the precise manner in which Bill wishes to make the essential acknowledgments. We gave it a left-hand page, backing the Dedication (also supplied) to save pages in front matter and not make it too conspicuous.

You will see a note on the bastard title offering suggestions to the printer about the nature of the crosses used throughout the book—on jacket, binding, title page, half-title pages and even where two-line space breaks occur in the text. This is terribly important. We must avoid the use of denominational crosses and want simple, the simpler the better, wooden crosses throughout. Where the crosses appear at the opening of each of the ten parts, they must be quite large and so placed as to give the opening chapter page a great deal of sinkage. Where we indicate three little crosses to mark a lapse of time or change of scene we want the crosses to be no larger than the upper case of the regular type measure used for text, no larger than an ordinary asterisk.

We would like to have a simple cross on a binding of blue for the front of the book. The backbone will merely bear the title, Bill's name, the Random House imprint, *but no crosses*.

Bill would like to offer the suggestion that the jacket be of a dark blue at the bottom and gradually getting lighter and lighter till at the top it is almost the color of a clear sky and imposed on the top half again the simple cross, perhaps in white, and in the dark-blue section beneath

A FABLE

William Faulkner

These are merely suggestions, and perhaps premature, but they embody what we sat up all last night talking about after ten steady hours of work at the script.

Our layout therefore will be as follows:

I Bastard
II Ad-Facer (List of Bill's books)
III Title
IV Copyright
V Dedication (supplied)
VI Acknowledgment
1 H.T.
2 Blank
3–? Text

My guess is that we will come within 14 forms of 32's or 448 pages or 480 at most.

You will notice that no provision is made for a Note on the Author. This is at Bill's special request. It will therefore be omitted.

At the end of the book there appears a three-line date and place notice, which we would like to have set in a small face, flush left, somewhat like this:

December, 1944
Oxford—New York—Princeton
November, 1953

Whenever you decide to set, I will be responsible for all proofs, if Bill won't be available to read them. If he is, we will do them together.

You will notice that all the chapter heads except one—the last, TOMORROW—bear date lines. We would want them set quite inconspicuously, certainly not in caption style, as the days themselves must be. The purpose of the date lines, obviously, is to help keep the reader oriented in time.

[no signature]

969 Letter from Howard Hawks to Faulkner, November 16, 1953, signed ribbon typescript, 2 pages. From Paris.

Dear Bill,

Just back from Cairo and wired you how pleased I am that you are coming. Am trying to pick a good place for us to work, maybe in Switzerland, and will wire you when I know what is good. Egypt is great, perfectly beautiful and very interesting. This can be an amazing picture.[1] Here's a little description which you probably already know.

Egypt is a river, outside of the land alongside of the river it's a desert and all life is centered around the river. Old days the Nile used to overflow and the land was inundated except for the villages which are always built on higher ground, naturally or artificially. During flood times the people worked for the Pharaoh. The Pharaoh was God, he controlled all the people, fed them, and according to his nature, ruled them. If he were warlike they fought, if he were artistic the arts became worth while.

They had one consuming belief, that of a second life and all of the Pyramids and mastabas were only to ensure an uninterrupted future existence. So they went to unbelievable lengths to build these final resting places and to hide their tombs from possible intruders. To give you an idea of size the big pyramid has 2,500,000 stones, each averaging 2½ tons. These stones were cut to tolerances of 1/100 of an inch.

They took their stones from quarries (one of which had a tunnel 15 miles long), dragged the stones to the Nile, floated them on boats, dragged them across the desert to the Pyramids and then succeeded in hoisting them 4 & 5 hundred feet into the air.

We will try and show all of this and it ought to be fun.

When you come maybe you can bring me half a dozen cartons of Kent cigarettes and a couple of bottles of vitamin B No. 1 pills, they are hard to get over here.

As to clothes, it is going to be cold in Europe and hot in Egypt. Bourbon is a little tough to get, but I've got some scouts looking out.

Will be glad to see you, and in the meantime, if you want any information, just cable:

Hotel Plaza Athenee
23 Avenue Montaine, Paris.

or

Warner Bros.
5 rue Valasquez, Paris.

Regards,

Sincerely,
/s/ Howard
/t/ Howard Hawks

[1] *Land of the Pharaohs,* for which Hawks had enlisted Faulkner to do the filmscript.

973 Letter from Estelle Faulkner to Dorothy and Saxe Commins, "Monday" [November or December 1953], signed autograph manuscript, 2 pages.

Dear Dorothy and Saxe—

It was shocking to Jill and me to get home and find that Saxe had been so desperately sick—Thank God his recovery is assured—What indifferent friends you both must think us!

Bill wrote saying that you, Saxe, were recuperating in Princeton and that he had been down to see you, but it wasn't until Jill, Tori and I got in from Mexico Friday, that I found Dorothy's letter of September 15th—Am sure Bill just forgot to forward it—

Even though I couldn't have been of any help, being so far away—could have at least written and telephoned and kept in touch—

Saxe was so very good to us in our trouble last fall, I feel doubly guilty in our neglect of him—even though I knew nothing of his serious illness—*Should have written from Mexico to you all, anyhow!* Then, some one could have sent us a wire, at least—

The children and I had a wonderful two and a half months' stay—Had a charming apartment in the city, met most attractive people and were fortunate enough to see many parts of Mexico guide fools fail to exploit—

Jill and I hope to go back some day—Don't know whether Jill lost her heart to the country, or to one of her many admirers!

Tori, the little school-friend of Jill's, who made the trip with us, had to hurry home to collect a trousseau for an early February wedding—hence our premature return to the States—

Our plans right now depend greatly on my mother's health which is failing visibly, day by day—We will certainly be in Oxford until after Christmas, then I suspect Jill will get restless again—

Gloria, Malcolm and Jill send their love—

And from me, Love to you all, and Frannie, Bill—Eugene—

Always devotedly
Estelle

974 Letter from Estelle Faulkner to Saxe and Dorothy Commins, "Wednesday—Dec. 9th," signed autograph manuscript, 2 pages, with envelope addressed in Mrs. Faulkner's hand and postmarked Oxford, December 10, 1953.

Dearest Saxe—

And, of course, Dorothy—you two are so inseparable in my mind that, writing to one, always means both of you—

It was sweet and good of you, Saxe, to bother to write when I know it was an effort, but Jill and I felt so relieved, and positively *joyous*, you sounded so like a well and radiant man again—Bless you—and may you always be strong and happy—

Jill is working these weeks before Christmas for a friend of mine who has a dress shop here—She seems sort of mis-cast in the role of sales-lady, but seems to be enjoying it, and very proud of her weekly pay-check—

My mother's illness necessitates long hours away from home for me, so Jill's employment is a god-send in a way—However, both Jill and I have the happy faculty of never becoming lonely even in this big untenanted house—

We have found a young woman at the University who has no place to go for the Holidays and are hoping to make them pleasant for her by sharing Santa Claus—How we would love having the Commins family!

Naturally Mama's condition is a source of grave concern, but she is most insistent that we celebrate as usual, and is even convinced that she will feel well enough to participate—Such courage usually wins!

Please, when you see them, give Mr. Haas, Don and Bennett[1] my warmest regards—Do hope though, that you are giving New York a wide berth still—

It is comforting to Jill and me to know that we have a true and trusted friend in you, and it may be that a little selfishness prompts our deep concern over your welfare—However, we prefer it to be Love—

And, it *is* Love, and Merry Christmas to Dorothy and you, Eugene, Frannie and Bill—

Always devotedly
Estelle

[P.S.] No word from Bill since the Friday before he was to leave on Monday—Did he get away?[2]

[1]Robert Haas, Donald Klopfer, and Bennett Cerf.
[2]Faulkner departed from New York on November 30 to join Howard Hawks in Paris and begin work on the script of *Land of the Pharaohs*.

935h Letter from Phil Stone to Carvel Collins, December 14, 1953, carbon typescript with typed signature, 2 pages.

Dear Carvel:

Thank you for your nice letter of December 10.

. . . .

I am much amused that they are going to publish those sketches that Bill made for the Times-Picayune during 1925. They are certainly not worth publishing. John McClure and George Healy, at my request, got this work for Bill and my recollection is that he got $5.00 apiece for these sketches.[1]

I observe in the paper that Bill has gone to France to do a job on a script that is laid in Egypt. I don't know whether he is going to Egypt or not but the report in the paper said he would not be back until March. I don't think it will be necessary for him to go to Egypt in order to write the script because any Faulkner can tell you everything about Egypt even though he has never been there. Strictly between us and completely off the record, I am just about fed up with Bill and as far as I am concerned I don't care much if he never comes back.

I have not read the new book[2] but he brought us part of the manuscript several years ago and it has some wonderful Faulkner writing in it. My guess is the whole book will be something like that but not successful as a book from a literary standpoint, that it will lack overall design as all of Bill's longer works do and, principally, that it is a book requiring humility, which trait I have never seen in any Faulkner.

. . . .

Your friend,
Phil Stone

[1]Collins edited the *Times-Picayune* sketches (plus "New Orleans" from the *Double Dealer*) in *William Faulkner: New Orleans Sketches* (New Brunswick, N.J.: Rutgers University Press, 1958).
[2]*A Fable*.

1954

981 Letter from Faulkner to Dorothy and Saxe Commins, "4 Jan 54," signed autograph manuscript, 1 page, with envelope addressed in Faulkner's hand and postmarked Suvretta, St. Moritz, Switzerland.

Dear Dorothy and Saxe,

The job here[1] is going all right, but I was right about not wanting it. I am already sick to the teeth of rich American expatriates from income tax, who have moved intact their entire Hollywood lives to Europe. Got away from it Xmas, Stockholm and London & Paris. Just got back tonight.

Have had no word from home yet, so I suppose everything is all right. Have made no arrangement about this money yet, so will you please transfer $2500

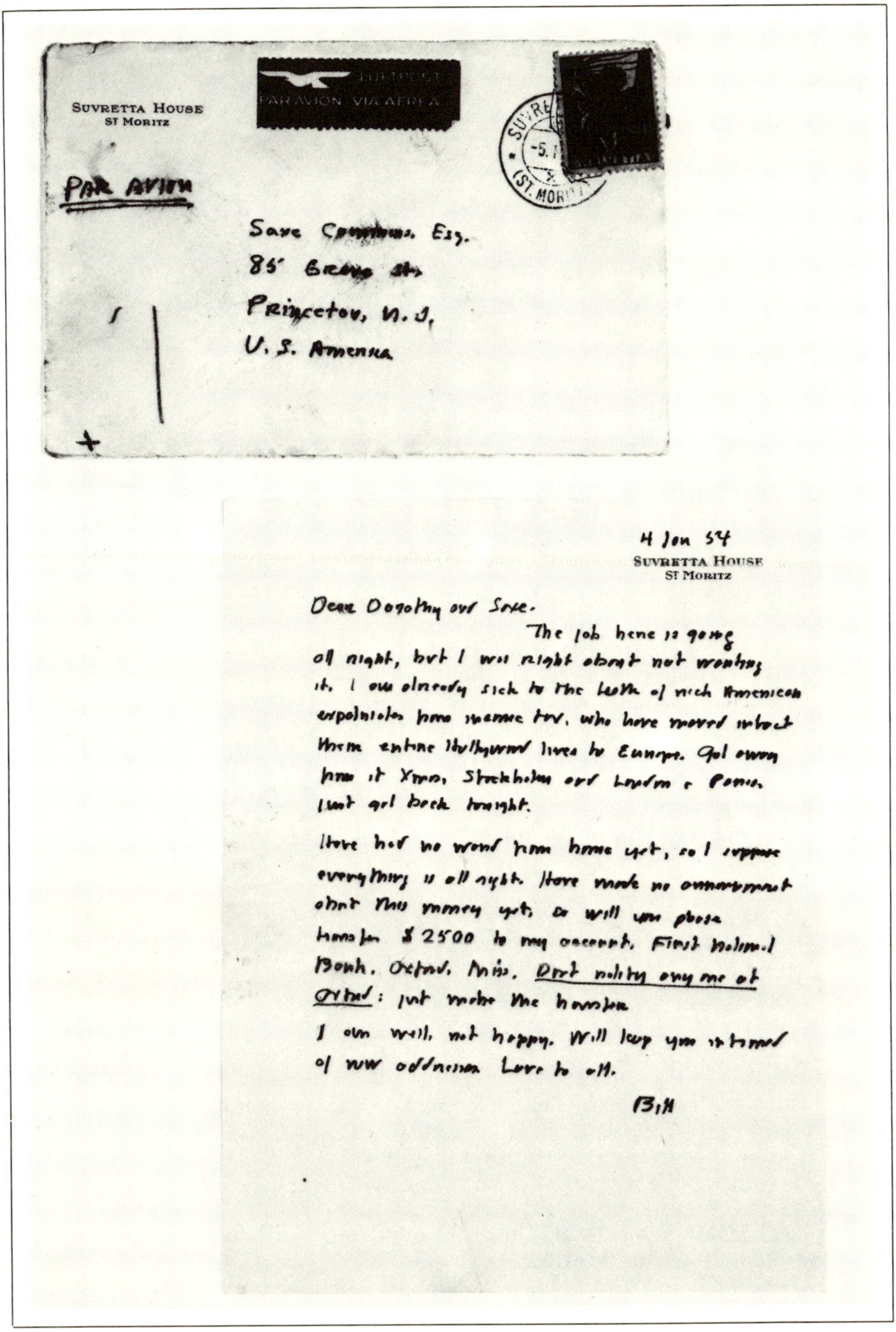

Suvretta House
St Moritz

Par Avion Via Aerea

Par Avion

Saxe Commins, Esq.
Princeton, N. J.
U. S. America

4 Jan 54

Suvretta House
St Moritz

Dear Dorothy and Saxe:

The job here is going all right, but I was right about not wanting it. I am already sick to the teeth of rich American expatriates from movie too, who have moved about their entire Hollywood lives to Europe. Got away from it Xmas, Stockholm and London & Paris, just got back tonight.

Have had no word from home yet, so I suppose everything is all right. Have made no arrangement about the money yet, so will you please transfer $2500 to my account, First National Bank, Oxford, Miss. Don't notify anyone at Oxford; just make the transfer.

I am well, not happy. Will keep you informed of my address. Love to all.

Bill

25. Letter from Faulkner to Dorothy and Saxe Commins, with envelope (item 981)

to my account, First National Bank, Oxford, Miss. *Dont notify anyone at Oxford*: just make the transfer.

I am well, not happy. Will keep you informed of new addresses. Love to all.

Bill

[1] Faulkner's assignment on *Land of the Pharaohs.*

982 Letter from Estelle Faulkner to Saxe Commins, dated "Oxford—Jan. 29," signed autograph manuscript, 2 pages, with envelope addressed in Mrs. Faulkner's hand and postmarked Oxford, January 29 [?], 1954.

Dear Saxe—

This is a most embarrassing thing for me to do—enclose this threat from Levy's[1] in Memphis—but as I have no authority to write checks on Bill's account—can think of nothing else to do but ask you to send them the money for Bill—

As soon as I opened the letter, phoned the credit manager and explained that Mr. Faulkner was in Europe and I had no way of getting in touch with him immediately—

Mr. Condon was very nice about it—asked me to disregard the pending unpleasantness—but to ask Bill to send a check as soon as possible—

Jill had a note from B. written in Rome on the 22nd—but said they were going on to Africa in a few days—

I sent his unpaid bills in care of Gallimard in Paris, soon after we got home and I found such a frightening pile of them—Perhaps he didn't get them—

Our allowance is adequate, but so far haven't managed to save enough to take care of old accounts—This one from Levy's dates from 1952, so I hardly blame them—

Please believe how sorry I am to have to ask this of you—

Love from Jill and me to you *all*—

Estelle

[1] A department store.

983 Letter from Estelle Faulkner to Dorothy and Saxe Commins, "Saturday" [January 1954], signed autograph manuscript, 2 pages.

Dearest Dorothy and Saxe—

Jill and I have been muchly concerned over Saxe's venture *back* into work in New York—and have wanted to write before this, asking about you both—for we know the anxiety Dorothy must face—

For the past three weeks I've had a friend of mine here at Rowan oak trying to nurse, both her body and mind into some semblance of health and happiness again—Mary lost her husband some time ago, and still is in a pitiable condition from shock and lack of interest in living—

Between home, and sitting several hours with my mother a day—have had little time to write—Jill too, is very busy—Has an editorial job on our local newspaper,[1] and is taking short-hand, a history course and conversational French and Spanish at the University—

Please let me apologize for my 'phone call at such a busy hour for you—Am sure you were at dinner and maybe had guests! At any rate, talking to you helped so much—

Jill is flying to North Carolina the 10th of February to be in a school-friend's wedding, but we've given up the idea of going on to New York and down to Princeton—I am sorry not to see you for a few hours again—More than four days away from school and her paper would be too much for Jill, and besides, we wouldn't dare now to take the car—We assumed from the talk around that Bill had gotten Joan a job with the picture company—

Of course you are proud to the bursting point of Eugene![2] So are we—and are amazed sometime to find ourselves telling of his honours as though he sort of *belonged* to us too! When you have the time and inclination, let us hear how you *all* are—please include Frannie and Bill—

This scrawl has been written in a half-darkened room at Mama's—Perhaps you can decipher some of it—I love you very dearly

Estelle

[1] *The Oxford Eagle.*

[2] As a graduate student in physics at Columbia University, Eugene Commins had been awarded a Guggenheim fellowship.

985 Letter from Estelle Faulkner to Saxe Commins, "February 6th," signed autograph manuscript, 2 pages, with envelope addressed in Mrs. Faulkner's hand and postmarked Oxford, February 6, 1954.

Dear Saxe—

As always, you are right—I had no reason whatsoever to think that you could pay Levy's off without Bill's consent and approval—Please believe me most contrite—For a day or so I was panic stricken, and called upon you without considering how unethical my request was—

Have saved two hundred dollars out of our household allowance and will go ahead and pay the demand—I had hoped to use this money only for an emergency, should one arise, as Bill did not provide for money to cover anything other than our usual expenses—

He was fully aware that Jill and I had a charge account at Levy's—There's nothing more to say—other than please forget my lapse and forgive me—

We are most concerned over Dorothy's accident—How I wish it possible for me to be with her and pamper her as thoroughly as she did me last spring—

Don't, for heaven's sake, let anything else dire happen to the Commins—you are much too fine to be touched by misfortune—

Bill couldn't have a defter hand or a better mind than yours, to steer the Fable to completion—I'm sure he is resting quite easily on that score—although the strain on you must have been nerve-racking—Jill and I are grateful to you—

Thank you for your long, understanding letter—

With sincerest love

Estelle

[P.S.] If you kept it, please sometime return the Levy paper—Thank you—

986 Letter from Estelle Faulkner to Saxe Commins, "Thursday—11th," signed autograph manuscript, 2 pages, with envelope addressed in Mrs. Faulkner's hand and postmarked Oxford, February 11, 1954.

Dear Saxe—

Thank you very much for your letter and the Levy thing you returned—Am so distressed that Dorothy has been afflicted with a cold—A shame for her to have to suffer all the misfortunes of lesser mortals—Dorothy is far too saintly for anything but life's best—Kiss her for me—

Have been busy getting the gardens and grounds in shape for serious planting this year—For the past two springs I felt physically unable to do much, and as Bill was away most of the time, Rowan oak has suffered from neglect—I *do* want 1954 to be different—

Your letter, Saxe, gave me pause—I was just on the verge of writing Bill that I was suing for divorce—I still believe it the only wise thing to do—on his account, as well as Jill's and mine—

Bill has been at home very little the past four years, and a good bit of that time spent here, has been a nightmare of drunkenness—He must be very unhappy—so the only cure I know of is to help him get free—legally—Heaven only knows he has been free in every other sense—

Jill (she will tell you this very frankly) and I are happier and *more at ease* when Bill is away—Since his unfortunate disclosure to Jill about his current affair—she hasn't felt too secure around him—As for me—I'd do anything for peace—and my own sense of *doing the right thing*—

Since your letter—as I said—I'm wondering just what the right thing is—

Having every confidence in the world in your judgment, and sensibilities where Bill is concerned—will wait for advice—if you'll be so good—

Please believe that I'm only endeavoring to make everyone concerned, a little happier—

Love to all the family—
Devotedly

Estelle

987 Letter from Faulkner to Saxe Commins, "27th. February, 1954," signed ribbon typescript, 1 page. From Cairo, Egypt.

Dear Saxe,

This letter of Joor's explains itself.[1] If you can itemise the doctor and the hospital bills and get the information to him, by telegraph if necessary, before the deadline, please do so.

I am fairly well—working. I don't think very highly of Egypt.

Love to Dorothy and everyone else.

As always,
/s/ Bill

[1] W. W. Joor, a tax lawyer and accountant from Oxford, handled Faulkner's income tax returns for several years.

988 Letter from Estelle Faulkner to Saxe Commins, "Sunday morning," signed autograph manuscript, 4 pages, with envelope addressed in Mrs. Faulkner's hand and postmarked Oxford, February 29 [*sic*], 1954.

Dear Saxe—

Whether this compulsion to write about Billy is wise, or not—I don't know—But, as long as you've gone through so much of the anguish with me, I feel it only fair to tell you what *I believe* to be wrong—

Three, (almost four now), years ago Bill met, liked, and took an absorbing interest in a young woman from Memphis—Joan Williams—whom you know—She was an aspiring young writer, Bill was working on his play,[1] and told Jill and me at Easter-time that she was going to collaborate with him in finishing it—We *both* were a little amazed—as Pappy heretofore, brooked *no* interference—Billy visited Joan at her school (Bard) and in Memphis—had her down here, *once*—Her work on the play evidently came to nought—Billy *has* taught her to write, I'm sure, as she, with his help, is having things published—

It was this fall that we found how deeply involved they were—Billy is completely enamoured, and Joan professes her love in no uncertain terms—*Bill had Malcolm open and read her letters to him*—and Mac, shocked, gave them to me[2]—I returned them to Bill, but he knows that Jill and I know—He chided Jill for not having ambition like Joan, and several other comparisons that aren't worth mentioning—

This, I believe, Saxe, is Billy's trouble—He is afraid to face reality because of Jill—Jill worshipped him—still does—youth is resilient and she'll forget soon that Pappy hurt her—*if* he will permit it—

As for me—I'm hurt, but not despairing—*Nothing* can alter my love and devotion—nor upset my faith in Bill's actual love for me—although right now, he swears he doesn't care—I'm throwing myself on your mercy and kindness, to understand—All I want is Billy's good—and to prove it, I'll do *anything* that is best—The only thing that I shudder at and might try to evade, is a divorce—and *that,* only on Jill's account—

Billy *should* be at home with a *good* nurse—a man he could trust to help him, and I could look after his creature comforts—But, should he come home now, he and Joan both would feel frustrated, as this trip had been planned for some time[3]—I *am* shirking responsibility, because I just don't know what to do—however, I promise *you* this, that whatever you decide, I'll be brave about it and hold up my end—

This is a shocking letter, Saxe, and I'm sorry—but you *had* to know to get things in focus—Use your discretion about telling Billy that I wrote it—Had I told you all this when you were here,[4] perhaps it would have been better, but I thought for awhile that I could cope with the situation alone—I can't—Billy's continued drinking makes it most grave—

May God help me if I've misrepresented anything, though, even to me, it is all unbelievable—

I'll wait anxiously to hear from you—My fingers are shaky—after a sleepless night—Can you decipher my scrawl?

Always my love to Dorothy, and to you—love, gratitude and confidence

Estelle

[1] *Requiem for a Nun.*

[2] Cf. Faulkner's account of how Estelle learned of his affair. See page 94.

[3] Apparently Estelle believed that Joan was with Faulkner during his assignment on *Land of the Pharaohs.*

[4] Presumably a reference to Commins' trip to Oxford in October 1952.

989 Letter from Estelle Faulkner to Saxe Commins, "Sunday night" [March 1954], signed autograph manuscript, 4 pages (3 leaves).

Dear Saxe—

After your wonderfully spirit-lifting letter, I am mortified to find how many days have gone by without an acknowledgement from me—

Jill has had unexpected house-guests this week—She came home from North Carolina Monday, and a week's absence from school and her newspaper, doubled her work, naturally—Therefore Mama had all the entertaining to do—Very pleasant and diverting too, however time consuming—

I am so vastly relieved, Saxe, that I had the temerity to shift my burden on to you—as it were—I asked for advice, and believe, with all my heart, in your willingness to give me unbiased counsel—And, certainly I'm not fool enough to seek guidance, then disregard it—

Bill's letters (three so far) have been notes—mostly business, about taxes etc. Not even the cold comfort of a formal salutation—just plain statements and instructions—

To say that I'm at loss to explain this would be foolish—What can I think but that he is trying to drive me to a break? I'd rather not be driven—still it's hard to be completely indifferent and ignore him—I am far from callous—worse luck—

And, please believe this—When I thought seriously of going to my lawyer, I had no intention of hurting anyone—I was going to ask for a divorce on grounds of incompatability—even though it appears rather ridiculous after twenty-five years!

Nevertheless I believe Mr. Roberts would have been persuaded—

I am much too old and poised (I hope) to give vent to personal animosity—In fact, am not sure that I feel any—Certainly I do not blame Joan—In all probability, had *I* been an aspiring young writer and an elderly celebrity had fallen in love with me—I would have accepted him as avidly as Joan did Bill—

Who am I, to judge her anyway? I don't—

And in a way, I feel sorry for Bill—He *is* in a mess, and I daresay is going to have a bad time of it—

My one thought was *really* to get all three of us, Bill, Jill and me, out of a tragic—and in some ways—comic—situation, in as dignified a manner as possible—

You are usually—no, always—so right—It makes me very proud to have you put confidence in me, in that you speak—I listen, and act accordingly—I think, Saxe, I could never disobey your advice in *anything*—

Bill's article, "Mississippi," in next month's Holiday explains the two Bills—He is so definitely dual I think—Perhaps artists must needs be—

Dearest love to both Dorothy and you—

From now on (by the grace of God)
Placidly yours
Estelle

[P.S.] This scrawl is to Dorothy too—of course

991 Letter from Estelle Faulkner to Saxe Commins, "Friday—March 12th" [1954], signed autograph manuscript, 1 page.

Dear Saxe—

Thank you for your letter—My last one to you hardly called for an answer—in fact I'm sorry it was ever written—I overstepped the bounds of good taste sadly, and humbly ask forgiveness—

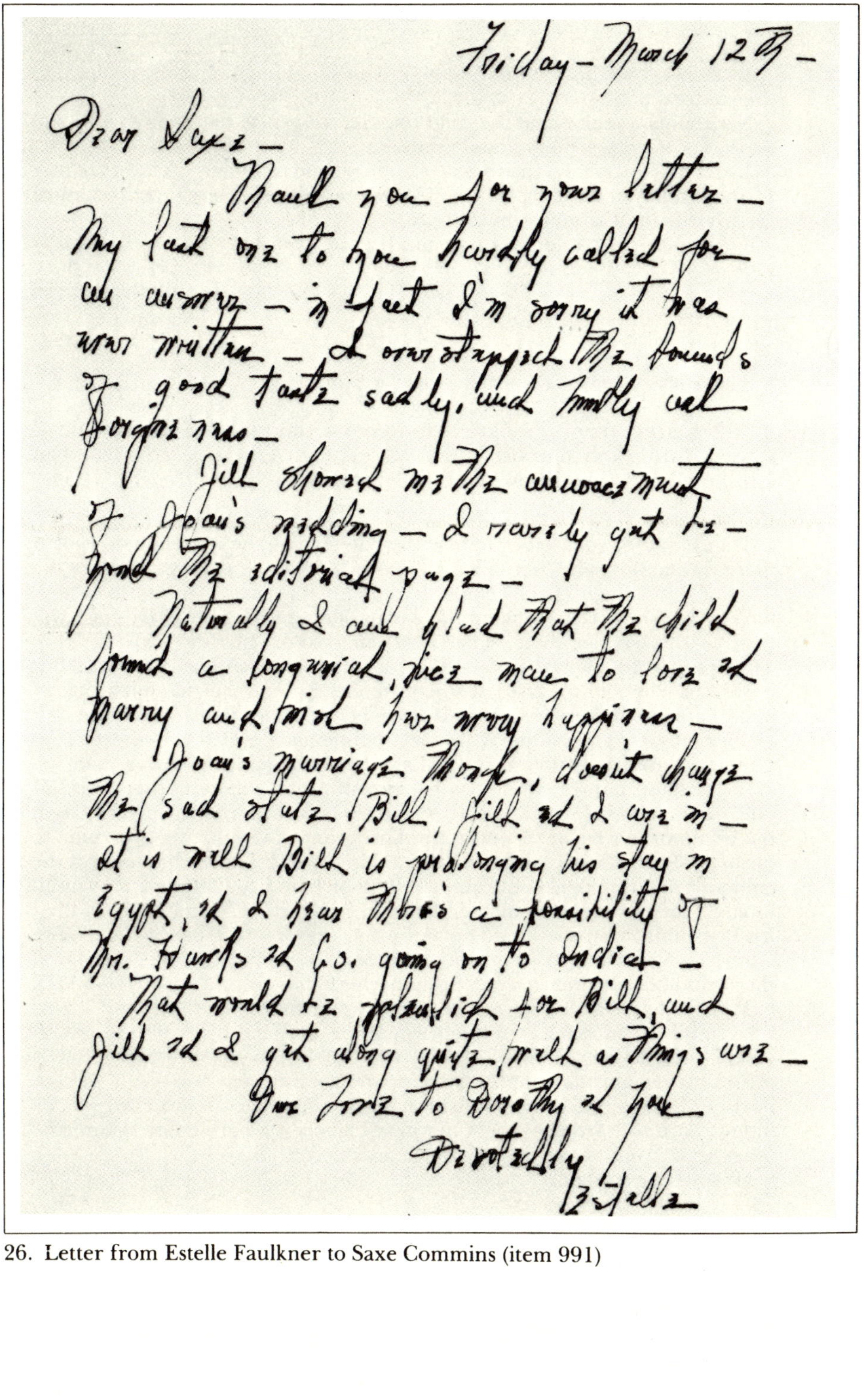

Friday - March 12th -

Dear Saxe -

Thank you for your letter - My last one to you hardly called for an answer - in fact I'm sorry it was ever written - I overstepped the bounds of good taste sadly, and humbly ask forgiveness -

Jill showed me the announcement of Joan's wedding - I rarely get beyond the editorial page -

Naturally I am glad that the child found a tranquil, nice man to love and marry and find her own happiness -

Joan's marriage though, doesn't change the sad state Bill, Jill and I are in - It is well Bill is prolonging his stay in Egypt, and I hear there's a possibility of Mr. Hawks and Co. going on to India - That would be splendid for Bill, and Jill and I get along quite well as things are -

Our love to Dorothy and you

Devotedly

Estelle

26. Letter from Estelle Faulkner to Saxe Commins (item 991)

Jill showed me the announcement of Joan's wedding[1]—I rarely get beyond the editorial page—

Naturally I am glad that the child found a congenial, nice man to love and marry and wish her every happiness—

Joan's marriage, though, doesn't change the sad state Bill, Jill and I are in—It is well Bill is prolonging his stay in Egypt, and I hear there's a possibility of Mr. Hawks and Co. going on to India—

That would be splendid for Bill, and Jill and I get along quite well as things are—

Our Love to Dorothy and you
Devotedly
Estelle

[1] Joan Williams and Ezra Bowen were married on March 6, 1954.

992 Letter from Faulkner to Saxe Commins, "Sunday 14th," signed autograph manuscript, 2 pages, with envelope addressed in Faulkner's hand and postmarked Pyramids, Egypt, March 14, 1954.

Dear Saxe—

Thank you for your letter. I knew about it.[1] I think she is too honest, even if there was nothing else, not to let me know. We knew a year ago that her life was not right, she was not demon-driven enough for art, writing to suffice, too much middle class background saying home, marriage, children. I was not free to marry her, even if I had not been too old. So I—we—expected this. That was my trouble last winter 1953[2]: the art should have been enough. But it was not. She told me last fall when she met Bowen, that she might marry him, that she would tell me herself—not let a stranger do it. Which she did: wrote me here about middle April [*sic*] that she had decided, and the date. So I knew. I want her happy. If she is, I am the best friend Bowen ever had.

Incidentally, a queer thing has happened to me, almost a repetition; this one is even named Jean.[3] She is 19, daughter of M.C.A. cap.[4] living in Paris in the house of her bachelor uncle, the European representative. She came to me in St Moritz almost exactly as Joan did in Oxford. But she has none of the emotional conventional confusion which poor Joan had. This one is so uninhibited that she frightens me a little. I left St Moritz to spend Xmas in England, assuming that she would be gone, since she was supposed to be back in Paris New Years to go back to school. But she was still in St Moritz. She stayed there until her momma in Venice found where she was, and ordered her back to Paris by telephone. She came to Rome when we moved there, and stayed there until her momma found out where she was, and ordered her back to Paris by telephone. I expect any day now for her to come to Cairo. She is charming, delightful, completely transparent, completely trustful. I will not hurt her for any price. She doesn't want anything of me—only to love me, be in love. You will probably meet her next fall when we are home again. The other affair would have hurt of course, except for this.

My love to everyone.

Bill

[1] Joan Williams' marriage.
[2] Faulkner entered this date between the lines, apparently in afterthought.
[3] Jean Stein.
[4] Jules Stein was the founder of the Music Corporation of America.

994 Letter from Estelle Faulkner to Dorothy and Saxe Commins, "March 30th," signed autograph manuscript, 3 pages (2 leaves), with envelope addressed in Mrs. Faulkner's hand and postmarked Oxford, March 30, 1954.

Dearest Dorothy and Saxe—

Jill and I have had a "series" of casual house-guests lately which may explain my failure to thank Saxe for a lovely letter—I'm sorry—

Having a big house, our friends feel free to lodge any over-flow they might have—and our next-door neighbor, as well as Gloria and Malcolm, have been swamped with company the past few weeks—The little effort involved is very rewarding—Chief Justice Frankfurter[1] was one of our guests—I completely lost my heart to him—Judge Frankfurter came down to lecture at Ole Miss and we entertained him to accommodate Dr. Farley—dean of the law school—

I was so interested in your account of Judge Lotimyier [?], Saxe—and took the liberty of sending that part of your letter on to Cornell (Judge Franklin—but my whole letter seems to be Judges!)

I remember the old gentleman with a great deal of pleasure, and *your* paragraph was such a splendid piece of writing—I wanted Cornell to get the graphic picture too—

Judge Franklin's Virginia place is so near Washington—I'm sure that he will get in touch with the "gnome"—How expressive—and you are right—he must be at least ninety—

Between entertaining, I've managed to make a few spring dresses for Jill and me, and really have done well with my gardening—Have always liked to work out of doors—

Do write sometime and tell us about your lovely place—Jill *must* see your house before she ever plans one of her own!

We would like so much too, news of Franny and Bill, and *very* important—Eugene—

Bill F. writes that he will be away until June at least—Am glad for him that he can stay away awhile—

A heart full of love to you *all*

Estelle

[P.S.] Did you like Bill's Mississippi? The mother of the "son-of-the-absconded-banker"[2] cut me dead in our local super-market!

[1] Felix Frankfurter, associate justice, United States Supreme Court, 1939–1962.

[2] See "Mississippi," in *Essays, Speeches & Public Letters by William Faulkner*, ed. James B. Meriwether (New York: Random House, 1965), p. 36.

1009 RCA Radiogram from Faulkner to Saxe Commins, April 12, 1954. From Paris.

FORGOT JUDAS MISERY DESIRE REWRITE ONE SECTION[1] PLAN ARRIVE 20 APRIL OR WILL CABLE TO SEND SECTION HERE—BILL

[1] Reference here is to the next-to-last scene in *A Fable*. After the book was in galley proof, Faulkner rewrote the scene in question to add the Judas character.

1010a Letter from Robert Coughlan to Phil and Emily Stone, April 13, 1954, signed ribbon typescript, 2 pages.

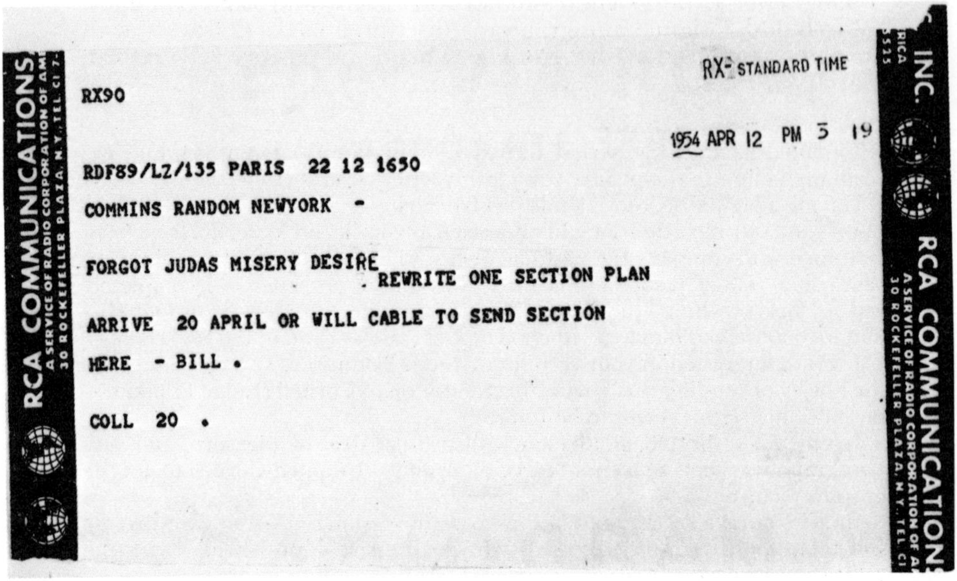
RCA COMMUNICATIONS

RX90

RX= STANDARD TIME

1954 APR 12 PM 3 19

RDF89/LZ/135 PARIS 22 12 1650

COMMINS RANDOM NEWYORK -

FORGOT JUDAS MISERY DESIRE . REWRITE ONE SECTION PLAN

ARRIVE 20 APRIL OR WILL CABLE TO SEND SECTION

HERE - BILL .

COLL 20 .

27. Telegram from Faulkner to Saxe Commins regarding *A Fable* (item 1009)

Dear Phil and Emily,

As you know, I've been converting the Life articles on Bill into a short book for Harpers. It's finished and will be off to the printers around the first of May. But there are several points that I can't nail down in my notes or from printed sources, and since Moon Mullin [*sic*] has moved and I can't call on him for checking, I'm imposing on you herewith, with apologies but in hopes that you can help me out.

1. Aunt Bama. Is her name really Bama, or is that short for Alabama? Where does she fit into the family—great aunt? On which side? Her name now is Mrs. Walter McLean (correct spelling?). Is she still living?

2. In Bill's article on Mississippi in the current (April) issue of Holiday, he indicates that he finally became Master of the annual hunt. I didn't know they had a Master: if anybody was in charge, I supposed it would be Ike Roberts as "camp boss." How about that? Also, I have listed Leo Calloway, Joe Butler, Red Brite, Bob Evans, John Cullen, and Ike Roberts as more or less regular members of the hunt. Does that sound right to you? And could you tell me the occupations of Butler, Brite, Evans, and Cullen?

3. In the Holiday article he speaks also of sailing on the Gulf: ". . . one summer being blown innocently over in catboats . . . the next summer he returned because he found that he liked that much water, this time as a hand in one of the trawlers . . . he learned the barrier islands too; one of a crew of amateurs sailing a big sloop in offshore races . . . a professional now, living in New Orleans, he commanded for pay a power launch belonging to a bootlegger . . . etc." This was all news to me. I had heard from one of his Hollywood friends that he spoke of being a rum runner in New Orleans, but I thought

that probably this was one of his fairy stories. If it's true, I assume it happened when he was living in the French Quarter after you, Phil, and he had gone down there. Had he been there the summer previous, to account for this earlier sailing he mentions? Could you fill me in a little on all this?

4. What year did he first go to Hollywood? And what was the movie he went out to do then—Sanctuary (The Story of Temple Drake) or Turnabout; or what? Did he, as the Judge[1] told me, drive out to California at that time in a Model T, with his negro houseboy? Do you happen to know the books and stories of his own that he has adapted for the movies?

5. The first child, as I understand, was named Bama (or Alabama?) after the aunt. What year was she born, and how long did she live?

6. In the Holiday article he describes at some length his adventures with a Mr. Sells Wales. Is this true; and if so, how did he happen to fall in with Mr. Wales?

This is quite a load, Phil, and I hate to bother you with it, but you're the only one who really knows the answers to some of these questions.

I was talking with his publisher the other day, and he says he hasn't heard from Bill and doesn't know how soon he'll be coming back—he's over due now. Says also he has a hunch that Bill will never go back to live in Mississippi: that Bill believes he can't write there anymore. What a shame that would be. As you know, he finished A Fable up here. Random House thinks it's "a masterpiece." I'm afraid I think it's a flop. I wish he would do what you've wanted him to do, finish the Snopes series. He's no damn good when he writes about things far from Yoknapatawpha.

Phil, I sent the Nobel Speech to your friend.

With best regards to you both,

Sincerely,
/s/ Bob

[1] Faulkner's uncle, John Wesley Thompson Falkner, Jr.

1010b Letter from Phil Stone to Robert Coughlan, April 15, 1954, carbon typescript with typed signature, 3 pages.

Dear Bob:

We have your letter of April 13 and were glad to hear from you.

Remember that we want an autographed copy of the book when it comes out. You have been so kind to us that you should not hesitate to write me at any time about anything that you want to know.

1. Aunt Bama is really short for Alabama. She was the sister of Bill's grandfather, J. W. T. Falkner. Unless she has died in the last few weeks she is still living at Memphis and is a grand old lady. I think you have the correct spelling of her name but you can get it from the Memphis telephone directory which I do not have.

2. Bill becoming the master of the hunt is all bunk. Those boys don't have any Master of the hunt but if they had one it would be Ike Roberts. By the way, I saw Ike up town yesterday but he is rather feeble. Evans is a farmer and I think Butler is too. I shall find out about the occupations of Cullen and Brite and try to write you today or tomorrow about that.

3. This is also largely bunk. It is just the usual manifestation of a Falkner inventing romantic stories about himself and the Falkner tribe. It refers to a couple of summers when Bill was invited to go down on the Coast with my brother Jack (W. E.) Stone and his wife Myrtle (who now lives here). I am pretty sure he was never a hand in one of the trawlers, am doubtful that he ever helped sail any big sloop in off-shore races, and know that he never did any rum-running.

He was in New Orleans practically all the time, probably all the time, after he and I went down there in January, 1925, and he sailed from there for Europe in July, 1925. John McClure or George Healy of the Times-Picayune can check this for you.

4. I don't remember just when he went to Hollywood and the fragmentary correspondence I had with Bill during this time burned when the old house burned. I think he went before Sanctuary was published and am pretty sure that he did not drive out there with his negro houseboy. I don't remember now what books and stories of his own that he adapted for the movies. I believe that Darryl Zanuck of Fox could and would give you this information.

5. The first child was named Alabama after Mrs. McLean. Apparently she was prematurely born and only lived a few short weeks. I think she was born in 1930 or 1931, but the Department of Vital Statistics at Jackson should be able to give you the exact information.

6. The adventures of Sells Wales are entirely fiction so far as Bill is concerned. The man he refers to was named Sel Jones who had a plantation at Black Bayou in Tallahatchie County between Clarksdale and Greenwood and who was a legendary character and who did all the things that Bill tells about, but Bill got all this information from me and never saw Sel Jones in his life. Nor is it true that he ever was employed by the Receivers of the Lamb-Fish Lumber Company or received any pay from them. My brother was one of the Receivers and Bill just went along as a voluntary companion for Frank Kelly of Chicago, the other Receiver, and Bill and Frank drank whisky together. If Frank Kelly is still living you might get some things from him that would be most amusing. His brother, Jack Kelly, was City Attorney in Chicago under Mayor Dever.

Of course the stuff about Bill playing the Civil War with spools and shells is all imaginary because I was the one who did this and Bill never did it in his life. This is just of a piece with his tale about what he told General Longstreet. Bill never saw General Longstreet in his life. I was the one who told General Longstreet this one summer when we were at the Hyde Park Hotel in Chicago and I was eight or nine years old. In fact, Bill never seemed interested in the history of the Confederacy at all until I began pumping him full of it around 1919 and 1920 and showed him what splendid romantic material it was for a writer.

I also think that Bill is never coming back to Mississippi and, just between us, I don't care personally whether he does or not. I agree with you that it will be a great mistake, but I think the Nobel prize has ruined Bill and that what he writes anywhere from now on is not going to be worth much, but there is no use in me trying to tell him because you can't tell a successful Falkner anything.

I have not seen the completed manuscript of A FABLE but my guess is that my opinion would be about half way between yours and the opinion of Random House. I think the book will lack overall design, which we think all of Bill's longer books lack, but from what we saw of the manuscript it will be full of some marvelous Faulkner prose. I also think, as I believe I wrote you before, that this is the type of book which could never be great without humility and I repeat that I never saw a Falkner who had any trace of humility.

Thanks a lot for sending the Nobel speech to Judge Green.

We think of you and speak of you often at home, and we wish you would come to see us again and bring your family.

Your friend,
Phil Stone

P. S. Since dictating the above Mr. J. B. Howell, the Chancery Clerk, informs me, as I thought, that John Cullen only does concrete work and that Brite works at the Minnow Shop of Duke, just across the street from our Episcopal Church.

I think another reason Bill wants to stay up around New York is that there he meets only his idolators and does not have to meet anyone who knew him when. Another reason (strictly off the record) that Bill is not likely to come back here is that I think he is permanently getting rid of Estelle.

1010c Letter from Phil Stone to Robert Coughlan, April 16, 1954, carbon typescript with typed signature, 1 page.

Dear Bob:

I inclose you a clipping from the Commercial Appeal of yesterday.[1] I am very doubtful that Estelle knows what she is talking about but she may be right. She may expect Bill home around July [*sic*] 1, but I don't.

Your friend,
Phil Stone

[1] "Faulkner Will Aid Talented Students," Memphis *Commercial Appeal,* April 15, 1954, p. 14. The article, which announced the establishment of a trust fund by Faulkner to support scholarships and other worthy causes, included the following information: "Mr. Faulkner now is in Cairo, Egypt, working on a script for a film. He is expected home around June 1."

1011 French Cable Company cablegram from Faulkner to Saxe Commins, April 19, 1954. From Paris.

PLEASE BOOK HOTEL TUESDAY NOTIFY OXFORD

BILL

1012 Letter from Estelle Faulkner to Saxe Commins, "Monday—April 19th," signed autograph manuscript, 3 pages, with envelope addressed in Mrs. Faulkner's hand and postmarked Oxford, April 19, 1954.

Dearest Saxe—

As always, you are so kind and thoughtful—sending us The Reader[1]—Jill and I thank you from the depths of our hearts—It is a beautiful book—quite worthy of your mastery in editing—Bill Faulkner is a fortunate man!

Your letter distressed us—Have you been ill again? May God forbid—This is rather selfish—but I, among many, I'm sure, would be bereft of the best and truest of friends should anything happen to you—so do take care and get completely well again—

It was good hearing all about Dorothy and the children—We *do* love you *all*—

One of Jill's admirers came up from Mexico last Monday for, I presumed, a short visit—Mr. Luria [?] is still with us—The situation is extremely awkward for I'm afraid he is a suitor, and Jill's heart is decidedly elsewhere—In fact Jill is only waiting for Bill's consent to marry—That, I insisted upon—However, Bill communicates with us so seldom, I may have to see the logic of Jill's arguments—and not wait much longer to announce the engagement—

Jill will write to Dorothy and you, all about her new-found radiance—Perhaps you can tell from her letter just how deeply in love she is—

Again, let me express our concern over your health—I would worry more, had I not complete faith in Dorothy's powers to charm one into living forever—

Write to us only when you feel it an easy thing to do—even a card, sometime—

All send Love
Devotedly
Estelle

[P.S.] Saxe, and to you I say—A Fable owes its completion to your untiring, loving work with Bill those last weeks in Princeton—I realize, only too well, that he was in no emotional nor physical condition to do it without *you*—Bless your dear heart—

[1] *The Faulkner Reader* was published April 1, 1954.

1014 Letter from Faulkner to Saxe Commins, "Wednesday" [April 28, 1954], ribbon typescript with typed signature, 1 page.

Dear Saxe:

I reached home Sunday night, 10:30, a record—Princeton to Roanoke, Virginia, 6 pm Saturday, 430 miles, Roanoke to Oxford, 703 miles Sunday night; I dont intend to do it again.

Am making pictures of the cross file lettered onto the wall here,[1] will send them if you should like or be able to reproduce them in the book.

Jill plans to marry in August. Would you and Dorothy come down for it?

Still have the stomach, but hope it will improve here.

Enclosed is the matter I spoke of. Please seal it away for me.

Regards to all.

Bill

[1] The outline of *A Fable* on the wall of Faulkner's office at Rowan Oak.

1015 Letter from Faulkner to Saxe Commins, undated [probably late April 1954], signed ribbon typescript, 1 page.

Dear Saxe:

What I wanted to know was, who in the east I might have neglected to send a book[1] to, so I can rectify when I come up in May. Did I send Joan Williams (Mrs Bowen now) one; also to sign books for any at Random House who should have one. But mainly, people outside Random House. If any sort of record of the mailings was kept, I can attend to it.

Please ask Harold[2] to send the checks to me here. In fact, I was glad to hear this part. I had a sort of recollection that you gave me an envelope from him with a check in it while I was there, but have not been able to find it. You didn't give me such an envelope then, right?

/s/ Bill

[1] Presumably *The Faulkner Reader.*
[2] Harold Ober, Faulkner's agent.

1017 Letter from Saxe Commins to Faulkner, May 3, 1954, unsigned carbon typescript, 1 page.

Dear Bill:

When I reached the office this morning, I found your letter on the desk. My God, how did you do it?! 1133 miles within 36 hours is just beyond belief. Are you sure you're all right and are not suffering any consequences of the strain? How is your back?

Indeed Dorothy and I *will* come down in August for Jill's marriage. Neither Dorothy nor I would miss that for anything—we'll be there! Give her our deep love and best wishes for all happiness.

Everything quiet here and in Princeton. I saw Professor Einstein yesterday, and he asked particularly about you. He wanted to be remembered with all respect.

Love,
[no signature]

1018 Letter from Faulkner to Saxe Commins, "Sunday" [probably early June 1954], signed ribbon typescript, 1 page.

Dear Saxe:

Before the mss. FABLE is shopped around to movie prospects, be sure everybody understands about Bacher,[1] that he is to have first chance to refuse it. I agree with Bennett, there is no movie in it that I can see now, but Bacher must have first chance to buy or use or have a share in making the movie.

As I told you, we agreed that I would do it as a book, to belong to me completely; then he and I together would share in it when it became a film.

I dont know how you can do this. That is, can you ask for bids, and take the best offer? If so, we might give him the chance to meet the best offer, if he wishes to, inside a limit of time—hours or days. Or if he had rather let Random House sell it, and he to share in the price—my part of the money of course, not Random House's. Would it be better for you to do this—Random H.—or shall I get in touch with him by mail? Or has R.H. a representative in Los Angeles, to handle it.

That is, to me, he has a moral claim to the first refusal, provided Random House and I get the top price. If he cannot meet the top price, or does not want to, or cannot handle the matter without delaying things, to our cost, then he can have a share of my part of the sale price. That is, Random House is not to suffer, and neither is he.

Talk this over, and let me hear from you.

He may be able to work along with you or your agent in selling it, and work himself into the producing deal, we to get our price, and he to get his share without cost to us, which would settle everything.

Am well, too damned hot here. Will write you later re Missy as soon as the thing is formally announced, etc. Love to all in shop, and to Dorothy and the children.

This business is going to cost, so I will need money probably.

Yours,
/s/ Bill

[1]Producer William Bacher, who, along with director Henry Hathaway, originated the idea upon which *A Fable* is based. Though no contract was ever drawn up, Faulkner had a verbal understanding with Bacher and Hathaway that they would share in the movie rights to the book.

1019 Letter from Saxe Commins to Faulkner, June 12, 1954, signed ribbon typescript, 1 page.

Dear Bill,

Jim Putnam, President of PEN,[1] called me up a little while ago from New York to ask whether you would consent to appear at their big conference in New York in September. I told him at once that you were making no engagements until you will have completed the last volume of the trilogy. In spite of this virtual rejection, he made me promise that I would write you and have you confirm or overrule my reasons for your inability to appear.

I have done my duty. I have kept my word. You can write across the bottom of this note how you feel about it and I'll do what's necessary so far as Putnam and PEN are concerned.

Nothing else of consequence except our love.

Ever
/s/ Saxe

[1]The acronym PEN stands for "poets, playwrights, editors, essayists, and novelists." Founded in 1921, the international organization seeks to promote friendship and intellectual cooperation among authors in all countries.

1019 Letter from Faulkner to Saxe Commins, undated [mid-June 1954], signed ribbon typescript, 1 page. Appears at bottom of letter from Commins to Faulkner, June 12, 1954.

No, cant attend PEN meeting. Work going along, but slow, as I am busy getting Jill's horse ready to enter a horse show here last of July. Hot as bejesus but all well.

The corner pipe shop, Shirmer I think the name is, had some wire pipe cleaners in the window last spring. You may remember: they looked like small cylindrical wire brushes, like pistol cleaning rods. Will you send me two or three of them? Much much love to Dorothy and all of you from all of us.

/s/ Bill

1020 Letter from Faulkner to Saxe Commins, "Friday" [June 18, 1954], signed ribbon typescript, 1 page.

Dear Saxe:

We left here last Friday for Washington, for Missy's announcement party there,[1] got back home last night and found the books,[2] the one you sent and the package. They are very fine, I am as proud as you are; if we are right and

85 ELM ROAD

PRINCETON · NEW JERSEY

June 12, 1954

Dear Bill,

Jim Putnam, President of PEN, called me up a little while ago from New York to ask whether you would consent to appear at their big conference in New York in September. I told him at once that you were making no engagements until you will have completed the last volume of the trilogy. In spite of this virtual rejection, he made me promise that I would write you and have you confirm or overrule my reasons for your inability to appear.

I have done my duty. I have kept my word. You can write across the bottom of this note how you feel about it and I'll do what's necessary so far as Putnam and PEN are concerned.

Nothing else of consequence except our love.

Ever

Saxe

No, cant attend PEN meeting. Work going along, but slow, as I am busy getting Jill's horse ready to enter a horse show here last of July. Hot as bejesus but all well.

The corner pipe shop, Shirmer I think the name is, had some wire pipe cleaners in the window last spring. You may remember: they looked like small cylindrical wire brushes, like pistol cleaning rods. Will you send me two or three of them? Much much love to Dorothy and all of you from all of us.

Bill

28. Exchange of letters between Saxe Commins and Faulkner (item 1019)

it is my best and not the bust which I had considered it might be, I will ask nothing more.

All well here. The wedding invitations will go out soon, the date is 21 Aug. You and Dorothy are expected whenever you will come. Malcolm and Ria still want you to come and stay long enough for a good visit and to see some of our country.

I will need money, probably a ghastly amount. Am solvent now, but I will suggest you send $5000.00 any time before Aug. 1st. No, about July 1st. as Jill and her mother seem bent on making a production out of this, and her trousseau wedding stuff, bridesmaid's dresses, champagne etc will run to quite a piece of jack I fear.

Will write again later. I'll tell about the Wash. party later, damndest collection of prosperous concerned stuffshirt republican senators and military brass hats and their beupholstered and becoiffed beldames as you ever saw. Fortunately hardly any of them ever heard of me, so I was let alone.

/s/ Bill

[1]At the home of Paul Summers' foster parents, in Rockville, Maryland.
[2]Complimentary copies of *A Fable.*

1021 Western Union telegram from Faulkner to Saxe Commins, June 19, 1954.

PLEASE CALL DON KLOPFER AT ONCE TO [S]TOP REPORTER[1]COMING DOWN NEXT WEEK LETTER TO DON IN MAIL TONITE

BILL

[1]For *Time* magazine, which was planning a cover story on Faulkner to appear in conjunction with the publication of *A Fable.*

1023 Letter from Faulkner to Saxe Commins, "Friday" [probably July 2 or 9, 1954], signed ribbon typescript, 1 page.

Dear Saxe:

The Dept. of State are paying the transport, the Brazilian govt. my expenses, to Sao Paulo, Aug. 7–16 and return, to attend a centennial beanfeast,[1] me to strike a blow of some sort for hemispheric solidarity. I will need my dinner jacket, the coat and pants are hanging in 'Gene's closet. I think the shoes were among the clothes I had stolen in Egypt. But in case, they are patent leather slippers, not new. If they are not in the closet too, can someone from R. House have a pair sent to me? I want English shoes, Church is the maker, evening shoes. There is a shop on the west side of Madison, somewhere between 50th St and Tripler's, I have seen Church shoes in the window, Tripler may have them, in fact, I think they have. If you could bundle the suit up and take it in with you, it and the shoes could be crammed into a packing box and sent to me, dont worry about creases as I will have it pressed here. I hate to have to worry you, but I didn't know about Brazil when I left the suit there.

The shoes will be 6½, B width or C, that is, not too narrow. That is, my foot is short, I can wear No 6, D.

About the trip here. Dont worry. You and D. will be met without difficulty any hour you reach Memphis, to stay as long as you will.

/s/ Bill

[P.S.] Not pumps: lace shoes, patent leather evening shoes, with lace-up fronts. Can you arrange with shop to let me return them if wrong fit, etc?

[1]The program of the quadricentennial of the city of São Paulo included an international writers' conference, which Faulkner attended.

1024 Letter from Lawrance Thompson to Saxe Commins, July 4, 1954, signed ribbon typescript, 3 pages, with envelope postmarked Ripton, Vermont, July 5, 1954.

Dear Saxe,

You asked me to tell you how Faulkner's FABLE hit me, and I must confess that it disappointed me, greatly. I had hoped that it might well be what you claimed for it: the zenith of Faulkner's attainment, and one of the most notable contributions to American letters in our time, and a classic. But, according to my reactions, after a first and careful reading, A FABLE is nowhere near so good as LIGHT IN AUGUST or THE SOUND AND THE FURY. I will even be so bold as to predict that A FABLE will eventually take much the same sad place in the Faulkner canon as OVER THE RIVER AND INTO THE TREES has already taken in the Hemingway canon. Let me give you a few hints as to why I am so disappointed.

First, in characterization: there is no major character in A FABLE which seems to me to be adequately realized. For example, consider only the major character, the Corporal. From the beginning, or at least as soon as the reader learns about the central situation, the mutiny, and the relation of the prime-moving Corporal to that mutiny, the reader anticipates and waits for and watches for some first-hand evidence, provided by the Corporal-in-action, which may gradually accumulate until the reader is convinced that this extraordinary person has those extraordinary powers which are attributed to him, and which he must have had, to bring about the mutiny. Such evidence is never given. Instead, we are merely asked to take the words of other characters, that the Corporal *does* have extraordinary powers. Instead, again, we are asked to lean on "allegory"—the allegory of the Corporal-as-banker—and that is not convincing on the first level, and so loses its force on the allegorical level of meaning.

Second, in the central action or situation: the mutiny, and the episodes which unfold as effects or consequences of the mutiny, are somehow unconvincing, unrealistic, even "fabulous," perhaps because we start once again by being told *about* the situation, and are asked to wait for an adequate presentation of motives or of a motor-character. Of course those of us who have been reading Faulkner for years are so familiar with his technical principle of circling, or of going back and back over the same situation, again and again, each time adding further information and perspective, that we wait patiently, assuming that we shall gradually be made to visualize the motives of that mutiny in a convincing light. But the convincing light is never shed, and that is another disappointment.

Third, in structure: the architecture of the total action is clumsy, disproportionate, confused. (Not "confusing": this is one of the "easiest" Faulkner books to read, in so far as the first level of meaning is concerned, and (for those of us habitually accustomed to the techniques of allegory) one of the "easiest" books to read, in so far as the allegorical level of meaning is concerned.) The obvious framework of the separate days of the week, allegorically correlated with the week of the Passion, does give an illusion of neatness and order; but if considered on the initial and immediate level of the unfolding of the specific action, the reader cannot help but notice that too much emphasis is given to characters of relative unimportance and not enough emphasis is given to characters of major importance. (The "Horse Thief" episode or digression represents the best writing in A FABLE; but not enough use is made of the central character, there, to justify that splendid digression.)

Fourth, in style: with the exception of the "Horse Thief" digression (which may well be an early piece of writing patched into this novel), the style is that of a tired, weary Faulkner. It rarely takes wings and gets off the ground to soar. Instead, it is labored and further weakened by too many vestigial traces of the Faulknerian rant and the Faulknerian jargon which have always been considered on the debit-side of Faulkner's art-ledger. I have in mind certain pet words, phrases, ideas, which he has overworked, for years, with the result that their occurrence and recurrence here become "damnable iterations."

Perhaps stylistic weaknesses should be listed, here, as the underlying and all-important weaknesses, because they may be seen as causing and determining those other weaknesses of characterization, action, structure. For example, in characterization, Faulkner permits character after character to talk like Faulkner, to rant like Faulkner, and to mouth Faulknerian clichés. So the separate characters frequently blur into each other, and into Faulkner. Take another example, which involves both action and structure, as controlled by style: Faulkner has always seemed only one remove from a dramatist, because he has so frequently presented his narratives through episodes which give us characters pushed out on the stage, so to speak, or into actions where they characterize themselves. This is, essentially, a dramatic principle of characterization. But in A FABLE, the principle of narration tends toward mere description, and as a result the reader gets the sense that he is watching the action through the wrong end of a telescope.

Fifth, in Faulkner's use of parable, symbol, allegory: the analogy between Faulkner's immediate story and the ancient Biblical myth of Christ's passion should achieve several different kinds of enrichment; but it fails to achieve them, for reasons which are easily described. Let me digress, briefly. In theory, whenever an author chooses to establish a sustained and cumulative analogy—either specific or symbolic—between his immediate story and some familiar traditional story, a double-action should take place: the new story should provide an implicit enrichment of the old story, and simultaneously the old story should provide an implicit enrichment of the new story. In theory, this double-action is achieved when the interplay of the analogies keeps making the reader *feel* that the new story makes him understand certain aspects of the old story in a way he has never before understood them; that the old story makes him understand certain aspects of the new story in a way he has not previously understood them. Now I assume that Faulkner intended to put this theory into practice, and I assume that Faulkner felt that he had achieved this double-action. But it doesn't "come off" for me, even though I happen to like the allegorical mode of literature and even though I am deeply impressed by the profound implications of the Christ myth, as it has bearing on human experience, human action, human history.

Faulkner's weakness, in his use of the allegorical mode here, is that he has not found a central action, in his own story, which can adequately compare with the central action, in the Christ story. As a result, he spends much time dragging the Biblical analogies in, by the heels, so to speak, and then he invites the reader to find some significance in the overtly hinted and painfully obvious analogies between the two stories. His task, as artist, was to make us *feel* the significance of those analogies, rather than to make us go groping and searching for the significance.

As a consequence, the so-called "allegorical" element in A FABLE is merely decorative, and not functional. It approaches the slap-happy decorative mode of the bastard-baroque. For example, I'd call it bastard-baroque to let our hero's sister (or rather half-sister) inform the reader (obliquely) that this hero was conceived out of wedlock and was born on Christmas eve, in a stable, exactly 33 years before his "crucifixion." The analogy is clear, but it is laid on from without, and it is quite meaningless. Again, it is bastard-baroque to find ourselves reading the details of "The Last Supper" on pages 333ff, with all the crudely pointed references to the Judas who betrayed our hero, and the Peter who denied him. The analogy is clear, but again it is laid on from without, and it is also meaningless. Perhaps the height of the Faulknerian bastard-baroque occurs when the barbed wire arranges itself in the pattern which is analogous to Christ's "crown of thorns." For Faulkner, this may have profound significance and illumination; but for even an allegory-enjoying reader, the attempt to make this meaningful is feeble.

You must remember that I am a rabid Faulkner admirer, and I consider him a great artist. But Faulkner is nowhere near his best, in A FABLE. No wonder that he spent nine years trying to make this book jell, because he himself must have realized, repeatedly, that he had not succeeded in making it jell. I should imagine that he must have become so discouraged, at certain times, that he was ready to burn the whole damned thing, and I wish he had burned it, because it will never do his literary reputation anything but harm.

In conclusion, I regret to say that I think you and Random House are stuck with a dud. Of course the dud may prove to be a tremendously successful best-seller, but I doubt it. Anyway, no matter whether I am right or wrong, I regretfully confide to you that I have decided not to use A FABLE in my "Four American Authors" course at Princeton, this autumn. Even so, if you are willing, I would still like to have you come and talk to my boys about A FABLE because I shall begin the course by urging them all to read A FABLE on their own, and I shall not prejudice them for or against it, until they have had time to read it.

Please forgive me for speaking frankly from my "blindness," and please do not let our disagreement over A FABLE have any ill effects on our friendship.

Very cordially yours,

/s/ Larry

1025 Letter from Estelle Faulkner to Dorothy and Saxe Commins, "Saturday—24th," signed autograph manuscript, 3 pages (on 1 folded leaf), with envelope addressed in Mrs. Faulkner's hand and postmarked Oxford, July 24, 1954.

Dear Dorothy and Saxe—

A belated note, but a loving and sincere one—Bill, Jill and I are counting on your coming down for the wedding—in fact, want you more than anyone (any *two*) save possibly, the groom—

Ella Sommerville[1] [*sic*] is most anxious to have you all as her house-guests during the festivities, and will write, of course, just as soon as you let us know your definite plans—

We *all* hope that you can fly down Wednesday or Thursday before the 21st—then stay and visit *us* at Rowan oak as long thereafter as possible—

Jill is radiantly happy—Bill is pleased over his coming trip to Brazil, and [I] know we'll be prouder than ever of him—A Fable is a marvelous book—I feel so indebted to you, Saxe, for its beautiful completion—

Do write as soon as you can, and Ella will send off her letter to you immediately—Malcolm will probably meet your plane—He has spoken for the honour—

As always—my Love
Estelle

[1] Ella Somerville had been, with Faulkner, a member of the Ole Miss dramatic group, the Marionettes, in the early 1920s. One of Oxford's leading literati, she numbered among her close friends not only Faulkner but also Stark Young, Eudora Welty, and Ben Wasson.

S-37 Letter from Carvel Collins to Saxe Commins, July 28, 1954, signed ribbon typescript, 1 page.

Dear Mr. Commins,

Following up the idea you kindly gave me when Perry[1] and I had dinner with you and Mrs. Commins in Princeton, I got in touch with Francis Brown, who seemed pleased at the suggestion I write a review of *A Fable* and assigned me 2500 words.[2]

I turned in thirty words short of that so no one would cut it, but Brown had left for vacation without telling his assistant that the review was to be the longest of the year. The assistant, who likes William Faulkner personally but is apparently hostile to his fiction, without letting anyone know until the thing was printed, cut hundreds of words. In two phone calls since it was too late to do anything about it, I've learned that by his cuts he reslanted the piece in ways you and I—and Mr. Faulkner—will not like. I am writing you to apologize for this unfortunate mishandling of the novel and of your excellent suggestion.

Very best regards to you and to Mrs. Commins.

Sincerely,
/s/ Carvel Collins
/t/ Carvel Collins

[P.S.] I've enclosed a pamphlet[3] discussing one feature of *The Sound and the Fury* hoping that you will not consider it too wild.

[1] Perry Miller, English professor at Harvard.

[2] Collins' review, "War and Peace and Mr. Faulkner," appeared in the August 1, 1954 issue of the *New York Times Book Review*.

[3] *The Interior Monologues of The Sound and the Fury.*

S-38 Letter from Faulkner to Phillip E. Mullen, "Friday night" [late July 1954], signed ribbon typescript, 1 page.

Dear Phil:

Thank you for calling and giving me that much warning.[1] I cant stop this one coming here and asking questions about my private life, anymore than I was able to stop the ones from Life. I may not be able to do this, but I will try. Tell him he must not worry my mother. She is too old to have to suffer this sort of thing. The ones from LIFE told her lies in order to get into her house, pry into her privacy. If this happens again, I will help this one make some news indeed. I realise it is not his—the individual reporter's—fault; he must accept the assignment, or risk being fired probably. What a pass have we come to, that one of the most terrifying things in modern American life is what they call 'Freedom of the Press'. One individual can defend himself from another individual's freedom and liberty, but when big powerful monied organizations confederate under shibboleths and catchwords like liberty and democracy and religion, within the structure of which the individual practitioners are automatically freed of any moral responsibility whatever, then God help us; we damn sure need it.

Hope to see you when you come up.

/s/ Bill

[1] Mullen had called from his home in Canton, Mississippi, to warn Faulkner about the impending arrival of *Newsweek* staffwriter Bill Emerson, assigned to do a feature article on Faulkner in conjunction with the publication of *A Fable*. Though Faulkner typically refused to cooperate, Emerson completed the article, published as the cover story in *Newsweek* on August 2, 1954.

1029 Letter from Faulkner to Saxe Commins, "Thursday" [probably July 1954], signed ribbon typescript, 1 page.

Dear Saxe:

Please drop the enclosed stamped letter into the mail. Also, will you send to Miss Stein, same address, a copy of A FABLE under your cover?

Will write in fuller detail soon re wedding, etc. All well here. Love to Dorothy.

/s/ Bill

1064a Letter from Phil Stone to Carvel Collins, August 16, 1954, carbon typescript with typed signature, 5 pages.

Dear Carvel:

Your pamphlet on The Interior Monologues of THE SOUND AND THE FURY was sent to me by the Department of Humanities, I suppose at your request.

Of course, in view of what I know about the situation and the conversations Emily and I have had with you before, we read it, thought it was very well done, and were quite amused. I know it is not going to do any good but just the same I am writing this letter, as we lawyers say, "for the record." Since I am so busy and just got to read the pamphlet last night, the letter is bound to be sketchy.

Your theory is good and I am sure I cannot convince any Faulkner enthusiast that it is wrong, but the trouble about it is the same trouble that besets so many beautiful theories, and that is that it happens to be contrary to fact. As you know from your researches, Bill and I are the only people in the world that know some of these facts.

Page 29. Actually the original germ of the book was in an idiot of the Chandler family, one of the old families here. The Chandlers lived on that large lot just back of the old Nielson home on South Lamar, and some of them lived there until recently when they sold the property. This particular brother was an idiot from birth and they would not send him to an institution but cared for him with the help of a negro man and kept him at home. He was older than I am and died several years ago, I think about ten or twelve years ago.

Page 29. What you said about Joyce having a great deal to do with the book is true but the reason it is true is because about that time, in the late 'teens and early 'twenties I was drilling into Bill that Joyce was a pioneer and that fiction would never again be the same after *Ulysses.* In fact, when the portions of *Ulysses* were published in The Little Review I gave them to Bill to read and talked to him endless hours about it.

Pages 29 and 30. Bill is not ill-read but he certainly is not widely read and never has been. This is very natural when you consider that a professional writer does not care to spend his leisure time reading books. It is especially true with Bill because, as Emily and I have tried so often to tell you, Bill is strictly an empirical writer and has no theory of aesthetics at all. I know that this is atheism to the Faulkner idolators but it is another fact that happens to be true. That is why some of his writing can be so bad. As to the idea that he never plans a work of fiction, that depends on a definition of the word "plan." If the word is defined as starting out with a conscious well-organized structure of plot, he does not plan the work of fiction. That is why his short stories are so much better than his novels and why he has never written a novel that was anything, from the standpoint of overall design, except a series of episodes.

Page 30. I doubt very much that Bill ever read *The Divine Comedy* at all, but I was amused at your statement. He was, as I have said before, made very familiar with the work of Joyce because I attended to that.

Page 31. The only debt he owes to Joyce in THE SOUND AND THE FURY is the debt an empirical writer would owe, a matter of method purely. As to the inaccurate clock, the amusing thing about that is that the old negro woman who was the prototype for Dilsey and who lived with Bill until her death (a very fine character she was) actually had done the same thing for an inaccurate clock that the Faulkners had, so that idea came from the prototype of Dilsey and not from Joyce and *Ulysses.*

Page 32. The genesis of THE SOUND AND THE FURY did not come from Macbeth at all. It could not come from Macbeth because Bill was reading this stuff to me three or four nights a week over a period of three or four months and Macbeth was never mentioned. I thought I told you the way the title was evolved, that when Bill finished the book he still did not have a title and that we thought about it and finally I suggested, since it was a tale told by an idiot, that we call it THE SOUND AND THE FURY. Bill agreed since he could not think of a better title. I realize that you have to shift gears to fully understand how impossible it was in those days for me not to know what Bill was doing and why he was doing it. Remember at that time he was entirely dependent on me not only for faith in his ultimate success, but for ideas and advice concerning the actual writing because he had no one else to whom he could turn. You know me and know that I have to know why. So I always made Bill tell me why. This does not mean that he always agreed with me. He frequently disagreed with me and more often than not he was right because of his insistence as a writer, but I did know all that was going on and if there had been a hint of Macbeth carrying such an important part as you suggest I certainly would have known of it, and there was not the slightest hint until we got through. Actually, in addition to the Chandler idiot, the germ of the story was the piece he wrote in New Orleans and about which I had forgotten.[1] This frequently happened in his writing, just as SANCTUARY and THE HAMLET both grew out of a series of sketches he had been experimenting with over a number of years.

Page 32. As for the monologue of the idiot being put last, such a suggestion from people who are supposed to know about writing simply amazes me, stuns me. The reason the monologue of the idiot was put first was not because of following any pattern laid down by Freud or by Joyce, but simply because of the fact that if it had been put last there would have been no tension to hold the reader. This is so obvious that I am just stunned that anyone should not see it, and it is exactly the reason an empirical writer like Bill would have, being a very good writer. I do have the advantage that no one else has ever had or ever will have because this was read to me night after night over a period of time. I told you that I could not make head nor tail of it and asked Bill and he kept telling me to wait, and as soon as we got into the part about Quentin the whole thing began to unfold like a flower. This is just exactly the effect that Bill was trying to get. But the reason was technical and not psychological.

Page 33. You speak about Benjamin being fascinated with the light and the repetition of that. This did not have to come from Freud at all. Even Thackeray did it with the Marquis of Steyne in Vanity Fair. It would be true of any idiot, even one born a thousand years before Freud, because the idiot lives entirely by his senses. I tried to get Bill interested in Freud but I never could get him to read it because, as I insist again, my dear friend, as a writer absolutely without theory, his repetition of the light and of the shadow mentioned on page 34 are simply instances of the effects he gets from frequent repetition.

Page 34. It happens that Jason did not come from Freud but from my own brother James Stone, Jr. And between him and my mother, as I told you, there was a typical harmless but complete Oedipus and Jocasta complex. Anybody who knew Jim Stone could recognize him from the way Jason talks in THE SOUND AND THE FURY and many have actually done so.

Page 35. I repeat again that all this stuff about Bill following the chart of Ulysses is nothing but pure theory. I admit that the theory is plausible, but if Bill did it it was purely a subconscious result. I wrote you that he told us several years ago one night when he came out home that he had never read Freud and had never heard of Jung. There was no reason for him to tell this to Emily and me unless it was a fact, and all I know about Bill and about these incredible Faulkners bears it out.

Page 36. It is not at all safe to assume that Bill read Freud. The truth is that the literary group in New Orleans, with the exception of Spratling and Sherwood Anderson, were to Bill a comedy group and he paid very little attention to anything they said. In fact I had for years, as I have told you, warned him against "literary people."

Pages 38 and 39. I have already covered these things about THE KINGDOM OF GOD and about the reason for Benjamin's monologue opening the novel. It happens that Benjamin was carrying a narcissus just because Bill always liked the flower. You may remember Narcissa Benbow in Sanctuary. If it hadn't been for this it is quite likely that Benjamin would have been carrying an Easter lily.

Page 40. Bill not only did not have to bother about the technicalities of Freud; he didn't bother any more than he bothers now about contradictions of time and incident in his own works. You still just don't believe what I tell you about these incredible Faulkners and how they are all given to rushing in where angels fear to tread and how often they get away with it successfully. Of course Bill portrays Benjamin with unattractive characteristics because any idiot would have such.

Page 40. Of course Benjamin has no sense of time. No idiot would have and any idiot, as I have said, lives only through his senses. Idiots did this even before Freud.

Page 42. As to the episode of driving the wrong way around the courthouse square, this again is just like an animal. You can confuse a dog, even an intelligent one, by reversing customary procedure.

Page 42. The remark about Benjamin "been three years old thirty years" is an instance of wry humor and the significance of the narcissus I have already touched upon.

Page 43. The conversation about Benjamin in the middle of the page simply reflects the old superstition still held by negroes that people who are afflicted mentally know things beyond the ken of the so-called sane.

Pages 43 and 44. The Chandler idiot was also inarticulate and was constantly watched and controlled and did not think in words. Bill knew all about the Chandler idiot and idiots did this way long before Freud.

Page 46. Jason does act with more decision than Jim Stone would have acted but he does act entirely for the benefit of Jason as Jim Stone always did and he was tied to his mother as was Jason. You are wrong about Mrs. Compson not loving anyone. She loved Jason beyond a doubt.

Page 53. THE SOUND AND THE FURY is a sociological account secondarily and that is all it is or was, consciously.

Pages 55 and 56. This part about Dilsey is simply good writing. She was a fine woman and all who knew her loved and respected her.

My dear friend, Freud and Macbeth had no more to do with the conscious writing of this book or with any part of it than you did and you didn't even know Faulkner then.

. . . .

Your friend,
Phil Stone

[1] "The Kingdom of God," published in the April 19, 1925 *Times-Picayune.*

1064c Letter from Phil Stone to Carvel Collins, August 24, 1954, carbon typescript with typed signature, 2 pages.

Dear Carvel:

I reckon when you are trying "to make the record" you should help make it when you are wrong also.

You have had Emily and me in a perfect stew since you left because there doesn't seem to be any way to explain your theory about *The Sound and The Fury* being based upon a design laid out on the pattern of the crucifixion and the days preceding except that this was done consciously. I see no way that it could have been just a coincidence.

I still have not abandoned my theory entirely to the effect that Bill does not have in his novels an overall esthetic design. We are still too confused to write you what we have in mind but when we think it out I shall do so.

What I am driving at vaguely is that the type of design of which you spoke, and which you seem to have fully proved, is not a functional dynamic design but is, rather, a pattern rather than a design, something like an embroidery pattern. Still, you have me licked on this one and you may prove me wrong about the other but I shall write you again as soon as we think it out.

I want to give you one word of caution which may be right and which it may help you to consider. You said that Bill was a "secretive" writer. This is undoubtedly true but I think it is a result and not a cause. I think that the real thing is that Bill is a taciturn writer. I base this opinion on my close association with him for so many years. In other words I think that if I had asked Bill what was the significance of the dates to the different parts of *The Sound and the Fury* he would have told me right off.

In those days I had to be so careful to check up with him on little things like dates I do not know why in the world I failed to ask him about these dates but I remember clearly that I did not do so.

We enjoyed our brief visit with all of you and do hope that you will come again soon and stay longer.

Your friend,
Phil Stone

1075 Letter from Harold E. Howland, U.S. State Department official, to Faulkner, September 2, 1954, signed ribbon typescript, 1 page.

Dear Mr. Faulkner:

Many thanks for your August 15 letter and the fine things said about us.

I was delighted to note that you might conceivably be available to visit some of the other strategic countries of the world under the auspices of our educational and cultural exchange program.[1] You could gain for our country an immeasurable amount of understanding and respect if you would and I therefore hope we can get together to discuss this further. I'd be quite agreeable to go to New York to talk this over with you there if you find a Washington visit inconvenient. Or, perhaps, it might be more convenient if you should be traveling from New York south, with a brief stop-over in Washington, for me to meet you at the Washington airport for a short chat.

The reports from Peru and Brazil have been most glowing accounts of your success there and the entire Department of State is indeed grateful that you took the time from your crowded schedule to assist us in our efforts to gain respect and enhance our country's prestige abroad.

Sincerely yours,
/s/ Harold E. Howland
/t/ Harold E. Howland

[1]Faulkner had just returned from a trip to Peru and Brazil on behalf of the State Department.

1076 Letter from Harold E. Howland, U.S. State Department official, to Faulkner, September 2, 1954, signed ribbon typescript, 1 page.

Dear Mr. Faulkner:

I'd like to have our fiscal officers prepare a voucher so that I can obtain for you some per diem allowances which I believe you have coming. If you will sign the enclosed voucher in the space marked for the payee's signature, I will have our fiscal office prepare the necessary form. The information we need is:

(1) date and hour of departure from São Paulo
" " " " arrival at New York
" " " " departure from New York
" " " " arrival at Memphis
" " " " departure from Memphis
" " " " arrival at Oxford

(2) Did you use sleeper berth on your return trip?

(3) Do you have the carbon copies of your tickets? If, so, please send them to me.

All good wishes,

Sincerely yours,
/s/ Harold E. Howland
/t/ Harold E. Howland

1079 Western Union telegram from Malcolm Franklin to Faulkner (c/o Random House), September 14, 1954.

MARK ARGYLE[1] ARRIVED 201PM 13TH WEIGHT 8 POUNDS. RIA AND BABY FINE. WILL WRITE

MALCOLM

[1]Son of Malcolm and Gloria Franklin.

1080 Letter from Muna Lee, U.S. State Department official, to Saxe Commins, September 15, 1954, signed ribbon typescript, 4 pages.

Dear Mr. Commins:

Enclosed are translations of a half-dozen of the many excellent stories resulting from William Faulkner's press conference at Lima during his brief Peruvian stopover.[1] Thomas Driver, Public Affairs Officer at our Embassy there, wrote me:

> "Faulkner was far more composed and *'listo'* than the press boys. They all seemed to have 'buck fever.' It was, however, a really bang-up press interview. . . . Later on, the reporters told us it was the finest press interview within their memory."

You may be interested to know that the interpreter at the interview, at his own urgent request, was a young Peruvian, Cârlos Zavaleta, who has been doing graduate work at Columbia University on a student-grant scholarship. Last year at Columbia Mr. Zavaleta attended a seminar on William Faulkner in preparation for the thesis which he is now writing and expects to present at the end of the present session.

In an official report on Mr. Faulkner's visit, the Embassy reported to the Department of State that

> "The Peruvians were most impressed with Mr. Faulkner's high idea of the purpose of writing and his deep faith in humanity. Several articles on Mr. Faulkner have been promised in future issues of magazines."

The official report states further:

> "The highlight in Mr. Faulkner's visit was the informal reception to

which approximately 35 writers, artists, etc. were invited on the basis of their interest or work in the intellectual field in Peru. In a private reception room at the Hotel Bolivar, chairs were grouped informally in front of a table on which locally available editions—in English and Spanish—of Mr. Faulkner's works were displayed. . . . At first, Mr. Faulkner was a little on guard and reluctant to speak, but gradually . . . as he noted that he was among interested and informed colleagues, he opened up. The note of the gathering became more relaxed, the questions and answers flowed more freely, and the pace of the interchange of ideas was stepped up. Again, Mr. Faulkner was very habile at dodging embarrassing questions. For example, when asked his opinion on certain South American and European authors, he preferred to state that he was not familiar with them to expressing an evaluation of them. . . . What little interpreting was necessary—since most of those present understood English even if they could not speak it—was done effectively by Carlos Zavaleta. [Officers of the Embassy and the United States Information Agency] preferred to remain in the background and to let the Peruvians have free sway. They certainly made the most of this unique opportunity and bombarded Mr. Faulkner with questions for two solid hours. The time went by so quickly and so interestingly, however, that it was necessary to interrupt in order to bring the session to an enforced end. . . ."

Mr. Faulkner's visit to São Paulo was equally successful and equally contributory toward cordial cultural relations, as we have heard from several thoroughly informed sources. However, President Vargas' suicide and resultant disturbances have delayed official reporting on cultural events, so press clippings and a formal despatch on the visit have not yet arrived. In a telegram, however, the United States Information Agency informed the Department:

"Faulkner's UNIAO remarks August 12 warmly received capacity audience. . . . Answered many impromptu questions. 'I have no fixed writing habits; always have pad and pencil in pocket; may write in saddle, while waiting at table.' Favorite musicians Mozart, Beethoven, Prokofieff. Dostoevsky strongly influenced Faulkner's works. Likes Fry's *The Lady Is Not for Burning.* Finds Eliot's *Family Reunion* a weak play. Promised to return to São Paulo spring 1955, two months visit Amazon area. Confessed writing *Sanctuary* for immediate cash. Prefers *Light in August,* but feels 'All my works failed' and still 'hopes to write great work'; considers *A Fable* 'good work, although weak in spots.' Advised young Brazilian writers, 'Always write the truth as you see it'. At collective press, radio and television interview on August 11 stated, 'I am a farmer, not a writer. . . . All men are equal on one score: all suffer the same anguish and pain. . . . Solidarity is imperative for men of all creeds, color, and social conditions.' Considers race problem throughout world most important for solution. Believes Babbitt still exists all countries. Favorite books *Don Quixote* and Bible. . . . Faulkner enjoyed several Brazilian dishes; spent day Campinas Coffee Fazenda; visited São Paulo Agricultural Experiment station, prize winning cattle and horses. Photostat message to city released to local press. . . ."

The return trip from Brazil was up the east coast. The plane landed at the Caracas airport for so brief a time (I believe, a half hour) that no plans had been made to burden Mr. Faulkner with an interview there. However, in this no one had reckoned with the Venezuelan press, which flocked to the airport and were evidently met by a smiling and composed William Faulkner, since the Cultural Officer of our Embassy at Caracas telegraphed on August 16:

"William Faulkner announced that he would begin studying Hispanic American literature and would soon return to South America.[2] Faulkner held a press conference during his stopover at Caracas, returning from the International Writers Congress at São Paulo. He said that he had been deeply impressed by the intellectual energy of youth in South America, and that it had waked in him desire to know the area better. In March and April Faulkner plans to visit the Peruvian and Bolivian Andes, the Brazilian interior, and the Caribbean coastal region. Faulkner said that the main object of his coming trip would be to learn more about what is American. At the press conference, Faulkner repeated his deep concern with respect to man, and the necessity of writing about his heart and soul. All the newspapers greeted the illustrious writer cordially, publishing pictures and articles prominently on the first page."

The well-known Brazilian novelist, Erico Veríssimo, who is chief of the Cultural Division of the Pan American Union here at Washington, told me last week that William Faulkner's visit had been immensely stimulating to Brazil, and that in spite of political tensions, the newspapers are still publishing long articles showing its impact. (Mr. Veríssimo himself is writing the introduction to the translation of *Red Leaves* which is a feature of the forthcoming edition in Portuguese of *Perspectives, USA*). A day or so later, Carlos Dávila, the newly appointed Secretary General of the Organization of American States—of which the Pan American Union is the Secretariat—former President of Chile, and himself a distinguished writer and critic, said the visits of William Faulkner and Robert Frost to South America had established a new level of distinction in inter-American cultural relations; and are immensely valuable, among other things, in counteracting international communist propaganda attempts to depict the United States as not only lacking culture but inimical to it. Both Mr. Dávila and Mr. Veríssimo expressed the hope of meeting Mr. Faulkner, whose works they greatly admire, when he visits Washington.

In the Department of State also we are looking forward with keen interest to his visit. Impressions received during his South American visit and his suggestions for cultural interchange will be most valuable.

Yours sincerely,
/s/ Muna Lee
/t/ Muna Lee

[1] Enclosed were translations of five articles from Lima newspapers: "William Faulkner Arrives Today," *La Prensa,* August 7, 1954; "Visit of the Dedicated Novelist William Faulkner Excites Interest in Lima," *La Crónica,* August 7, 1954; "William Faulkner, 'Southern Gentleman,' Advocates the Disappearance of Racial Discrimination," *La Crónica,* August 8, 1954; "Racial Discrimination Is Repugnant to Me, William Faulkner Declared," *La Nación,* August 8, 1954; and "A Writer's First Obligation Is to Speak the Truth," *El Comercio,* August 8, 1954.

[2] Faulkner never made this proposed trip, but he represented the State Department on a visit to Venezuela in April 1961.

1082 Letter from Jill Faulkner Summers to Dorothy Commins, September 19, 1954, signed autograph manuscript, 2 pages (on 1 folded leaf), with envelope addressed in Mrs. Summers' hand and postmarked Charlottesville, September 20, 1954.

Dearest Miss Dorothy—

For the past weeks we've been in the process of moving into & making inhabitable the apartment here in Charlottesville. It's beginning to take shape now—to such an extent that we took the bull by the horns & entertained for the first time today.

Paul has known many of the young men here in law in past years so we invited a few in late this afternoon for drinks & small chow. The handsome tray & glasses performed their offices magnificently & acted as marvelous ice breakers. Truly they are fascinating with the coin design & among our favorite wedding gifts. (Paul, as a matter of fact, insists on having his after class cooler off-er from one.)

I can say "thank you" for the present, but I shan't even attempt to tell you what it meant to us both that you & Mr. Saxe should want to be with us on our important day. Your presence made the event perfect & complete, for you well know I lost my heart to you many years ago when you showed such warmth & love to a little girl overawed by the big city.

Much love—

Jill

1084 Letter from Jill Faulkner Summers to Faulkner, September 20, 1954, signed autograph manuscript, 2 pages (1 leaf), with envelope addressed in Mrs. Summers' hand and postmarked Charlottesville, September 21, 1954.

Dear Pappy—

You've always scrupulously kept your word—to me—so there's really no reason I should mention this, but just for the record, you have opened an account for Mama at the Oxford bank so she will feel free to do as she wishes? (& be able to do so) We agreed that was the best solution—remember?

I mailed the passport[1] early last week but haven't called home since so don't know her present plans.

I'm so very happy now, I want your help in making Mama happy.

The apartment is finished—or at least to the extent of our present finances—so we've really settled down to being a family—Paul, Jyp, & me. Classes began today so I've had my first taste of being Mrs. Summers all alone & can see no danger of imminent boredom—my days are all too full.

Tomorrow is our anniversary[2] so I've planned a most formal dinner. That will properly initiate our house keeping.

Give my best to everyone at Random House[3] & especially to Mr. Saxe & Miss Dorothy.

Please, Pappy, I'm depending on you to do everything possible to give Mama happiness. I'm afraid she feels I'm more or less lost to her.

Love—

Missy

[1] For Estelle Faulkner, who was planning a trip to visit her daughter and son-in-law, Victoria and Bill Fielden, in Manila.

[2] That is, the one-month anniversary of their marriage.

[3] This letter was addressed to Faulkner at the Algonquin Hotel in New York.

1085 Letter from Genzaburo Yoshino, Editor-in-Chief, *Sekai*, to Faulkner, September 22, 1954, signed ribbon typescript, 1 page. From Tokyo.

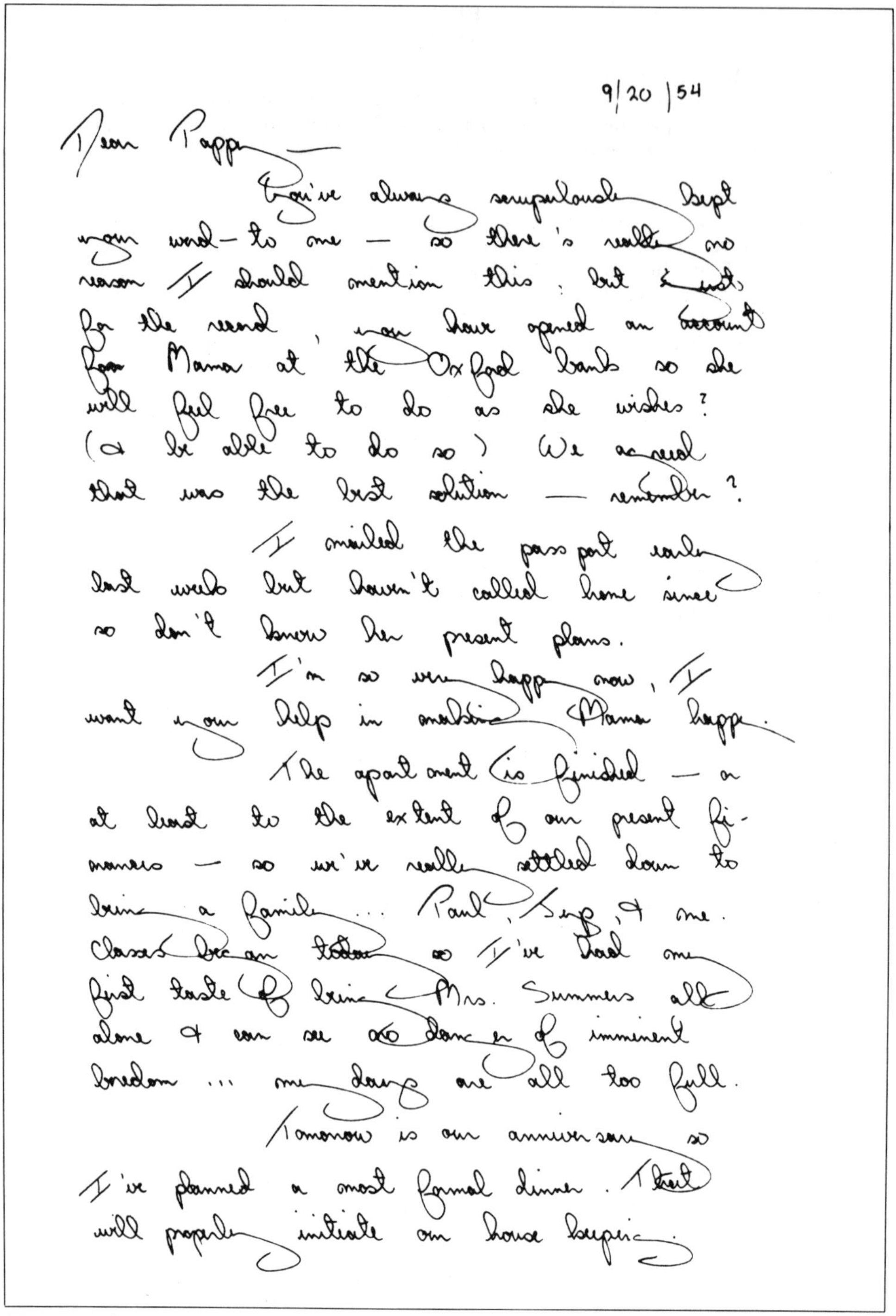

9/20/54

Dear Pappy —

You've always scrupulously kept your word — to me — so there's really no reason I should mention this, but just for the record, you have opened an account for Mama at the Oxford bank so she will feel free to do as she wishes? (& be able to do so) We agreed that was the best solution — remember?

I mailed the passport early last week but haven't called home since so don't know her present plans.

I'm so very happy now, I want your help in making Mama happy.

The apartment is finished — or at least to the extent of our present finances — so we're really settled down to being a family ... Paul, Snip, & me. Classes began today so I've had my first taste of being Mrs. Summers all alone & can see no danger of imminent boredom ... my days are all too full.

Tomorrow is our anniversary so I've planned a most formal dinner. That will properly initiate our housekeeping.

29. Letter from Jill Faulkner Summers to Faulkner (item 1084)

Give my best to everyone at Random House & especially to Mr. Saxe & Miss Dorothy.

Please, Pappy, I'm depending on you to do everything possible to give Mama happiness. I'm afraid she feels I'm more or less lost to her.

Love —

Missy

Dear Mr. Faulkner:

It is a great honor and joy for me to write to you who are one of the most beloved American authors among Japanese readers.

As you know, the hydrogen bomb tests, conducted by the United States military authorities repeatedly since March 1, 1954, in the South Pacific area, have caused great shocks and fears among the Japanese people. While the aftermaths of the Hiroshima and Nagasaki events nine years ago are still heavy on us, the Bikini explosions, fatally affecting the crew of a Japanese fishing boat and causing a long-drawn period of radio-activated rainfalls over the Japanese islands, are further intensifying our people's sense of insecurity and helplessness.

Under such circumstances, our people's desire for peace is becoming stronger and ever more articulately pronounced. On the other hand, however, our Yoshida regime, tied up with the United States foreign policies, is persistently carrying out its rearmament plans.

Our magazine *SEKAI* (which means "The World"), since its first publication in 1945, has been the foremost magazine in our country, treating political, economic and cultural subjects and speaking firmly and unyieldingly for peace, and is enjoying enthusiastic support from general intelligentzia, workers and students.

We are planning to make the January 1955 issue of our magazine *SEKAI* a special number devoted to "the Problems of Contemporary Civilization." Would it be possible for me to ask you to be kind enough to contribute to this issue your manuscript in the form of personal correspondence between you and a Japanese writer? Mr. Jun Takami, one of our foremost novelists, kindly complying with our request, has written a letter addressed to you, which I enclose herewith. We should feel most grateful if you would write for us a reply possibly in about 2,000 words to this letter and send it to us so that it would reach us before November 10th, since our Jan. 1955 issue must be ready for publication very early in December.[1]

For your manuscript, we should like to offer a net sum of $40, to be remitted through the foreign exchange agency of the Japanese government. We know this is an extremely small sum, but at present, due to our government's foreign exchange control, we are very sorry not to be able to pay more.

Anxiously and gratefully awaiting to hear from you, I am,

Faithfully yours,
/s/ Genzaburo Yoshino
/t/ Genzaburo Yoshino

[1] Apparently Faulkner never responded to this request.

1085 Open letter from Jun Takami, Japanese novelist, to Faulkner, September 25, 1954, signed ribbon typescript, 3 pages. From Tokyo.

Dear Mr. Faulkner:

The speech you made at your Nobel prize reception ceremony was something that came straight to the hearts of us living in these distant islands of the Far East. It filled our hearts and souls with deep compassion.

You called to "the young men and women already dedicated to the same anguish and travail." You continued to say that "the young man or woman writing today has forgotten the problems of the human heart in conflict with itself which alone can make good writing because only that is worth writing about, worth the agony and the sweat."

We writers of Japan had read your novels with devotion and endearment. Some of us had been greatly influenced by them. But we had failed to see your inner power that created "out of the materials of the human spirit something which did not exist before." We had been arrested more by the new, great literary style of your works and were anxious to imitate it. We were young and ambitious for new literary adventures.

Then you spoke out, warning such superficial followers of your style of their neglect of "the old verities and truths of the heart, the old universal truths lacking which any story is ephemeral and doomed." These you pointed out as the only thing that mattered to a writer. We were struck by your words, by your strong recalling of the old and universal truths about literature.

You went on to say that young writers today had forgotten the problems of the human heart because they were consumed by the fear of "when will I be blown up?" Your mention of that fear had a stronger ring in the ears of the Japanese people than those of any other people in the world. We had already twice been "blown up" by atomic bombs. Ours was not a mere anticipant fear but one founded on terrible actual experience.

Our memories of the deadly experience of 1945 had begun to dwindle a little when came the Bikini affair[1] and dragged us back to that fear—nay, a far more intensified fear about the catastrophe of humanity ever close at the back of us. This time again, it was not a vague, imagined fear but an actual and concrete one embodied in the fatal injuries suffered by the entire crew of a Japanese fishing boat that happened, at the time of one of the explosions, to be near but outside the off-limits line of the test area.

The sufferings of these fishermen have proved so fatal that they have made the entire Japanese people easily anticipate a similar fate to crawl on them at any time, their dark imagination having been further darkened by the visitation of radio-activated rainfalls that followed the Bikini explosions. Tuna fish of the South Pacific, a favorite food article of the Japanese people, has been found often dangerously radio-activated and shiploads of it, caught after great labor and at enormous risks, have been and are still being thrown away as unfit to eat. You will understand the Japanese people's vivid feelings toward hydrogen bombs.

Moreover, even after the passage of these nine years, people in Hiroshima are still dying of the atomic effects. Many of them apparently seemed all this time to have clearly escaped the poisoning, but suddenly and most unexpectedly they begin to suffer and fall off. These accumulative reports from the "blown city" are weighing down heavier than ever on the dark outlook of our people.

Toward the close of the Pacific War I was in China. In Hancow I witnessed an unforgettable incident. I saw a long line of coolies carrying big bags of salt to a warehouse from a ship moored by the bank of the Yangtse. Now and then the salt spilt off the bags to the ground and at each fall of the glistening white stuff a crowd of rag-covered women and children rushed to the spot and, with the quick use of the tiny broom each had ready, raked up the dirty salt into the bag also each carried in his or her hand.

To my curious inquiry about this strange sight, my companion, a Chinese writer, told me that these people would carry their acquisition home and boil it in water until clean salt was recovered. They would use it for their cooking or sell it to others. In the remote inland of China, far from the sea, salt was always a valuable foodstuff, which, in the bad conditions prevailing under the Japanese occupation, had become as precious as lifeblood itself.

My Chinese companion went on explaining that not every poor woman and child was entitled to join the salt-picking, that those on the scene were the coolies' wives and children who alone had the privilege to the spilt treasure. The coolies there were dropping the contents of their loads on the ground on purpose for their families to come and pick up.

I then noticed some watchmen, each with a thick piece of rope, thrashing at the crowd of salt-pickers, apparently to prevent the coolies' tricks. Had these coolies been paid enough to support their families they would not have exposed their wives and children to this cruel treatment. My heart ached at this sight of misery—the misery brought by the misrule of the Japanese army.

It was only a glimpse of the vast affliction brought by the Japanese army on the occupied China. It was a glimpse, no doubt, but still it well represented the effects of the crimes of our militarists. Out of my anguished heart I begged for forgiveness of my companion and of the entire Chinese people.

I wondered then how a Chinese writer could go on writing a story in the midst of such national distress. Soon, however, I saw that it was only my vulgar view which did not see into the depth of another writer's heart. So crushing was the effect of the existing misery on human hearts.

I thought then that probably this kind of human misery was exactly what Chinese writers like my companion should write about, since it struck the hearts of Chinese people more strongly and intimately than any others'. They should not turn aside from it for the reason that this misery was ephemeral and therefore not fit for their making of literature which should not be ephemeral. Rather, was it not the duty of Chinese writers, as writers and human beings, to catch these passing phenomena of great affliction and embody them in an enduring literature?

Later, in the midst of the awful tribulation that came on our people following our national surrender—in the midst of such tribulation as a foreign observer would have wondered how any one in its midst could write anything at all—I went on writing novels, which, however, did not treat the misery of the actual surroundings of that time. Was it because we Japanese were, unlike the Chinese people, facing then another category of misery—an affliction by which our people had to be punished?

The desperate horror and helplessness with which we Japanese are forced at present to accept the hydrogen bomb tests are indeed a cause of further affliction for us. But is this also the kind of tribulation by which the Japanese people must be punished?

I am sure there must be some, or probably a great many, people in the United States who are opposed to further testing of these catastrophic bombs. But their voices do not reach us. What come to our hearing are such comments as the possibility of the Japanese fishing boat having been engaged, at the time of the Bikini event, in espionage activity on the outskirts of the test area and the injuries suffered by this fishing crew having been exaggerated out of proportion to the actual happening. These comments are hurled at the victims as well as at the entire people in a manner which reminds us of your exquisite phrase, "victories without hope and, worst of all, without pity or compassion."

Toward the statements of this nature given out by the United States government, our Yoshida ministry acts exactly in the way I saw the Chinese watchmen act toward the poor coolies' wives and children picking spilt salt on the Hancow road. This is something which never brightens the downcast outlook of the Japanese people.

I well remember what you said about the sole importance of "the problems of the human heart in conflict with itself." But my heart is too often disturbed nowadays by external facts of misery so thickly surrounding me. As a Japanese I love my country just as Americans love their country of America. I love Japan as much as I love literature. And I cannot but grieve at the affliction of my people.

I cherish my country just as I cherish humanity. So I grieve for the misery of my people in the sense that it is the misery of humanity.

What can or should a Japanese writer do with this anguish of the heart? I should be happy and grateful if you would speak to us.

Most sincerely yours,
/s/ Jun Takami

[1]Bikini, an atoll in the Marshall Islands, was used from 1946 to 1956 as the site of atomic bomb tests conducted by the United States government. An explosion on March 1, 1954, followed by an unexpected shift of wind, exposed 31 American test personnel, 236 Marshall Islanders, and 23 Japanese fishermen to extremely high levels of radioactive fallout. One of the fishermen died as a result of the exposure.

1081b Letter from Phil Stone to Osmar Pimentel, São Paulo, Brazil, September 27, 1954, carbon typescript with typed signature, 1 page.

Dear Senor Pimentel:

I have your interesting letter of September 18 and I first want to congratulate you on the lucidity and clarity of your English. I certainly could do nothing like that with Portuguese.

Your question about what Faulkner meant[1] is quite natural since you were not familiar with the local situation. What he meant by the noun "grapes" was the cluster of large round light bulbs, about six inches in diameter, which hung from the light poles in groups of five. These, being round, were naturally similar to large, bloated grapes.

If I don't make myself clear and if I can help you any further, don't hesitate to write me.

Yours truly,
Phil Stone

[1]Pimentel had asked about Faulkner's use of the phrase "bloodless grapes" at the opening of "That Evening Sun."

1086 Letter from Faulkner to Jean-Louis Barrault, September 27, 1954, carbon typescript with typed signature, 1 page.

Dear M. Barrault:

I hereby authorize you to offer your own dramatic adaptation of my novel AS I LAY DYING in the French language for production in the Theatre Maringy in Paris.

The terms for the right to offer this dramatic adaptation are to be arranged through Gallimard, publishers, or Mrs. William Bradley of Paris, France.

With my best wishes for the success of your production and my assurances of respect.

Sincerely,
William Faulkner

1088 Letter from Harold Ober to Saxe Commins, September 30, 1954, unsigned ribbon typescript, 1 page.

Dear Saxe:

Dr. Paolo Grassi, Manager of the Piccolo Teatro della Citta di Milano, is prepared to purchase the Italian stage rights (including adaptation rights of the book that aren't yet dramatized in the original) in REQUIEM FOR A NUN, by Wm. Faulkner.

He's prepared to agree to the following terms:

(a) an advance of 200.000 Lire on the signature of the agreement.

(b) first opening to take place within 24 months of the date of the agreement.

(c) box office split: 70% to the Author, 30% to the Piccolo Teatro (which is a very good split, as it amounts, including the higher opening night royalty, to about 7.25% instead of the usual 5% or 6%)—All royalties net (i.e. after deduction of the commission that has to be paid, under law, to the Italian Society of Authors, and which amounts to 13½%). I think this is fair enough.

Sincerely,
[no signature]

1010g Letter from Phil Stone to Robert Coughlan, October 6, 1954, carbon typescript with typed signature, 1 page.

Dear Bob:

I did take off time to read your little book on Bill[1] and I think it is a very good job.

However, the remark you quote from Clifton Fadiman[2] about Bill's method of writing shows that Fadiman is stupid about writing, as I thought before now. One of the best things about Bill's writing is the deliberate withholding of information. This creates suspense and also makes the reader feel that he is sharing himself in working out the solution. This is more or less the same method that is used in detective stories and is absolutely sound. Of course what other unfavorable critics have said about other aspects of Bill's writing is also sound.

Estelle was in the office day before yesterday to get me to help her get a passport to visit "Cho-cho"[3] in the Philippines, and she told me that Bill was in New York and that she was going to try to get away before Bill got back. What this means I don't know, but it probably means nothing, as most of what Estelle says means.

Emily sends her best to you and your wife.

Your friend,
Phil Stone

[1] *The Private World of William Faulkner* (New York: Harper, 1954).

[2] Coughlan quotes (p. 122) from Fadiman's review of *Absalom, Absalom!* (*New Yorker*, October 31, 1936, pp. 62–64), in which Faulkner's method is defined as "Anti-Narrative, a set of complex devices used to keep the story from being told. . . ." Compare Stone's negative judgments of Fadiman in this letter to his remarks in his April 6, 1956 letter to Fadiman.

[3] Estelle and Cornell Franklin's daughter, Victoria.

1090 Note from Maud Falkner to Faulkner (c/o Random House), undated, signed autograph manuscript, 1 page, with envelope addressed in Mrs. Falkner's hand and postmarked Oxford, October 11, 1954.

This is a nice one:

"May the wind be at your back,
May the road rise up to meet you,
And may God always hold you in
the palm of his hand."

I love you.
Moms

1091 Letter from Faulkner to Saxe Commins, "Monday" [October 25, 1954], signed ribbon typescript, 1 page.

Dear Saxe:

I sent the Freedom of Press piece to you, rewritten, today. It still stays on my mind though, and now I think I know why. It is not an article, but a lecture. It is a section of a kind of symposium, maybe 5 or 6 lectures, on THE AMERICAN DREAM: WHAT HAS HAPPENED TO IT? So read it and send it back to me. I have more and more offers to lecture, my price is up to $1000.00 from colleges now, and I may take it up, use this one for the first of a series, to be a book later, on what has happened to the American Dream which at one time the whole earth looked up, aspired to.

What do you think of the idea? Anyway, send the article back. Or better: just hold it there, do not submit it, as I have the carbon.

/s/ Bill

1092 Letter from Faulkner to Saxe Commins, "Tuesday" [probably October 26, 1954], signed ribbon typescript, 1 page.

Dear Saxe:

E. leaves for Manila Friday, still says she does not want to go, but ticket bought, trunk shipped, and apparently she is. Nice to be able to spend 3000 bucks doing something you constantly remind the owner of the 3000 bucks you dont really want to do.

Received this a.m. a wide flat parcel from Random H. which I have not opened because it may be the records[1] and I dont want to have to wrap them up again as I dont want them. I dont want one at all, I thought they were for you and Linscott and Miss Stein, though I dont know why you want them either. If you can ascertain that they are the records, let me know and I will send them back and you can have them distributed. That is, keep yours and give Linscott his and hold Miss Stein's until I can give you her address as she may be out of town by then.

Enclosed also a foreign letter I received this a.m. Dont know why it was sent to me, nor what I am supposed to do.

And lastly, a correction for page 3 of the piece, ON FREEDOM OF THE PRESS which I mailed to you yesterday. Count 6 lines up from 'it' at end of first paragraph, to line beginning. . . . cups (in vino . . . This phrase should read: cups (*in vino*: which, if this was his true opinion, who to blame etc etc etc from hard incessant work to discover the pleasure *and courage and hope* to be got etc etc etc. that is, add

All well here, Ria or Buddy writing you soon. Too hot still; me for some place like Maine or Canada for the rest of my life I think. Love to Dorothy
/s/ Bill

[P.S.] No, disregard the crossed-out paragraph,[2] and send the article back to me. On thinking about it, I realise it is not complete as is, but contains germ of a much better one of wider less personal scope, not on FREEDOM OF PRESS but on Freedom, American style—the sort of misused freedom and liberty which produced the McCarthys[3] and from which people like Oppenheimer[4] suffer. Read it if you like, but dont submit it, send it back; I am rewriting from the copy.

[1] Presumably copies of *Faulkner Reads from His Works,* which Faulkner had recorded for Caedmon Publishers on September 30, 1954.

[2] Faulkner deleted with grease pencil the paragraph containing the revision of the "Freedom of the Press" essay.

[3] In the early 1950s Joseph McCarthy, a U.S. Senator from Wisconsin, led an investigation of government officials considered to be "security risks" because of their former association with Communists.

[4] J. Robert Oppenheimer, the physicist who had headed the project to develop the atomic bomb, was dismissed from the Atomic Energy Commission in 1954, having been accused of associating with Communists and opposing the development of the hydrogen bomb.

1093 Western Union telegram from Faulkner to Saxe Commins, October 27, 1954.

PLEASE HOLD FREEDOM OF PRESS ARTICLE. LETTER IN MAIL TODAY
BILL

1094 Letter from Gloria Franklin to Dorothy and Saxe Commins, October 31 [1954], signed autograph manuscript, 4 pages (on 1 folded leaf), with envelope postmarked Oxford, November 1, 1954.

Dear Miss Dorothy and Mr. Saxe,

I can't begin to tell you again how useful the dresses and blankets you sent have been to me. Thanks to you, I have not had to buy any other clothes for him—and thank heavens, he is growing a mile a minute and there will be so many things to get for him shortly. Pappy told me you never received my letter that I mailed on the 23rd of September—as I put a return address on it and I haven't had it returned to me, I never gave it a second thought but that you had heard from me. I am awfully sorry—but I guess letters can go astray.

Mark is such a healthy and good baby—we are so fortunate! I am enclosing two pictures taken when he was a month old. You can see—he's all boy—as Pappy said when he first saw him—you could never mistake him for a girl. . . .

With a sigh of relief I say—Mama left yesterday.[1] I was keeping my fingers crossed right up to the end. Mama claimed she wouldn't eat unless we came down there every night to eat with her—and with me still being tired from carrying the 25 extra pounds for the length of time I did—and getting about 3–4 hours sleep each night since I arrived home from the hospital—have to take Mark out each night and rearrange his schedule to meet the situation. I must confess, I was getting pretty tired of her. But Mac and I both agreed—anything to keep peace and get her on her way would be worth it, I reckon it would and did pay off. I don't know how long Pappy will be able to stand it alone in the house—with no one to cook for him etc.—Mac and I have our hands full—and with help only for a few hours a week—I don't have time to have Pappy for meals. He says he is staying and going deer hunting—that will be to the end of Nov.—I sort of wish he would go back to N.Y.—I don't think I'm selfish in wanting my husband and my baby completely to myself for just a little while—cause Mama will return in March—

Pappy is doing fine, so far, he has been in good spirits and I think utterly amazed that Mama really left him. Perhaps a taste of being alone in that house would serve him right and do him good—and I hope when he finds that no one is going to entertain him, he will return—that would be just one more thing off of our mind to worry about—

Please let us know when your grand child arrives—I know that will be another most welcomed and well loved baby!—But don't wait 'til then to let us hear from you—I know how busy you are—with so many people to take an interest in and to love—I would like to add that never a day goes by but Mac and I think of you and the peace and contentment you gave us.

Love,
Gloria

[1] For Manila.

1081d Letter from Phil Stone to Osmar Pimentel, November 6, 1954, carbon typescript with typed signature, 2 pages.

Dear Senor Pimentel:

I have your very nice letter of October 30, which I deeply appreciate. You don't owe me any thanks because I was very glad to give you the information and it was no trouble.

As for the English language, I confess that it seems to me that it lacks a great deal in lucidity and clarity. I can easily understand why it is one of the most difficult languages for a foreigner to master. This is especially true since I had seven years of Greek in college and since that is the most accurate language that I have ever known. About the only thing logical about the English language is that it is illogical.

As for Faulkner, you are correct in thinking that for twelve years I was his only believer. I deserve no credit whatever for this because to anyone with a fair amount of sense and a fair knowledge of literature it was perfectly obvious that the man could write. You can talk about disappointments and silent ignoring, but we really had them. We could get nobody to help, nobody interested. All we got was silence for twelve years, except for one little poem that was published in the New Republic Magazine. Sherwood Anderson was the man who finally got William Faulkner published and he did it simply by forcing on his own publisher, Horace Liveright, the manuscript of SOLDIERS' PAY. It was only with THE SOUND AND THE FURY that Faulkner got any little recognition and only with SANCTUARY that he made any money. He was ignored and sneered at and laughed at here in Oxford for years. People even said that I must be writing his stuff because he didn't have sense enough to do it. As I have said many times, anyone should know that I did not write it because if I had written it it would have been punctuated better.

Now it is amusing to see how the idolators flock around him, some of the very same people who used to avoid him like he had the plague. They even turn on me because I don't think he is as good a writer as most people think now. I think he is the best of his generation in English fiction, but I don't think the generation compares so well with other generations of English literature.

With reference to the book,[1] I shall never write it. In the first place, I don't have time.

In the second place, I am not a writer.

In the third place, it would have to be very much about his personal life which he does not care to have aired.

. . . .

You are right in thinking that there is a great deal of shallow rot being written about Faulkner and his work. There are only three things that I have seen that are worthy of any serious consideration.

The first of these is the preface by Malcolm Cowley to THE PORTABLE FAULKNER, published, I think, by the Viking Press, New York. However, Cowley has taken seriously a lot of Bill's romancing about himself and the Falkner family and swallowed a lot of things which are pure fiction.

Robert Coughlan, a roving editor of LIFE Magazine, has published a very good little book, THE PRIVATE WORLD OF WILLIAM FAULKNER. Coughlan is a very capable and accurate reporter and the book is worth your reading.

The man who has made himself the real authority on Faulkner by a great deal of hard work is Professor Carvel Collins of the Massachusetts Institute of Technology, Cambridge, Massachusetts. He is doing some monographs from time to time about Faulkner's work and will eventually produce a book. I do not entirely agree with him because I think he also overestimates Faulkner, but he is certainly the most accurate authority. His address is: Carvel Collins, 14-N432, Massachusetts Institute of Technology, Cambridge 39, Massachusetts. Possibly you would like to write him. If you do, tell him that I suggested that you write him.

If you should ever come to this part of the country we should like for you to visit us, and if we ever get enough money to come to Sao Paulo we shall certainly look you up.

Yours truly,
Phil Stone

[1] Pimentel had asked when readers might expect to see a book on Faulkner by Stone.

1095 Letter from Faulkner to Saxe Commins, "Monday" [probably early November 1954], unsigned ribbon typescript, 1 page.

Dear Saxe:

Have mailed today SOLDIERS PAY MOSQUITOES SARTORIS PYLON THE UNVANQUISHED for the leather binding.[1]

Read the enclosed,[2] if you approve, send it to Ober, with any suggestions you like, though his judgment will be all right with me where to submit it.

Love to Dorothy.

[no signature]

[1] Faulkner had arranged to have a set of his works bound in leather for his daughter Jill.

[2] Probably the "Freedom of Press" essay.

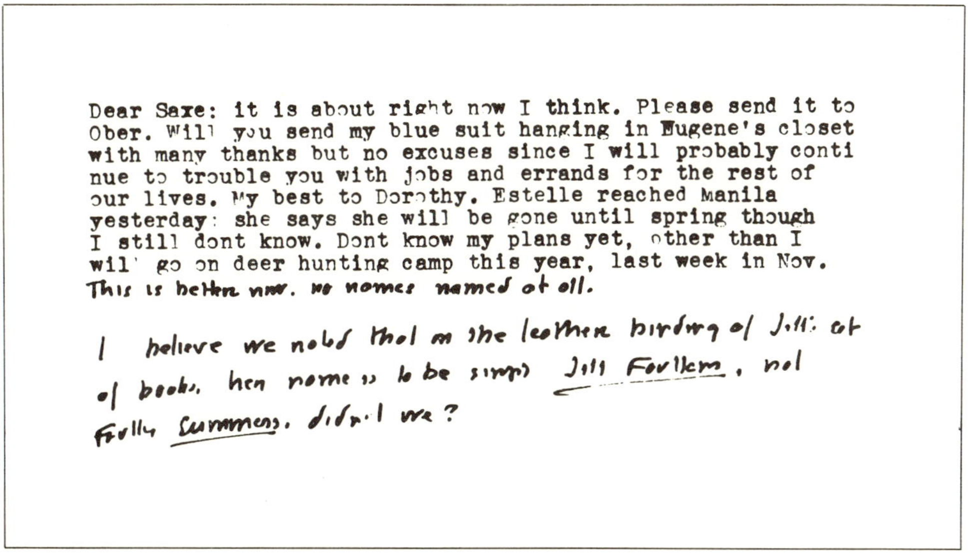
Dear Saxe: it is about right now I think. Please send it to Ober. Will you send my blue suit hanging in Eugene's closet with many thanks but no excuses since I will probably conti nue to trouble you with jobs and errands for the rest of our lives. My best to Dorothy. Estelle reached Manila yesterday: she says she will be gone until spring though I still dont know. Dont know my plans yet, other than I will go on deer hunting camp this year, last week in Nov.
This is better now. no names named at all.

I believe we noted that on the leather binding of Jill's set of books, her name is to be simply Jill Faulkner, not Faulkner Summers, didn't we?

30. Letter from Faulkner to Saxe Commins (item 1096)

1096 Letter from Faulkner to Saxe Commins, undated [early November 1954], unsigned ribbon typescript with two sentences added in holograph, 1 page.

Dear Saxe: it is about right now I think. Please send it to Ober. Will you send my blue suit hanging in Eugene's closet with many thanks but no excuses since I will probably continue to trouble you with jobs and errands for the rest of our lives. My best to Dorothy. Estelle reached Manila yesterday: she says she will be gone until spring though I still dont know. Dont know my plans yet, other than I will go on deer hunting camp this year, last week in Nov.

This is better now, no names named at all.[1]

I believe we noted that on the leather binding of Jill's set of books, her name is to be simply *Jill Faulkner,* not Faulkner *Summers,* didn't we?

[no signature]

[1] Presumably a reference to the revision of the "Freedom of Press" essay.

1097 Letter from Estelle Faulkner to Dorothy and Saxe Commins, "November 9th" [1954], signed autograph manuscript, 3 pages (on 1 folded leaf). From Manila.

Dearest Dorothy and Saxe—

At long last am with Cho-Cho and Bill—have been almost a week now—

My trip out by plane was very pleasant, and am sure, as soon as I become acclimated, will find Manila delightful—

The Fieldens have a charming home on the Bay—a lovely garden that runs down to the beach—interesting neighbors—splendid servants—so I *should* have a good time—Alas—I'm plagued with home-sickness—Did hate so to leave Bill, Mark, Gloria and Malcolm—

We are so anxious to hear from you about Franny, and pray everything goes well—Please *do* let us know—

Saxe, if it isn't too much bother, I would like, very, to give Bill a good Atlas for Christmas—Am sure that Pappy will be only too glad to have it charged to him—Could you arrange to have one sent out to me? Bless you!

I firmly intended sending this picture to you before I left Oxford, but my last weeks there were busy, and neglected to—Isn't it sweet?

Had the extreme pleasure of seeing Jill and Paul in their own home on my way out—Don't believe I could have left the country otherwise—

Write sometime when it isn't a chore—we would like to know how you are—you, Eugene—Frannie and Bill and *of course* about the baby—

Vicki and Bill send love
you have mine—
Always devotedly
Estelle

[P.S.] A borrowed pen as you see!

1098 Letter from Jill Faulkner Summers to Saxe Commins, November 10, 1954, signed autograph manuscript, 2 pages (on 1 folded leaf), with envelope addressed in Mrs. Summers' hand and postmarked Charlottesville, November 11, 1954.

Dear Mr. Saxe—

Thank you, sir, for your opinion & advice. It is probably the best, since I hadn't consulted my spouse on the matter (wanted to know the prospects first) & he quite possibly would not have approved of the idea. I am going on & compile them just for us, however.

Your news is all so good I could fairly pop with happiness for the Commins family. Please extend our congratulations to Eugene (you both must be very proud) & love to Franny. Let us know when the baby arrives—all the particulars.

We're hoping you will visit us someday—either here in Charlottesville or when we are settled in Oxford. I claim you as family.

Love—
Jill

1099b Letter from Phil Stone to James P. J. Murphy, Audubon, New Jersey, November 24, 1954, carbon typescript with typed signature, 1 page.

Dear Mr. Murphy:

Mr. Faulkner always gives me the autographed copies of his books as they come out but he does not like to autograph for other people, and I never ask him to do so. In fact, since he won the Nobel Prize he seldom comes to see me.

Yours truly,
Phil Stone

1104 Letter from Estelle Faulkner to Dorothy and Saxe Commins, "Monday December 13th," signed autograph manuscript, 2 pages, with envelope addressed in Mrs. Faulkner's hand and postmarked Manila, December 16, 1954.

Dearest Dorothy and Saxe—

We, Vicki, Bill and I, are anxiously awaiting news from you about the new Baby—I, especially, am hoping and praying that everything went well and Frannie is as radiantly happy and strong again—as *all* the best wishes could make her—

Feel so guilty having let Saxe's charming letter go unanswered til now—

Manila is a strenuous place to live, as the Fieldens live it—but Nature stepped in, on my behalf—laid me out with bronchitis for ten days—so I stored up enough energy and rest I hope, to propel me through the Holidays—

The artificially induced gaity of the Far East is very pronounced here—a feverish clutching at nothing, that is little short of terrifying—As I sit here now, looking out on Manila Bay with its warships and carriers—every one of them ready for instant action—I feel an insecurity verging on panic—But, in a little while, I'll go on out to tea, cock-tails, dinner and what-have-you, and join in all the inconsequential chatter of the internationals—

Have just heard from Ria that Bill is in New York—Am sure he'll enjoy being with you again—

Jill—bless her! writes often, and it does my heart good to know how happy she is—Vicki (Jr.) is spending the Holidays with friends in Paris, and seems quite reconciled at last, to her school—

I hope to spend a week with her in Switzerland on my way home—

Do have a Merry Christmas—I will think about you *all*—Frannie and Bill ([indecipherable]) Eugene and you two with sincerest love—

Always
Estelle

[P.S.] Kindly give my regards and greetings to Professor Einstein—Meeting him was one of the greatest privileges I've ever had!

1105 Letter from Estelle Faulkner to James W. Silver, "December 15th," signed autograph manuscript, 1 page, with envelope addressed in Mrs. Faulkner's hand and postmarked Manila, December 16, 1954.

Dear Jim—

I very seldom ever
Try my hand at being clever—
But lately, at a church bazaar
Mine eyes beheld this Fine Cigar—
And so, all Caution cast adrift—
I bought this Trifle as a gift
For you, my friend, who can't gainsay
That Sometime there might come the day
(or Night) when you will bless the Bloke
Who—invented things to smoke—

Now Dutch[1] may not approve of it
(My dubious venture into Wit)

If not, then pass it as a joke
As tasteless, as *may* be this smoke—

Love and Merry Christmas
to you *all*

Estelle

[1] Mrs. Silver.

1955

1119 Letter from Estelle Faulkner to Dorothy and Saxe Commins, "Jan. 4th—" [1955], signed autograph manuscript, 2 pages, with envelope addressed in Mrs. Faulkner's hand and postmarked Manila, January 5, 1955.

Dearest Dorothy and Saxe—

A very Happy New Year to you—and of course it will be! Congratulations and much Love to the entire family too—How wonderful to have Baby Jean—Am sure she is *everything* Saxe claims for her, and it will be something else for me to look forward to this spring—my meeting with Miss Bennett—give her a nice, gentle kiss for me—

Christmas out here was so unlike Christmas at Home that the Day passed without any pangs on my part—The next day, however, we all drove up to Baguio, in the mountains; and the sight of pine trees, and open fires in the hotel, brought waves of home-sickness and longings for the other part of my family—I do feel though, my being here helped Vicki and Bill over a bad time—Hope I was successful in concealing the fact that I was blue!

Jill wrote that Pappy spent Christmas in Princeton—What a treat for him—You are so wonderfully kind and generous to us—Thank you—

Victoria and I are going to Hong Kong on the 17th, for a week or ten days while Bill goes to the island of Negros to visit tobacco plantations—Have promised Sister I'll stay in Manila until after her birthday on the 5th of February—Then, I feel as though I'd like to start my long journey back to the States—

Hope to spend a week in Siam, and if at all feasible go down to Cambodia—I care little about India and the Near East so plan to dash through those countries to Rome—I'm writing to ask Bill to please advise about a hotel in Rome—will you too?—as I am traveling alone, and would like to stay in Rome a week or so, want some place easy to find my way to and from—Not being a linguist, will doubtless find it difficult to go to all the places I'd like—anyway—intend seeing and doing all I can—

After Italy, Switzerland, France, then home—

The Philippines aren't lovely islands like the Hawaiian group, and of course, it will be a long time before Manila fully recovers from her fearful bombings—The climate is bad except for the hardy—Life is made easy by plentiful servants, and there seems to be limit-less opportunities to make money and enjoy the society of strange and wonderful people—

Saxe, I beg of you, not to feel as though you should answer every letter I write—My inconsequential notes are written because I want you both to know how often I think of you, and with what Love—

Always devotedly
Estelle

[P.S.] Haven't received the Atlas—Perhaps Christmas rush—detained—
[P.P.S.] Jill is ecstatic over the Books—so am I!

31. Faulkner with Jean Stein and Saxe Commins at National Book Award presentation, New York, January 25, 1955

1124b Letter from Phil Stone to Judith S. Bond, February 18, 1955, carbon typescript with typed signature, 1 page.

Dear Miss Bond:

I have your letter of February 16.[1]

I know that I still have my own autographed presentation copy of "The Marble Faun" and I think I have another similar copy, but I am not sure. I am having to leave today for Chicago to attend the Midyear Meeting of the House of Delegates of the American Bar Association so I may not have time to look up the other copy. I shall ask my wife to do so while I am gone. If I have the other copy I will not take less than $75.00 for it.

It may interest you to know that in 1925 (I think that was the year) I was in Chicago, went around to see Miss Monroe, had lunch with her, told her that the literary star in America was passing from the Midwest to the South, and tried to get her to publish free in POETRY some parts of Bill's "Marble Faun." She wouldn't do this but she later wrote a little editorial about what I had told her.

Yours truly,
Phil Stone

[1] Miss Bond, the curator of the Modern Poetry Library at the University of Chicago, was seeking a copy of *The Marble Faun.*

1125 Letter from Estelle Faulkner to Saxe Commins, "February 27th" [possibly 1955], signed autograph manuscript, 1 page.

Dear Saxe—

The papers[1] you asked me to sign before a notary, and send on to Jill, will be forwarded to her in the morning—

I have so little free time to attend to personal matters that by the time I located a notary public, it was too late to get papers in today's mail—Am sure Jill will send them on to you soon—

Malcolm was home from Jackson for the week-end, and seemed fairly resigned to continuing his work for the University for a time—anyway—Appreciate your concern, and you can imagine how heart-sick I've been over him—

Thank you for telling me about Bill and his work—know he's enjoying it—

Love to you and Dorothy
Always
Estelle

[1] Unidentified.

1130 Letter from Faulkner to Saxe Commins, "Wednesday," signed ribbon typescript, 1 page, with envelope addressed in Faulkner's hand and postmarked Oxford, March 16, 1955.

Dear Saxe:

Whatever you decide about the deal[1] will suit me. But I dont think I will try to write movie scripts on them. I have never learned how to write movies, nor even to take them very seriously. I dont think I need the money at present, and that is the only reason I would have to try the job, or any movie job. Just say to Geller that I have too many commitments at present to consider a movie job this year anyway.

All pretty well here, I go to hospital tomorrow to try to find what is wrong inside, and will advise you.

Have talked to Estelle, who saw Vicky.[2] She says Vicky most definitely does not want Swarthmore, and perhaps she is right. Vicky says she wants a school with football team, junior prom, etc. The child never wanted Switzerland. That was her mother, who is a middleclass snob. She was never interested in what Vicky would learn at a Swiss school; she merely wanted the privilege of saying at cocktail parties 'My daughter is in a private school in Switzerland.' I think myself that Vicky is not equipped for Swarthmore, either by temperament or competence; she does not want knowledge, wisdom. Perhaps she belongs at some place like the Univ. of Ohio or California. And if she does, having been compelled where she did not want to go once, maybe she should have some choice of her own now; at 17 it is long ago too late to do much with a child, in my experience. It is sad, but I am afraid that Vicky belongs to that race which does not look on school as a privilege, but merely as a payment for a bribe; that is, 'I'll go to your school if you make it worth my while.'

I'll try to talk to her though, if I have a chance to accomplish anything. But I am afraid that, for your own peace of mind, you had better just give these Franklins up.

Love
/s/ Bill

[1]The possible sale of the film rights of *The Sound and the Fury* and *Soldiers' Pay* to Hollywood producer Jerry Wald.
[2]That is, Faulkner's step-granddaughter, Victoria Fielden.

1131 Letter from Estelle Faulkner to Dorothy and Saxe Commins, "Sunday—March 20th" [1955], signed autograph manuscript, 2 pages.

Dear Dorothy and Saxe—

It is very hard for me to realize that I've been Home three weeks—and feel more than ashamed of my failure to write before now—

Saxe was sweet to take time off from Random House and make me a little visit—How I treasure the friendship and love you two bestow upon us!

Naturally, have had a busy and pleasant life since coming back to Oxford—Seeing family and friends, and catching up on a delayed acquaintanceship with the new grand-son has filled my days delightfully—

Malcolm, Saxe, has not answered your letter, nor thanked you for the material sent, not from any lack of sincere appreciation, but because the child is perhaps loathe to admit, even to himself, that what you suggest is beyond him! However, I believe *now*—he will write and explain—

It is really too bad—Malcolm and Victoria can't exchange personalities—Cho-Cho has so much ambition and force, and Malcolm has an excellent mind, utterly devoid of any desire for material advancement—

It is nice being at Rowan oak again—Bill and I have worked in the grounds—trying to get the place looking lovely for Jill's first visit Home—and having no house servants, save Broadus!—I have been busy in the house too—

After four months of leisure, feel quite competent to undertake most anything—

Can hardly wait to see you all again—and see, and get to know Jean—

As soon as my things arrive from Manila will send the little gifts I got for Dorothy and Frannie—

With a heart *full* of Love to each and all of you—

Devotedly
Estelle

1133a Letter from Phil Stone to Dave Womack, Mississippi state representative, March 28, 1955, carbon typescript with typed signature, 1 page.

Dear Mr. Womack:

I read with much interest your letter[1] with reference to the letter of my friend Bill Faulkner concerning the school problem, and also read the other two letters in the paper the same day.

I was very much amused at your stating that you bowed to Bill's higher intellect. This is funny indeed because, as Bill himself said in an unguarded moment, he is nothing but a writing man, and his ignorance on many subjects is so profound that it would shock you. I have been puzzled and perturbed the last few years at his habit of writing to the editors concerning subjects about which I know that he knows practically nothing.

I certainly don't see how he could possibly know anything about the school system because he did not quite finish the eighth grade and never got a degree from any school. The only way that I can figure out his habit of writing letters to the papers is that he is not getting as much publicity now as he did when he had just won the Nobel Prize. I know he insists that he does not want publicity, but I think he is about that, as I have told him, Mr. Greta Garbo.

I have no doubt that he is very likely to come forward with a plan to perfect the whole school system, but any Falkner, not just Bill, would within three days present to God a plan for the reorganization of Heaven. The Falkners all can give you all the information as experts about everything in the world, and the less they know about the subject the more assured they are about voicing their opinions.

Of course you people are doing the best you can down there and any one of you knows more about this subject in ten minutes than Bill does or ever will know in a lifetime. So don't take him seriously.

Of course on account of our forty years' close friendship this letter is not for the press but simply for your private eye.

Yours truly,
Phil Stone

[1] In the Memphis *Commercial Appeal* of March 27, 1955. Womack was responding to Faulkner's letter in the March 20 issue.

1147 Western Union telegram from Faulkner to Saxe Commins, April 20, 1955.

ALBERT EINSTEIN WAS ONE OF THE WISEST OF MEN AND ONE OF THE GENTLEST OF MEN. WHO CAN REPLACE HIM IN EITHER, LET ALONE IN BOTH

BILL

S-39 Letter from Faulkner to Phillip E. Mullen, undated [possibly April 1955], signed ribbon typescript, 1 page.

Dear Phil:

Thank you for letter and pictures. Enclosed is a clipping from Ben Wasson, Greenville, and a letter. The letter is interesting. I fear that some of my fellow Mississippians will never forgive that 30,000$ that durn foreign country gave me for just sitting on my ass and writing stuff that makes my own state ashamed to own me.[1]

Yours
/s/ Bill

[1] Blotner (*Selected Letters of William Faulkner,* p. 312) dates this letter "probably Jan. 1951," but Mullen has linked the letter to Faulkner's controversial anti-segregationist stand (see *Osceola* [Arkansas] *Times,* December 25, 1980, p. 4).

S-40 Note from Saxe Commins to Faulkner, undated [possibly mid-May 1955], signed autograph manuscript, 1 page.

Bill:

Harold Ober phoned to say that he got $2500 for the story,[1] with a promise of even more if there will be another one.

Call me if there is anything you need.

Saxe

[1] Possibly "Kentucky: May: Saturday: Three Days to the Afternoon," published in the May 16, 1955 issue of *Sports Illustrated.*

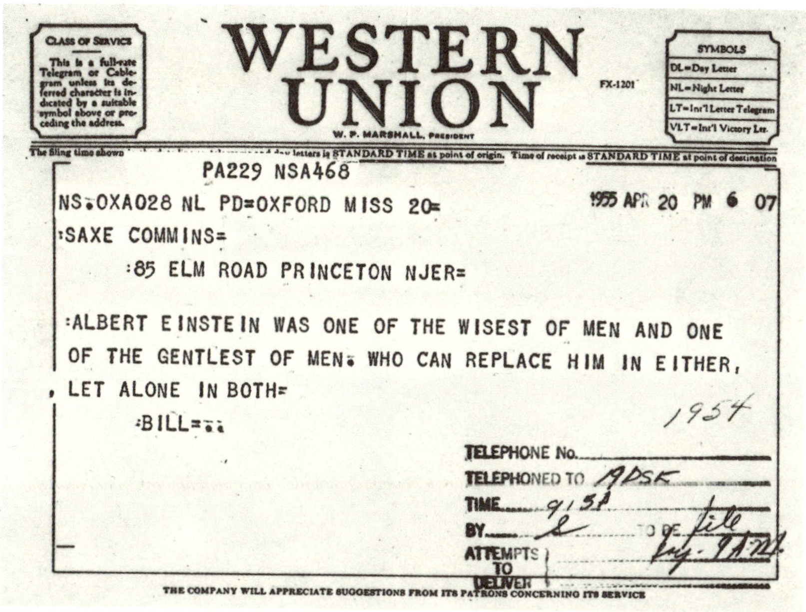
CLASS OF SERVICE
This is a full-rate Telegram or Cablegram unless its deferred character is indicated by a suitable symbol above or preceding the address.

WESTERN UNION

W. P. MARSHALL, PRESIDENT

FX-1201

SYMBOLS
DL=Day Letter
NL=Night Letter
LT=Int'l Letter Telegram
VLT=Int'l Victory Ltr.

PA229 NSA468

NS.OXA028 NL PD=OXFORD MISS 20= 1955 APR 20 PM 6 07

SAXE COMMINS=

:85 ELM ROAD PRINCETON NJER=

:ALBERT EINSTEIN WAS ONE OF THE WISEST OF MEN AND ONE OF THE GENTLEST OF MEN. WHO CAN REPLACE HIM IN EITHER, LET ALONE IN BOTH=

:BILL=

1954

TELEPHONE No.

TELEPHONED TO

TIME

BY

ATTEMPTS TO DELIVER

THE COMPANY WILL APPRECIATE SUGGESTIONS FROM ITS PATRONS CONCERNING ITS SERVICE

32. Telegram from Faulkner regarding the death of Albert Einstein (item 1147)

1153 Letter from Estelle Faulkner to Dorothy Commins, "Monday 30th," signed autograph manuscript, 2 pages, with envelope addressed in Mrs. Faulkner's hand and postmarked Oxford, May 31, 1955.

Dear Dorothy—

It seems a very long time since you kindly offered to give a concert in Oxford[1]—

I talked to Mr. Bowen[2] about it at once, but, being near the end of the school year, everyone on the campus was so busy that nothing was done—

Last Sunday (a week ago) A. G. (Mr. B) came down, and we talked about our good fortune very seriously—Bill suggested that he give a $500 scholarship in music[3] to a worthy young man or woman, and, that the proceeds, over and above the cost of your appearance, go also to that cause—

A.G. suggested (and I heartily agree) that your concert be sponsored by our local cultural clubs—There are three, and we believe more interest, and incidentally more money, would come from the town folk than from students—

Please let us know as soon as convenient just what date in November we could set for our treat—and, your fee—That is important—Naturally, I am looking forward to a nice *long* visit from you and Saxe—and November *is* our lovely month—

Could you send us some press notices etc. to impress our yokels? Alas! people in Oxford know so little of what goes on in the outer world—still, they are amazingly quick to respond to proper stimuli—

This is a hurried letter—Bill is waiting to mail it for me—He is thoroughly

33. Faulkner at a Kentucky horse farm, May 1955

engrossed right now in re-conditioning his sail-boat, "against" Jill's arrival in a week—He is fine—I am unusually well, and busy with house and garden—

Dearest love to all the family—

Do, *please*, let us hear—

Devotedly

Estelle

[P.S.] The concert, of course, would be given at the University—Fulton Chapel—I have already arranged that—

[1]Mrs. Commins, a concert pianist, presented the program in late November 1955.

[2]A. G. Bowen, Jr., was director of University Extension, University of Mississippi.

[3]Public announcement of the Dorothy Berliner Commins Music Scholarship from the William Faulkner Scholarship Fund was made by the University of Mississippi on March 15, 1956. The first award was presented two months later.

1161 Letter from Faulkner to Saxe Commins, "6 July" [1955], signed ribbon typescript, 1 page.

Dear Saxe:

I am undertaking the Japanese assignment[1] for the State Dept., expenses paid and some salary too this time, and I will go on to Europe from there. So I will make plans to take care of finances here before I leave. I will want $5000.00, to send my dead brother's daughter to school this year, for my mother's and Estelle's allowances. Please send five.

Will leave here about July 28th, I think to Washington first for briefing, dont think I will be able to come up, as I am due in Tokyo Aug. 1st. I will be in Europe about Sept. 1st, dont know how long I shall stay, maybe until Xmas, though I have not made that definite statement here yet.

All well here, am doing some sailing with Jill and Paul. Give Dorothy my love. Every night I compose in my mind the letter I intend to write her, which I dont ever do. My only poor excuse is, Dorothy already knows what I would say in it.

I wont be able to see our book[2] this year until I reach home, probably.

/s/ Bill

[1]To participate in the Summer Seminars in American Literature at Nagano, Japan.

[2]*Big Woods,* which Faulkner dedicated to Commins.

1165 Letter from Estelle Faulkner to Dorothy Commins, "Aug. 15th," signed autograph manuscript, 2 pages, with envelope addressed in Mrs. Faulkner's hand and postmarked Oxford, August 15, 1955.

Dearest Dorothy—

Please believe how distressed I am over my failure to write—However, by now, am sure that you've heard directly from the University about your concert—*Everyone* is thrilled over the great honor you are bestowing upon us; and *I* am selfishly exulting, that not only we will hear great music, but I will have the pleasure of having you as my guest!

Am praying Bill will be here then, and have every reason to believe that he will—We are taking it for granted—Saxe will come down too—He simply *must,* for remember, you both promised us a fall visit—

I was in Memphis in the hospital when your letter came—same old trouble with my tummy—Malcolm got panic-stricken and 'phoned Jill in Washington—She and Paul came down immediately, and are with me at *home,* now—

Am feeling very much better and intend watching my diet *carefully* from now on—Doesn't pay to tempt ulcers into erupting—

My trunks came at long last from Manila, and will get a little package off to you and Frannie soon—Am sorry about the delay, for it *may* be Jean has already outgrown the baby things I got for her—*Do* hope not—

I solemnly promise not to let you down again, Dorothy—and feel as though you might believe that I'm not aware of the sacrifice you are making for Bill and the University—Really, I've never been more touched by your beautiful unselfishness—

With a heart full of love to you and Saxe

Always devotedly
Estelle

1175 Letter from 'Bama McLean to Vance Broach, October 6, 1955, signed autograph manuscript, 2 pages (1 leaf).

Dear Vance

Only a note today as no time for letter writing—

I want to call your attention to Look Magazine of Oct 4th which carries an article of "A Group of 100 of World's Most Important People" in which William F. is included—together with only 2 women, Mrs Roosevelt & Elizabeth, Queen of England. To my mind perhaps the greatest honor Billie has achieved.

Another family tribute is explained in enclosed letter. I sent clippings concerning my father, your great, great grandfather to Duclos & on his article he was awarded a scholarship to University of Michigan![1]

. . . .

Hurriedly
Bama

[1]Donald P. Duclos subsequently produced a doctoral dissertation entitled "Son of Sorrow: The Life, Works, and Influence of Colonel William C. Falkner, 1825–1889" (University of Michigan, 1962).

1196b Letter from Phil Stone to William Van O'Connor, November 15, 1955, carbon typescript with typed signature, 1 page.

Dear Mr. O'Connor:

I have your letter of November 11.[1]

Bill read some Hawthorne but I don't think he read a great deal. The truth is, I don't think he is extremely well read in anything.

I think I still have two copies of The Marble Faun but the title had nothing to do with Hawthorne at all. I know because I am the man that put this title on it.

Yours truly,
Phil Stone

[1]O'Connor, an English professor at the University of Minnesota and a noted Faulkner scholar, had written that he was working on an article treating Faulkner and Hawthorne and was curious to know if Stone felt that Faulkner was influenced by Hawthorne. O'Connor's article was published as "Hawthorne and Faulkner: Some Common Ground," *Virginia Quarterly Review,* 33 (Winter 1957), 105–123.

1198b Letter from J. Merton England, Editor, *Journal of Southern History,* to Bell I. Wiley, November 30, 1955, typed copy of original, 2 pages.

Dear Bell:

. . . .

When you mentioned the possibility of printing the three papers on the segregation decisions[1] I gave a snap judgment that it would be good to have them in print but that I didn't think the *Journal* should publish them. I still feel that way. And after giving a good deal of thought to the matter on the way back from Memphis and since, I do not believe the Association should publish them. Nor do I think they should be published *for* the Association.

I do not think we should go into any kind of a publications program, even a limited and perhaps single-shot one, without a thorough discussion by the Council, an organized discussion based upon committee recommendations. A polling of opinion by mail cannot serve as a substitute for such a discussion. Perhaps we can get a good many of the Council together in Washington.

I do not believe the Association should go into the business of publishing, except for its official journal. We are not staffed or equipped to publish works and to promote their sale. I do not think we should attempt to compete with scholarly publishers. We could, of course, encourage scholarly historical work by awarding prizes to manuscripts and perhaps by subsidizing their publication, as the American Historical Association has done and as the Mississippi Valley Historical Association is considering doing. But there should be a definitely formulated policy, arrived at by thoughtful consideration of committee recommendations.

The principles I have stated above are general ones that I think are valid and should apply before we publish anything other than the *Journal.* Everything that follows is *obiter dicta,* but I think I should also give my reasons for objection to our publishing the segregation decision papers.

I am proud of Jim Silver[2] for arranging the program where these papers were given. It was a fine session—the best we have ever had, I think. A great many of our members, though, would not agree. I heard several comment that it wasn't "history," it was "propaganda" or "crusading." I disagree with their prejudices, but I still have some tolerance for their engrained intolerance. Most of them have a lot of affection for the Association, even though they think it went astray on this occasion. I have hope for most of these people. They have already come a long way toward a recognition of simple justice. If we published these papers, though, we would be rubbing salt on some pretty sore hides. We would have to expect some nasty bickering in the future, and we should also anticipate a good many resignations from the Association. Having a program on an important Southern problem of current interest is one thing, and quite justifiable, I think; for the Association to publish the papers, which many don't regard as "history," is another.

I think we should be pretty wary of beginning something which might become an embarrassing "precedent." It's not likely to happen, but suppose that the next year, or the next, there were another similar session, equally dramatic, in which the speakers championed the popular Southern views on segregation. What justification would we have for refusing to publish these papers if we were urged to and if the "precedent" were thrown at us? It certainly wouldn't be an adequate answer to say: The Memphis speakers were "right," but these are "wrong." We would really be laying ourselves open to the "crusading" charge then.

Maybe what a lot of this boils down to is that I agree with Adlai[3] that "moderation" is a good word. Year in and year out Ben[4] and I—Ben much more than I, thank goodness—have to live with and get along with our members, petty and ornery as many of them are. When some of them get cantankerous, we're the ones who are apt to catch it in the neck. I like some controversy now and then to keep me awake, but I don't want it as a steady diet. Some of our members, I know, think I do some crusading too in the acceptance of articles for the *Journal* and in the choice of book reviewers, but I'm much more sure of my ground on those scores than I would be in defending the publication of the three Memphis papers.

Finally, any such publication as this would throw a heavy burden on Ben. He has enough Association business to do without having to promote, sell, and distribute something else. And he needs time to get his research and writing done.

I would like to see the papers published by a university press or a journal devoted to contemporary problems. But I strongly oppose their publication under the imprint or *for* the Association.[5]

Best regards! Hope to see you in Washington.

Sincerely
J. Merton England

[1]The addresses delivered by Faulkner, Benjamin E. Mays, and Cecil Sims at the meeting of the Southern Historical Association in Memphis, November 10, 1955.

[2]James W. Silver, history professor at the University of Mississippi, was program chairman for the Memphis meeting. A personal friend of Faulkner, he had arranged for Faulkner's appearance on the controversial program.

[3]Stevenson.

[4]Bennett H. Wall, Secretary-Treasurer of the Southern Historical Association.

[5]The pamphlet, *Three Views of the Segregation Decisions,* was published by the Southern Regional Council of the Southern Historical Association in late 1956. For additional details on the publication of the pamphlet, see Bell Wiley's letter to James Silver, January 20, 1956, printed below.

1199 Letter from Faulkner to Saxe Commins, undated [probably late November 1955], unsigned ribbon typescript, 1 page.

Dear Saxe:

I just found my copy of the enclosed.[1] If Manny[2] knows nothing about this, I cant imagine how it could have happened. The best idea seems to be Montadori's [*sic*][3] own: have Random House, with my acquiescence or authority, ask Brest what gives, and have him instruct Garzani[4] to do what we want. I myself never heard of Brest or Garzani either before this, and if Random House granted no rights, no rights obtain. Please see to it at once if you agree, cable Montadori in my name, chg to me, that the matter is in hand for solution.

Dorothy's concert went well, people still talk of it, she may have been a pioneer here for better music, familiarity with good music, etc., taking it out of the 'cissified' into the common, the dignified, the 'natural'.

Will you ask Mary or Miss Coomes[5] to phone Dunhill and ask if they have sent my repaired pipe to me here.

[no signature]

[1]Unidentified.

[2]Emmanuel Harper, Random House accountant.

[3]Alberto Mondadori was Faulkner's Italian publisher.

[4]Probably Livio Garzanti, who published the first Italian translations of *Soldiers' Pay* (1953) and *Sartoris* (1955).
[5]Random House secretaries.

1200 Letter from Faulkner to Saxe Commins, undated [probably December 1955], signed ribbon typescript, 1 page.

Dear Saxe:
Thank you for sending the Collins letter. No, I cant make a commencement address.[1] But yes, I will make the recording.[2] Will he wait until after the holidays, when I will know where I shall be, whether I will be here or come East. That is, if I cant come East before he leaves for Mexico, we will arrange to suit him.

All well here, Tempy, the horse, is jumping pretty well. I have a polo player's girdle to wear, and my back stands the work. She is rough as hell yet, jumps too quick and hard; I spend about half the time a foot in the air with no stirrups, but she will settle down and maybe I can show her in horse shows this summer.

Doing a little work on the next Snopes book. Have not taken fire in the old way yet, so it goes slow, but unless I am burned out, I will heat up soon and go right on with it. Miss. such an unhappy state to live in now, that I need something like a book to get lost in.

Love to Dorothy and the children.[3]

/s/ Bill

[1]Faulkner was being considered as a possible speaker for the commencement exercises at Harvard.
[2]Collins had requested that Faulkner tape a reading from his fiction for use on a radio broadcast.
[3]The last two paragraphs of this letter have been printed in *Selected Letters of William Faulkner,* p. 390.

1956

1208 Letter from Estelle Faulkner to Dorothy and Saxe Commins, "Jan. 5th," signed autograph manuscript, 2 pages, with envelope addressed in Mrs. Faulkner's hand and postmarked Charlottesville, January 7, 1956.

Dearest Dorothy and Saxe—
Do I seem an awful ingrate? I am *not,* and know, should you have been with me for the past few weeks, my forgiveness would be assured—

Never, have I received a gift that thrilled me more than the wonderful Picasso album, and, coming from you two, makes it doubly valuable—Please believe how very grateful and pleased I am, and be glad with me that the joy can be renewed, every time I pore over the pictures—

Bill, I'm sure, will write too—He is down on the Mississippi Gulf coast right now, and I seized the chance to run up here to be with Jill and Paul for a week or so—

Jill looks wonderfully well—is so happy and excited over the baby—and of course *I* am beside myself with anticipation also—

She and Paul have a charming little house—the guest house on a big Virginia estate—and is ideally ready for the baby to come along to complete things—

Vicki and her roommate from Pine Manor spent the Holidays with us, so of course my Christmas was delightful, even though Jill couldn't get South—

With Mama's illness, Mrs. Faulkner's convalescence and lack of servants at Rowan oak, I've been head over heels in activity—which was good for me, but until I arrived in Charlottesville last night, have had no leisure to write—

Dorothy, Oxford is still patting itself on the back for the opportunity they had hearing you play—Surely your ears burn frequently?

Wish I had the time (and money) to run up to see you in Princeton for a few days—It seems years since I have—Saxe, particularly—

Do write sometime—I love you *all* very dearly, and think about you and wish good things for you 'most every day of my life—

Jill joins me in sincere Happy New Year to you—

Always devotedly
Estelle

1209a Unfinished letter from Faulkner to "Mr [W. C.] Neill," dated "Oxford, Mississippi / Jan. 12, 1956," unsigned ribbon typescript, 1 page, canceled with red grease pencil.

Dear Mr Neill:

My copy of your letter to Congresswoman Green[1] was at hand when I reached home today.

Thank you for it, but I doubt if we can afford to waste even on Congress, let alone on one another, that wit which we will sorely need when again, for the second time in a hundred years, we Southerners will have wrecked and ruined our native land[2]

[1] Edith Green, U.S. representative from Oregon.

[2] A completed version of this same letter (see *Selected Letters,* p. 391) adds the phrase "just because of niggers." In the complete version "destroyed" is substituted for "wrecked and ruined."

This incomplete copy of the letter appears on the verso of page "15" of a typescript draft of "On Fear: The South in Labor: Mississippi." The key statement in the letter, "when again, for the second time in a hundred years, we Southerners will have wrecked and ruined our native land," appears, in slightly altered form, in that essay. A carbon copy of the unfinished letter (also in the Brodsky Collection) appears on the verso of page "14" of a typescript draft of "On Fear."

1198d Letter from Bell I. Wiley to James W. Silver, January 20, 1956, signed ribbon typescript, 1 page.

Dear Jim:

A letter from Edward Reed of the Fund for the Republic,[1] received today, states that the organization has appropriated $1,000 for publication of the segregation papers.[2] The Southern Regional Council, to whom the money will be paid, will publish the pamphlet with its imprimatur. An Atlanta firm will do the printing. The Fund proposes to give the SHA [Southern Historical Association] and the SRC 5,000 of the pamphlets for distribution and to reserve 5,000 for itself. It may give some of its own 5,000 to one or both the SHA, SRC, but this will be decided later. I should think that of the 5,000 given to the SRC, SHA, the SHA would get at least 2,000, and possibly 2,500, but these details will have to be worked out in consultation with the SRC. I don't know how we'll take care of Hoffman and his crowd or of extra needs that you may have. I should think that you might have a good chance of getting some of the Fund for the Republic's 5,000 if you'd write to Edward Reed, The Fund for the Republic, 60 East 42nd St., New York, 17, New York.

Reed writes that "Our Counsel points out that the reference to Richard Wright in Mr. Faulkner's talk (p. 4 on the typewritten script) is possibly libelous and should be omitted. I hope that you will be able to take this up with Mr. Faulkner and see that it is removed in the printed version of the talk." I don't know why no mention was made of the reference to Robeson, unless it be on the ground that Robeson is an avowed Communist (Is he?). Anyhow, I would appreciate your phoning Bill and see if he will agree to omitting the phrase "or Richard Wright" and writing me at your earliest convenience.[3]

Reed states that he'd like inclusion of a statement in the introduction acknowledging the underwriting of publication by the Fund for the Republic, which is okay by me, and he requests, but does not require, to see the proof, with a view to deciding what distribution the Fund for the Republic will make of its 5,000 copies.

Favorable action on this matter came as a distinct surprise to me, as I had concluded that the long delay meant negative action. I'm very happy that at last we can go ahead. I'll have to get to work and write members of the Council, and draft an introduction.

Cordially,
/s/ Bell
/t/ Bell Wiley

[1]This educational corporation was founded in 1952 "to defend and advance the principles of the Declaration of Independence, the Constitution, and the Bill of Rights." The organization, supported by an initial grant from the Ford Foundation, conducted seminars and adult education activities, participated in television programs, sponsored national and international conferences, and published books and pamphlets on various topics.

[2]The papers presented by Faulkner, Benjamin E. Mays, and Cecil Sims at the November 1955 meeting of the Southern Historical Association in Memphis.

[3]Faulkner did delete the phrase from the published version of his speech. The passage in question appears on page 149 of *Essays, Speeches & Public Letters.*

1211 Letter from Faulkner to Saxe Commins, "Friday" [January 1956], signed ribbon typescript, 1 page.

Dear Saxe:

The letter[1] about Mr Van Wyck Brook [*sic*] was probably on their letterhead; I recognise them and they get thrown into the waste basket without being opened. I imagine that's what happened to it. But I dont know anything to write about him. I didn't know him personally and never read anything he wrote. So there is nothing I can say, if you will be kind enough to decline for me. Also found yours about the Negro journalist.[2] Of course I will see him. I dont like any journalist but it is his trade, not his color, that I dont like.

All well here. The Snopes mss.[3] is going pretty good. I still have the feeling that I am written out though, and all remaining is the craftsmanship, no fire, force. My judgment might be extinct also, so I will go on with this until I know it is no good. I may even finish it without knowing it is bad, or admitting it at least.

Am planning on maybe coming up for a week about 1st February, dont know yet. Love to Dorothy and all.

/s/ Bill

[1]Unidentified.
[2]Possibly a reporter for *Ebony*. See Faulkner's letter to Commins, item 1246 below.
[3]*The Town*.

1212 Portion of letter from Faulkner to Editor, Memphis *Commercial Appeal,* undated [possibly January 1956], carbon typescript, 1 page, canceled with red grease pencil.

Dear Sir:

In the first half of the nineteenth century, before slavery was abolished by law in the United States, Thomas Jefferson and Abraham Lincoln both held that the Negro was not yet competent for equality.

That was more than ninety years ago though, and nobody can say whether their opinions would be different now or not.

But assume that they would not have changed their belief, and that their opinion is right. Assume that the Negro is still not competent for equality, which is something which neither he nor the white man knows until we try it.

But we do know that, with the support of the federal government, the Negro is going to gain the right to try and see if he is fit or not for equality. And if we cannot trust him with something as mild as equality, what are we going to do when he has power—the power of his own fifteen millions of unanimity backed by the federal government, which has compelled his right to test his capacity for equality, from those who are on record through the voice of the white citizens' councils that they will go to any length short of force, to stop him, when the only check on that power will be that federal government which is already his ally?

In 1849, Senator John C. Calhoun made his address in favor of secession if the Wilmot Proviso was ever adopted. On Oct. 12th of that year, Senator Jefferson Davis wrote a public letter to the South, saying: "The generation which[1]

[1]This portion (roughly the first half) of this letter, numbered page "1," appears on the verso of page "8" of a typescript draft of "On Fear: The South in Labor: Mississippi." A complete, revised version of this same letter has been published in Eileen Gregory, "Faulkner's Typescripts of *The Town,*" in *A Faulkner Miscellany,* p. 138.

The letter was never published in the *Commercial Appeal* and probably was not even mailed. Faulkner incorporated the letter, with only minor alterations in wording, into the "On Fear" essay.

1214b Letter from Phil Stone to Donald P. Duclos, February 9, 1956, carbon typescript with typed signature, 1 page.

Dear Mr. Duclos:

I have your letter of February 6.[1]

I don't doubt at all your sincerity in this matter but I have so much to do that I just don't have time to keep up with all the doings of the Falkners.

Bill's great-grandfather, W. C. Falkner, died either before my birth or in my childhood and I don't know much about him. By the way, Bill is the only descendant of the old man who was named after him: William Cuthbert Falkner.[2] We had most of the writings of old Colonel Falkner but they were burned when our old house burned in 1942, as were all but three of the autographed first edition author's copies of Bill's books that he always gives to me. I suggest that you write Judge J. W. T. Falkner here. He is Bill's uncle and probably knows more about the original old Colonel than anyone.

You are right in thinking that the old Colonel was a romantic figure but from conversations with the anti-Falkner group as well as with the Falkners I think the old man was probably a grasping, pushing stinker. Such a result is not unusual among the Falkners.

Yours truly,
Phil Stone

[1] Duclos had requested information concerning Faulkner's great-grandfather, Colonel W. C. Falkner.

[2] According to some sources, the old Colonel's middle name was Clark, not Cuthbert.

1230a Letter from Phil Stone to Clifton Fadiman, April 6, 1956, carbon typescript with typed signature, 2 pages.

Dear Mr. Fadiman:

I have been meaning for a long time to write you concerning your article on William Faulkner in your book "Party of One."

I disagree with many of your conclusions generally, but I just have to write you and congratulate on having the insight and the guts to proclaim that sometimes the Emperor does not have on any clothes. You may conclude that I am writing from a sour point of view. This is the reaction I provoke when I try to tell Bill's idolaters that, while Bill is probably the best writer of contemporary American fiction, he is being very much overrated. Of course their reaction to my dissent is silly because for twelve years I talked to deaf ears when I tried to tell people that he was being much underrated. Furthermore, I confess that I am human enough to enjoy saying "I told you so" to those people who turned deaf ears in those dark days.

I seldom get to New York but if and when I do I should like very much if you could find time for us to have a quiet afternoon conversation about Bill. By chance it happens that no one knows as much about the facts concerning him and his writing as I do because I labored with him for twelve years.

In the first place, Bill does not have a style. He has only a personal mannerism and to the Procrustean bed of this mannerism he fits his subject matter. In my opinion this is very much the reverse of sound aesthetics because, as many of us have said before, the style should grow out of the subject matter naturally. The same man who wrote "Lost Illusions" and "Cousin Bette" also wrote "The Lily of the Valley."[1] Also the same man who wrote "King Lear" and the "Falstaff" series of plays wrote "The Tempest." It is always true of the greatest in fiction that they fit their styles to the subject matter.

In the second place, Bill has no sense of overall design and has never written a novel. His novels are merely a collection of episodes.

In the third place, all but a few of his characters are mere puppets. They are, as he said of Popeye in "Sanctuary," like figures cut out of tin. They seldom are developed by what happens to them and come out at the end of the book almost exactly like they came in. This is certainly not true of Balzac, Thackeray, Fielding or Defoe.

You may wonder why, since Bill and I were so intimate so long, that I don't have more influence upon him now. In order to understand that you would have to know the tribe of Falkners. They are the most incredible people of whom you ever heard, and no Falkner will take any advice as long as he is successful.

Yours truly,
Phil Stone

[1] Honoré de Balzac.

1230b Letter from Clifton Fadiman to Phil Stone, April 11, 1956, signed autograph manuscript, 1 page.

Dear Mr. Stone:

Thank you for your most interesting letter, which has an authority that no analysis by an outsider, such as myself, could possibly have. The only part of your letter which is not clear to me is your estimate of Mr. Faulkner ("the best writer of contemporary American fiction") as contrasted with your three rather crushing judgments: (1) He has no style; (2) His novels are merely collections of episodes; (3) Most of his characters are puppets.

I rarely go into New York except by compulsion, but I know it would be pleasant for us to have a talk if it can be arranged. I should be happy to do so.

Sincerely
Clifton Fadiman

1230c Letter from Phil Stone to Clifton Fadiman, April 16, 1956, carbon typescript with typed signature, 1 page.

Dear Mr. Fadiman:

I have your letter of April 11 and was interested in hearing from you.

I would have to write you too long a letter to explain what I mean about Bill's work. Shortly, it is that I don't think the contemporary crop is very good compared to the old masters. The principal model I held up to Bill was Balzac although I realize that Balzac should now wear a new coat, but Bill did not follow this much. I don't like to quote myself because that is, to my mind, an indication of intellectual petrifaction, but I have not yet found a better description of Bill as a writer than my own: that he is entirely an extrovert writer.

I do hope that I shall get to New York some time and we shall have a chance to talk about it when I can make my meaning clearer. I am so busy with my own work that I don't have much time to write long letters.

I can understand your feeling about New York. I think it is a nice place to go to but not a nice place to stay.

I am sending copy of this letter to my son who is at Hotchkiss because he is interested and because Bill is one of his godfathers.

If and when I get to New York I shall take the liberty of telephoning you.

Yours truly,
Phil Stone

1243 Letter from Faulkner to Saxe Commins, undated [probably early June 1956], signed ribbon typescript, 1 page.

Dear Saxe:
This is about ⅓ of it.[1] Will be in Washington for president's conference 10-11-12,[2] may come on to NY after if necessary, or may return here until about 20th.
The committee business will interfere but I will keep at the mss. typing, cleaning it up, I hope to have it in by Dec. 1st, maybe sooner.

Title page: THE TOWN

next page like this:

VOLUME TWO

SNOPES

Dedication, 1st volume was to same Stone.

To Phil Stone

He did half of the laughing for thirty years.

I still cant tell, it may be trash except for certain parts, though I think not. I still think it is funny, and at the end very moving; two women characters I am proud of.

/s/ Bill

[1]The typescript of *The Town*.
[2]The "People-to-People" program initiated by President Dwight D. Eisenhower to improve international relations. Faulkner served as chairman of the Writers' Committee.

1246 Letter from Faulkner to Saxe Commins, "Saturday noon" [June 1956], ribbon typescript with typed signature, 1 page.

Dear Saxe:
Our horse is Fabius, but I am afraid I wont get the bet made, cant find the bookie.
Talked to Morrison, the EBONY reporter yesterday on phone, asked him to phone you Monday. His description of how they will use the picture of me and his author sounds all right: nothing about race: just a budding writer paying her respects to a veteran writer.[1] That's all right with me.
Will see you in July I imagine.

Bill

[1]No such photograph accompanied Faulkner's "If I Were a Negro," which appeared in the September 1956 issue of *Ebony*.

1247 Letter from President Dwight D. Eisenhower to Faulkner, "June [blank], 1956," ribbon typescript with typed signature, 1 page.

Dear Saxe:

This is about 1/3 of it. Will be in Washington for president's conference 10-11-12, may come on to NY after if necessary, or may return here until about 20th.

The sommittee business will inhtterfere but I will keep at the mss. typing, cleaning it up, I hope to have it all in by Dec. 1st, maybe sooner.

Title page: THE TOWN

next page likethis:

VOLUME TWO

SNOPES

Dedication, 1st vlkume was to same Stone.

To Phil Stone

He did half ofthe laughing for thirty years.

I still cant tell, it may be trash except for certain parts, though I think not. I still think it is funny, and at the end very moving; two women characters I am proud of.

Bill

34. Letter from Faulkner to Saxe Commins (item 1243)

Dear Mr. Faulkner:

I am writing to ask your help.

Our Government, as you know, has relatively modest apparatus for trying to make the United States' objectives and principles better understood throughout the world. I have asked Congress for additional funds to strengthen this activity during fiscal '57.

But, clearly, there will never be enough diplomats and information officers at work in the world to get the job done without help from the rest of us. Indeed, if our American ideology is eventually to win out in the great struggle being waged between the two opposing ways of life, it must have the active support of thousands of independent private groups and institutions and of millions of individual Americans acting through person-to-person communication in foreign lands.

Secretary Dulles[1] and Mr. Theodore C. Streibert, Director of the U.S. Information Agency, join me in this conviction that there is something important which every U.S. citizen—man, woman and child—can do to help make the truth of our peaceful goals and of our respect for the rights of others known to more people overseas.

In a very real sense, to be successful we must wage peace with all the vigor and resourcefulness and universal participation of wartime.

It is my intention to call upon all U.S. citizens to help their Government in this task; but before doing so I would like to bring together at the White House a group of distinguished American leaders to assist with the organization of various phases of the work. I earnestly hope, therefore, that it will be possible for you to participate as one of these leaders and assume the chairmanship for writers' activities.

In accepting this appointment, you will be undertaking an assignment demanding of some time and effort on your part to make it successful. But it is patriotic work and work which I am convinced is of vital importance to our national interest. I seek your help confident that you will be able to impress this fact upon leading authors throughout the country and convince them that by taking part in creating understanding abroad they will contribute to lessening world tensions and to helping solve our problems.

With kindest personal wishes,

Sincerely,
Dwight D. Eisenhower

[1] Secretary of State John Foster Dulles.

1249 Western Union telegram from Faulkner to Saxe Commins, August 25, 1956.

NO RICH NOW PREFER PAY LOOK FIVE G NOT TO[1] FINISHED BOOK TODAY[2] WILL BREAK THE HEART THOUGHT IT WAS JUST FUNNY BUT WAS WRONG

BILL

[1] *Look* magazine had offered $5,000 for a picture story on Faulkner.
[2] *The Town.*

1254 Note from Faulkner to Saxe Commins, undated [possibly late September or early October 1956], signed autograph manuscript, 1 page.

Saxe—

I have the mss. with me. May come in later.[1] If not, will see you tomorrow.

Bill

[1]Apparently Faulkner left this note for Commins at his Random House office.

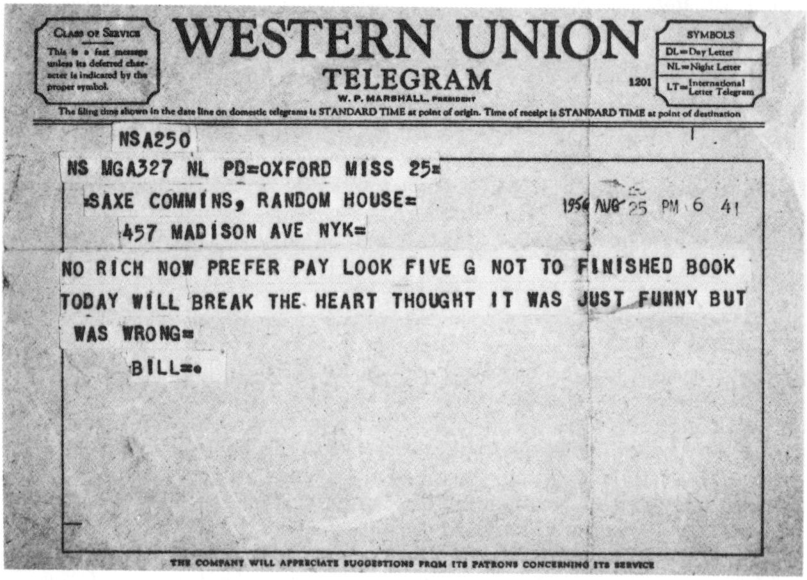

CLASS OF SERVICE
This is a fast message unless its deferred character is indicated by the proper symbol.

WESTERN UNION
TELEGRAM
W. P. MARSHALL, PRESIDENT
1201

SYMBOLS
DL=Day Letter
NL=Night Letter
LT=International Letter Telegram

The filing time shown in the date line on domestic telegrams is STANDARD TIME at point of origin. Time of receipt is STANDARD TIME at point of destination

NSA250

NS MGA327 NL PD=OXFORD MISS 25=

=SAXE COMMINS, RANDOM HOUSE=

457 MADISON AVE NYK=

1956 AUG 25 PM 6 41

NO RICH NOW PREFER PAY LOOK FIVE G NOT TO FINISHED BOOK TODAY WILL BREAK THE HEART THOUGHT IT WAS JUST FUNNY BUT WAS WRONG=

BILL=

THE COMPANY WILL APPRECIATE SUGGESTIONS FROM ITS PATRONS CONCERNING ITS SERVICE

35. Telegram from Faulkner to Saxe Commins regarding *The Town* (item 1249)

S-41 Letter from Faulkner to Van Wyck Brooks, undated [late September 1956], mimeographed typescript with imitation signature by proxy, 1 page.

Dear Mr Brooks[1]

The President has asked me to organize writers to see what we can do to give a true picture of our country to other people.

Will you join such an organization?

Pending a convenient meeting, will you send to me in a sentence, or a paragraph, or a page, or as many more as you like, your private idea of what might further this project?

I am enclosing my own ideas as a sample.

1. Anesthetize, for one year, American vocal chords.
2. Abolish, for one year, American passports.
3. Commandeer every American automobile. Secrete Johnson grass seed in the cushions and every other available place. Fill the tanks with gasoline. Leave the switch key in the switch and push the car across the iron curtain.
4. Ask the Government to establish a fund. Choose 10,000 people between 18 and 30, preferably Communists. Bring them to this country and let them see America as it is. Let them buy an automobile on the installment plan, if that's what they want. Find them jobs in labor as we run our labor unions. Let them enjoy the right to say whatever they wish about anyone they wish, to go

to the corner drug store for ice cream and all the other privileges of this country which we take for granted. At the end of the year they must go home. Any installment plan automobiles or gadgets which they have undertaken would be impounded. They can have them again if and when they return or their equity in them will go as a down payment on a new model. This is to be done each year at the rate of 10,000 new people.

Will you please communicate either with me or Harvey Breit who has accepted the chore of being a co-chairman?

Yours very truly,
/s/ William Faulkner
/t/ William Faulkner

P.S. In a more serious vein, please read the enclosed one-page description of Mr. Eisenhower's purpose.

[1] Brooks was only one of a number of writers to whom this mimeographed form letter was mailed. The text is Faulkner's, though the letters were mimeographed (with a hand-copied Faulkner signature) and mailed under the direction of Harvey Breit and Jean Ennis (a Random House secretary), who assisted Faulkner with the People-to-People project.

For a survey of Faulkner's official correspondence on behalf of the Writers' Committee of the People-to-People Program (and the inauthentic signatures appearing on all such letters), see Joan St. C. Crane, "A William Faulkner 'Machine' Signature," *American Book Collector,* 2 (July–August 1981), 13–14.

S-42 Letter from Faulkner to W. S. Merwin, October 1, 1956, typescript with mechanically produced signature, 1 page. On Random House letterhead paper.

Dear Mr. Merwin[1]:

Since it will be difficult for a quorum of us[2] ever to get together for a meeting and since we will all like it better if one meeting can accomplish our purpose as soon as possible let us set a tentative date for that meeting for October 9th. In the meantime if you will send in to Mr. Harvey Breit, THE NEW YORK TIMES 229 West 43rd Street, New York 36, New York, or Miss Jean Ennis, Random House 457 Madison Avenue, New York 22, New York, or me, in writing, a synopsis or any idea or ideas you have on which we can base a program for our purpose, Miss Ennis, Mr. Breit and I could go over the suggestions and do the collaborating on such preliminary spadework so that when we can call our meeting for approximately October 9th we can get the most done.

If you agree with this and will send in your synopsis or idea we can then make our definite announcement of a date for a meeting in October which will be convenient to most of us.

President Eisenhower is anxious to have a report of our intentions as soon as possible, which is the reason for this tentative date for our meeting.

Yours sincerely,
/s/ William Faulkner
/t/ William Faulkner

[1] Merwin was one of a number of authors to whom this form letter was mailed. The Brodsky Collection also contains the copy of this same letter which was mailed to Van Wyck Brooks.

Like the other Faulkner letters regarding the People-to-People Program, this one contains an inauthentic signature.

[2] The Writers' Committee.

S-43 Letter from Faulkner to W. S. Merwin, October 11, 1956, typescript with mechanically produced signature, 1 page. On Random House letterhead paper.

Dear Mr. Merwin[1]:

It has been suggested that you cannot deal people-to-people through the Iron Curtain, but must deal with a government.

I think we are all agreed that this is a self-evident fact.

The whole purpose of this committee is that this is a self-evident fact.

Which do you think the more important?

1. The aim of this project, even though unattainable?____
2. The risk that the project itself might be used as a political catspaw?____

Our correspondents have sent in the following suggestions. Will you rate these suggestions as follows: 1) Excellent 2) Good 3) Poor 4) No. Please check the attached list and send it back to me.

I think we are all of one mind that there is no need in calling a meeting until we are agreed on what we are going to do in it.

Sincerely,
/s/ William Faulkner
/t/ William Faulkner

[1] Again, this form letter was mailed to various writers. The copy mailed to Van Wyck Brooks is also in the Brodsky Collection.

S-44 Letter from 'Bama F. McLean to Robert Daniel, undated [mid-October 1956], signed autograph manuscript, 1 page.

Dear Mr. Daniel—

It was a real disappointment not to see you this summer, & I welcomed your letter of Oct 9th, & but for being confined to my bed with a severe attack of lumbago, I would have responded more promptly—

Now—my father's name was W. C. Falkner—the "C" stood for Cuthbert,[1] according to family records—the "W" for William—Yes, I have the last printing of the "White Rose"[2] & I agree with your opinion of Robert Cantwell's introduction—William Faulkner has become a literary measuring stick! I find so many references to him in magazines—newspapers etc, when writers are speaking of present writers, & will say "He writes like Faulkner" perhaps or "he does not write like Faulkner."

I dont know whether I justify my use of "Faulkner's being a measuring stick," or not, but if my letter seems confused, remember I am in bed, writing from a cramped position—

I enclose a newspaper clipping concerning late news of William—I think he will enjoy going up to Va—as his only child lives on a farm, "Fox Haven Farm," near Charlottesville, & Jill has a baby a month or so old—a boy—& Billie adores this grand-son—hadn't heard he was having back trouble—

. . . .

Robert, I'd like to write more but my cramped position must be relieved—
So a reluctant Au Revoir

Fondly
Bama F McLean

[1] As noted previously, this middle name is a matter of dispute. Blotner records the name as William Clark Falkner (see *Faulkner: A Biography*, p. 9).

[2] *The White Rose of Memphis: A Novel* by W. C. Falkner, originally published in 1881, was reissued in 1953 with an introduction by Robert Cantwell.

1191 Letter from Estelle Faulkner to Saxe Commins, "Oct. 30th" [probably 1956], signed autograph manuscript, 2 pages.

Dearest Saxe—

As always, you were sweet to bother with Dot's[1] jingles—Don't think she will be disappointed, as she rather fancies herself as a serious writer, and did these rhymes principally for Malcolm's little boy—

Dot does write well, but have no idea that her subject matter is interesting enough to attract attention—or favorable comment—That remains to be seen—

I *do* thank you, and please say to Miss Bonino that I'm grateful for her trouble, too—

Bill tells me that he is going back to New York very soon now, and will attend to the material for Dorothy—How wonderfully unselfish she is to do all this for Jill and baby Paul!—*I* am overwhelmed by her generosity—

Have been so busy since we've been home—both inside the house and working in the grounds too—have had lots of on-the-spur-of-the-moment entertaining—*Remember,* you and Dorothy are coming down for one quiet visit—you promised us that, and I fully intend holding you to it—

Sometime when I can find the leisure, I'll write a proper letter to you both—Pappy is impatiently waiting for me to go downtown right now—

Love and more thank-yous
Always devotedly
Estelle

[1] Dorothy Oldham, Mrs. Faulkner's sister.

1262 Letter from Estelle Faulkner to Saxe Commins, dated "Oxford—Nov. 5th," signed autograph manuscript, 3 pages, with envelope addressed in Mrs. Faulkner's hand and postmarked Oxford, November 5, 1956.

Dear Saxe,

Here is the letter I've intended writing for some time—

I am sorry not to have been able to tell you about things—but both my visits to New York this fall were on the spur of the moment—as it were—and I had no time to get in touch with you to arrange for a quiet talk—

You must have been aware in the past, (or maybe Bill told you) that I drank a lot at times—in fact a most unpleasant, unpredictable, alcoholic I was—Especially, when I got upset over unfortunate occurrences etc—drink seemed to me an ideal escape—

I still don't know just *when* it became a *necessity* beyond my personal feelings, to stop drinking—but I got in touch with Alcoholics Anonymous in Memphis, and by the grace of God, and A.A.—I stopped—short, and have reason to believe, for good—

All last fall, winter, and into the spring when she died,[1] I spent every available moment with my mother—It was a strain, because I loved Mama dearly, and it's hard to see one's Mother die and be powerless to prevent it, or even do anything to prevent its inevitable suffering—

Jill was pregnant too—I was concerned over her health and was forced by circumstance to stay in Oxford, except for a short visit to Jilly in January—

The week after Mama was buried, Bill started on his drinking bout that very nearly ended in disaster[2]—You know about this, of course—

The first afternoon of his heavy drinking Bill and I took a long drive—We drove to the Lake[3] for him to see about an anchorage for our sail-boat, then on around the reservoir through Harmontown—back home—

It was on this drive that Bill told me about his affair with Miss Stein—Since then he has not mentioned it to me—nor I to him—

I am telling you all this, Saxe, to let you see for yourself that I *have* changed—With all the adversity of the last eighteen months—heart-ache and sorrow, I haven't had one drink and feel capable of dealing with whatever comes with some poise and dignity—Two years ago—I couldn't have—

I know, as you must, that Bill feels some sort of compulsion to be attached to some young woman at all times—it's Bill—At long last I am sensible enough to concede him the right to do as he pleases, and without recrimination—It is not that I don't care—(I wish it were not so)—but all of a sudden [I] feel sorry for him—wish he could know without words between us, that it's not very important after all—

The only possible fear I have is, that Jill might hear of this attachment—She adores Bill, is a puritanical little monogamist, and was so hurt by the Joan affair—I pray Bill will think of that and be discreet this time—

Actually, Bill and I have lived more amicably, and with better understanding the past year than ever before—

Perhaps it's because of my changed values, or because Bill feels better, having seen that I'm not upset over Miss Stein—

You might tell me sometime what *you* think—

Thank you for reading all this—it is what I wanted to tell you in Bennett's[4] office—and couldn't—

With a heart full of love to you and Dorothy

Always devotedly
Estelle

[1] Lida Oldham died on March 10, 1956.

[2] Faulkner collapsed on March 18 and was rushed to the Baptist Memorial Hospital in Memphis for emergency treatment.

[3] Sardis Lake, twenty miles west of Oxford.

[4] Bennett Cerf.

1263 Letter from Maud Falkner to James W. Silver, November 16 [1956], signed autograph manuscript, 1 page.

Dear Dr. Silver—

My ink has vanished, my refill has run dry, still I must tell you how so delighted I am that you sent me a copy, autographed, of your book.[1] I enjoyed it immensely—inscription and all—it fitted in perfectly with what I had been reading all summer.

Congratulations on an absorbing book.

Sincerely
Maud Falkner

[1] Unidentified.

S-45 Letter from Faulkner to Van Wyck Brooks, November 20, 1956, typescript with mechanically produced signature, 1 page. On The-People-to-People Program letterhead paper.

Dear Mr. Brooks[1]:

With regard to the President's proposal for a People-to-People Program, we have now gone over the material—both letters and filled-in questionnaires—that fifty-seven writers have been cooperative enough to send in. The suggestions are, of course, varied, but we believe that most of them fall into one of the following categories:

1. The idea of exchange—of books, periodicals and people.

2. The relaxation of governmental controls—such as the McCarran Act, passport and visa regulations, etc.

3. Miscellaneous—ranging from the freeing of Ezra Pound to a sounder foreign policy.

Now we would all agree that any exchange of books and ideas is to be encouraged and improved and intensified. But that is part of an old pattern. There are already government agencies busily doing that, not to mention the fact that all of us writers spend our lives doing that very thing, and so we can't very well do more than we have done.

We are looking for a new pattern, which should be not to export America, but to import representatives of the people who don't like us into America—to bring their families and children and live and work as American families do; let them and their children see how we live and what it is in our country which makes us, anyway, prefer it.

We would like to discuss this idea and ways and means of implementing it. Would you be willing to devote, say, one hour of a two-hour meeting to this main topic? We would then reserve the second hour for a discussion of other ideas. We are calling such a meeting for Thursday, November 29, from 4 to 6 p.m., at Harvey Breit's home, 116 East 64th Street, New York City.

Will you let us know if you would like to come, and whether you can?[2]

Sincerely yours,
/s/ William Faulkner
/t/ William Faulkner

[1] Brooks was only one of various writers who received this form letter, the text of which was actually written by Harvey Breit (see Blotner, *Faulkner: A Biography,* p. 1622).

[2] Brooks did not attend the meeting.

1264a Letter from Linton Massey to James W. Silver, November 26, 1956, signed ribbon typescript, 1 page.

Dear Dr. Silver:

Through the kindness of Bell Wiley I received some time ago a copy of THE SEGREGATION DECISIONS containing the paper read by William Faulkner at the meeting of the Southern Historical Association in Memphis over a year ago.

As a collector of the works of Faulkner since 1931 I have acquired material that occupies some twenty five feet of shelf space. I am naturally interested in acquiring the original of the paper mentioned above, which I have been informed is in your hands. Ed Younger says you might sell, or you might not. If you will, then I hope you will allow me to negotiate for its purchase.

Sincerely yours,
/s/ Linton Massey
/t/ Linton Massey

1264b Letter from James W. Silver to Linton Massey, December 2, 1956, carbon typescript with typed signature, 1 page.

Dear Mr. Massey:

I'll have to admit that I was rather intrigued with your letter of November 26, as well as with the enigmatic statement of Ed Younger.

Your inquiry poses something of a problem and right now I don't know what the answer is. Bill Faulkner and his family have been close personal friends of ours for almost twenty years. I'm not in love with the only Faulkner "manuscript" that I possess but I rather doubt the propriety of selling it. My wife turned down an offer of a rather large sum of money for an article on Faulkner "from a woman's point of view," and she says that I must not sell this. I'm inclined to agree with her.

Mr. Faulkner gave me the manuscript, an original, which he typed himself, about ten days before his appearance in Memphis. Before he made the talk he changed a considerable part of it—at the beginning—and then in December, about three weeks after the talk, he corrected my copy himself. I don't quite understand it but one of the seven or eight pages is a carbon. The rest is original, with his misspellings, words crossed out, etc. There is none of his handwriting on it. He also typed out for me on a sheet of yellow paper, the three short paragraphs which Bell Wiley added to his talk when it was printed. I have that, too, and I consider it one of the most powerful short statements Faulkner has ever made.

I'm not sure as to why I'm writing all this, except that you are interested in Faulkner. I have been tempted many times to write down an objective account of what I know of the man, but it would have to be something that could not be opened until after the principals were gone, and the size of that kind of job has scared me off. But I'm sure that no one will ever know the real Faulkner.

I'll keep your letter here and in time may write you about your offer again. Right now I don't think that I could do this and keep peace in the house.

Sincerely,
James W. Silver

1264c Letter from Linton Massey to James W. Silver, December 5, 1956, signed ribbon typescript, 1 page.

Dear Dr. Silver:

It was good of you to write me with reference to the Faulkner manuscript you own; and I certainly do not plan to burden you [with] endless appeals respecting its possible sale. At the same time I hope you will allow me a chance at it if ever you decide to part with it. As I remarked to you, I have been collecting Faulkner for a long time, with the market all in my favor up to the Nobel Prize award after which everybody wanted to get into the act. Were you to sell now you would come in at the top; when authors die they tend to fall out of fashion among collectors, with a consequent drop in the value of their first editions and manuscripts.

As a fair guess, judging from your description of your material, I should estimate its *retail* value at $100 to $125. at the present time. I paid $150. for a five page *holograph* mss. just a year or two ago.

I saw Ed Younger at a cocktail party last Saturday, one given for the Trinity College Fellow, Peter Laslett, whom you may remember; and Ed mentioned the fact that he would be seeing you shortly. His remark as reported in my letter was meant to be taken literally, for he truly did not know whether you would sell, now or ever.

In the meantime, please accept my sincere thanks for your very interesting letter. I am most grateful for your friendly note.

Cordially,
/s/ Linton Massey
/t/ Linton Massey

1268 Letter from Faulkner to Saxe Commins, "Monday" [probably December 10, 1956], signed ribbon typescript with holograph insertions, 1 page.

Dear Saxe:

I would make no change in the letter,[1] nor attempt to rectify anything except a glaring untruth, even if I needed to. To change a written statement is to become a censor, and any censor is a dictator, or wants to be.

I would suggest that, as soon as Miss Ennis has an answer from everybody, she notify me and send me any further comments like mine above, and I will send my copy of the letter, with the comments, in a covering personal letter to the President of the United States, whose committee we are.

Then I dont know what more we can do. Though as loyal citizens and cognizant by our craft of world conditions, he himself already knows he has only to call on us further.

Yours
/s/ Bill

[1]The summary report of the Writers' Committee of the People-to-People Program. Commins had drafted a copy of the report, issued the following month over the signatures of Faulkner, John Steinbeck, and Donald Hall.

1269 Letter from Faulkner to Saxe Commins, "Friday" [probably December 28, 1956], signed ribbon typescript, 1 page.

Dear Saxe:

The galleys[1] went back to you Wednesday. The signed pages today. I signed and numbered 450, signed 25 extra ones. Is that enough extra ones?

All well here, a pleasant Xmas, though I dont feel too good myself, may have to go back on my last spring's baby pap diet again. I dont know what is wrong with me, but something is.

Love to Dorothy.

/s/ Bill

[1]*The Town.*

1273 Western Union telegram from Faulkner to James W. Silver, c. 1956. From New York.

HAVE HEARD NOTHING. DID MALCOLM ACCEPT JACKSON? WIRE COLLECT YES OR NO. WRITE DETAILS. PLEASE CONTACT ESTELLE AND GET SAILBOAT SAILS MEASURE FRONT SNAP EDGE OF SMALL SAIL AND WRITE ME HOW MANY FEET. WANT TO BUY ANOTHER SAIL TO FIT THIS MEASUREMENT. SAXE AND DOROTHY SEND LOVE TO EVERYBODY. SAXE ALSO ANXIOUS ABOUT BUDDY

BILL FAULKNER

36. Saxe Commins at Random House, 1957

1957

S-46 Letter from Faulkner to Van Wyck Brooks, January 2, 1957, typescript with mechanically produced signature, 1 page. On The-People-to-People Program letterhead paper.

Dear Mr. Brooks[1]:

This is a distillate of the discussion held November 29 with the proposals which we will send to the President.[2]

Do you agree to this? Please let us know.

Sincerely,
/s/ William Faulkner
/t/ William Faulkner

[1] Brooks was only one of a number of writers to whom this form letter was sent.

[2] Accompanying this letter was a two-page summary report of the Writers' Committee meeting.

1292 Letter from Faulkner to Saxe Commins, "Wednesday," signed ribbon typescript, 1 page, with envelope addressed in Faulkner's hand and postmarked Oxford, January 23, 1957.

Dear Saxe:

While I was in NY for the meeting Nov. 29th,[1] a long distance call, A. B. Stein, New York, to Mrs Wm Faulkner, came. Stein said "I am no kin to her, but for $500.00 I can tell you something about a Miss Stein and your husband."

Estelle said she knew about Miss Stein and hung up. She was startled, off balance, because, for all our faults, people here in the south dont do things like that: ring the telephone of strangers with such intent to alarm, annoy. He also said he did not know me, but had seen me.

That was between 4 and 5 oclock, our time, in the middle of the week. Since then, he has called her three more times, same hour, which will be between 5 and 6 there, and when I am always away from home, usually hunting. He has not mentioned money again. In the second call he said, "Mr Faulkner will be in New York in February. I am going to Florida then, and will stop in to see you on the way."

As I say, Estelle is not used to this sort of thing, is too startled and frightened to have presence of mind to ask his address. I am not here at the time, and I imagine he would either hang up, not talk to me at all, or lie.

One week when he did not call, the same New York call came from a man who called himself Guernsey Smith, to Estelle, Mrs F., never to me, who wanted to know if she was going to Virginia[2] with me. She ends these calls as soon as shc can, but as I say, she has no such experience, is alarmed and frightened, with no presence of mind to try to find out who it is.

The last call came at a little after 4 p.m. yesterday, Jan 22. She refused to accept it. I must know who this is and stop it. Please go to the police, or get a private investigator if you can, and have this number traced. There cant be so many calls to Mrs Wm F. Oxford, Miss, put in at between 5 and 6 p.m. your time, on Jan. 22, that there may not be a record. Do anything you can, I will pay, find who this is and when I come up Feb 4th. I will attend to him.

Let me hear from you. If another call comes and I am away and cant take it myself, Estelle will try to get more detail. This is an outrage, persecution, not of me but of Estelle.

/s/ Bill

[1]The Writers' Committee of the People-to-People Program.

[2]Faulkner had accepted an appointment as Writer-in-Residence at the University of Virginia.

1293c Letter from Alexander D. Wainwright, Princeton University librarian, to Saxe Commins, February 12, 1957, signed ribbon typescript, 1 page.

Dear Mr. Commins:

Yesterday I helped to dismount the Pulitzer Prize exhibition, and I brought back the manuscript of *A Fable*. I understand from Jim Meriwether that we are to hold it here since it is to be included in the Faulkner Exhibition.

I would like again to thank you for lending it to the Grolier Club. I know that the courtesy of the loan was greatly appreciated.

Very sincerely yours,
/s/ Alexander D. Wainwright
/t/ Alexander D. Wainwright

1296 Letter from Estelle Faulkner to Dorothy and Saxe Commins, "Friday—15th Feb.," signed autograph manuscript, 3 pages, with envelope addressed in Mrs. Faulkner's hand and postmarked Charlottesville, February 18, 1957.

Dearest Dorothy and Saxe—

This must be a joint letter, but you two blessed people are so attuned, am sure you won't mind.

First of all, my heartfelt gratitude to Saxe for looking after poor Bill[1]—I am distressed beyond measure by two emotional upheavals ending in sprees, in such a short time—and can't help but believe that Bill has reached the breaking point with me—

I have offered him a divorce, and think after our stay here in Charlottesville he will see the wisdom of such a step—

Bill admits he wants freedom, but evidently realizes that he actually has it, for he will not even discuss divorce—now—

I would like to be free, not from Bill, for once I love it's forever—but from the utterly false, undignified position I've occupied the past six years—

I am tired of being the poor deceived wife in the background—to his loves, that is—Actually Bill has told me, in his cups, about his affairs, and I've tried very hard to rationalize my reactions and see *his* way as a *necessity*—and forget it all—

With Joan, it was difficult, because Bill insisted upon bringing her into our home, and flaunting her in our faces—even Jill's—

This time, Bill has had the good taste to (or so I thought until recently) keep his affair with Miss Stein secret, or at least, discreet—

Since those unfortunate telephone calls began—I now know that probably everyone in New York knows about them, and far from being the abstraction it was for months, has become very real—

As you see by now—with me, it is not a question of a hurt heart, but of an affront to that little dignity I've been able to salvage—In short, I'm sick of it all, and would welcome a clean decisive end—

Bill and I are both looking forward to a visit from you all—in fact I can hardly wait—and solemnly promise that you will find only pleasantness and love awaiting you—

I refuse to tear myself to pieces emotionally over things, people and circumstances over which I have no control—but realize how unwise I am at times and want, and earnestly seek, your advice—I have great faith in you both!

When you come down I can thank you properly for the Christmas gift—I was completely captivated with the beautiful book—and certainly blessed the unknown donor—never dreaming *you* sent it—

Really though, I should have known—shouldn't I? Such thoughtfulness, such taste, could only have come from the Commins!

Dorothy, take good care of Saxe, and you both run on down to Virginia for a wonderful, intimate visit—

And thank you for reading and putting up with such a letter—

Love and congratulations to Frannie and Bill—

Love, Love, Love to you
Always devotedly
Estelle

[1]Commins had nursed Faulkner through a siege of alcoholism at the Hotel Berkshire in New York, February 5–8, 1957.

1293d Letter from Phil Stone to James B. Meriwether, February 19, 1957, carbon typescript with typed signature, 4 pages.

Dear Jim:

Pardon me for not having answered sooner your letter of February 11[1] but I am so swamped with work, more so than I have ever been in my whole life, that I am as they said in "Alice in Wonderland": just running at breakneck speed and staying in the same place.

. . . .

With reference to *The Marble Faun,* I find that I do have another copy, besides the two that I am saving for Philip and Araminta, but the dust jacket is gone and this copy is not in good shape. When I get the letter from the man who is to write me about sending these things I shall send this copy along. For some reason it seems to be the only one that was not autographed by Bill. I am sure that Mr. Commins can get Bill to autograph it if you want that done. Personally, I am not going to ask Bill to do anything. When it comes, if the Princeton Library would like to buy it at the price of $140 it can do so because I gave one to the Yale Library, my own Alma Mater, and because you tell me that Harvard has one. I shall be glad to lend this for the exhibit and have it returned to me to keep so please don't let the Princeton Library feel that it is under any obligation to buy this.

When I send it I shall send the manuscript of *The Hamlet* which Bill gave to Philip, his godson, and also the manuscript of a story which he gave Philip and inscribed to him.[2] Of course I would not lose these for anything on earth. You may remember that I told you that I had a stack of stuff, letters and original manuscripts, about six feet high, which I was keeping for Jill and which burned when our old house burned in 1942. I thank you for the photostat from the Times-Picayune and shall keep it. I had the originals of all of these at home but they also were burned.

It is news to me that *The Town* was dedicated to me. Bill did offer to let me have the manuscript to read but, as I told him, for about three years I have never had time to read anything but law books and maybe the daily paper, and I did not know how long it would take me to complete the manuscript. I don't have the original manuscript of *The Hamlet* and the things I have listed are just about the only things I have since all but three of the autographed first edition author's copies, books that Bill has given me each time one came out, were burned.

Bill has told so many romantic stories about his career that I hardly think I would be popular there in revising some of them to fit the actual facts, especially as I know better than anyone else that the idol not only has feet of clay but sometimes has a head of clay.

Just when the Snopes idea was first propounded I cannot tell you except that it was some time in the 20's and before *Sartoris* was written. The idea was mine, as were a great number of the incidents, but I think Bill invented the name. The name had no connection with the Scopes trial.[3] The core of the Snopes legend was an idea I gave Bill back in the 20's, after *Mosquitoes* was written and before *Sartoris* was written and it was, as you know, that the real revolution in the South was not the race situation but the rise of the redneck, who did not have any of the scruples of the old aristocracy, to places of power and wealth. As to the stories, I don't know and can't remember now which of those were a part of the Snopes legend. Some of them were and Bill once wrote fifteen or twenty pages on the idea of the Snopes trilogy which he entitled "Father Abraham" but I think that has disappeared.[4] Of course I am interested in the Snopes legend because the most important thing I ever did for Bill was to give him a sense of humor. Contrary to the opinion formerly held and as I told you when you were here, actually I never wrote a line of Bill's books. I simply listened to the manuscripts he read, suggested changes and furnished him with a number of characters and incidents.

As to the French symbolist poets, Bill read a good many of them that I had, some in the original and most in translation, and I think they had some influence upon his own verse. As to facts, Carvel Collins is just about as accurate as anybody.

I did have a number of letters and manuscripts of Bill, as I told you before, that burned.

It is amusing to me how people now overrate Bill just as they so consistently underrated him for years. I think Bill is the best of the contemporary lot but I also think that his final rating will be one of the best second-rate writers of fiction in English literature.

I don't see much of him these days because he very obviously does not care for my company and I don't know anything that suits me better. To put it mildly, my friend of former years has let the Nobel Prize greatly exaggerate his idea of his own importance and wisdom. This is also ironical since few people stop to think that Bill got the Nobel Prize for nothing he had written after 1940 and it would not surprise me if he did not play out entirely as a writer.

There are two recent incidents that may amuse you. Last fall there was visiting here a Jewish woman from Long Island who was born and brought up here in Oxford and who used to go with us to our parties when we were young people. You can understand that because you know how little prejudice against Jews there is in the South. Estelle invited Emily and myself over to have supper with Florrie, her hostess and some other old friends of Florrie from Memphis. Bill acts so insufferably that I first decided not to go at all but I changed my mind because I was afraid Florrie would think that I did not care to see her. So we went. Bill fixed the drinks all right but acted like a lump on a log as he usually does and exerted himself in no other way to entertain his guests. During the conversation about old times Florrie asked Bill if a certain lady who used to live here was the prototype of a certain character in one of Bill's stories. Bill leaned back and said in his most Olympian manner that the lady was not, that he, Bill, could invent much more interesting people than God ever made. Emily said if it hadn't been in Bill's house, she would have murmured "Poor God." I told her I would have added: "He done the best He knowed how."

The incident is amusing for another reason which is that almost all the characters Bill has used in his books were invented by me and not by Bill.

The other day a lady who is teaching at the University asked Bill to come and talk to one of her classes, but he informed her loftily that he never did that sort of thing. When she reminded him he was going to Virginia to do very much the same thing, Bill replied that when he made a public appearance he always wanted to do that in a time of crisis when he could do some good. When I see Bill again I think I shall ask him to be sure to appoint a deputy and give us the deputy's name and address so when he, Bill, got on one of his two-weeks' drunks the whole world would not fall to pieces for lack of management. The arrogance and egotism of these Falkners is incredible. Even more incredible is their success with it. Pope said that fools rush in where angels fear to tread,[5] but Falkners rush in where fools fear to tread and usually get away with it.

We have lots of things to tell you but this letter has already been too long. I don't know what Philip will do when he gets through college and am going to let him do what he wants to do. I can understand you and Mrs. Meriwether wanting to come back South, and you know how many Yankees are coming first because of the race situation up there. That situation is quite pleasant in Mississippi.

I hope we shall see you and her both before long so we can have another enjoyable visit laughing about how ridiculous are the ideas of the South that are held by most people out of the South.

Your friend,
Phil Stone

P.S.: I forgot to tell you that I have promised Philip that I will, if possible, go up to Hotchkiss in May and talk about Bill to the English classes there. I don't know that I shall be able to do this but if I shall be able to do only one of these two things I shall have to give Philip preference over Princeton.

[1] Meriwether had addressed several questions to Stone concerning the Faulkner materials to be displayed in the upcoming exhibit.

[2] "The Wishing Tree."

[3] The famous court contest in 1925 in which John T. Scopes, a Tennessee science teacher, was tried for having taught the doctrine of evolution in his classes.

[4] This manuscript was acquired in 1953 by the New York Public Library from a bookdealer and was published, with an introduction by Meriwether, for the library by Red Ozier Press in 1983.

[5] Alexander Pope, "An Essay on Criticism," line 625.

1297 Letter from Faulkner to Saxe Commins, "Thursday" [February 1957], signed ribbon typescript, 1 page.

Dear Saxe:

We are mighty glad you and Dorothy are coming down next week. Meantime, will you call Dr. Gilbert,[1] I dont have his address or I would write him myself, and tell him I am going to Greece on this job,[2] and will he arrange, maybe through Weylin Chemists, corner of Madison and 53rd. I think, for you to bring me some Miltown and ¾ gr. seconal.

The book looked fine.

/s/ Bill

[1] Dr. Benjamin A. Gilbert, the New York physician who had treated Faulkner on numerous occasions.

[2] A good-will tour for the U.S. State Department's International Educational Exchange Service.

1244h Letter from Phil Stone to Carvel Collins, March 8, 1957, carbon typescript with typed signature, 1 page.

Dear Carvel:

I have your letter of March 4.[1]

Twenty-five or thirty years ago it may be that I did translate some Greek to Bill in some conversations, but I don't remember about that. So far as I know he never asked me for any translations but it is possible that he might have read some standard English translations of Homer.

What I quoted to Bill in the original Greek was the lament of Oedipus Tyrranus after he had found out the truth about himself and blinded himself.

We do want to see your article when it comes out.

You must come to see us or we are going to quit you.

Hurriedly yours,
Phil Stone

[1]Collins had asked whether Stone ever translated any Greek for Faulkner.

1293h Letter from Linton Massey to Saxe Commins, March 10, 1957, signed ribbon typescript, 1 page.

Dear Mr. Commins:

Before the wretched typewriter ribbon I am momentarily cursed with expires altogether, I want to renew the thanks I gave you here for your great kindness in releasing those galleys of THE TOWN for my Faulkner collection, through the good offices of Mr. Klopfer, whom I have taken the liberty of addressing, and Margie Cohn of the House of Books. You did not really see my treasures; there will be other times, I am sure. We were enchanted to meet you and Mrs. Commins: we can only hope to renew our friendship as opportunity offers. You are both of you, very warm-hearted persons capable of drawing from your friends a very intense loyalty.

. . . .

Do remember us, Mary and me, to Mrs. Commins. It has made us happy to know you both.

Sincerely yours,
/s/ Linton Massey
/t/ Linton Massey

1299 Letter from Harold Ober to Saxe Commins, March 12, 1957, signed ribbon typescript, 1 page.

Dear Saxe:

We expect within a few weeks a check on the option payment on THE SOUND AND THE FURY. This will be $2835. for Bill as 10% goes to Random House.

We will also have a check for $2973.02 on REQUIEM FOR A NUN from the Paris production. This we will have within a few days.

We will probably have $2835. on the option payment on THE HAMLET. I am not certain of this and we wouldn't get it for another month or two.

If Bill changes his mind on A ROSE FOR EMILY I think we could get $4000. for television rights.

Sincerely,
/s/ Harold

1304a Letter from William Sloane, Director, Rutgers University Press, to Saxe Commins, April 9, 1957, signed ribbon typescript, 1 page.

Dear Saxe:

I believe I mentioned to you the fact that we are publishing those fifteen Faulkner sketches which appeared in 1925 in *Times Picayune,* with an explanatory and introductory article about them and Faulkner by Carvel Collins.[1] I know I can write very freely to you and not beat around the bush so I will say that these Faulkner pieces show almost no traces of the later talent and they are, in fact, nothing more than examples of the sort of mood journalism that was popular in the mid-twenties in such papers as the *Times Picayune*. We are not anxious to force the issue on this book or pretend to have anything more than what we have, which is something for the record. Better we should do this volume right and quietly than let somebody else come along and exploit the last three sketches and harass Faulkner collectors and the like.

What I am writing to you about is how many copies of this book you think we ought to print and bind. The whole thing will run to about 50,000 words. I know you wouldn't dream of doing such a thing at Random House, but assuming that you had to for some reason or other, what would your figure be, assuming also you asked the sales force to do nothing to force it? Any advice gratefully appreciated.

Yours,
/s/ Bill
/t/ William Sloane

[1]*New Orleans Sketches*, published by Rutgers University Press in 1958.

1304b Letter from William Sloane to Saxe Commins, April 17, 1957, signed ribbon typescript, 1 page.

Dear Saxe:

I am most obliged for your letter of April 12 and your suggested quantities. I was in error when I said fifteen—of course sixteen is the right number. All three of the unreprinted pieces are to be included. My guesses are about 500 copies over yours since the three unreprinted ones are the best, the Minneapolis volumes[1] are not readily available and one encounters such a horrendous penalty for binding 500 sets of sheets that I'd rather gamble the two hundred bucks and bind them all at once. Still we are very close and the chances are the printing will be 2,000 and the binding the same. One area which is hard to appraise is the export one; we are doing very much better in this area and of course the printing of 2,000 leaves us net with 1,800 to sell. It would be murder to go back on press and we will print from type. If a miracle should occur, we will just have to do another printing by offset and incur a second loss. However, that is what we are supposed to be for.

. . . .

I have left instructions that every piece of paper connected with the production of this Faulkner item be kept in a single place here with the idea of filing it in the end with your collection of Faulkner materials so that no piece of it winds up in the hands of somebody like the late lamented Captain Cohn.[2] If there is anything I dislike it is having nuisance items get into the collector's market and serving as levers on some guy who is unfortunate enough to have enough money to be held up for the purchase of trifles. I hope this meets with your approval.

Yours,
/s/ Bill
/t/ William Sloane

[1]*Mirrors of Chartres Street* (Faulkner Studies, 1953) and *Jealousy and Episode: Two Stories by William Faulkner* (Faulkner Studies, 1955).

[2]Louis Henry Cohn, bibliographer of Hemingway and owner of House of Books in New York.

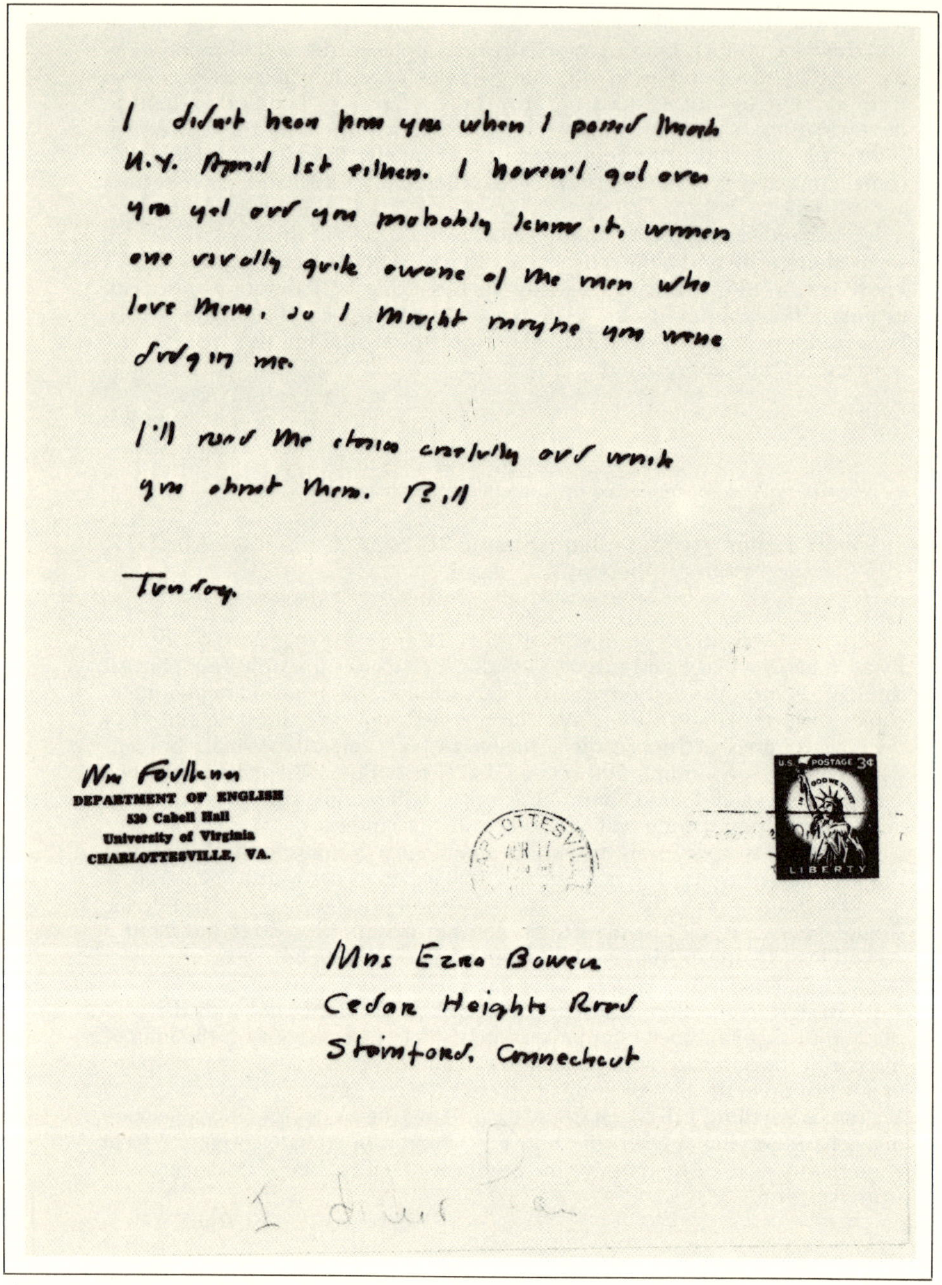

I didn't hear from you when I passed through N.Y. April 1st either. I haven't got over you yet and you probably know it. Women are usually quite aware of the men who love them, so I thought maybe you were dodging me.

I'll read the stories carefully and write you about them. Bill

Tuesday.

Wm Faulkner
DEPARTMENT OF ENGLISH
530 Cabell Hall
University of Virginia
CHARLOTTESVILLE, VA.

U.S. POSTAGE 3¢
IN GOD WE TRUST
LIBERTY

Mrs Ezra Bowen
Cedar Heights Road
Stamford, Connecticut

37. Letter from Faulkner to Joan Williams Bowen, with envelope (item S-47)

S-47 Letter from Faulkner to Joan Williams Bowen, "Tuesday," signed autograph manuscript, 1 page, with envelope addressed in Faulkner's hand and postmarked Charlottesville, April 17, 1957.

I didn't hear from you when I passed through N.Y. April 1st either. I haven't got over you yet and you probably know it, women are usually quite aware of the men who love them, so I thought maybe you were dodging me.

I'll read the stories carefully and write you about them.

Bill

1293o Letter from Phil Stone to William S. Dix, April 18, 1957, carbon typescript with typed signature, 1 page.

Dear Mr. Dix:

With further reference to your letter of March 8,[1] my wife is this afternoon getting off by express the two volumes of the typed manuscript copy of THE HAMLET which were autographed to Philip, Bill's godson. She is also getting off the story, THE WISHING TREE, which Bill wrote and inscribed to Philip. Please acknowledge receipt of these when you get them. I don't think the inscription to Philip that "he will be faithful, fortunate and brave" means anything in particular except that they were nice words that Bill happened to think of at the time.[2]

You may be interested to know that my wife has gone through some early letter files dated in the '20's and found some manuscript poems of Bill's, a good deal of correspondence between him and myself at that time and some cancelled checks of bills I paid for him. I don't want to risk sending this information and I would not like to have it where someone can copy it because I want to keep it for my wife to use later. Also I am not going to nurse a bunch of manuscripts if I am able to come to Princeton. If she will come along and bring them we shall have them there on the 11th.

It is still uncertain that any of us can come and it will probably be uncertain until around May 1. As soon as I find out definitely I shall write Mr. Meriwether.

Yours truly,
Phil Stone

[1] Dix, the Princeton University librarian, had written Stone about the Faulkner documents to be displayed in the Princeton exhibit.

[2] Stone apparently did not realize that these words which Faulkner wrote on the manuscript of *The Hamlet* had previously appeared in *Mayday,* which Faulkner had written in 1925 or 1926.

1305 Letter from Estelle Faulkner to Dorothy Commins, "Tuesday—23rd," signed autograph manuscript, 3 pages, with envelope addressed in Mrs. Faulkner's hand and postmarked Charlottesville, April 24, 1957.

Dearest Dorothy—

How grieved I am for you—Bill only told me today or I would have 'phoned or written sooner—You always have my Love, and please know just now, you have all the sympathy an understanding heart can feel—and give—

I shouldn't add to your gloom, but feel certain that you and Saxe are interested in Malcolm—so will tell you—

Malcolm, when I got to Mississippi several weeks ago, was in a desperate state, mentally and physically—I stayed at home long enough to see that being in Oxford was the worst possible thing for him, so, on the pretext of wanting him to drive me back to Virginia—we came on—

When Bill finally came to his senses, Malcolm had already done some unfortunate things here, so Bill sensed immediately that medical aid was imperative, and *helped me no end* by persuading Malcolm to go to a hospital—

He is in a sanatorium in Richmond—We saw him Sunday, and the improvment even in ten days is marked—so at last I feel hopeful—The boy was on the verge of a complete nervous collapse, but perhaps we got help in time—If sometime you can, and will, a short note or card from you would bolster his courage and morale a great deal—Malcolm adores Bill—always has—and has proven his devotion through the years, especially when Bill had been drinking—That was why I was doubly upset over this last act of Pappy's—

At any rate I got Bill to a hospital on Sunday, and by the following Thursday, Bill and I drove Malcolm to Tucker's Sanatorium in Richmond and helped him get settled—

Sometimes I wonder whether or not I'll ever lead a sane, normal life—Doubt it—involved as I am—

I see that Joan Williams is bombarding Bill with her manuscripts once more—and most likely he'll re-write them for her—That, however, is not for me to bother about—

I would still feel cleaner—rid of it all—Bill included—

Come back to Charlottesville when you can—your little visit was a marvelous tonic for me! and what pleasure your being here gave so many—

Am expecting Victoria (Cho-Cho) Monday—

It is possible that I'll meet her in New York Sunday or Monday—spend a day or so then come on down—Will telephone you, *should* I go up—

Again Dorothy, please know how I love you, and were there words I could write to convey solace and peace to you my pen would write on forever—but alas! I know no such magic words—

Best always
Your devoted friend
Estelle

1342 Letter from Estelle Faulkner to Dorothy and Saxe Commins, "Tuesday night" and "Friday," signed autograph manuscript, 3 pages, with envelope addressed in Mrs. Faulkner's hand and postmarked Charlottesville, May 10, 1957.

Dearest Dorothy and Saxe—

You will, I know, forgive me for waiting so long to write—I've wanted so to believe that I could manage some way to come to you on the 10th for the party,[1] but family affairs have me completely tied down—

Jill and Paul had promised long ago to go to see Paul's sister's new baby christened—and *I* had said of course, they could leave Baby Paul with me—It is my misfortune the christening festivities and the exhibition excitement should come the same week-end—However, *that* isn't all—I am sure I could have worked out something were Malcolm's troubles not so bad, and just now, so pressing—

Victoria (Cho-Cho) came last Tuesday, and we very naturally went to Richmond the next day to see Malcolm—It was a bad move, for since then he has become anxious to leave the hospital, and only Bill's marvelous control has kept him there—We can't be sure just how long that will last—

Malcolm is in a very bad condition both mentally and physically though there is definite improvement—and his doctors believe several months at Tucker's are vitally important for a complete recovery—Judge Franklin[2] is more than useless—so I look for no help there—

Friday—

By now you probably have seen Linton Massey—It is sad for me *not* to be at liberty to come—I wanted to do some little something to help Dorothy—bless her! You two *have* helped Malcolm—

Vicki has complicated things, but thank God for Bill—

Simply can't write more now—

All my Love
—Estelle

[1]In conjunction with the opening of the Faulkner exhibit at Princeton University, May 10, 1957.

[2]Cornell Franklin, Malcolm's father.

1346 Letter from Phil Stone to Jim Dan Hill, May 18, 1957, carbon typescript with typed signature, 1 page.

Dear Dr. Hill:

I am writing to thank you for your column on my friend William Faulkner which appeared in the Memphis Commercial Appeal today.[1]

There are many things concerning the matter and manner of writing which you say and with which I do not agree because I still think that when it comes to the writing of fiction Bill is tops in the United States at present.

But it was certainly a relief to read your article. I am tired of the nauseating obsequiousness that proclaims an indication of genius everything that Bill does and writes and every little remark he makes (usually borrowed from someone else), just as the same people who are praising him now were completely mistaken when I tried without success for twelve years to tell them that this was a man who had talent and would be famous some day now idolize everything he writes and says. It is not exactly a case of the emperor and his new clothes but it looks to me as if the so-called literati would see that sometimes his greasy overalls are not formal clothes.

Yours truly,
Phil Stone

[1]"Mr. Faulkner's 'Town'," Memphis *Commercial Appeal,* May 18, 1957, p. 6. Hill's article is a scathing review of *The Town.*

1293w Letter from Phil Stone to James B. Meriwether, May 25, 1957, carbon typescript with typed signature, 2 pages.

Dear Jim:

Thanks for your letter of May 21. I really don't have time to write letters but I shall have to write this one.

. . . .

I am sure you will not like the article from President Hill and I know of course that you will realize I do not agree with most of it, but just the same there is so much unthinking adulation of Bill and of his writing that is simply following the present fad and that is nauseatingly unsound.

Of course we want you and your wife to come by this summer. The reason for us wanting you to telephone is to be sure that we shall be at home and to enable me to try to get my work up ahead of time so that I can spend more time with you. Don't talk about five minutes. Come and stay awhile.

When we get to the leaflet,[1] which I herewith return, it is a little difficult for me to tell you just exactly what I mean in such a short space of time.

Taking them up as they are underlined.

The first mention about the design is, I think, purely an afterthought. Certainly I tried for years to drill into Bill's head the importance of dynamic design but if he ever realized it or paid any attention to it I have no recollection of it. He does not have a dynamic design in anything except his short stories and that is his great failure as a novelist. He does have patterns, as Carvel Collins has pointed out in his analysis of THE SOUND AND THE FURY, but these are static patterns to which the story is fitted regardless, just like fitting things to a Promethean [*sic*] bed.

Next, SARTORIS did not mark the inception of the design. It marked the inception of the saga and not a difference in design at all.

Third, nearly all of the Faulkner novels are alike in that they all have the same crisis and are all written in the same personal mannerism which is not a style and which is not fitted to the sound and tone of the particular book.

I cannot agree at all about Bill having variety. He has too much sameness and he has improved very little in twenty years. When one does not improve one grows backwards. There is no alternative.

Nor does he seem to me to experiment with new forms. He keeps on doing the same thing he has done over and he repeats and imitates experiments and successes right along.

The basic trouble with Bill is that he has no dynamic design such as Balzac shows. The stories do not grow of the ground. They are foisted on the ground. Next, he has few characters who develop at all, but most of them remain just the same at the end of the book as they were in the beginning. They are like he said of Popeye: "cut out of tin."

Read his books carefully, disabuse yourself of your preconceived ideas and of the present adulation and note how this is true. Of course he is the best of the generation, but the generation is not very good and his future place in English literature will be that of a splendid second-rate writer.

Of course I know you won't agree with any of this, but I take comfort in remembering how nobody agreed with me from 1917 until 1930 when I said that Bill was going to be a famous writer.

Your friend,
Phil Stone

[1] "The Literary Career of William Faulkner: An Exhibition," the leaflet which accompanied the Princeton exhibit of Faulkner materials.

1293x Letter from Phil Stone to James B. Meriwether, May 28, 1957, carbon typescript with typed signature, 1 page.

Dear Jim:

I find that the marked copy of the Faulkner pamphlet was omitted from my last letter, and I herewith inclose it.

Of course the comments I had to make to you were very hasty and not very clear, but they just keep me going so fast these days that I don't have time to sit down and do other things carefully. I do want to add that when it comes to the short story, Bill can hold his head up with anybody who ever wrote a short story in English. He is just about the best there is when it comes to writing a short story.

Your friend,
Phil Stone

1244m Letter from Phil Stone to Carvel Collins, July 19, 1957, carbon typescript with typed signature, 1 page.

Dear Carvel:

A few days ago I made to Emily and Philip a prophecy which I shall now make to you. This is it.

For some time now Bill has not been getting publicity. My prediction is that between now and October 1 he will do or say something startling that will again attract public attention. Watch for it. I have no idea what it is because I have not talked with Bill since he got back from Virginia.[1]

You said you were coming to see us, but I do not believe it. However, I am glad that you have not come yet because I have been tremendously overwhelmed with work and still am. But I now have a young law student to help me and I have bought a dictaphone and think in two or three weeks I shall not be so overrun.

We are doing all right and will enjoy seeing you.

Your friend,
Phil Stone

[1] Faulkner had returned to Oxford on June 27.

1259e Letter from Phil Stone to O. B. Emerson, August 30, 1957, carbon typescript with typed signature, 2 pages.

Dear Mr. Emerson:

Thank you for your nice letter of August 26.[1] I shall answer it as best I can but it will have to be brief, since I seem to be working all the time now. In fact, I am up at the office now putting this on the dictaphone at night.

With reference to what I said about Bill a long time ago I say now that he is very much overrated and one of these times, perhaps in the next ten years, the people who are idolators now will come back to my point of view and probably worse. In other words, they will probably go to the other extreme.

With reference to the dedication to THE TOWN, what Bill is saying is a recognition of the fact that I invented the idea of the book, a great many incidents and some of the characters. This was between 1925 and 1930 and we had a lot of fun laughing over these people and their doings. Believe me, they are very little exaggerated. We have people like that right around here now.

You can be sure that I shall not be the Boswell of Bill or of anybody else.[2]

While I am writing this, you watch out for my wife, Emily Whitehurst Stone, some of these days. That gal can really write although she still has not been able to hook a publisher.

Shakespeare did have a great deal of influence on Bill.

As to THE MARBLE FAUN, there was not a great deal of criticism of it but there was some. I put away all these reviews because Bill would not take care of them, but they burned when my old house burned in 1942 and burned the twelve large files that I had of Bill's stuff including many original manuscripts.

As for Bill not reading reviews, I have an idea that he reads the favorable reviews.

I am not sure about the coffin incident,[3] but I remember dimly that at some funeral of some of Bill's people there was water in the grave and they had to bore holes in the coffin to sink the coffin.

I don't know about anyone being thrown off a wagon.[4]

I don't remember the story regarding Flem Snopes of which you speak.[5]

I can't agree with you about A FABLE. I think it is quite a failure although it contains some beautiful Faulkner prose. The reason I think it is a failure is that no one can write a successful book on the life of Christ without having a sublime humility and God never put humility into any Faulkner I ever saw. If you want to see how much better the job can be done, read Oscar Wilde's DE PROFUNDIS.

Best of luck.

Yours truly,
Phil Stone

[1] Emerson, who was completing his doctoral dissertation on Faulkner at the University of Alabama, had questioned Stone about various aspects of Faulkner's work.

[2] Emerson had quoted an article in the November 6, 1932 Memphis *Commercial Appeal* in which Louis Cochran had referred to Stone as Faulkner's "future Boswell."

[3] Emerson had asked whether there was anything in Faulkner's past experience which might explain his fascination for accidents involving coffins.

[4] Emerson had alluded to a coffin being thrown off a wagon in *Absalom, Absalom!*.

[5] Emerson had asked about the story in which Flem Snopes dies and goes to Hell. The incident appears at the end of the "Eula" section of *The Hamlet.*

1353 Letter from Jill Faulkner Summers to Saxe Commins, "Sunday," signed autograph manuscript, 1 page, with envelope addressed in Mrs. Summers' hand and postmarked Charlottesville, September 2, 1957.

Dear Mr. Saxe—

This is a rather awkward letter to write. Just after we were married three years ago, Bennett[1] wrote a very nice note of congratulation & said that he (I assumed Random House) would like to furnish a library for us. We hesitated to take advantage of so generous an offer & decided to do so only with restraint. Thus far I've sent two requests for books, I believe.

If I misinterpreted Bennett's letter please don't hesitate to say so & the check will be mailed immediately. Above all we don't want you to foot the bill.

I must apologize for writing no sooner but the books and your letter arrived just as we started moving & this is my first opportunity to sit down & collect my wits.

Please let me know as soon as possible about the bill.

Love to you both as always—

Jill

[1] Cerf.

1354 Western Union telegram from Faulkner to Saxe Commins, September 14, 1957.

PLEASE SEND TWENTY THOUSAND ALL WELL HERE. LOVE TO DOROTHY

BILL

1244n Letter from Phil Stone to Carvel Collins, September 16, 1957, carbon typescript with typed signature, 1 page.

Dear Carvel:

Please refer to the second paragraph of my letter to you under date of July 19 and read the enclosed clipping.[1] My guess came true with sixteen days to spare.

I can understand why people will disagree with me about my opinions of Bill's writing, but it is strange to me that people still refuse to realize the fact that nobody knows Bill as I do. Perhaps it is part of that Yankee trait to believe nothing that does not fit in with their previously adopted formula and to disregard all facts that do not fit such formula.

. . . .

Your friend,
Phil Stone

[1]Stone had predicted that Faulkner would shortly "do or say something startling" to gain the attention of the public. The enclosed clipping was a copy of Faulkner's letter to the editor published in the Memphis *Commercial Appeal,* September 15, 1957. The letter reflected Faulkner's pro-integration stand.

1355a Letter from Phil Stone to James B. Meriwether, September 16, 1957, carbon typescript with typed signature, 1 page.

Dear Jim:

I realize that this letter will probably reach Princeton before you do, but I had to write it before I forgot it.

You may remember that I told you when you were here that between that time and October 1 Bill would do something to attract some publicity since he has not been getting publicity lately. I enclose you a clipping from the Memphis Commercial Appeal for Sunday, September 15. So my prophecy came true with 16 days to spare.

I can see why the idolaters differ with me concerning my opinions of Bill and of his writing, but what I cannot see is why they don't realize that I know more about Bill than does anyone else in this world.

Best of luck.

Your friend,
Phil Stone

1356 Letter from Faulkner to Editor, *New York Times,* October 7, 1957, carbon typescript with typed signature, 2 pages.

Sir:

The tragedy of Little Rock[1] is that it has at last brought out into the light a fact which we knew was there but which, until it was dragged forcibly out of hiding, we could ignore by pretending it wasn't there. This is the fact that white people and Negroes do not like and trust each other, and perhaps never can.

But maybe this is not a tragedy after all. Now, by having this fact out where we will have to look at it and recognise it and accept it, maybe we can realise that it is not important for us to like and trust each other. That it is not even [of] prime importance for us to live, rub along somehow, in amity and peace together. That what is important and necessary and urgent (urgent: we are reaching the point now where we haven't time any more) is that we federate together, show a common unified front not for dull peace and amity, but for survival as a people and a nation.

It may already be too late; as a nation and a people we may already be on the way down and out. But I do not believe it. I decline to believe that in a crisis we cannot rally our national character to that same courage and toughness which the English people for instance did when as a nation they stood alone in Europe for the national principle that men shall and can be free. Ours will be a bigger task not because the threat is greater but because we will have to stand up not as one nation among a continent of nations nor even in a hemisphere of nations, but as the last people unified nationally for liberty in an inimical world which already outnumbers us.

Against that principle which by physical force compels man to relinquish his individuality into the monolithic mass of a state dedicated to the premise that the state alone shall prevail, we, because of the lucky accident of our geography, may have to represent that last community of unified people dedicated to that opposed premise that man can be free by the very act of voluntarily merging and relinquishing his liberty into the liberty of all individual men who want to be free. We, because of the good luck of our still unspent and yet unexhausted past, may have to be the rallying point for all men, no matter what color they are or what tongue they speak, willing to federate into a community dedicated to the proposition that a community of individual free men not merely must endure, but can endure.

William Faulkner
Oxford, Miss.

[1] Federal troops were used to ensure the peace during the integration crisis at Central High School in Little Rock, Arkansas, during the fall of 1957. Faulkner's letter appeared in the *New York Times* on October 13, 1957.

1357b Letter from Phil Stone to George Thatcher, October 9, 1957, carbon typescript with typed signature, 1 page.

Dear George:

I have your letter of October 8, and was very glad to hear from you.[1]

With reference to having THE MARBLE FAUN republished, I doubt if Bill would be interested in this and, frankly, I don't think THE MARBLE FAUN is good enough to justify republication.

As for approaching Bill, the only way I know of for you to approach him is to write him directly.

Since he got the Nobel Prize it seems to me that he has a chronic case of Nobelitis and I rarely see him. Since he has taken the position he has in turning his back on his own people and his native land, I don't care to ask him anything.

Your friend,
Phil Stone

[1] Thatcher, the owner of The Dixie Press, Gulfport, Mississippi, sought Stone's assistance in arranging for a reissue of *The Marble Faun.*

1359a Letter from Maude McGregor, secretary to Mr. and Mrs. Zachary Scott, to Saxe Commins, October 17, 1957, signed ribbon typescript, 1 page. From London.

Dear Mr. Commins:

Mrs. Scott has asked me to send you the attached itinerary of the dates for "Requiem For A Nun."[1] We have also sent a copy of this to Mr. Faulkner.

Yours sincerely,
/s/ M. McGregor

[1] The enclosed itinerary read as follows:
"*November 11th:*
Opens out-of-town at Bournemouth for one week.
November 18th:
Out-of-town at Blackpool for one week.
November 26th:
Opens at the Royal Court Theatre, Sloane Square, London for four weeks.
December 21st:
Close at the Royal Court Theatre."

1360 Letter from Faulkner to Dorothy Commins, "Wednesday" [October 30], signed ribbon typescript, 1 page, with envelope addressed in Faulkner's hand and postmarked Oxford, October 31, 1957.

Dear Dorothy:

I will arrive Princeton Wed. Nov. 13th. Will telephone or telegraph more exactly later.

I take you at your word that I wont be in Eugene's or Franny's way in the house. Will hope to get a foothold of my own so that I can always vacate the room when they want to come out.

Jill and her little boy are here now. We will leave here Monday Nov 11th, to drive to Charlottesville, should arrive there Tuesday 12th. and I will get an early train Wed. a.m. for Princeton if possible, if not Trenton. Will wire or telephone to ratify.

I dont want Saxe to do this himself, *bring* them out, ask him to ask Jimmy or the shipping dept. at the office to send out my three suits in the closet in his office, the blue, the brown, the gray tweed one, to your house in Princeton.

Saxe, get us tickets for the game Sat. 16th, I think the game is at Princeton that day, isn't it?[1]

/s/ Bill

[1] Faulkner subsequently changed his plans. As Blotner reports, Faulkner stayed in Charlottesville and attended the Virginia-South Carolina football game on November 16 (see *Faulkner: A Biography*, pp. 1677–1679).

1361 Letter from Faulkner to Saxe Commins, "Sunday" [possibly October 1957], signed ribbon typescript with final sentence added in holograph, 1 page.

Dear Saxe:

Thank you for your letter. I know I am always welcome in Dorothy's house, and I intend to spend much time there. But I dont intend to take up room all the time. So I am asking Mike[1] to get me a room in the Princeton Inn, for headquarters. I may not use it much, but I must not be in the way when any of your children want to come out home.

Malcolm is not doing at all well. He does nothing at all, will not go to work, stays in bed all day long until his mother makes him get up, then sits around in a sullen, surly, moody way, saying nothing for days. Occasionally he rouses up a little, but we cannot persuade him to go to a hospital or see a psychiatrist, as all the doctors say he must. I personally think he has quit, given up, will never be any better. Estelle is worried very much, it will be good for her to get away for a while. She will go to Va. with Jill while I am in Princeton. My guess is though that she will have to take Malcolm there with her, just as she did last spring.

I will come up about the 10th–15th. Will certify later.

Will you see what this is that Harvey wants.

/s/ Bill

[1]Whitney J. Oates, a classics professor at Princeton University. Faulkner was making arrangements for his visit to the Princeton campus in November.

1359b Typed copy of letter from George L. Lazarus to Ruth Ford, December 8, 1957, ribbon typescript, 1 page.

Dear Miss Ford:

Although I know it is an impertinence I thought I must write you a line of thanks for the most moving experience you afforded me when I came to see the play on Friday.[1]

I wouldn't presume to attempt to express my gratitude from the theatrical angle. I seldom go to the theatre now, but purely as a Faulkner lover. I have sat and worshipped at his feet ever since I was a young man and, as a matter of fact, have as good a collection of his works as exists in England, including my great treasure, the manuscript of Absalom, Absalom, which Professor Carvel Collins of the Massachusetts Institute of Technology is especially coming over to study in the very near future.

Until I saw the play on Friday "Requiem" had never meant very much to me, largely I think because I was too inexperienced and stupid at reading dramatic dialogue to get the full meaning out of it.

However, all this has changed now and thanks to the great performance I was privileged to see last week I realise now that Faulkner has written a great play.

My apologies once more in having written to you. Please don't bother to answer. You must be a very busy person.

Yours sincerely,
George L. Lazarus

[1]Lazarus, a noted English book collector, had attended a London performance of *Requiem for a Nun.*

1367 Letter from Faulkner to Johnette Tracy, undated [early December 1957], signed ribbon typescript, 1 page.

Dear Mrs Tracy:

His aunt, Dorothy Oldham, wrote the letter.[1] She failed to sign it simply because she showed it to Estelle and me for approval, and Estelle added a postscript and sealed it before she realised Dorothy had not signed it. We all took it for granted that Malcolm would know who it was from, since he knows me better and longer than to think I would write him that sort of letter myself.

Whether the idea in the letter is justified or not, I dont know. But I felt and still feel that his aunt, who loves him and who has been hurt very much by the fact that something went on in this business that none of us knew about apparently. Decency demanded that Gloria should have told Malcolm as soon as the thought occurred to her, that she planned to marry Lamar as soon as she was divorced. Simply gratitude should have compelled her to tell him at least an hour before the wedding, that she was going to. We have all watched for years. . . , and I think his aunt had every right to blow her top. I also think in the end it will help Malcolm. He has been babied too much in his life. That's why he got himself into the mess he did.

Thank you for your letter. I hope you will see Malcolm and assure him that I did not and would not have written him such a letter myself, but that if his aunt Dot felt she must, I felt she had that right.

/s/ William Faulkner

[1] For an explanation of the situation to which Faulkner has reference in this letter, see the following item.

1368 Letter from Johnette Tracy to James W. Silver, undated, signed ribbon typescript, 3 pages (2 leaves), with envelope postmarked Jackson, Mississippi, December 13, 1957.

Dear Jim,

. . . . I have never had a Xmas tree, but this is such a dump, and I thought it might give Malcolm something to do, too, so we are going to get one on Saturday.[1] I don't know whether he'll go back to Oxford for the day or not. I say this for you only—not to be repeated to anyone for reasons I'm sure will be obvious to you. He was here for Thanksgiving, and we felt he'd had a nice time, and in fact, I thought he was more relaxed and happy than I'd seen him in years. I was really somewhat encouraged—on a small scale only of course—when the next evening he called me and said he'd had an anon letter from Oxford, which was terrible, and proceeding to read it to me, I certainly agreed. . . . Well, he thought WF wrote it—he was half out of his head at least, and said to me that's how southerners look at things, and settle things that way, etc. I tried to get him to come over and bring the letter, as I could tell he was in such a state he'd do something—and of course, I knew WF never wrote that blah—though I've known they believed it, he is not so hysterical. I told M. if anyone in his family wrote it, Aunt Dot did—and not to worry about what she thought of family honor until she paid back the two hundred dollars she borrowed from me, etc. Well he wouldn't come, and after awhile I called back, and he had just telephoned to L. and Gloria in NO and challenged L. to a duel with pistols, and God knows what—he drew a blank and remembered nothing except saying he'd made a fool of himself, and he cried, and he couldn't come. But soon he called me, and said he was coming. So I took a look at the letter, which showed me nothing new—and I guess I sat up most of the night—he was absolutely *non compos*—with his history to talk to him like that is utterly foolish—I asked him why he destroyed—this is just an example—and maybe you asked him this, too, those snake slides. He said—this was a different time, of course, and he was rational—that when G. told him she was finished last spring, he made a big fire, and then he said, and God knows I agree—I did my best to scare her, and guess I succeeded to some extent—she was lucky to be alive. Well, anyhow, this night, he talked of ambushing L., and shooting him, committing the perfect crime, which could not be pinned on him, and how G. had deliberately driven him crazy—this is typical paranoia, and dangerous as hell. So I told him, as I have many times, how much more honorable to do nothing, say nothing. . . . Finally he said I'd calmed him down—and he did seem to be all right. But that—he'd been drinking every night, according to him, in some beer joint, and then going home and sitting up and drinking—sent him on a big toot, and in this town that just means he'd wind up in the Jackson city jail, or if he got by, two or three weeks of that, and he'd be ready for anything. I was scared of the whole business, and besides whoever wrote one might write another, and another, and so finally I went to see Dr. R. and told him about this, and asked him if he thought it was a dangerous situation, as my husband and I did, and he did, so I tried to get M. to go to see Dr. S.—the man he saw before. But he wouldn't, and things went from bad to worse—he did keep on the job but showed up late, and so on. So at last I did the only other thing I could think of, that is, I wrote to his family, describing this letter, which of course I had no idea came from them really, except that I didn't think anyone else in Oxford would know enough to write some of the things in it, but I just said it was an anon letter, and M. thought he had to do damage to L. and G. for the sake of the family honor; and would WF please tell M. he didn't write that. So, the next day, M. said they called him, and he wouldn't talk to them—which I guess is true, because the day after I received a letter from the great man in which he told me that the letter was written by Aunt Dot, shown to them for approval, his wife adding a postscript, and sealing it before they realized that she hadn't signed it yet, and they had no idea M. would not know who wrote it, knowing him, WF, too well to think he would, etc. Well, I'd never seen the postscript, and asked M. what happened to it, and he said he tore it off the letter before he brought it over—the reason for this as nearly as I can tell was that he wanted me to talk him out of the idea that WF wrote it, for which I can't blame him—it was dreadful, and I shudder to think how it hurt him, but he thought if I saw his mother's note, I'd think well WF must have written it, just as he did, and wouldn't convince him WF didn't. Well, that is about it anyhow. But I bet they hated me when they heard from me characterizing their letter as terrible, monstrous, and a few other choice adjectives. WF said in the long run this would help M., he'd always been babied, etc. etc. He would not write this, but felt Aunt Dot had a right to, etc. So anyhow, he wouldn't write it, and that was the main thing. I showed that to M., and for all I know Aunt Dot's letter did help—as long as he knew where it came from—intemperate though it was, as he wouldn't feel he'd have to shoot L. for the family honor even if she did say so—and also I'd been doing a lot of work on him myself about drinking. So he quit that night, except for one bottle of beer, so he says, and he acts and looks so much better that H., whom I didn't tell this to, in the event it didn't last any time, remarked to me how much better he looked. Well, I answered the great man's letter and said that I had never seen the postscript and we thought it was just an anon letter, and of course I didn't question his aunt's right to write what she pleased. Which I hope will smooth that over as much as it need be—so that if I meet them on the street in O. we can all speak. But I hope I put the fear of God into them, and they won't make any more incendiary statements. I keep thinking M's present state might just be another manifestation of his disease, and one I just never saw, but you would be amazed at the change in him, and I don't think it's from getting a lot of tough talk from Aunt Dot, I think it's because we have tried to give him a little honest love and affection, and he's just blooming like the rose. That crowd was always so busy blaming G. for everything, and still is, and hating her to stop and do anything for him—and vice versa for that matter. I showed the Rices WF's letter, too, and they kept saying what's the matter with those people. I told Dr. R. when I went to see him about this first that I would hate to have the contents of Aunt Dot's letter get out, and he said they wouldn't say anything, and I'm sure they won't, but he also said the family will put it out themselves at this rate.

Well anyhow I guess we shall have an Xmas tree if all goes well. M. says he lives from day to day, and he's not alone in that. But how my heart goes out to him; is there anything really that he hasn't had to take—it's no wonder he's the way he is.

. . . .

/s/ Johnette

[1]The Tracys, close personal friends of Malcolm Franklin, were seeking to help him through the difficult period of his divorce. Mrs. Tracy obviously felt that the letter by Miss Oldham had exacerbated an already dangerous situation.

1369 Letter from Harold Ober to Saxe Commins, December 18, 1957, signed ribbon typescript, 1 page.

Dear Saxe:

I am afraid I am going to have to trouble you by asking you to sign the enclosed five copies of a letter to Fox authorizing them to pay the commission due James Geller on THE HAMLET. Like the others you signed, these will need to be signed before a notary, and I hope that the kind man at the Princeton Library will help you with this. Will you then return all five copies to me in the enclosed, self-addressed envelope? I am sorry about this, but I thought when I was in Princeton that they were all the same, but one set referred to THE SOUND AND THE FURY, and the other to this one, THE HAMLET.

We miss you here in the city, and we hope you are continuing to feel well. As you know, I very much enjoyed my stay with you and Dorothy.

Miss Davis wants me to send you her best wishes—and Merry Christmas from both of us!

Sincerely,
/s/ Harold

1359c Letter from Ruth Ford to Saxe Commins, December 20, 1957, signed ribbon typescript, 1 page. From London.

Dear Saxe:

I was so happy to get your letter yesterday and will answer early in the new year.

38. Ruth Ford as Temple Drake (photograph by Anthony Armstrong-Jones)

Here are some marvellous reviews of the play.[1] Again, please read them all and let Cerf and Linscott read them, if they like, and then be the angel that you are and send them to Bill for me. I know that, if he receives an envelope from *you,* he will open it but I am not sure what would happen to an envelope arriving from London, and I do so want him to see and read all of these reviews.

Our four weeks at the Royal Court are up this Saturday, December 21st. We have had an enormous success, playing to standees every night. We will move into a theatre in the West End as soon as there is a suitable one available, which we hope will be only a matter of a few weeks, then we hope to have a long run in London. When we finish here we have a lot of great plans for the play, which I will write you about.

I hope you enjoy fabulous health in the New Year and send loving wishes and blessings to you and your family at Christmas time.

/s/ Ruth

P.S. The Royal Court Theatre has a policy more or less like the Phoenix. Plays are scheduled for a certain number of weeks and then they have to make way for the next one.

[1] The British production of *Requiem for a Nun.*

1359d Typed copy of letter from William Bush to Ruth Ford, December 22, 1957, ribbon typescript, 2 pages.

My dear Mrs. Ford:

After your gracious reception of last evening, I cannot resist the desire to communicate with you.

I am a Southerner as are you. Yet so often I have felt the perenniel rebellion at it—the search for Truth in other pastures, scorning the ways, the ideas of our forebears, being intellectually formed by a public school education under progressive Denitz and positivist teachers to think that the south—our south—once did a very foolish thing and deserved to suffer for having been so stupid. I have rejected my education and I have come to see the greatness of our defeat, the greatness of suffering for honour.

Suffering—that is the key word. It is Temple Drake as you showed her. It is life—that life, that pulsating, utterly believable life which you incarnated in Temple Drake last night. Although my admiration for Catherine Sellers in the Paris production is limitless, you added a bitterness, a boredom which only we who have run from ourselves in the midst of American respectability can grasp. You were *barren,* and endowed with no grace save that which came to you from your sin, your tenderness only that from an affair which the world held in horror, your love only that of sheer passion without even the maternal instincts to support you. Your scenes with Nancy were magnificent, manifesting at the same time an affectionate tenderness and an awareness of southern conscience which only a native could grasp. I had thrice wept before Faulkner's greatness in this work before last night; first upon reading it, then twice on seeing it in Paris. But never before have my eyes been *constantly* moist. This was due to you, to your timeless incarnation of the suffering of all of us from the lie within ourselves.

After last night I know that there is another southerner besides Faulkner who sees, who understands, who is not afraid to see in suffering a greatness scorned by a materialistic and progressive society.

I *cannot,* I will not accept the fact that we have not produced this work in America with anything but a sense of shame and humility; and, if I dare be so presumptuous in speaking against our own America, I cannot feel that in ignoring this work we have manifested any progress in understanding the external mysteries: suffering, expiation, love, sin—in short, good and evil.

I feel less alone with my shame and my humility before this negligence after having seen you. Faulkner has given—and, because he alone was able to give what he has given us, he *is* alone and indomitably has accepted the necessity to be so. But you penetrated his solitude, you burned with it, and hence I felt caught up in it as if you and Faulkner and I were those southerners, those *Americans* (and how often don't we have to swallow the insulting insinuations of the Europeans simply because we are too well bred to be impolite before their barbed remarks which they probably think us too naive or too childish to grasp!) who stood for a few hours before the profoundest of mysteries; that of good and evil.

I am grateful and I shall cherish the joy with which my heart burned as I sensed not only a pride in Faulkner but also a pride in you; that you, as it were, gave me a support along this solitary road to truth, a support which is never so sweet as when it comes from another who has come from a southern formation, who is a companion not only in spirit but in the truth of geographic affinities.

I no longer feel alone with Faulkner. Thank you.

Wm. Bush

1958

1359e Letter from Ruth Ford to Saxe Commins, January 6, 1958, signed ribbon typescript, 1 page. From London.

Dear Saxe:

You won't have to read any more of these now![1] This is "the lot," as they say in England.

Zachary and I are making a quick business trip to New York, leaving tonight and will call you on our arrival. I am longing to see you.

Please send these clippings, along with the others, on to Bill.

Love
/s/ Ruth

[1] Reviews of the London production of *Requiem for a Nun.*

1388 Letter from Harold Ober to Saxe Commins, January 13, 1958, signed ribbon typescript, 1 page.

Dear Saxe:

I have two checks from Fox representing the payments due Bill Faulkner at this time on both THE SOUND AND THE FURY and THE HAMLET.[1] They're made out to Bill's order, as you will see. I wonder if you will be kind enough to endorse these to the order of this firm and return them to me in the enclosed, self-addressed envelope?

Many thanks—and as always my best wishes to both you and Dorothy!

Sincerely,
/s/ Harold

[1]Enclosed with this letter were vouchers numbered 1867 and 1868, each in the amount of $5,985.

1304c Letter from William Sloane to Saxe Commins, January 14, 1958, signed ribbon typescript, 1 page.

Dear Saxe:

In a day or two, if not sooner, you will be receiving an advance copy, considerably belated, of WILLIAM FAULKNER: NEW ORLEANS SKETCHES with a Carvel Collins introduction which I hope you will feel does scholarly credit and literary justice to the whole enterprise. I certainly would welcome any reaction from you as to your feeling in the matter. Happy New Year and thank God this particular project is accomplished, dared and done.

I will collect what materials are lying about in connection with the projection of the book and have them shipped down to you for destruction or addition to your Faulkner collection as you decide. This will keep anything and everything out of the hands of the less desirable kind of rare book dealer.

A wonderful 1958 to you.

Yours,
/s/ Bill
/t/ William Sloane

1391a Letter from Harold Ober to Saxe Commins, January 23, 1958, signed ribbon typescript, 1 page.

Dear Saxe:

I enclose two memos about dramatic rights—one of LIGHT IN AUGUST and one of AS I LAY DYING. Also copy letter from Peter Glenville who wants an option on the picture rights of ABSALOM ABSALOM. He is a very good director and among the other plays he has directed are Huxley's GIOCONDA SMILE, Sartre's CRIME PASSIONELLE, Saroyan's THE TIME OF YOUR LIFE and William Archibald's THE INNOCENTS.

Do you think there is any use pursuing these inquiries? In other words do you think Bill would want to have plays done from LIGHT IN AUGUST or AS I LAY DYING?

As for ABSALOM I think Glenville might make a *good* picture which I don't expect from any of the books of Bill's that have been sold for large prices.

Finally, do you think there is any use writing Bill about any of these inquiries?

Sincerely,
/s/ Harold

1391b Letter from Harold Ober to Saxe Commins, January 28, 1958, signed ribbon typescript, 1 page.

Dear Saxe:

Thank you for your letter. We agree with you entirely about the dramatic inquiries. There was an item in one of the newspapers the other day to the effect that Jerry Wald of Twentieth Century-Fox (who bought THE SOUND AND THE FURY and THE HAMLET) is interested in ABSALOM, ABSALOM. If he is, I am sure he would pay more money than Peter Glenville could. I would like to see one of these two pictures before deciding what to do about ABSALOM. I presume, however, that Bill cares more about how much he gets for a picture than what kind of a picture it is, because he knows that very few pictures are really good. But I would be inclined to go a little slow on ABSALOM.

Sincerely,
/s/ Harold

1393a Letter from Arnold Weissberger to Ruth Ford, January 28, 1958, signed ribbon typescript, 1 page.

Dear Ruth:

I hope I won't seem unduly fussy in suggesting that I would be happier if your understanding with Mr. Commins were put in writing.[1] You know and Mr. Commins knows and I know what Mr. Faulkner intends, but lawyers and agents can only be guided by what the contract says, and the contract as it now stands does not certainly give you the rights that Mr. Faulkner wants you to have. There would be some difficulty, also, in establishing an oral amendment to a written agreement.

It is my suggestion, accordingly, that we get a written amendment to the agreement that will provide that no one may produce "Requiem for a Nun" or any part of it in any medium at any time or place in the English language without your express consent.

Do you want to talk to Mr. Commins about this?

Love to you and Zach.

/s/ Arnold

[1]See Ruth Ford's letter to Saxe Commins, February 12, 1958, and related letters, printed below. Weissberger, Miss Ford's theatrical lawyer, was the senior partner in the New York law firm of Weissberger and Frosch.

1391c Typed copy of letter from Peter Glenville to Harold Ober, February 3, 1958, ribbon typescript, 1 page.

Dear Mr. Ober:

Thank you very much for your letter of the 29th of January, the contents of which I fully understood.

There are two books of William Faulkner's in which I am extremely interested. One is ABSALOM, ABSALOM and the other is LIGHT IN AUGUST. Both are difficult books to realize in view of their very intricate story patterns, but it occurs to me that LIGHT IN AUGUST is perhaps the easier one to tackle first. My suggestion would be that we fix a price for the purchase of the rights, which I suggest should be between $35,000. and $50,000. and that you should give me an option of nine months for a down payment of ten per cent of the figure agreed upon. I could then see my way clear to devote the following months to giving my time and engaging a script writer to work on a film treatment of the story that would satisfy motion picture requirements whilst keeping the artistic core of the work intact.

I would be most happy if you could see your way clear to agree to an arrangement of this sort as I am very anxious to start work on one of these stories, and, I certainly feel that I have a better chance of achieving a watertight script of LIGHT IN AUGUST within a reasonable time than ABSALOM, ABSALOM, which I feel is an extremely long and difficult undertaking, especially if one wants to remain true to the original work.

I shall look forward to hearing from you.

Yours sincerely,
Peter Glenville

1391c Letter from Harold Ober to Saxe Commins, February 5, 1958, signed ribbon typescript, 1 page.

Dear Saxe:

I think I sent you a letter from Peter Glenville so you know who he is. Here is a copy of another letter from him.[1] I feel fairly sure that the pictures to be made from THE SOUND AND THE FURY and THE HAMLET will be poor ones, certainly, according to the reviews, PYLON was terrible. So I would be inclined, the price being as good or better, to let Peter Glenville do one of Bill's older books with the hope of getting a better picture. What do you think?

Sincerely,
/s/ Harold

[1] See the previous item.

1304d Letter from William Sloane to Saxe Commins, February 5, 1958, signed ribbon typescript, 1 page.

Dear Saxe:

. . . .

We have been having a good initial reception of WILLIAM FAULKNER: NEW ORLEANS SKETCHES. Our advance orders came to about 1200 and every mail is bringing in more. This without any special pressure—I promised you we would employ none—and yet our mere mention of the title has produced a substantial number of overseas orders and a good initial take with libraries and institutions as well as the book trade. I should not be surprised if we wound up selling 3,000 or better of the little book. I can't imagine that this will please Faulkner to any notable extent but it certainly will gratify Carvel Collins.

Yours,
/s/ Bill
/t/ William Sloane

1392 Letter from Harold Ober to Saxe Commins, February 11, 1958, signed ribbon typescript, 1 page.

Dear Saxe:

Everybody I know has or has had a cold lately and I know how miserable it makes one feel so don't look at this material until you feel like doing so.

I have written Mr. Gwynn[1] to find out about how many pages are available.

Some of Bill's answers are interesting but I should think that a whole book would make difficult if not tiresome reading.

As you know, I wrote Mr. Gwynn that if this should be published in book form it could be done only by Random House.[2]

Sincerely,
/s/ Harold

[1]Frederick L. Gwynn, professor of English at the University of Virginia, who had contacted Ober about the possible publication of Faulkner's remarks to various classes at the University of Virginia.

[2]*Faulkner in the University: Class Conferences at the University of Virginia 1957–1958*, ed. Gwynn and Joseph L. Blotner, was published by the University of Virginia Press in 1959.

1393a Letter from Ruth Ford to Saxe Commins, February 12 [1958], signed autograph manuscript, 2 pages (1 folded leaf). From Austin, Texas.

Dear Saxe—

This is a letter from my lawyer, Arnold Weissberger. He and Mr. Ober worked out the contract between me and Bill,[1] that you signed. Arnold feels that, now that I am going into production in London again—and the contracts are ready to be signed for the American production—that since a co-producer will now be with me, I must for my own protection have this amendment to my contract with Faulkner, so that my position is clearly defined to the co-producer.

Zachary and I are leaving for the airport—flying back to N.Y.—so I'll mail this from there.

We plan to fly to London around Feb. 20th—will, of course, call you before leaving—

Forgive haste—

All love to you & Dorothy.

Ruth

[1]For the stage production of *Requiem for a Nun.*

1394 Letter from Phil Stone to Maud Faulkner, February 14, 1958, carbon typescript with typed signature, 1 page.

Dear Miss Maud:

I got your note and I thoroughly agree with you. It sounds like Alice in Wonderland when you consider that the taxpayers have had to pay out over $800,000 apiece to keep nine negro children in a school when they, the negro children, have a brand-new million-dollar school just a few blocks away which is a better school than the one they are now in.[1] How crazy can we get?

I don't think we are going to have any integrated schools in Mississippi any time soon, and it is my own feeling that the NAACP is breaking its own neck and that everybody is getting tired of it. It would not surprise me if, by 1970, the NAACP were as dead as the Ku Klux Klan in the '20's. It is just making a complete nuisance of itself all over the country and they do not represent anything like a majority of the negroes in the country, nor even a majority of the negroes in a single state in the Union. The Yankees certainly are scared of a loud noise, aren't they?

I hope you are getting along well.

Your friend,
Phil Stone

[1] Stone has reference here to the federally-enforced integration of Central High School in Little Rock, Arkansas.

1393b Letter from Anne Louise Davis, of Harold Ober Associates, to Saxe Commins, February 18, 1958, signed ribbon typescript, 1 page.

Dear Mr. Commins:

I have your letter to Mr. Ober, who is out of town this week, but we discussed it yesterday morning on the telephone, and I later had a talk with Mr. Weissberger about it.

The second paragraph of Mr. Weissberger's letter disturbs both of us very much, because we feel that there should be some restriction to the hold that Miss Ford has on the play. Now, we both understand that the play was written for her, and we understand that Mr. Faulkner wants her to have the first chance to play in it, but we feel for his own protection that she should not have the entire control over it. Mr. Weissberger admits that what Miss Ford really wants, in effect, is to have the play deeded over to her.

The Dramatists Guild recently faced a related problem, and held a long session on the issue, and they feel very strongly that this kind of an arrangement would be disastrous to the property, and they think Mr. Faulkner should maintain the primary control over his property.

Miss Ford's present contract gives her the right to take the play to the West End of London, and then, provided that the requisite number of performances has been given, she may take out a Dramatists Guild contract for an American production, so as far as this goes she is very adequately protected.

At any rate, I truly think that the only way you can resolve this problem is to wait until Mr. Faulkner arrives in Princeton, and then point out to him that it would not be wise to grant the rights that Miss Ford wants. Mr. Weissberger and Miss Ford want this settled before she leaves for Europe the end of this week, but we don't see how it can be. I return the two letters you sent on.

I hope you are feeling much better!

Sincerely,
/s/ Anne Louise

1393c Letter from Ruth Ford to Saxe Commins, undated [February 1958], signed ribbon typescript, 1 page. From London.

Dear Saxe:

Attached is the correspondence between my lawyer Arnold Weissberger, Mr. Ober, and the lawyer for the Royal Court Theatre. If you could please have the patience to read through these letters, you will see the position clearly stated. I cannot help but feel that Ober is taking an unreasonable stand on this. His refusal to recognise the Royal Court as a West End theatre is based purely on the unimportant point of geography. My contract with Faulkner calls for "50 performances in a West End theatre" so, unless Bill will recognise the Royal Court as a West End theatre and accept the 32 performances that were actually given there as a fulfilment of our contract (there were 16 performances on the road prior to London, making a total of 47 [*sic*] performances) I cannot meet the requirements of my contract with Faulkner and will, therefore, lose my English rights.

As you know, I chose the theatre and the director and the set designer and so forth, that I thought would be the best for "Requiem" and I was proven right, wasn't I? The press couldn't have been better nor could the play have been more successful so it seems to me that Mr. Ober must recognise these points.

Love
/s/ Ruth

1393d Letter from Harold Ober to Saxe Commins, February 25, 1958, signed ribbon typescript, 1 page.

Dear Saxe:

I am just back from ten days in the south. I think that Ruth Ford must have gone back to England as she was supposed to leave last Thursday. I really don't think that Ruth Ford needs anything more than she now has. Even if we wanted to, we couldn't allow the play to be done in English anywhere else because the contract she has wouldn't allow us to do so. We have agreed to give her the right to do the play in English in Europe, and what else can she need?

If I were you, I would do nothing. We have talked to Weissberger, and I will talk to him again.

The publicity people for THE LONG HOT SUMMER (THE HAMLET) have been calling me, wanting to interview Faulkner, and if they couldn't get hold of him, to interview me to get some publicity for the picture. I don't imagine Bill wants to give any interviews, and if that is so, will you just write me a note saying that he doesn't want to do so.

Also, Barbara Cohen of Caedmon Records called to find out whether the rights may be available for them to do a record based on readings from AS I LAY DYING. They would make the script and submit it for Bill's approval. We don't know how you and Bill will feel about this. We have checked with Manny Harper[1] and neither he nor we know of any conflicting commitments on this novel. Will you let me know how you feel about this?

Sincerely,
/s/ Harold

[1] Random House accountant.

1396 Letter from Estelle Faulkner to Dorothy Commins, "Tuesday—Feb. 26th" [1958], signed autograph manuscript, 1 page.

Dearest Dorothy—

How wonderful to know that you and Saxe are coming down to see us!

I didn't interrupt Bill's long distance talk with Saxe yesterday, for I know they had business to discuss—so am hastening this note off to let you know how welcome your visit will be—Can hardly wait—

Jill and Paul are *anxiously* eager to have baby Paul know you, and naturally I'll be very proud to show off our newest grand-son—

Someday, I hope to get to see, and know, Frannie's babies—Bill says they are lovely—

Much love, and we will meet you the afternoon of the eighth—

Hurriedly
Estelle

39. Faulkner and Saxe Commins, Princeton, Spring 1958

1401a Memorandum from Dan D. Coyle, head of the Department of Public Information, Princeton University, to his staff, March 3, 1958, signed carbon typescript, 1 page.

Mr. Faulkner has strongly requested that any publicity pertaining to his brief visit be limited to the attached,[1] which he approved today. The combination of a tight schedule in the University and the pressures of his own work will make it impossible for him to grant any interviews, to pose for pictures, to take time for anything except appointments arranged under the direction of Professor Oates. Any out-of-the-ordinary questions, possibly involving literary or publishing angles with which we might not be familiar, may be referred to Mr. Faulkner's close friend and editor, Saxe Commins.

Both Faulkner and Commins were pleased with what Commins called the "dignity and restraint" of the attached squib.

/s/ DDC
/t/ Dan D. Coyle

[1]The attached press release reads as follows:

William Faulkner, distinguished American novelist, who in recent years has won both the Nobel and Pulitzer Prizes in Literature, will be in residence here at Princeton University for the next two weeks under the sponsorship of the Council of the Humanities.

Mr. Faulkner, it was explained today by Professor Whitney J. Oates, chairman of the Interdepartmental Committee of the Council of the Humanities, will participate in several graduate seminars as well as in preceptorial conferences in undergraduate courses in American literature. He will also be available for individual consultations with students in the Department of English.

1393e Letter from Ruth Ford to Saxe Commins, March 7, 1958, signed ribbon typescript, 2 pages. From London.

Dear, dear Saxe:

I hope this letter finds you completely well and Spring aknockin' at the door. I was so distressed when I talked to you the day before leaving to discover that you had been ill again. I know that Dorothy is nourishing you with love and strength and I feel that you must be responding to all of that.

Our situation here is rather distressing. There seems to be no theatre available to "Requiem." The theatres here are getting fewer and fewer, just like New York. We cannot go into a large house because that would be bad for our play and the small ones are filled with long runs or the owners and managers of the ones that are available are putting in their own plays first. Also, the turnover here is not as vast as in New York. Plays seem to run here for ever. The worse they are the longer they run. So, we have just about accepted the fact that we won't be playing out our run here. Our potential audience here is great and we are very sad indeed that, up to today, we cannot find a theatre to house us. Maybe, after our New York run, we can come back to England.

Our American producers will be here in a lump next week and we will get down to the business of organising our American pre-Broadway tour, with an opening on Broadway now set for the first week in October.

There are several points in the contract that Ober drew up between Ruth Ford and William Faulkner that disturb me and I would very much like to put the case before you as simply as possible so that you and Bill can see my point. I loathe boring either or both of you with all of this but I just cannot seem to get through to Ober and make myself clear. He has given me the kind of contract, all the way down the line, that he would give to Darryl F. Zanuck and Irene Selznick or whoever. He refuses to take into consideration the background and the history of this play and that it is not just purely and simply a hard-bound business deal, but concerns a play that Bill wrote for me and I somehow understood from Bill that it was in my hands to do with as I wished, naturally not doing anything in any way that would harm him or the play. Nor does he take into consideration that this is my adaptation, on which I worked extremely hard, and that I wish to play the part of Temple as long as I can, in as many places and countries as I can, exclusively. As you know, my lawyer wrote him a letter saying that, in order to have protection on this, I should have an additional paragraph to the contract stating that "no-one can perform this play or any part of it, in any medium, in the English language, anywhere, without my consent." I know you sent this letter from our lawyer on to Ober. I don't know whether he was out of town or not, but Miss Davis called my lawyer and said that she "wouldn't dream of giving me any such rights" and that she "was sure that Mr. Ober would agree with her." Why she took this stand, I don't know. Anyway, as you know, that is about the time I had to leave to come back to London.

Now that an American producer will be doing the play, they could, if they so decided, send out a road company while I am playing New York, or even send another company to England. Naturally, I would not want this to be done because I want to play the road and England and whatever and whenever for as long as I can—say, reasonably, within a period of five years.

So, I would be happy if Bill would give this his consideration. You know I worked so hard on the script and tried for six years to get this play produced.

As you know, no first-class American producer would touch it—they were scared to death of it—but, of course, the moment it was a success here, they all started screaming and grabbing for it. So many years of my life have been involved and devoted to this play. All I want now really is the chance to play it because, as you know, I passionately love it.

Please give Bill my love—and Dorothy and dear Saxe, for you too, of course, love—from Zachary too.

/s/ Ruth

1403a Letter from Harold Ober to Phil Stone, March 11, 1958, signed ribbon typescript, 2 pages.

Dear Mr. Stone:

I saw Mr. Faulkner in Princeton on Saturday and he asked me to tell you that he would be home on Thursday March 20 and that he would call you when he got there.

He asked me also to write you about adding a codicil to his will. The contract which he signed for the sale of moving picture rights of THE HAMLET contains the following clause.

"The Owner will add a Codicil to his last will, containing a provision to the effect that if there shall accrue in favor of the Executor of said will the right to renew or extend any copyright or copyrights in said literary property or in any portion thereof, then said Executor shall renew or extend said copyright or copyrights within the period required by law, and promptly after each such renewal or extension and without cost or expense to the Purchaser, said Executor shall assign to the Purchaser, for such renewed or extended term, all of the rights in said literary property which are the subject of the within option."

"The Owner shall not revoke, cancel or modify the foregoing provision of said Will, and if the Owner executes any later Will or Codicil, the Owner shall include the foregoing provision therein and shall deliver to the Purchaser a copy of such later Will or Codicil."

I enclose a copy of the Codicil which the Picture Company would like to have added to his will.

The reason for this is that the first 28 years of copyright on THE HAMLET will end in 1959 and if Mr. Faulkner should die before the end of the first 28 years of copyright his heirs might not confirm the terms of the picture contract for the second 28 years. This would leave the picture company in the position of having paid for and having spent a great deal of money to produce the picture and not being able to exhibit it and get their money back.

When you have added the Codicil to the will and it has been properly executed will you write me a letter to that effect so that I may complete the stipulation of the moving picture contract.

Sincerely,
/s/ Harold Ober

1393f Letter from Saxe Commins to Ruth Ford, March 14, 1958, unsigned carbon typescript, 1 page.

Dear Ruth,

I discussed your letter of March 7th with Bill last night and his response can be summed up in this manner: He had given you his word that the English version of *Requiem* was for you and that he will always abide by that word. He thinks that should suffice and sees no reason for a written amplification or amendment to what is understood by Harold Ober, by you and certainly by himself. No one else can undertake it without his consent, whether it is in New York, on the road or in England and the Continent. This right to consent or refuse he must retain and cannot relinquish it by conferring it on anyone else.

Of course he realises all that the play means to you and wants you to have the success you so richly deserve. He believes that we should cross each bridge as we come to it and that you should go ahead on the old basis, knowing that he will keep his word.

Bill's visit in Princeton has been a great success so far as the students are concerned and certainly as far as Dorothy and I have had the great joy of his company in our house for two weeks. He goes back to Charlottesville tomorrow and thence to Oxford, returning to the University of Virginia in mid-April. We've never had such a considerate guest.

I do hope that you will yet find a theatre in London, although from what you say the outlook is dim. When you open in New York in October, all these trials will be forgotten.

Please give Dorothy's and my love to Zachary and keep a good share for yourself.

Always
[no signature]

1393g Letter from Ruth Ford to Saxe Commins, April 10, 1958, signed ribbon typescript, 1 page. From London.

Dear Saxe:

Thank you for your letter of March 14th. I am *covered* with humiliation that you and Bill should have, for a moment, felt that I had no trust and faith in Bill's word when, as a matter of fact, I would stake my life on Bill's word. I am so sorry there has been so much confusion and bother to both of you on this matter. All those requests were really because of my lawyer's insistence. You know how boring and hard-headed and one-track lawyers can be. They have never heard of the "spoken" word—it is the written word or nothing with them. They were just trying to protect me from any misunderstanding between myself and my producers, not between me and Bill. Anyway, I go *blind* trying to read contracts. I am just not at all talented in that way. It is all just like Greek to me. If my lawyer had just simply explained to me that *nobody* can do this play without Bill's consent, then all of these back and forth letters and requests would have been completely unnecessary. Anyway, let's call it all a closed book now and forget it. I couldn't be happier nor feel more secure. I was touched to tears by the little hand-written P.S. of Bill's.

Zachary and I are booked to leave on the Ile de France from Southampton July 23rd, arriving New York July 30th. We need three or four weeks to reactivate our lives and start the ground-work casting for "Requiem." We will, of course, call you when we arrive.

Spring is determined *not* to arrive in England. As a matter of fact, judging by the newspapers, it seems to be determined not to arrive anywhere. Anyway, I do hope warm weather and beautiful, sweet, soft air will be reaching you soon and finding you well and strong. Tell Dorothy I will answer her letter in a few days. I know what a great joy it was for you both to have Bill there for two weeks. I am sure the joy was equal to you all.

Zachary and I send you both warm love,

/s/ Ruth

1408 Letter from Jill Faulkner Summers to Dorothy and Saxe Commins, April 21 [1958], signed autograph manuscript, 1 page.

Dearest Miss Dorothy & Mr. Saxe—

How very very sweet of you to remember both of us on Tad's birthday. Perhaps I should say all three of us for Paul is enjoying the book on the orchestra[1] as much as Tad. (Last night they spent all the "reading before bed time" on it & we were both completely absorbed.)

My scarves are lovely & so perfectly compliment my predilection toward simple suits for each & every occasion. Thank you.

We have some wonderful news & although it is a bit previous we do want you to know before everyone but grandparents. We are expecting another child next fall. Mama & Pappy are so excited & we're all sort of hoping for a little girl this time.

Paul's business is improving slowly but steadily so we're really beginning to put down roots in Charlottesville. Again let us urge you to come down for a visit—soon.

Love from all three of us—

Jill

[1] Possibly Mrs. Commins' children's book, *Making an Orchestra* (New York: Macmillan Company, 1931).

1411 Letter from Estelle Faulkner to Dorothy Commins, "Wednesday—April 30th," signed autograph manuscript, 2 pages, with envelope addressed in Mrs. Faulkner's hand and postmarked Charlottesville, May 2, 1958.

Dearest Dorothy—

After such a long lapse—a note from me—and rather an embarrassed one!

I do want to thank you for the handkerchiefs Jill tells me you so thoughtfully sent, along with little Paul's charming "orchestra"—handkerchiefs I never had the thrill of seeing—never got—

It happened like this—

The Summers were here the week following Tad's birthday, and that Sunday, the 20th, was Helen Summers' natal day—so Jill saved some of the baby's gifts in order that they might celebrate together—

In the ensuing confusion of tissue paper, ribbon, boxes etc—(which Paul, being most orderly, immediately threw away) evidently your sweet remembrance to me was lost—I am desolate—At that, though, it gives me a glow, to know you still love me despite my horrid failure to write—

Why I am such a poor correspondent is a question for a psychologist—I think of you and Saxe daily, and quite envied Bill his two weeks with you in Princeton—

This spring in Charlottesville has been so interrupted by our four week stay in Mississippi and minor illnesses in the family—that I haven't had the fun we had last year—For one thing, the house we have is hopelessly small, and entertaining must needs be limited—

I'm hoping and *praying* that Bill *will* see his way clear to buy a place up here—Then you can come (if you will) and stay and stay and stay—How I'd love that!

We've found an ideal house and grounds that *I* already feel at home, in and on, but of course I realize how serious a move it will be, for Billy—and say little—I've sort of trained myself to be reasonably satisfied anywhere—but to be near Jill and her little family means a great deal—

This little news from me *is* truly written on the fly—

I love you both, dearly—

Always
Estelle

1403d Letter from Phil Stone to Anne Louise Davis, May 15, 1958, carbon typescript with typed signature, 1 page.

Dear Mrs. Davis:

I have your letter of May 13, and shall govern myself accordingly.[1]

I thought I wrote Mr. Ober that I prepared a codicil for Bill to sign before Bill got back from Virginia. I thought Mr. Ober had told Bill about it and he has been around here for a while, but he never came by the office. I am glad to do this and I do things like this for Bill free, but I have too much to do to run Bill down. Bill is just too much trouble sometimes anyway. If Mr. Ober wants Bill to sign the codicil he had better get in touch with him himself from your office and tell him to do so. Also, a lot of my law practice is out of town and I am frequently gone and I think it best for me to be here if and when Bill executes the codicil, to be sure that it is done correctly.

Yours truly,
Phil Stone

[1]Miss Davis sought Stone's assistance in getting Faulkner to execute a codicil to his last will and testament regarding the assignment of motion picture rights to *The Hamlet* to Twentieth Century-Fox Film Corporation. See Ober's letter to Stone, March 11, 1958, printed above.

1414 Letter from Anne Louise Davis to Saxe Commins, July 14, 1958, signed ribbon typescript, 1 page.

Dear Mr. Commins:

Thank you so much for signing the two copies of the agreement providing for the Brazilian production in the Portuguese language of Mr. Faulkner's REQUIEM FOR A NUN. I've sent these off to South America.

This morning, I received from them our copies signed by Gert Meyer, the principal, and just so we'll have the record straight and complete, would you also be kind enough to sign these two copies and return them to me in the enclosed, stamped envelope? Thank you!

Mr. Ober has been out of the office with a bug, but I think he'll be back tomorrow or the next day. I stayed home last week myself, and while it was fiendishly hot, at least I wasn't in the city, and I got a lot done, and it was a change. I hope you are staying well.

With best wishes,
Sincerely,
/s/ Anne Louise
/t/ Anne Louise Davis

1412k Letter from Maud M. Brown to Faulkner, July 16, 1958, signed autograph manuscript, 1 page.

Dear Billy,

You told me, I know, that The Wishing Tree[1] was mine to do with as I pleased. Through all these years I've cherished it as something personal because Margaret loved it so much. The manuscript is yellow and dogeared from her handling of it. I have never before considered publishing it but now I believe it should be published. Since a copy was on exhibit at Princeton[2] it has become an object of public curiosity.

Dr. Silver tells me that no publisher will consider it without your written permission. Will you give me that permission?[3] I should like to see it published with a dignified presentation instead of as a showpiece in an exhibit.

I am glad you are back in Oxford and hope you will stay here though I hear rumors to the contrary.

Sincerely yours,
Maud M. Brown

[1] The presentation copy which Faulkner had given to Mrs. Brown's daughter in 1928.

[2] The copy exhibited at Princton was the presentation copy Faulkner gave to Philip Alston Stone in 1948.

[3] Faulkner never responded to either this letter or the follow-up letter Mrs. Brown wrote on December 1, 1958. The texts of these letters printed in this volume are based on copies Mrs. Brown provided Professor Silver in 1960.

1415 Western Union telegram from Estelle Faulkner to Dorothy Commins, July 17, 1958.

DEAREST DOROTHY WE ARE SHOCKED AND HEART BROKEN.[1] JILL AND BABY ARE HERE. JILL IS CRUSHED AS WE. BILL OR I WILL COME IMMEDIATELY IF IN ANY WAY OUR PHYSICAL PRESENCE WILL HELP KNOW THAT WE IN MISSISSIPPI MOURN TOO OUR LOVE

ESTELLE JILL BILL

[1] Over the death of Saxe Commins, July 17, 1958.

1416 Western Union telegram from Faulkner to Dorothy Commins, July 18, 1958.

THE FINEST EPITAPH EVERYONE WHO EVER KNEW SAXE WILL HAVE TO SUBSCRIBE TO WHETHER HE WILL OR NOT QUOTE HE LOVED ME UNQUOTE

BILL FAULKNER

1412b Letter from Ralph Graves, an editor for *Life* magazine, to James W. Silver, August 8, 1958, signed ribbon typescript, 1 page.

Dear Professor Silver:

John Osborne has given me the Faulkner manuscript[1] that you entrusted to him. I am indeed interested in the possibility of publishing it in LIFE. It is very long for us to cope with, of course, but I assume that we would just have to cope unless Mr. Faulkner felt that it should be cut.

I am writing to raise all the basic questions: Would Mr. Faulkner be agreeable to publication? Under what conditions? And what price would be placed on it by Mrs. Brown or Mr. Faulkner or both?

I realize that it may take you some time to provide the answers. If it is all right with you, I will keep the manuscript until I hear from you.

Sincerely,
/s/ Ralph Graves
/t/ Ralph Graves

[1]"The Wishing Tree," for which Silver, on behalf of Maud Brown, was seeking a publisher.

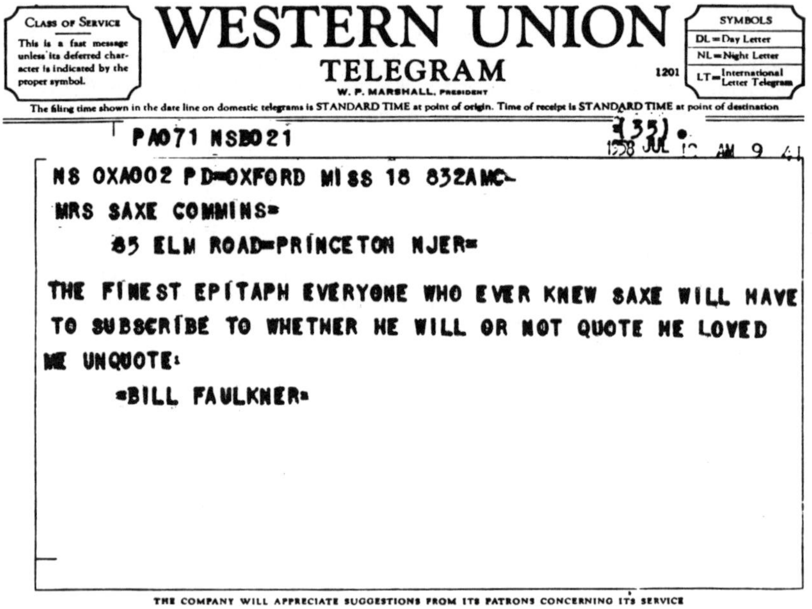

CLASS OF SERVICE
This is a fast message unless its deferred character is indicated by the proper symbol.

WESTERN UNION
TELEGRAM
W. P. MARSHALL, PRESIDENT

1201

SYMBOLS
DL=Day Letter
NL=Night Letter
LT=International Letter Telegram

The filing time shown in the date line on domestic telegrams is STANDARD TIME at point of origin. Time of receipt is STANDARD TIME at point of destination

PA071 NSB021

1958 JUL 1? AM 9 41

NS OXA002 PD=OXFORD MISS 18 832AMC=
MRS SAXE COMMINS=
85 ELM ROAD=PRINCETON NJER=
THE FINEST EPITAPH EVERYONE WHO EVER KNEW SAXE WILL HAVE TO SUBSCRIBE TO WHETHER HE WILL OR NOT QUOTE HE LOVED ME UNQUOTE:
=BILL FAULKNER=

THE COMPANY WILL APPRECIATE SUGGESTIONS FROM ITS PATRONS CONCERNING ITS SERVICE

40. Telegram from Faulkner on the death of Saxe Commins (item 1416)

1412c Letter from James W. Silver to Ralph Graves, August 13, 1958, carbon typescript with typed signature, 1 page.

Dear Mr. Graves:

I was glad to hear that John Osborne had turned over to you the manuscript of the "Wishing Tree." And to know that you are interested in it.

It seems to me that there is just about a fifty-fifty chance that Wild Bill will come through with the publication rights. I talked at length with Mrs. Brown who has *written* to Faulkner. (Just after I talked with her, I spent a couple of hours with him, but did not think it strategic to mention the matter.) But Mrs. Brown and I think it best to wait till about September 1 and then if she hasn't heard anything, we'll try another approach.

The story behind this story is, I think, an intriguing one. About 1928 Mrs. Brown had an afflicted child, a girl of about nine, who died two or three years later. Bill Faulkner brought the story to the door one day, saying that he had written it for Margaret. There is a lot of sentimental stuff about what it meant to the child, etc., but I'll skip that. But it does seem to me that this gives a side to Faulkner that the outside world knows little about. For instance, he was local scoutmaster for years—and I understand a good one until the mothers took him in hand after Sanctuary came out. Anyway, what I'm getting at is that there is a fine story to go along with this story—if we can get permission to publish.

In 1949 [*sic*] Faulkner borrowed the manuscript and made another copy, for Phil Stone's boy, I think.[1] That copy was shown at the Princeton exhibit and I don't know where it now is. But the original manuscript and the story was *given* to Margaret Brown some thirty years ago.[2]

I will keep you in touch with developments here, and hope that I shall have something encouraging to write. I think it can be worked out.

Sincerely,
James W. Silver

[1] Faulkner also made an additional copy, which he presented to Ruth Ford's daughter, Shelley.

[2] Silver was not aware that the Brown copy was actually the *second* copy of the story; Faulkner had presented the original manuscript to Victoria Franklin, Estelle Franklin's daughter.

1403e Letter from Phil Stone to Harold Ober, October 10, 1958, carbon typescript with typed signature, 1 page.

Dear Mr. Ober:

Bill Faulkner at last came by and executed the Codicil[1] in duplicate. I herewith enclose the original of the duplicate Codicil.

I told Bill to keep the other original duplicate but, as he said, he probably will misplace it, and wanted me to put it in my lock box for him. I shall put it in Lock Box No. 46 at the Bank of Oxford of this place, in a sealed envelope on which is typed: "Codicil to the Will of William Faulkner."

Please acknowledge receipt.

Yours truly,
Phil Stone

[1] Relating to Twentieth Century-Fox's movie rights to *The Hamlet.*

1418 Letter from Whitney J. Oates to Dorothy Commins, October 21, 1958, signed ribbon typescript, 1 page.

Dear Do:

This is just to let you know that I finally did reach Bill Faulkner on the telephone and had a very nice talk with him. He is planning to arrive in

Princeton on either November 16th or November 17th and he promised to wire me his exact time of arrival so that I can meet him.[1]

. . . .

All love to you and the Bennett family.

As always,
/s/ Mike
/t/ Whitney J. Oates

[1]Beginning on November 16, Faulkner conducted six days of preceptorials and student conferences on behalf of the Humanities Program at Princeton. Oates, a classics professor at Princeton, was chairman of the program.

1412k Letter from Maud M. Brown to Faulkner, December 1, 1958, signed autograph manuscript, 1 page.

Dear Billy,

Last summer I wrote you a letter of which I enclose a copy.[1] After I had mailed it I learned that you were in transit, as it were, to Virginia at just that time. I have wondered if my letter ever reached you. I do not want to seem to pester you but I still feel about this as I did when I wrote this enclosure. The Wishing Tree is a very charming piece of literary workmanship and deserves a better fate than merely to have a place on my shelves. Besides, knowing how Margaret loved it, I should like for other children to know it too.

Sincerely yours,
Maud M. Brown

[1]Mrs. Brown's letter of July 16, 1958, printed above. Faulkner never consented to the publication of "The Wishing Tree," which was issued posthumously by Random House in 1967.

S-48 Letter from Faulkner to Phillip E. Mullen, undated [possibly early December 1958], signed autograph manuscript, 1 page.

Phil—

This gentleman will explain what he needs.[1] I believe you can help him more than anyone in my absence. Best to you.

Bill

[1]This letter of introduction was perhaps supplied to the Australian professor mentioned in Faulkner's December 8, 1958 letters to James W. Silver and Phil Mullen (see below).

1420 Letter from Faulkner to James W. Silver, undated, signed autograph manuscript, 1 page, with envelope addressed in Faulkner's hand and postmarked Charlottesville, December 8, 1958.

Dear Jim—

An Australian history prof, in the University of Sydney, N.S.W. will call on you between Xmas and 12th Night. He will not be a burden, he only wants contacts to learn what he can of the South, economy, tenant farming, etc. I will appreciate what you can do. Will be home for bird shooting about 2 Jan. Regards to Dutch.

Bill Faulkner[1]

[1]Faulkner wrote this letter on the verso of an 8-by-5¼-inch fragment of a sheet of stationery bearing the letterhead of "The-People-to-People Program." Cf. the following item.

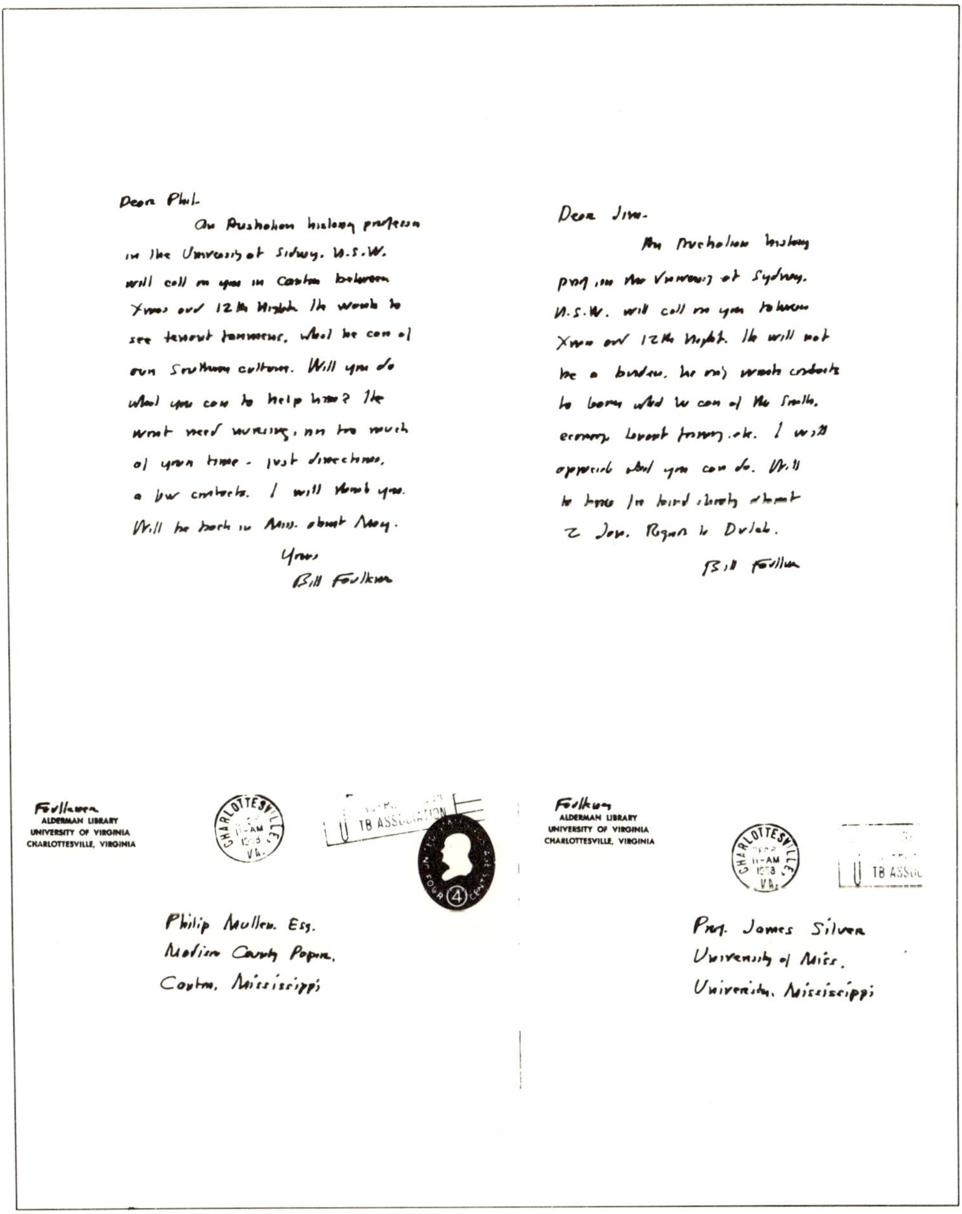

41. Letters from Faulkner to Phil Mullen and James Silver, with envelopes (items 1420 and S-49)

S-49 Letter from Faulkner to Phillip E. Mullen, undated, signed autograph manuscript, 1 page, with envelope addressed in Faulkner's hand and postmarked Charlottesville, December 8, 1958.

Dear Phil—

An Australian history professor in the University of Sidney [*sic*], N.S.W. will call on you in Canton between Xmas and 12th Night. He wants to see tenant farmers, what he can of our Southern culture. Will you do what you can to help him? He wont need nursing, nor too much of your time—just directions, a few contacts. I will thank you. Will be back in Miss. about May.

Yours
Bill Faulkner[1]

[1]This letter is written on an 8-by-5¼-inch fragment of stationery which appears to be the other half of the same leaf used by Faulkner to write James W. Silver with the same request. See the previous item.

1412k Letter from Maud M. Brown to Faulkner, December 1, 1958, signed autograph manuscript, 1 page.

Dear Professor Silver:

It has been rather a long time since I have been in touch with you, and I wondered if you had been able to make any progress on the Faulkner fairy tale? I realize, of course, that this is a long-range thing with much careful negotiation to be done, but I didn't want you to think that we had lost interest.

Sincerely,
/s/ Ralph Graves
/t/ Ralph Graves

1421 Letter (on printed Christmas card) from Estelle Faulkner to Dorothy Commins, "Dec. 13th," signed autograph manuscript, with envelope addressed in Mrs. Faulkner's hand and postmarked Charlottesville, December 15, 1958.

Dearest Dorothy—

This is assuming that you had Paul's wire about our newest grand-son—William C. Faulkner Summers—I am pleased now, but at first was quite disappointed as I *did* want a little grand-daughter, badly—

Bill leaves Jan. 3rd for Mississippi again, but I plan to stay on here until April—

If at all possible, and should you care to, do come and spend some time with me—Jill and Paul will move into their new home sometime early in January, but I dare say a good bit of Jill's time will still be at Farmington where grand-mama can be of use!

We *all* want you to come, and are looking forward to being with you once more—

May the Holiday season bring you some joy and peace of mind, is my prayer for you—

I know how sorely you've been wounded—

My Love as always
Estelle

1412e Letter from James W. Silver to Ralph Graves, December 22, 1958, carbon typescript with typed signature, 1 page.

Dear Mr. Graves:

For a couple of months I have been hoping that something would develop, more or less out of a clear sky, about the Faulkner manuscript.[1] But it hasn't and doesn't look as though it will.

Mrs. Brown *wrote* to Faulkner back in August, as I informed you about that time. She heard nothing, although I'm sure that she ran into Faulkner on the town square in the succeeding couple of months. I was busy during the fall and saw very little of either of them. Faulkner left town about the middle of November, after the marriage of his niece,[2] and Mrs. Brown took the occasion to write him again, assuming that he had not seen the first letter. Actually, it is possible that he hasn't seen either. But when Mrs. Brown took off for a Christmas visit about a week ago she had not heard from Faulkner and the premise must be now that she won't hear from him.

The only suggestion I have at the moment is for you to contact Faulkner's agent. I'm sure that *Life* knows who he is because it has made several contracts with Faulkner in the past. This might work although I don't have very high hopes from it. If it doesn't work, then the last alternative, it seems to me, is for Mrs. Brown or myself to *talk* with him until he does or does not give his consent. I rather doubt whether I would ever do this, mainly because of family connections, but it may be the only practical last resort. But I would like to have you see whether anything can be done through Faulkner's agent. This might work.

Sincerely,
James W. Silver

[1] "The Wishing Tree."
[2] Dean Faulkner and Jon Mallard were married on November 9, 1958.

1959

S-50 Western Union telegram from Arnold Weissberger to Ruth Ford, January 7, 1959.

MY WORDS OF PRAISE I WILL NOT HOARD
WHEN CHEERING THE VERSATILE TALENTS OF FORD
BRAVOS AND LOVE[1]

ARNOLD

[1] This telegram was sent to Miss Ford c/o Shubert Theatre, New Haven, Connecticut, on the occasion of the opening of *Requiem for a Nun.*

S-51 Letter from Edward E. Colton to Harold Ober, Arnold Weissberger, and Ben Aslan, January 26, 1959, signed carbon typescript, 1 page.

Dear Harold, Arnold & Ben[1]:

In view of the fact that "REQUIEM FOR A NUN" is opening[2] this week, I recommend that Twentieth Century be given an ultimatum to either accept the contract on the basis you are willing to make a deal, or otherwise forget about the deal. I think it inadvisable not to bring the matter to a head before the play opens.

I await your instructions.

Cordially yours,
/s/ Edward E. Colton
/t/ Edward E. Colton[3]

[1]Benjamin Aslan was an associate of the New York legal firm of Fitelson and Mayers.

[2]That is, on Broadway, January 30, 1959.

[3]Colton, senior partner in the New York law firm of Colton, Gallantz & Fernbach, was negotiator for the sale of the motion picture rights to *Requiem for a Nun*.

S-52 Letter from Arnold Weissberger to Harry J. McIntyre, of Twentieth Century-Fox Film Corporation, January 27, 1959, unsigned carbon typescript, 2 pages.

Dear Harry:

Ed Colton has conveyed to me substance of his conversation with you this afternoon. I have also talked to Harold Ober and this letter is written both on behalf of William Faulkner and my client, Ruth Ford.

1. There have been delivered to you certain outstanding contracts with respect to foreign productions of "REQUIEM." Mr. Faulkner will not make a motion picture deal for this property unless the grant to you is subject to the rights of the parties under these contracts. He will agree to use his best efforts to obtain from the grantees of foreign rights any modifications in their contracts that you would like to see or any clearances, but he cannot make guarantees or warranties to that effect.

2. Mr. Faulkner is unwilling to make any warranty with respect to the copyright status of the novel or play in countries outside of the United States.

3 Mr. Faulkner can only quit claim to you the motion picture rights with respect to translations and versions of the property written by others than himself. He cannot make representations or warranties as to whether he has acquired any rights to such translations or versions or with respect to the rights acquired by him therein.

4. The motion picture cannot be released by you prior to June 1st, 1960, or the date of the termination of the continuous run of the play in New York City and on tour (whichever date is earlier). The continuous run of the play shall not be deemed to have ended if the play is not presented between June 1st and September 15th, 1959, if at the time of the closing of the play within that period there is a bona fide intention on the part of the stage producers to resume the run of the play as a first class attraction in New York City or on the road prior to September 15th, 1959.

5. Mr. Faulkner's liability for breach of any and all representations, warranties and covenants made by him must be limited to the contract price.

6. The stage producers must receive credit on the film. The credit can be on the same frame as Mr. Faulkner and Miss Ford. The producers of the play are The Theatre Guild and [Julius] Fleischmann and [Richard] Myers and all three must receive credit.

With the foregoing basic points of difference between you on the one hand and Mr. Ober and myself on the other it is essential that we know before the opening of the play whether you are prepared to conclude the deal on the conditions set forth above. If you are not prepared to make a deal on these conditions then it must be understood that there is no obligation on the part of Mr. Faulkner or Miss Ford to make a deal and Mr. Faulkner and Miss Ford will be free to dispose of the motion picture rights to the property as they see fit.

If it is impossible to have a final contract before the opening of the play but if you will assure us as to your agreement on the conditions set forth in this letter, this will be satisfactory to Mr. Faulkner and Miss Ford.

I am enclosing an extra copy of this letter for your convenience in considering it.

Faithfully yours,
[no signature]

S-53 Letter from Arnold Weissberger to Ted Strauss, of Twentieth Century-Fox Film Corporation, January 27, 1959, unsigned carbon typescript, 1 page.

Dear Ted:

I am sending to you herewith, for your information, the Connecticut and Boston notices for "REQUIEM FOR A NUN" which are, as you will see, unanimously favorable.

In Joe Moscowitz' absence I must now bring to your attention the situation with respect to the contract. Mr. Colton, Mr. Ober and I have been in negotiation with Harry McIntyre. Harry has raised objection to certain provisions in the contract which are, in fact, substantially identical to previous provisions in contracts between 20th Century-Fox and William Faulkner. It is not my purpose in writing to you to take up matters that have been discussed with Harry, but we feel that this matter must be settled tomorrow without fail. The play opens on Friday, and either we have a preproduction deal or we do not. If we do not have a deal before the opening, then we are prepared to take our chances on making a better deal (either with 20th, or another company) after the opening.

Cordially yours,
[no signature]

S-54 Letter from Harry J. McIntyre to Arnold Weissberger, January 29, 1959, signed ribbon typescript, 1 page.

Dear Arnold:

This will acknowledge receipt of your letter to me of January 27, 1959, concerning our discussions relating to the form of the contract whereby this company is acquiring motion picture and allied rights in REQUIEM FOR A NUN.

In view of the provisions of prior agreements we have had with Mr. Faulkner, this will confirm my telephone advice to you this morning that this company accepts the substance of the 6 items in your letter. However, we do not wish this action on our part to be considered a precedent for any future agreements for the acquisition by us of such rights.

Moreover, in view of the agreement by this company to the substance of the 6 points in your letter of January 27th, it is my understanding that this company will not be asked to make any changes in addition to the ones we have already covered. Accordingly, I shall immediately prepare the revised documents for execution and should have them ready the early part of next week.

Sincerely yours,
/s/ Harry McIntyre
/t/ Harry J. McIntyre

S-55 Letter from Arnold Weissberger to Harold Ober, February 6, 1959, unsigned carbon typescript, 1 page.

Dear Harold:

Harry McIntyre was out earlier this week with a virus infection, but I called him today on his return to his office, and he promised to get out the "REQUIEM" contract as soon as he could.

It will interest you to know that yesterday when I talked to Ted Strauss at Fox about another matter, he indicated that he thought the play "had taken a terrible beating" and was about to close. I told him this was not at all the case—that the play had gotten some excellent notices and was faring quite well.

The point is, of course, that we can now see what Fox's attitude would have been on these contractual negotiations if we had not clinched the deal before the play opened.

Kind regards.

Cordially,
[no signature]

S-56 Letter from Albert Erskine to Faulkner, February 6, 1959, signed ribbon typescript, 2 pages (1 leaf).

Dear Bill,

Mink[1] arrived safely Wednesday afternoon; I've now read and annotated the first two chapters, a process which, because of frequent references to Hamlet and Town, took longer than you might think.

The note which you sent with the MS was in the middle of it, so that I found it only inadvertently and after reading almost up to it. That one day which you estimate will suffice for going over the MS will not be nearly enough—unless you and I mean something different by "discrepancies."

Since I've never worked on a MS of yours except through intermediaries (and was discouraged from asking as many questions as I wanted to by being assured that you not only didn't want to but wouldn't hear them) I cannot know until I try just how much editor you want or will put up with. But I assure you that so far as I can make it so it will be as much or as little as you yourself want. I don't need to tell you that I've never been given an assignment that gave me more pleasure.

It has been about ten years since I read The Hamlet, but I remember its essentials pretty well, and in the last few days I've refreshed my memory on a lot of details. I've spent the last two weekends, however, making a slow note-taking trip through The Town in anticipation of the arrival of the new MS. So I'm pretty fresh on The Town, and I was already alarmed at the discrepancies that exist between it and The Hamlet before I'd seen the first page of Mink, in which what I at least call discrepancies (matters of fact, event, names of characters, etc) are doubled and redoubled.

Which brings me back to my speculation about whether you and I mean the same thing when we say discrepancies. No conversation we ever had came anywhere close to this topic, but James Meriwether, with whom I had a long session just after Christmas (in which I learned about his involvement in the editing of The Town and got considerable respect for his qualifications as a textual expert), told me that you were definitely concerned about avoiding discrepancies at least within the confines of the Snopes trilogy, if not in its relation to other Yoknapatawpha novels and stories. This impression of his is restated in a letter today in which he offers his assistance—which with your approval I will accept, since I don't care how many hands get into the job if they contribute to its being done well. If I ever had any illusion of infallibility I've long since lost it.

This letter has already gotten longer and the time of day, because of many interruptions, later than I'd expected, so that the actual (what I call) discrepancies I haven't even come to discuss. So I'll send this along now as an introduction to my Memorandum on Discrepancies, which I'll try to do tomorrow or Sunday and send along separately, and a copy of same to Consultant Meriwether for his collection of textual notes. Then you'll know at least what I mean by discrepancies, and I can probably tell from your response what you mean. (I'm afraid one of the tribulations of being assigned a new editor is being bored the hell out of by questions and memoranda, but maybe these will become less necessary in the future and therefore less frequent. For your sake, I hope so, but please bear with me meantime: my purpose in all this is not just to test your patience.)

All best,
/s/ Albert

[1]The opening section of *The Mansion.*

S-57 Letter from Lawrence Langner, of the Theatre Guild, to Ruth Ford, February 13, 1959, signed ribbon typescript, 1 page.

Dear Ruth:

As you know, in view of the poor business in New York, and the excellent reception of the play in Boston and New Haven, we are planning to make a long tour next Fall. We would like to try to make the play run as long as possible in New York City,[1] and to this end all those connected with the project are making sacrifices, hoping to recoup again in the Fall.

The purpose of writing this letter is to ask you whether you would ascertain whether Mr. Faulkner would forego his royalties for the next two weeks which would avoid having to dig too deeply into the capital needed to send the play out next season.

You, yourself, have been most generous in helping us. We would ask you to thank Mr. Faulkner in anticipation of his consent.

Cordially yours,
/s/ Lawrence
/t/ Lawrence Langner

[1]The Broadway production of *Requiem for a Nun* closed on March 7, after only forty-three performances.

S-58 Western Union telegram from Ruth Ford and Zachary Scott to Arnold Weissberger, February 15, 1959.

DEAR ARNOLD:

FOLLOWING IS MY WIRE TO OBER QUOTE DEAR MR. OBER: MADE CONTACT WITH WEISSBERGER TOO LATE ON FRIDAY TO GET BACK TO YOU. WE WISH TO MAKE FIRM COMMITMENT TO PURCHASE "LIGHT IN AUGUST"[1] FOR $50000 5000 DOWN AND BALANCE IN INSTALLMENTS SUITABLE TO FAULKNER. WEISSBERGER WILL CALL YOU FIRST THING MONDAY MORNING OR WOULD YOU BE GOOD ENOUGH TO CALL HIM ON YOUR ARRIVAL AT YOUR OFFICE. REGARDS UNQUOTE.

RUTH FORD AND ZACHARY SCOTT

[1]That is, the movie rights to the book.

S-59 Letter from Zachary Scott to Arnold Weissberger, February 16, 1959, signed autograph manuscript, 2 pages (1 leaf).

A—have just spoken to L. L.[1]—the "temporary closing notice"[2] goes up tonight—to come down Thursday, if necessary concessions are made.

The Shuberts[3] have come down from $5000.00 to $3000.00—& R & I are cutting our salaries to the bone.

L. L. thinks we can (if we can get union ok on stage hands reduction) run our show at approximately $8,500—& go on for several weeks longer.

Will get in touch with you later after things are ironed out.

Best

Zach

[1]Lawrence Langner.
[2]For *Requiem for a Nun.*
[3]Owners of the Golden Theater, where *Requiem for a Nun* was playing.

S-60 Letter from Ruth Ford to Arnold Weissberger, February 16, 1959, signed ribbon typescript, 1 page.

Dear Arnold:

It seems the breaking point on "Requiem" is $17,500. The first week we took $16,043 and the second week $15,777, which is a loss of $3,180 over two weeks. This is the beginning of our third and last Theatre Guild Subscription week. The entire cast is being asked to take cuts. I am enclosing a letter to you from Lawrence Langner.[1] Could you please explain this situation in a letter to Ober and send this letter on to him. I understand from you that the author can be requested to forgo his royalty for two weeks after the first three weeks.

Entre nous, our stop clause at the Golden is $17,000 which, as you see, we have failed to make for two consecutive weeks, which means that the Shuberts could give us our walking papers, but our producers have made a deal with them, because there is no other play wanting this theatre for the moment, so we can apparently stay in the Golden until, I believe, around the 21st April when Adolf Green and Betty Comden will return in "A Party." That is, if we can get all our expenses down to nothing, which means the cast down to the minimum—try to get rid of a few stage hands—and if Faulkner will forgo his royalties. In other words, all of us are going to make every effort possible to stay as long as possible because, of course, the longer we stay the better it is for our tour in the Fall, which we are definitely going to make in all Theatre Guild Subscription cities and everywhere else that we can play and Faulkner will, of course, at that time get his full royalties and that will be for a period of at least nine months. In other words, the producers would like Faulkner to forgo his royalties beginning February 23rd for two weeks. That, I understand from you, can be done. Then am I correct in believing that anything beyond that will have to be done through the Dramatists Guild? Please get an answer for us from Ober as soon as possible. If Faulkner does not forgo the royalties I am sure we couldn't stay on. As it stands now the cast is already cutting down to minimum, a week before he is asked to do anything.

Love,
/s/ Ruth

P.S. Can you find out, possibly from Ober, what date Faulkner arrives. As I understand it, he is due here sometime in February.

[1]See item S-57.

S-61 Letter from Zachary Scott to Harold Ober, February 17, 1959, carbon typescript with typed signature, 1 page.

Dear Mr. Ober:

I hope you were not too startled by my telegram a day or so ago.[1] I was anxious to keep news of the transaction between Mr. Faulkner and ourselves from the papers for several reasons.

As you know, Mr. Harvey Breit and we are mutually interested in this property and plan to make a film of it that will be worthy, in every sense, of Mr. Faulkner and his talents.

We are forming a production company toward this end but, until things are clearly in focus, we prefer to have no knowledge of our plans known.

I simply wanted you to know that we are not buying this book as a money-making scheme, in any sense of the word—we simply want to see a film made which we think can be the best film yet made.

Very sincere regards from both Mrs. Scott and myself.

Yours very truly,
Zachary Scott

[1]See item S-58, printed above.

S-62 Letter from Lawrence Langner to Arnold Weissberger, February 19, 1959, signed ribbon typescript, 1 page.

Dear Arnold:

Will you please convey to Mr. Faulkner the thanks of The Theatre Guild for the waiver of his royalties for the two weeks commencing February 23, 1959. This will insure the play running for a longer period of time.

With best wishes.

Cordially,
/s/ Lawrence
/t/ Lawrence Langner

S-63 Letter from Ruth Ford to Arnold Weissberger, March 16, 1959, signed ribbon typescript, 1 page.

Dear Arnold:

Regarding the two enclosed letters,[1] will you please let me know if a decision on this can be made by me or if it is now in the hands of the producers. If the producers have to agree to this reading of "Requiem For A Nun" will you please pass on the letters to the Theatre Guild.

As you can see by the enclosed clipping Richard Zanuck[2] is in town in connection with the film "Compulsion," and they are going ahead fast with "Requiem." He is already discussing the treatment with several writers and it seems that now is the time to do something about all of this or never. If you know Richard Zanuck I would very much like it if you could set up an appointment for me to see him and talk to him. Let me know about this as soon as possible.

We must find out as quickly as possible what kind of contract the Theatre Guild and Myers want to offer us for the road tour in the fall and get that straight so that we can go ahead with other plans for the fall if it does not work out because, as we told Myers, unless we get an exceptionally good deal where we can make money beyond our expenses, we are not going to tour. Negotiations of contracts are always so involved and take so long I think we had better get started on this at once.

Love
/s/ Ruth

[1] The enclosures related to a request from J. David Madden, director of The Playcrafters, Appalachian State Teachers College, Boone, North Carolina, for permission to do a reading performance of *Requiem for a Nun.*

[2] Twentieth Century-Fox film executive.

S-64 Letter from Lawrence Langner and Richard Myers to Arnold Weissberger, April 8, 1959, signed ribbon typescript, 3 pages.

Dear Arnold:

After a considerable amount of study and consultation we would like to present two plans for a fall tour of REQUIEM FOR A NUN. We trust that you will discuss these with Ruth and Zachary and advise us of your reaction at your first convenience.

As you are probably aware the production to date has represented a loss of $30,000 to the investors and I know that the Scotts share our determination to return as much money as possible to the investors.

Accordingly, we will briefly outline herewith the two separate and distinct proposals for the tour. You will see that Plan 1 calls for production of the tour by the REQUIEM Company and outlines the particulars under which the REQUIEM Company would wish to present the tour. Plan 2 calls for a lease by the REQUIEM Company of the first class touring rights to a new Company and the specific terms of this lease are to be outlined at a later point in this letter.

PLAN 1

(a) That the contract signed previously operate as the basis of a new contract. However, in the weeks where the gross is less than $20,000, that Miss Ford's salary drop at the rate of $50 a week until she reaches a base of $500.

(b) That Mr. Scott's salary would follow the same fashion until he reaches a base of $750 a week. This would place their salary on the following scale:
Miss Ford—at $15,000 a week, $500
at $25,000 a week, $1,000

Mr. Scott—at $15,000 a week, $750
at $25,000 a week, $1,250

(c) That Miss Ford waive her 2½% royalty until the production cost has been recouped. Both Mr. and Mrs. Scott would still receive their 7½% of the gross over $25,000 after the production costs have been recouped.

(d) Miss Ford would continue to receive $75 per week as a reimbursement for her dresser.

PLAN 2

(a) The REQUIEM Company would lease to Miss Ford or her assignees the right to produce the road company. The company would make available the entire physical production exclusive of lighting equipment; the use of the phrase "the Theatre Guild and Myers & Fleischmann production of"; the Theatre Guild subscription at the usual rate in the following choice cities:

Philadelphia, 2 weeks, $45,000 guarantee

National Theatre, Washington, D.C., 2 weeks, $22,000 guarantee

Shubert Theatre, Detroit, Michigan, 2 weeks, $20,000 guarantee

Blackstone Theatre, Chicago, Illinois, 3 weeks, $60,000 guarantee

(b) The privilege of managerial consultation with the REQUIEM Company at all reasonable hours.

(c) In return for the lease of these rights your production would pay to the REQUIEM Company a flat fee of $1,000 per week.

It is our anticipation that properly publicized and exploited the tour can enjoy an artistic and economic reception equivalent to that which we received in New Haven and Boston.

Please be assured that we would be most happy to arrange a tour under either of the above plans and we look forward to your early response to our proposals.

Cordially yours,
THE THEATRE GUILD AND MYERS & FLEISCHMANN
/s/ Lawrence Langner
/t/ Lawrence Langner
/s/ Richard Myers
/t/ Richard Myers

S-65 Letter from Frank Perry, of the Theatre Guild, to Arnold Weissberger, April 9, 1959, signed ribbon typescript, 1 page.

Dear Arnold:

Attached is the enclosure[1] I mentioned on the telephone.

Thank you very much for your kindness in holding up the letter until this inadvertent omission had been corrected.

Regards,
/s/ FP
/t/ FP

[1] Printed below.

ENCLOSURE TO LETTER
Financial Considerations—REQUIEM National Tour

As indicated in the attached letter[1] a great deal of work and study on the part of the Theatre Guild and Myers and Fleischmann has accrued the following economic and budgetary information which, in supplement to the attached letter, should prove of interest.

1. The approximate cash cost of reopening the show on a national tour, exclusive of bonds, is $12,500. This would mean that a total of $22,500 would be withheld as financing for the national tour thus allowing a $10,000 reserve and sinking fund.
2. It is estimated that at the salary scale indicated for the two stars and with considerble reductions in pay for the roles of Gowan and Nancy, the production would break even at approximately $21,000. (Business in Boston averaged $30,000 for the two weeks).
3. Naturally the venture would become a profitable one if it is able to do an average business of $25,000 per week. It seems perfectly reasonable to expect this kind of business, but it must be borne in mind that both the producers and the investors must be protected from the occasional "off week" in which the production might fall below $20,000. This is, of course, the reason for the sliding scales expressed in the attached letter.
4. We are attaching the tentative budgets which we have used and referred to in the letter and this enclosure for your additional consideration.

[1]That is, Langner and Myers' letter to Weissberger, April 8, 1959, printed above.

S-66 Letter from Ruth Ford to Arnold Weissberger, April 13, 1959, signed ribbon typescript, 2 pages.

Dear Arnold:

The losses that Zachary and I have sustained over a period of seven years in connection with "Requiem For A Nun" are incalculable. Included in that are all the movies, plays and T.V. shows and what-not that we have had to turn down for long sustained periods, keeping ourselves free for a hopeful production of "Requiem." From the time we went into rehearsal for "Requiem" in London in October 1957 neither of us worked again until we went into rehearsal here in December 1958, being led to believe that a West End theatre would become available and/or a September rehearsal date would be made here. Both of us kept ourselves free which meant that for over a year we turned down all offers. In other words, we have practically devoted our lives to this play for seven years. We have had the blood, sweat, tears and the agony of it, along with the joy of our London success and our prestige success in New York. We have given this play all of our love, dedication and energy. Now the play has to give something back to us. From now on we are only in it for money and, if we cannot make any money out of it, we feel that we will have to close the chapter on "Requiem For A Nun."

I told all of this to Richard Myers several times and would have told it to Lawrence and Armina,[1] but they were away. I did ask Richard to pass this information on to them.

Zachary has never worked on the road for less than $1,750 plus a percentage of the gross and I think that this part on the road should pay any actress who can do it $1,500. Going on the road with this play is just too hard a way of making a living. We would have to make besides the living—money. It is very expensive going on the road. In order to really endure it one has to stay in the best hotels with the best service, best food and so on. A very expensive proposition—and, of course, we would also want to, and have to, take our secretary with us. Of course, I know that, besides playing the role eight times a week, I would be busy, and Zachary too, every spare minute, just as we were in Boston and here in New York, doing interviews, T.V., radio and personal appearances and so forth, so it is really a job that goes on every day from 11 in the morning to 11 at night—twelve hours of the most gruelling kind of intensity.

Our producers are business people and I am sure they understand that at times one has to make money. I hope that they will not feel that we are selfish and callous and uncaring. Over the past seven years I think we have proven that we are none of these things but now, in order to go on, the situation financially has to be reversed.

This letter, of course, is an extension of our telephone conversation: that Zachary and I would both want a guarantee of $1,500 a week—no sliding scale—and that I would get my 2½% royalty.

Love
/s/ Ruth

[1]Lawrence Langner and his wife Armina Marshall, both of whom were associated with the Theatre Guild.

S-67 Letter from Lawrence Langner and Richard Myers to Arnold Weissberger, April 16, 1959, signed ribbon typescript, 1 page.

Dear Arnold:

We have given the most careful consideration to Ruth's letter, enclosed with yours of April 14, and must agree with her that this has entailed a great amount of work for her over the past seven years, and I know that but for her devotion and Zachary's devotion, the play would not have come to a fruition. We see the reasonableness of her situation, but on the other hand we have to base our decision on the same basis as that of Ruth and Zachary and the sheer business end of it.

We do not feel that it would be fair for us and our investors to proceed on the basis of Ruth's letter. On the other hand, we do not wish to do anything which would prevent Ruth and Zachary from making a tour if they can arrange this with someone else. We shall therefore hold the scenery in storage for the next four weeks at our expense and will not notify the booking office of any change in this situation so that, if they wish to pick it up at that time, they can do so.

We will of course be glad to extend our subscription to such extent as we would be authorized by the Joint Committee of A.T.S. [American Theatre Society] and the Council of the Living Theatre.

Cordially yours,
/s/ Lawrence Langner
/t/ Lawrence Langner
/s/ Richard Myers
/t/ Richard Myers

P.S. I am enclosing the amounts earned by Ruth and Zachary as a result of the present engagement.[1] I understand the motion picture money can be taken as capital gains.

/t/ LL

[1]According to the enclosed statement, Miss Ford had earned $21,502.ll (including $12,150.00 for the sale of the motion picture rights to the play) and Scott $7,118.71.

S-68 Letter from Ruth Ford to Richard Myers, April 17, 1959, carbon typescript with typed signature, 2 pages.

Dear Richard:

I am so sorry that Zachary and I were presented with a deal for the tour of "Requiem For A Nun" that we did not see our way to agreeing to but, as I told you several times, we couldn't afford to devote another year to the play unless we could really profit from it financially. I understand that, from the point of view of the producers, this tour also has to make sense but, if it cannot make sense for both sides, then unhappily and unfortunately we will have to forget it. Zachary and I wanted so much to at least pay your backers back but, of course, we cannot do this at too great an expense to ourselves. They did not do so badly because we did have the movie sale.

I do not know if you saw the acting contract that Zachary and I made with the English company that did not come through. It was a contract made in good faith and the producers, at the time, certainly intended to produce the show. However, by the time the show was produced by you and the Theatre Guild this contract had been cut in every way to less than half for us. We were never happy, as I am sure you know, over the financial deal that we finally made but, wanting so much to get the show on, we went ahead. It would be completely infeasible for us to resume the same contract for the road. Just to give you an idea what kind of salary Zachary makes, I attach a memo of some recent offers made to him from M.C.A. All the offers he gets are comparable to these. He couldn't possibly put himself in a position where he could make $750 a week on the road as a star in this play. He only accepted his salary deal, in the first place, because of me and wanting so much to get this play on for me and, of course, I did the same. Anyway, let us think about going on to bigger and better—if that is possible—things.

. . . .

Ruth

S-69 Letter from Ruth Ford to Arnold Weissberger, April 27, 1959, signed ribbon typescript, 2 pages.

Dear Arnold:

Thanks for your letters and things. Now, about "Requiem." It does seem a pity not to take it on the road since we have Theatre Guild subscription which guarantees us $147,000 for nine weeks—that is without another penny being taken in. If we do the same kind of business that we did in Boston and New Haven we should practically sell-out in these places. You know, in 2½ weeks in Boston and New Haven we did $81,000. The scenery is ready and sitting there and the costumes are ready and sitting there.

I am sure that the budget of running expenses that the Guild sent on to us could be cut down. They say it would require $21,000 to break. It didn't even require that to break in New York and the last weeks that we were running we dropped a number of stage hands, simplified the scenery for the third act and, on the road, they had the salaries lower for the other players. Also, they have down $1,700 a week author's royalty which I am sure Faulkner would cut to $500 a week and maybe we could get Tony[1] to cut from $300 to $100 if he knew it was $100 or nothing. They have down musicians $400. Do all of those theatres *require* musicians and does the company have to pay for them?

Anyway, it seems to me, with a good business man at the helm, there is good money to be made on the road with this play. If you have not yet spoken to Jerry Leider I wish you would. Also, it seems to me it would be a good proposition for the Phoenix Theatre.[2] They are sending "Mary Stuart" out on the road to make money for the Phoenix. It seems to me that we could do better than they could and, if they do not have Guild subscription, then there is no doubt about it. I tried to reach both Norris and T. last week with no success so, if you speak to either of them, I would be very grateful if you would mention this to them.

There is not too much time left as the Theatre Guild said they would hold the scenery for four weeks. They stated that on April 16th so nearly two of those weeks have already gone, which means we have got a little over two weeks left to arrange a tour. This really looks like a very good proposition for somebody and I wish we could find the right somebody.

Thanks and love.
/s/ Ruth

P.S. Thank you for telling Ben Aslan that I *did* have control of casting. What do *they* want to do? Cast Nancy Kelly[3] as Temple?

[1] Tony Richardson, the director of the play.
[2] An off-Broadway theater founded by Norris Houghton and T. Edward Hambleton in 1953.
[3] Noted Broadway and Hollywood actress.

S-70 Letter from Arnold Weissberger to Ruth Ford, April 29, 1959, carbon typescript with typed signature, 1 page.

Dear Ruth:

I talked to Jerry Leider, after receiving your letter of April 27th, about a tour of "REQUIEM." We have had several conversations since then, and have gone over the figures. Leider will take the matter up with the Council next week and then get back to us. Aaron[1] will carry on in my absence.

The question that Leider asks, and that you and Zach will have to answer, is whether, if you are made partners on the enterprise from a point of view of sharing in the profits without putting up any money, you are prepared to take the sliding scale on your salaries proposed by Langner. Leider indicated that while he could understand the basis for your salary demands, the proposal would not be economically feasible unless you were prepared to cut when the going was hard. On the other hand, if they were successful, you would share in the profits.

My own opinion is that the possibility of profits is not great. It is true that you did very good business on the pre-New York tour, but that may have been due to the fact that people wish to see a Faulkner play on its way to Broadway. Once a play has flopped in New York, however, it is not easy to sell it to people on the road and I question very much whether you will enjoy the grosses that you did before the New York run.

Under the circumstances, you must realize that the salaries that you accept may be all that you will get out of it. If it is your principle that you will go into this only to make money, the venture seems to me dubious.

Love,
L. Arnold Weissberger

[1] Aaron Frosch, Weissberger's partner.

S-71 Letter from Anne Louise Davis to Ruth Ford, May 4, 1959, signed ribbon typescript, 1 page.

Dear Miss Ford:

I am sure Mr. Weissberger must have told you that we are selling the stock and amateur rights of Mr. Faulkner's REQUIEM FOR A NUN to Samuel French.[1] There is an advance due (when the contracts are signed) of $1,000.00, 40% of which is due you, and which we will send Mr. Weissberger when we have received it. There is a clause in the contract that we arranged with Mr. Weissberger, saying that they may not release these rights until after you have completed your tour of the play, or June 1, 1960, whichever is earlier.

The immediate problem is to furnish French with a copy of the final script, and if you will be kind enough to send me one, we will very much appreciate it. I have talked with Mr. Weissberger about this, but since he is leaving for Greece in the morning, we decided it would be easier if I dropped you this note.

Many thanks, and with best wishes,

Sincerely,
/s/ Anne Louise Davis
/t/ Anne Louise Davis

[1] A leasing company.

S-72 Letter from Howard H. Rayfiel to Mr. and Mrs. Zachary Scott and Harvey Breit, May 27, 1959, carbon typescript with typed signature, 1 page.

Dear Mr. and Mrs. Scott and Mr. Breit:

I enclose herewith a copy for each of you of the revised agreement with Mr. William Faulkner concerning purchase of the motion picture rights in and to the above work [*Light in August*].

When you have had the opportunity to read the agreement, please be in touch with me so that we may discuss it.

Mr. Weissberger conducted the basic negotiation with Mr. Ober but left for Europe before the draft agreement was completed. Mr. Frosch and I, therefore, reviewed the agreement and had incorporated therein several additional matters. It is presently in form satisfactory for execution and initialing subject to your mutual approval.

Mr. Faulkner expects to be in New York on or about June 1, so I will ask Mr. and Mrs. Scott to execute and initial the original agreement and two copies, which I will then hold pending final approval. If approved, we may then have Mr. Breit execute it and will submit it to Mr. Ober on June 1, for Mr. Faulkner's signature.

Our check in the amount of Five Thousand ($5,000.00) Dollars must be made payable to William Faulkner and delivered to Mr. Ober along with the agreement submitted for Mr. Faulkner's signature.

I look forward to hearing from you at your earliest convenience.

Sincerely yours,
Howard H. Rayfiel

1446a Letter from Phil Stone to Harrison Smith, June 2, 1959, carbon typescript with typed signature, 2 pages.

Dear Hal:

On page 25 of the May 30 issue of your magazine[1] appears a letter from a Mr. Gerald H. Strauss of Columbia, Missouri, stating that the first publication of anything written by Bill Faulkner was the little poem (L'Apres Midi d'un Faune) which appeared in *The New Republic* in 1919. Mr. Strauss is correct about this and is also correct in what he says about *The Double Dealer* in New Orleans.

But the reason I am writing this letter is because I think that the entire incident may amuse you.

Bill had been writing and writing for several years at this time (1919) and I had been having the things typed and had been mailing them off. They all came back poste-haste. So when *The New Republic* accepted this little poem and paid fifteen whole dollars for it, Bill and I felt like the lucky country boy at his first crap game: How long has this been going on?

So we sent off some more poems, and more poems, to *The New Republic*. When none of them were accepted we decided that no more would be accepted and that we at least might have some fun.

So, without title and without Bill signing the poem, we copied John Clare's poem about the asylum in which he was then confined, Northampton, as I remember now.[2] It is in the Oxford Book of English Verse but very few people seem to know it. Our plan was to have *The New Republic* accept it and publish it and then secretly to notify *The New York Times* of the fact and let the dull *Times* rib the smarty *New Republic*.

I always wonder whether or not anybody placed it or whether it was sent back simply because they didn't think Bill could write that good a poem. Anyway, it came back with no reply by letter.

Then we copied off Coleridge's Kubla Khan. It was returned to us with the very accurate criticism: "We like your poem, Mr. Coleridge, but we don't think it gets anywhere much."

I do not know the address of Mr. Strauss at Columbia, but perhaps he will be interested if you will send him the copy of this letter which I enclose.

Yours truly,
Phil Stone

[1] The *Saturday Review*.
[2] "Written in Northampton County Asylum."

1446b Letter from Harrison Smith to Phil Stone, June 5, 1959, signed ribbon typescript, 1 page.

Dear Phil:

Thanks for your amusing letter. Almost everything about Bill's early life in Oxford finds its way into print and half a dozen or more of his early novels, beginning with "Sartoris," sell for extraordinary prices in the second-hand bookstores. I met one of his devotees, an elderly dame, at a party last night and thought I would never get rid of her.

I presume that you won't object to our publishing the letter.[1]

We haven't been able to find Gustave Strauss' address and have returned your copy.

I wish you would come to New York sometime or other. I would be delighted to put you up in my apartment. There are some wonderful shows in town.

Sincerely yours,
/s/ Hal
/t/ Harrison Smith

[1] Stone's letter was printed in the "Letters to the Editor" section, *Saturday Review,* 42 (June 27, 1959), 23.

1446c Letter from Phil Stone to Harrison Smith, June 11, 1959, carbon typescript with typed signature, 1 page.

Dear Hal:

Pardon me for not having answered your letter sooner, your nice letter of June 5, but we are busy in some Courts right now, and I have not had time to do so.

I know how you feel about Bill. I have had the same trouble and dozens of people, and I told Bill sometime ago that I was rather like the man whose uncle had died and left him a lot of money, that winding up Uncle Joe's estate was so much trouble that he almost wished that Uncle Joe had not died, and that I often wish that Bill had not won the Nobel Prize.

Of course you may use the letter if you wish.

I don't know the address of Mr. Strauss either, but perhaps he will see the letter in your magazine.

I don't get to New York often, but if and when I do I shall certainly try to call you. Best of luck.

Your friend,
Phil Stone

S-73 Letter from Faulkner to Ruth Ford, Zachary Scott, and Harvey Breit, June 15, 1959, signed ribbon typescript, 1 page.

Dear Miss Ford and Mr. Scott and Mr. Breit:

With reference to the contract between us dated June 15, 1959, covering the motion picture rights in my novel, LIGHT IN AUGUST, this is to request that all future payments due under this contract be drawn to the order of my agent: "Harold Ober Associates Incorporated, as agents for William Faulkner," 40 East 49 Street, New York 17, New York, whose receipt shall be binding on me.

Sincerely
/s/ William Faulkner
/t/ William Faulkner

S-74 Letter from Harold Ober to Howard H. Rayfiel, June 16, 1959, signed ribbon typescript, 1 page.

Dear Mr. Rayfiel:

I am enclosing herewith two copies of the contract on LIGHT IN AUGUST, signed by Mr. Faulkner, and also by Mr. Breit, but not signed by Miss Ford and Mr. Scott. When you have obtained their signatures on these copies, and also on the other three copies of the contract that you have in your office, will you please be kind enough to send two copies, signed by your three clients, to me? We have one fully executed copy here, but we need a copy for Mr. Faulkner himself, and a further copy for Random House.

Also enclosed is a letter from Mr. Faulkner addressed to your three clients, asking that future payments be made to this firm as his agents. This is to facilitate the payments to Mr. Faulkner and to Random House. I want to thank you for the two checks totalling $5,000.00 that you sent over yesterday, signed by Mr. Breit and Mr. Scott. Since Mr. Faulkner was here he could endorse these for us, but it is not always so easy to reach him.

You will find a notation on one copy of the contract that is enclosed to the effect that the notarization is missing on one of the signatures. I am sure that this can be easily rectified.

Sincerely,
/s/ Harold Ober

1447a Letter from Howard C. Will, Jr., Southern Area Director, The Great Books Foundation, to Phil Stone, June 25 [1959], signed autograph manuscript, 2 pages.

Dear Mr. Stone:

Last October I came here [to Memphis] to administer the Great Books program for ten Southern states. I also wanted to learn more about the South. I decided that I should know Faulkner's works well. I had read 4 of his novels years ago. I began anew, this spring, and have read almost everything. I thought his work would be an excellent conversation piece in my travels in the South. It is. But who told most Southerners *not* to read Faulkner? I find they hate him in direct proportion to the amount of reading of his works they have *not* read. As a result, I have had a busy campaign on here in Memphis to get people reading his work. His *Light in August* is on the 13th year of our Great Books reading list. I have used *Intruder* and *Sound and the Fury* here for leaders' Refreshers. We will be using *The Bear* at the Institute in Waterville, Maine, this summer.

During my spring leader training here, most of my trainees humored my pushing Faulkner. One, Brother Luke, who teaches at Christian Brothers College, heartily agreed with my efforts. His colleague, Brother Paul, always dissented in a satirical way. His last comments are enclosed. I thought you might be interested. When you are finished with them, would you be kind enough to put them back in the self-addressed envelope and mail it back.

Do you remember Dr. Charles Biggers, who taught philosophy at Ole Miss? He has been telling me that you are Gavin Stevens, is this correct? How are the Snopes doing these days?

Sincerely,
Howard C. Will, Jr.

1447b Letter from Phil Stone to Howard C. Will, Jr., June 29, 1959, carbon typescript with typed signature, 1 page.

Dear Mr. Will:

I have your letter of June 25.

I am sorry, but if I took the time to write and talk with people who want to talk with me about William Faulkner I would never get my law practice done. As it is, we are working four nights a week at it.

As for Gavin Stephens [*sic*], I think both he and Horace Benbow were partly drawn from me.

As for LIGHT IN AUGUST and INTRUDER IN THE DUST, I can't say much for them. It was all I could do to read LIGHT IN AUGUST and I shall never want to read it again.

It is interesting, and amusing, how few people realize that Bill got the Nobel Prize for nothing he had written since 1940.

Be sure to give my best to Charlie Biggers.

Yours truly,
Phil Stone

[P.S.] I herewith return the material which you sent.

1412f Letter from Bennett Cerf to James W. Silver, July 6, 1959, signed ribbon typescript, 1 page.

Dear Professor Silver:

According to Mrs. Calvin Brown, you have in your possession a manuscript of approximately 10,000 words in length that was written by William Faulkner back in the 1920's.[1] Mrs. Brown adds that it's a fairy tale that was written for her own child and that it has never been published anywhere.

As I am sure you know, we are William Faulkner's publishers in America. Obviously, we would not publish the manuscript referred to without the express permission of Mr. Faulkner himself, but before we even approach him on the matter, we would welcome the opportunity of reading the script ourselves. We would also like your opinion of this script: do *you* think it merits publication?

Might it be possible for us to borrow this manuscript from you long enough to read? Or, better still, could you send us a photostat of the script?

I await your reply with great interest. In the event that you would like to talk to me about all this before writing a letter, I suggest that you phone me, collect, at your convenience. The number is Plaza 1-2600.

Cordially,
/s/ Bennett Cerf
/t/ Bennett Cerf

[1]"The Wishing Tree." Mrs. Brown, with the assistance of Professor Silver, was seeking to have the story published.

1412g Letter from Bennett Cerf to James W. Silver, July 22, 1959, signed ribbon typescript, 1 page.

Dear Professor Silver:

Thank you very much for your letter of July 19th giving me all the facts on Bill Faulkner's THE WISHING TREE. Directly I had read this letter, I phoned Ralph Graves of Life, and he has promised to send me his copy of the manuscript. I'll keep you posted on developments.

I hope that it will be possible for you to stop in and say "hello" to me in person here in New York on your way back to Mississippi. I'll probably have a report to give you about the whole situation before then, anyhow.

Cordially,
/s/ Bennett Cerf
/t/ Bennett Cerf

S-75 Letter from Arnold Weissberger to Ruth Ford, August 6, 1959, unsigned carbon typescript, 1 page.

Dear Ruth:

I spoke to Miss Davis at Harold Ober's office, after my conversation with you yesterday, and told her that you had no objection in principle to making the deal with Samuel French, but that it was a matter of the timing. At present there was a prospect of Hurok's[1] touring "Requiem" the season after this, and if he were to do so, then obviously there could not have been prior stock and amateur performances. I said that you would probably know in October whether the tour was to take place or not. If it was not to take place, then we would proceed with French. If it was to take place, then French's rights would have to be held up, although there was the possibility that French might get limited rights in such areas as would not interfere with Hurok's tour. Miss Davis said she would report this to Abbott Van Nostrand at French.

. . . .

[no signature]

[1]Sol Hurok, New York impresario who arranged tours of various theatrical productions.

S-76 Letter from Arnold Weissberger to Mr. and Mrs. Zachary Scott, October 14, 1959, carbon typescript with typed signature, 1 page.

Dear Ruth and Zach:

Harold Shaw of the Hurok office has finally gotten back to me about "Requiem For A Nun."

He told me that after a good deal of consideration Hurok had finally decided that it could not do the tour next year. There were many problems, one of which was that any company that has a Negro actor or actress is automatically unable to play in large parts of the country.

Love,
L. Arnold Weissberger

S-77 Letter from Faulkner to Dorothy Oldham, undated, signed autograph manuscript, 1 page, with envelope addressed in Faulkner's hand and postmarked Charlottesville, November 9, 1959.

Dear Dot—

Herewith Andrew's $12.50.[1] All well here. The fall has been fine, and good for hunting.

Bill

[1]Payment for Andrew Price, the black handyman at Rowan Oak. Miss Oldham, Estelle Faulkner's sister, managed Rowan Oak when the Faulkners were away.

1412h Letter from Bennett Cerf to James W. Silver, November 11, 1959, signed ribbon typescript, 1 page.

Dear James Silver:

Thank you for your letter of November 8th and the valuable Faulkneriana enclosed therewith. I shall treasure this.

I have written to Bill Faulkner to ask him what he would think of our doing

THE WISHING-TREE, possibly in a limited edition of about 2000 copies. As soon as I have some answer from him, I'll communicate with you further. It may well be, however, that he will wait until the next time he comes up here to talk about it. Bill is not the most dependable letter writer whom I know!

I am happy to send you under separate cover the Faulkner titles that are missing from your library. There will be no bill. Please accept these books with the compliments of the house.

Cordially,
/s/ Bennett Cerf
/t/ Bennett Cerf

1412j Letter from James W. Silver to Bennett Cerf, November 17, 1959, carbon typescript with typed signature, 1 page.

Dear Mr. Cerf:

Thank you for your letter of November 11 regarding the possibility of the publication of Faulkner's THE WISHING TREE. I do hope that something comes of this, but if you can get anything out of Bill Faulkner, you're a better man than I am.

I called Mrs. Brown this morning to let her know about your letter. In the conversation she suggested that she would be visiting her daughter for the month of December—after the 5th. Her daughter is Mrs. John B. Douds, 10 Los Robles Court, Reading, Pennsylvania. Her husband is an English professor at Albright College. I'm sending this information to you in the thought that if your conversation with Faulkner is satisfactory, you might want to talk with Mrs. Brown. She has known Bill since the day he was born, or almost so, and has, in regard to this fairy tale, a story that you should get from her own lips. It still seems to me that the BACKGROUND for the story is almost as important as the story itself, and that its publication will confound some of Faulkner's critics.

I shall look forward to your generous addition to my Faulkner "collection." I am very grateful.

Sincerely,
James W. Silver

1412i Letter from Bennett Cerf to James W. Silver, November 17, 1959, signed ribbon typescript, 1 page.

Dear James Silver:

I have received this letter from Bill Faulkner:

"Dear Bennett:

"This story was written as a gesture of pity and compassion for Mrs. Brown's little girl who was dying of cancer.

"I would be shocked if Mrs. Brown herself wanted to commercialize it. But it belongs to her. I will not forbid her to sell it, but I myself would never authorize it being published, unless perhaps, the proceeds should go to save other children from cancer."

Under the circumstances, I certainly think we should do nothing about this story for the time being.[1] The next time Bill comes up to New York, however,

I'll discuss it with him in person in further detail. If there are any developments, I promise to let you know immediately.

I do hope I'll have the pleasure of meeting you in person one day soon.

Cordially,
/s/ Bennett Cerf
/t/ Bennett Cerf

[1] *The Wishing Tree* was posthumously published by Random House in 1967.

1481 Letter from Estelle Faulkner to Dorothy Commins, "Nov. 19th," signed autograph manuscript, 2 pages (1 folded leaf), with envelope addressed in Mrs. Faulkner's hand and postmarked Charlottesville, November 19, 1959.

Dear Dorothy—

Owing to an injury to my hand I was unfortunate to get in a motorcar accident this summer, have been unable to write—

Even now I'm still hopelessly illegible!—but *do* read this if you can—

Bill and I were in Charlottesville for the winter and in the house on Rugby Road—

At long last, we've gotten it furnished in at least a livable fashion, and want you to come down to see us when you can—

There is so much time to be reclaimed—we've missed seeing you dreadfully—

The University is having an exhibit of Bill's work[1]—rather like the one in Princeton—You might be interested in *that,* but I hope, most of all, you would like seeing all of us again—

Come when it's convenient and you feel up to it—Jill, Paul, Bill and I send love—

Always devotedly
Estelle

[1] "William Faulkner: Man Working 1919–1959," Alderman Library, University of Virginia, October 1–December 23, 1959.

S-78 Letter from Phil Stone to Faulkner, December 9, 1959, carbon typescript with typed signature, 1 page.

Dear Bill:

I intended to see you before you left[1] and to thank you for leaving a copy of THE MANSION by the office, but I failed to do so, and am writing you now to thank you for it.

Don't think I am not interested by the fact that I have not yet had time to read it. Freeland and I have been working four nights a week and I work every Sunday, so I don't have much time to read a book, but I do hope to get this one read during the holidays.

I enclose you two items[2] which you need not return and which may amuse you.

Your friend,
Phil Stone

[1] Stone addressed this letter to Faulkner c/o the University of Virginia.
[2] Unidentified.

Oxford, 4th Jan.

Dear Joan:

I read the mss. Haydn sent me to Virginia, with a great deal of expectation and hope. I was not disappointed in either. It is all right. It is a good first book but it will be a bad last one. So you must continue. Go on, write another. Not only because this one will not be good enough for your last book, but because the more you write the more you will learn to correct the faults, all minor, in my opinion, in this one.

It is a good story in concept because it is not regional nor topical, but universal. Next time, if you still keep your sights high, you will do it better since the more you write, the more you will learn how to express, milk dry, the love and hatred you have to feel, not for man in his behavior, but for man in his condition.

The main criticism is the one I made to you once before: your people do the right, the inevitable, things, but you yourself dont always seem to know why, or at least to tell me why they did them. That's minor thoug. As long as the people stand up and move, and the complexities they move among and the universal hopes and passions, it is all right. Only PROVIDED, you dont become satisfied and stop there. So you must get at the next one right away. Dont write this one again. Write ANOTHER one.

Bill

You still wont quite let yourself go. What are you trying to save? For what? Every time you give all, there is always plenty more.

42. Letter from Faulkner to Joan Williams Bowen (item S-79)

c. 1960

S-79 Letter from Faulkner to Joan Williams, dated "Oxford, 4th Jan." [probably 1960], signed ribbon typescript with autograph postscript, 1 page.

Dear Joan:

I read the mss.[1] Haydn[2] sent me to Virginia, with a great deal of expectation and hope. I was not disappointed in either. It is all right. It is a good first book but it will be a bad last one. So you must continue. Go on, write another. Not only because this one will not be good enough for your last book, but because the more you write the more you will learn to correct the faults, all minor in my opinion, in this one.

It is a good story in concept because it is not regional nor topical, but universal. Next time, if you still keep your sights high, you will do it better since the more you write, the more you will learn how to express, milk dry, the love and hatred you have to feel, not for man in his behavior, but for man in his condition.

The main criticism is the one I made to you once before: your people do the right, the inevitable, things, but you yourself dont always seem to know why, or at least to tell me why they did them. That's minor though. As long as the people stand up and move, and the complexities they move among and the universal hopes and passions, it is all right. PROVIDED, you dont become satisfied and stop there. So you must get at the next one right away. Dont write this one again. Write ANOTHER one.

/s/ Bill

[P.S.] You still wont quite let yourself go. What are you trying to save? for what? Every time you give all, there is always plenty more.

[1] Apparently the manuscript of her first novel, subsequently published as *The Morning and the Evening* by Atheneum Press in 1961.

[2] Hiram Haydn, a Random House editor.

1960

S-80 Letter from Faulkner to Mary W. Chapman, Secretary, Longreen Hunt, Germantown, Tennessee, dated "Oxford, Miss. / 4 Jan. 1960," signed ribbon typescript, 1 page, with envelope addressed in Faulkner's hand and postmarked Oxford, January 6, 1960.

Dear Mrs Chapman:

When I reached home from Virginia yesterday, I found the invitation for the Opening Meet,[1] and your kind letter. I thank you for them, am sorry they were not forwarded so I could reply in time, and regret that I was not with you. I only hope this will not stand in my way of being invited out with you at another time.

Please extend my thanks to Mr Anderson,[2] with my respects to Mrs Anderson and his family.

Yours sincerely,
/s/ William Faulkner

[1]The story of Faulkner's involvement with the Longreen hunting club is recorded in *Longreen: 25 Years of Horse Sports in West Tennessee,* ed. M. Winslow Chapman (Memphis: Towery Press, 1982).

[2]The Master of the Hunt.

S-81 Letter from Ruth Ford to Arnold Weissberger, undated [received January 25, 1960], signed autograph manuscript, 3 pages (on 1 folded leaf).

Dear Arnold—

So sorry to be so late getting back to you. About Colston & Leigh[1] (sp?)—before we can tell them very much, they have to tell *us* some things. As we have never done anything of this sort, we are in complete ignorance. Any facts & figures concerning Req. as a play seem to me to have nothing to do with a reading. We would need a minimum of 5 actors—Z. would play Gavin, R., Temple—Bertice[2] (if we could get her), Nancy—and the same actor could play Gowan & Pete and the same actor the Gov. & the jailor. Would we have to carry understudies? In a lecture tour, such as Cecil[3] made—I guess if he was sick, his lecture would be canceled. So—ask C & L if we need understudies, that would mean one for me & conceivably she could understudy Nancy & play in black face. (That was done in Paris production—A white girl, Russian, played Nancy, in brown face.) Then one understudy, I suppose, could cover all male parts and that could be the stage manager. Would this be *Equity* or not? *That* would make a difference. We need a minimum of furniture—only tables & chairs—a few props (which we could easily carry with us)—and play against a back drop. There are no costumes. I have my dresses and the men would wear their suits. Would we need an advance man, someone to go ahead and arrange everything? We haven't the slightest idea what we could get as salaries as we do not know what the colleges & universities will pay for one evening of this sort. C. & L. will have to tell us this. They must know, that is their business. Then, do they work on a commission? Also, how many nights or performances a week do we play? and how many weeks could we get? and is this sort of thing pre-sold, or guaranteed? Must be. Naturally, Z & I are not going to break our necks doing this unless it pays off for us. Would we all travel in a bus or how? Also could a *Negro* appear on the stage with us everywhere we play? Naturally we would like to play all through the South & Texas—at my University of Mississippi, at Oxford, where William Faulkner lives and I graduated there and at the University of Texas where Z. graduated. Would like to play Oberlin, where our daughter is in college. I mean, the opportunities for this seem *vast.* I can't imagine a college or university in America not *eating* this up.

So discuss this with C & L. & give us some information from there. And we will go on from there.

. . . .

Love
Ruth

[1]Colston Leigh operated a booking agency in New York.
[2]Bertice Reading, who had played the role of Nancy in the stage production of *Requiem For A Nun.*
[3]Cecil Beaton, renowned photographer, author, artist, and theatrical designer.

1498a Letter from Phil Stone to Faulkner, probably January 28, 1960, unsigned carbon typescript, 1 page.

Dear Bill:
If you want this,[1] just drop by the office any time and get this pamphlet. If I am not here Mrs. Hoffman[2] will know where it is.

[no signature]

[1]A copy of *La New Orleans e la Louisiana del Faulkner* by Angela M. Giannitrapani. Stone's note to Faulkner appears at the bottom of a carbon copy of a letter he had written to Miss Giannitrapani on January 28, 1960, thanking her for the pamphlet.
[2]Stone's secretary, Elaine Hoffman.

S-82 Letter from Arnold Weissberger to Ruth Ford, January 29, 1960, carbon typescript with typed signature, 2 pages.

Dear Ruth:
I have your leter with respect to the Colston Leigh proposal on "Requiem For A Nun," and I have just talked to Leigh. There is actually no need to go into details, because when I told him that one member of the cast had to be a colored woman, he told me to forget it immediately—that there was no chance of touring the attraction with the problems that would result from having a colored member of the cast.

Leigh then said, however, that he would like very much to explore the possibility of having you and Zach go out in some kind of reading or two-character production, and he asked me to have you consider the matter very seriously, and make suggestions. He said it would be too late in the season now to arrange for you to tour in the Fall next year, but you could certainly have a good eight to twelve week season starting in January. According to Leigh the community centers and subscription series are avid for new attractions, and he feels that you could be sold widely on a guaranteed basis. You could probably make a good deal of money this way, and if the attraction proves successful on the road, you might even bring it to New York for a limited engagement. Think about it, explore the possibilities, and then get back to me as soon as you can.

Miss Davis of the Ober office has been clobbering me again about when you are going to release "Requiem,"[1] and it seems to me that the time has now come to tell her that you will release it. Apparently none of the impresarios want it, and Colston Leigh has given a very good reason why its touring possibilities are limited. Under the circumstances I think it is desirable for you to at least be earning the income that you would get from the stock and amateur rights.

Shall I give Ober the go-ahead?

. . . .

L. Arnold Weissberger

[1]To Samuel French.

1412k Letter from Maud M. Brown to James W. Silver, February 5, 1960, signed autograph manuscript, 1 page.

Dear Dr. Silver,

I am enclosing with this note copies of my two letters to Mr. Faulkner[1] of which we spoke this morning. I have no way of knowing just how Mr. Cerf presented this matter to Mr. Faulkner but, if he had known exactly my attitude, I think he would not have made his cruel remark about my "commercializing" the story.[2] That does not sound like Billy to me.

Thank you for your interest!

Sincerely,
Maud M. Brown

[1] Mrs. Brown had written Faulkner on July 16, 1958, and again on December 1, 1958, requesting permission to publish the copy of "The Wishing Tree" which Faulkner had presented to her daughter Margaret in 1928. Faulkner had not answered either letter.

[2] See Cerf's letter to Silver, November 17, 1959, printed above.

S-83 Letter from Arnold Weissberger to Mr. and Mrs. Zachary Scott, February 12, 1960, carbon typescript with typed signature, 1 page.

Dear Ruth and Zach:

With respect to the Caedmon recording of "Requiem For A Nun,"[1] all subsidiary are, of course, owned and controlled by Faulkner himself. I should think there would be no question that he would allow you to make the recording, but we would have to go to him as a matter of form to get his permission and, indeed, Caedmon would have to make its agreement with Faulkner. (I know very well the fey young ladies who run Caedmon—I represented them for several years a number of years ago. Their recording director is a very good man, by the way).

Let me know what you want done about this.

Love to you both.

L. Arnold Weissberger

[1] Ruth Ford had contacted Caedmon Publishers about this possibility; however, although Barbara Holdridge of Caedmon expressed considerable interest in the project, the recording was never produced.

S-84 Letter from Herbert O. Fox, of Broadway Theatre Alliance, Inc., to Arnold Weissberger, March 1, 1960, signed ribbon typescript, 1 page.

Dear Mr. Weissberger:

Just before he embarked on his trip around the world, Freddie Schang[1] gave me your letter of January 8 regarding "Requiem for a Nun."

It is our opinion that the subject matter and the somewhat obscure content of this play as well as the seemingly lack of success in New York would make it a most difficult property to exploit on the road. We are well aware of its artistic merits but we cannot in our minds devise a method of touring it. One immediately thinks of the college market. It is our experience that this market can absorb one expensive Broadway project per year. As we have been scheduling "J.B." for a college type tour in 1960–61 since the middle of last summer, it would seem that even this approach is impossible.

Thanks very much for thinking of us, and please keep us in mind for other plays in the future.

Cordially,
/s/ Herbert O. Fox
/t/ Herbert O. Fox

[1]Of Columbia Concerts, another booking agency.

S-85 Letter from Arnold Weissberger to Ruth Ford, April 6, 1960, carbon typescript with typed signature, 1 page.

Dear Ruth:

Anne Davis called me after receiving my letter about the French catalogue "Requiem For A Nun," and said she certainly shared your indignation about the way the thing had been set up.[1] She was particularly offended by the misspelling of Faulkner's name, and said that she had lodged a vigorous protest with Abbott Van Nostrand at French.

She said she would be very appreciative, as would French, if you would write your own 200 word description of the play for the French catalogue, putting in everything that you would like to have in: that is to say, a description of the subject matter of the play, the fact that you were the adaptor, that it was written for you, and that on Broadway you and Zach starred in it.

Love,
L. Arnold Weissberger

[1]Miss Ford had complained to Weissberger about the numerous errors in French's description of the play. Among other things, Faulkner's name had been spelled "Falkener."

1412-1 Letter from James W. Silver to Bennett Cerf, April 15, 1960, carbon typescript with typed signature, 1 page.

Dear Mr. Cerf:

Several times I have come close to replying to your letter of November 17, 1959, regarding the possible publication of William Faulkner's "The Wishing Tree." For, although the matter is of no direct concern to me, financially or in any other way, I have felt that Bill Faulkner was doing Mrs. Brown a tremendous injustice. I still feel this way, although I have hesitated to write you about it.

I have lived in this community for almost a quarter of a century and I have never found a person who has so thoroughly believed in Bill Faulkner or has so constantly defended him here where he has many enemies, as Mrs. Brown. She practically worships him, which, I think, may be understandable in view of the background of the story he wrote for her little girl.

Be this as it may, I'm now writing to you with a suggestion. Mrs. Brown is approaching her ninetieth year—just how close I'm not sure. It is obvious that she won't be around a lot longer. At the moment she is still very much alive mentally as well as physically. But when she goes the circumstances of the Wishing Tree will go with her. (Even Faulkner is wrong about some of the details, as he is about a lot of things.)

My suggestion is that you employ Mrs. Brown to write up the story as she remembers it. Pay her a thousand dollars, or five hundred, or whatever you can stand. Get every detail from her. Then, if you think it wise, put this away with the story for future publication. When the time comes for publication, use what she has written in whatever way you see fit. (She has done a good deal of historical writing, but her style isn't exactly felicitous.) But by following my suggestion, you would have authentic information on the writing of the story and Mrs. Brown, who needs the cash, would have something for having preserved a very charming manuscript.

In this case, were there profits from publication, at any time, they might well be turned over to some fund for cancer or something else. (As for the cancer business, I don't think that the child had cancer—although I suppose Bill *could* have been right on this.)

It seems to me that this procedure would please everyone and that even Random House might benefit considerably in the long run, or even the short run.

Sincerely,
James W. Silver

1412m Letter from Bennett Cerf to James W. Silver, April 20, 1960, signed ribbon typescript, 1 page.

Dear James Silver:

Thank you for your letter of April 15th, but we have learned from William Faulkner himself that he is not anxious at all to have THE WISHING TREE published in any way, shape or form. Unless he himself brings the matter up again, we think we should drop all thought of it whatever.

I am returning Mrs. Brown's notes, in accordance with your request. In the event that Bill Faulkner ever shows any sign of changing his mind, I'll write to you immediately.

Cordially,
/s/ Bennett Cerf
/t/ Bennett Cerf

S-86 Letter from Ruth Ford to Arnold Weissberger, April 22, 1960, signed ribbon typescript, 1 page.

Dear Arnold:

I am late thanking you for all the Samuel French "REQUIEM FOR A NUN" to-do. I will call Van Nostrand at French and see what the deadline is for all of that.

In the meantime, let me ask you—who keeps the books on this—Samuel French, Ober, or the Theatre Guild and who is responsible for seeing that my percentage is sent on to me? Does French do this by the year or by the piece or what?

Also, there is nothing in the correspondence about an off-Broadway production of "REQUIEM FOR A NUN." Did you take this up with Miss Davis? I mean, if it is not in somebody's contract with French that we will not permit an off-Broadway production, then we have no control over that, have we, and you and I and Zachary agreed that we did not want an off-Broadway production.

. . . .

Love
/s/ Ruth

S-87 Letter from Arnold Weissberger to Ruth Ford, April 27, 1960, carbon typescript with typed signature, 1 page.

Dear Ruth:

I have your letter of April 22nd.

Your participation in any proceeds from stock and amateur rights in "Requiem" comes through the producer. That is to say, the producer is entitled to 40% of all income from stock and amateur rights, and you are entitled to 25% of the producer's share. When the producer gets the money from Samuel French, the producer should forward your share to you.

French has the rights only with respect to stock and amateur productions. Any off-Broadway production would have to go through the Ober office, and they in turn would come to you about it.

. . . .

Love,
L. Arnold Weissberger

P. S. Anne Davis phoned to say that French never received the playing script of "Requiem" that you had promised to send last year. Just received copy of her letter to French and enclose copy of copy.

S-88 Letter from Ruth Ford to Abbott Van Nostrand, April 29, 1960, unsigned carbon typescript, 2 pages.

Dear Mr. Van Nostrand:

I am sorry we couldn't meet over the proposed printing of "REQUIEM FOR A NUN" by Samuel French. As no-one had told me the deadline on any of this and I didn't have a feeling of urgency from anyone, I assumed there was no rush but, since I am leaving for Europe on May 3rd, I thought I had better call and check. To my surprise and horror I discovered that your deadline was May 15th, which made mine practically as of this minute.

I have been working now for some days trying to get all of the material together that you will need.

The enclosed paragraph about the play for your catalogue, I would like put in, if you please, just as I have written it.[1] It is a few words shorter than "R. U. R." on page 146. I can think of no-one more worthy of space than William Faulkner, considered, not only in America but all over the world, to be, if not our greatest living writer, certainly one of the few, and one of the few great American writers of all time. I would very much appreciate seeing a proof of this before the catalogue goes to print.

I would also very much like you to include the enclosed four photographs in the book. In the Samuel French edition of "The Skin Of Our Teeth" you have reproduced four, and I am sure that is true of many other plays also.

Now, the version of the play that I want Samuel French to print is the published version printed in play form by Random House—word for word—exactly. There were a few minor alterations here and there in the script—a few minor changes, but the published version is the best. You can either have Miss Davis get a copy of this book from Random House and send it to you, or you can get one yourself from Random House or from any book store.

I would naturally like the dedication to appear in your version. Also, on the sheet that gives the cast list, would you please put that it was premiered at the Royal Court Theatre in London, November 26th, 1957, and was presented in

New York on the dates given in the book, with the names of producers and theatre.

I would very much like to see, if possible, a galley or proof of the play itself before it goes to press.

I am sending you the Prop List, the Light Cues, the Running Order, the Costume Plot and, in case you wish to include them, the Winch Cues. They are for the large louvered doors that are opened and closed by concealed wires off stage.

I must have the photographs returned to me. They are *extremely* valuable—being the only ones we have—and there is not a chance in the world of getting any others.

Please let me know if the slick page about the copyrights and credit to the photographer and so forth (the sheet opposite the dedication) will be reprinted in your version. I assume that it must be. In any case the photographer must be given credit. It might interest you to know that the photographer who did the photographs, Tony Armstrong-Jones, is Mr. Anthony Armstrong-Jones who is marrying Princess Margaret on May 6th.

In any listing of publicity of any kind concerning your publication of the play the name of Ruth Ford as adaptor must also be mentioned with William Faulkner as author.

If you have any further questions or problems before I fly away on May 3rd ring me.

Good luck and I hope we all make a lot of money.

Sincerely yours,
[no signature]

P. S. I have left space in the paragraph for the catalogue in which should be entered the *number* of foreign countries in which "REQUIEM FOR A NUN" has been performed. Will you please check this figure with Anne Davis.

[1]The enclosure reads as follows:

"REQUIEM FOR A NUN"
WILLIAM FAULKNER, Adapted for the stage by Ruth Ford. Written for her and dedicated to her. 5 m., 2 f. Unit set. Played in London and New York with great success, starring Ruth Ford and her husband, Zachary Scott. Acclaimed in [blank] foreign countries. This remarkable play by the great Nobel prize-winner unfolds a modern theme in classical dramatic form. Temple Drake from "Sanctuary" emerges into this new world of terrible retribution. Now married to the college boy who first led her the wrong way and suffering from the same demons of desire, she decides to run away with her latest passing fancy. To her Negro maid this is bad enough but, when Temple prepares to take her 6 months old baby with her, the maid is horrified. Rather than permit this she smothers the baby. All this we learn in Temple's confession to the Governor, to whom she has gone to plead for clemency on the maid's behalf, but the death sentence remains and the maid goes forth with faith in God. The final truth is a shattering experience for Temple. "It is a play for those who believe that the theatre can bring joy and illumination to the best minds working at their highest intensity . . . to hear Zachary Scott speak these words is a wonderful experience."—London Times, Harold Hobson. "It proves how raw and stunning the mature theatre can be. . . . Miss Ford is something worth writing for. She is electric and intense, bitter and remorseless. She is a superb woman and an artist of obvious integrity."—N.Y. World-Telegram & Sun. "Hangs icicles on 'Cat On a Hot Tin Roof'."—N.Y. Mirror.

S-89 Letter from Howard H. Rayfiel to Arnold Weissberger, June 9, 1960, carbon typescript with typed signature, 1 page.

Dear Arnold:

The Zachary Scotts and Harvey Breit must pay an additional $11,250.00 by June 15th to retain their rights in the above work [*Light in August*] by William Faulkner. They paid $5,000.00 last year of a total of $50,000.00, the balance to be paid off in annual installments of $11,250.00, this year's being the first such installment.

The Scotts have indicated that they want an extension but apparently do not understand that each year's payment is in effect consideration for a year's extension. I have not yet heard from Mr. Breit in response to my letter. Aaron thought, however, that you should have word of this in case you have any notions to be conveyed to them.

There are countless other matters upon which we have been working here, and I will prepare a detailed memo for your return.

Best regards to you all.

Cordially,
Howard H. Rayfiel

S-90 Letter from Anne Louise Davis to Howard H. Rayfiel, June 20, 1960, signed ribbon typescript, 1 page.

Dear Mr. Rayfiel:

In answer to the request contained in your letter of June 13, on behalf of Mr. and Mrs. Scott and Mr. Breit, Mr. Faulkner agrees to the deferment to September 15, 1960, of the payment of $11,250.00 due June 15, 1960, under the terms of the contract on LIGHT IN AUGUST, between the aforementioned and Mr. Faulkner.

Sincerely,
/s/ Anne Louise Davis
/t/ Anne Louise Davis

1436h Letter from Phil Stone to James B. Meriwether, July 7, 1960, carbon typescript with typed signature, 2 pages.

Dear Jim:

This is just a short letter to tell you that I received the Princeton University Library Chronicle. Your article[1] looks fine to me.

I have been so busy as usual reading law books that I don't know when I shall have time to look through this pamphlet, but I have found four errors in glancing through it already, to which I shall come later.

. . . .

With reference to the four errors which I have found on casual glance, they are as follows:

1. Page 118. As I remember, in 1919, Mr. Murry was not "Assistant Secretary" at the University, but was the Business Manager itself.[2] You had better check this, but I am pretty sure it is true.

2. Page 125. With reference to the boundaries of Lafayette County, the Tallahatchie River is only the northern boundary on a certain part of Lafayette County, what might be called the central northern line. Both on the east, the northwest and the west, that river is not the boundary.

The southern boundary of Lafayette County is not the Yocona (Yoknapatawpha being the proper Indian name) River at all. You may remember that this last river is only about six miles south of Oxford where you cross it on the way to Water Valley, and the county line is still at least about nine or ten miles south of that.

3. Page 127. With reference to THE SOUND AND THE FURY, I probably told you that the title was my own invention. Furthermore, I think I told you that I could point to the very spot on the University campus where I stood when Bill said that he didn't know why he kept on writing; that he was sure he would never make any money out of it and didn't even believe he would ever receive any literary recognition, that he probably wrote to keep from having to work. I told him that I was sure he was going to make it after all, but I didn't really believe it at the time. I knew if I said he wouldn't he would probably quit and give up. So I told him to go ahead and write what he damn pleased, just like he damn pleased, and see whether they took it or not, that even if he could not make money out of it he would probably get some literary recognition which might help.

You may remember that I also told you that I had an experience that no other human being has ever had or ever will have: this was that I sat night after night in Bill's little room in the little tower of the old Delta Psi chapter house and had him read THE SOUND AND THE FURY to me page by page.

4. Page 134. With reference to A GREEN BOUGH, all of those poems were actually written during the fall of 1924 and the spring and summer of 1925. The reason for their writing was that I was showing Bill what people like Housman did, and the poems were written with that in view. I think I may have told you that if you will look at them very carefully you will note how very few words are more than a single syllable.

Come to see us when you can.

Your friend,
Phil Stone

[1] "The Literary Career of William Faulkner: Catalogue of an Exhibition in the Princeton University Library," *Princeton University Library Chronicle*, 21 (Spring 1960), 111–164.

[2] As Meriwether pointed out in a subsequent letter, the 1919–1920 *Ole Miss* lists Murry Falkner as "Assistant Secretary."

S-91 Letter from Ruth Ford to Peter Glenville, August 9, 1960, unsigned carbon typescript, 1 page.

Dear Peter:

I had planned to tell you about this in person but, not knowing when we will meet, I think I had better drop you a note about it.

Zachary and I, with Harvey Breit, own the film rights to William Faulkner's "LIGHT IN AUGUST" which, of course, we think would make a most extraordinary and marvellous film. Certainly a modern classic—and a most contemporary and moving story of basic human conflicts.

I know that you are a real Faulkner fan and want to know if you are interested in acquiring this property for yourself or having a studio do it for you.[1] I also thought of writing to Laurence Harvey about it as I think he would be quite sensational as Joe Christmas. If you think this is a good idea, you might like to speak to him about it instead of me.

In any case please let me have a note or a call on your thoughts about this because—a letter from Arnold Weissberger to me today tells me that an independent producer in Hollywood is interested in acquiring the property and will be here in about two weeks to talk to him about it. I want to be sure that, if any of my friends are interested in this property, they are able to acquire it before or instead of an "outsider."

Love as ever to you and Bill. Always longing to see you both.

[no signature]

[1]Miss Ford may not have known that Glenville had previously expressed an interest in this property. See his letter to Harold Ober, February 3, 1958, printed in this volume.

S-92 Letter from Ruth Ford to Arnold Weissberger, August 25, 1960, unsigned carbon typescript, 2 pages.

Dear Arnold:

. . . .

Just a note about "LIGHT IN AUGUST." Did you ever hear from the independent producer, William Miller, that Miss Davis said was interested in "LIGHT IN AUGUST"? She said on August 4th that he would be here in about two weeks. . . .

In the meantime, what arrangements did you and Peter Glenville come to? Zachary and I want to sell this property (and Harvey will go along too) *because* we have no money to make the payments. As of September 1st we have earned this year exactly half what it costs us to live.

I have contacted the following about "LIGHT IN AUGUST." Some months ago, John Huston and Paul Kohner. Huston was definitely interested in the property but then he got involved in "THE MISFITS" and, naturally, this would be a difficult time to get word from him about it. Martin Jurow, who said no. I wrote to my friends, Joe Mankiewicz, Sam Spiegel and John Frankenheimer, but haven't heard from any of them. And Peter Glenville, who said he was definitely interested in the property, but you will know all about that if he called you as he said he was going to.

If you have any ideas about selling this property, go ahead and do so, but I think we should start at our price of $150,000—you know how Hollywood is—they would rather have something that costs more than something that costs less. After all, they paid $135,000 for "REQUIEM FOR A NUN" and on top of that had to pay another $50,000 for the rights of "SANCTUARY" in order to make the film, so that made $185,000. This is an infinitely better story than "REQUIEM" and would, I am sure, make a far better film.

I would love for Peter Glenville to have this property because I know he loves Faulkner, and we are very fond of Peter, but you and I know that he is famous for postponing projects and dilly-dallying and not coming to a decision, so I don't really feel like holding up anything for Peter. However, I would want to be sure not to present it to anybody that he is even vaguely interested in for either a producer or a star. We talked about Laurence Harvey—also several other actors. He was not Peter's choice but I feel that Laurence Harvey would be very interested in acquiring this story for himself and I would like to present it to him, but I don't want to do so if Peter is going to present it to him.

Have you ever read "LIGHT IN AUGUST"? It is a modern classic—a contemporary and moving story of basic human conflicts with elements of a chase and great suspense and couldn't be more timely.

So, dear Arnold, that's the story.

Love,
[no signature]

S-93 Letter from Arnold Weissberger to Ruth Ford, September 1, 1960, signed ribbon typescript, 2 pages.

Dear Ruth:

I had a long talk with Peter Glenville about "Light In August."

Peter said that he wanted to make it very clear that he loved the property, and that he wanted to do it. He had, in fact, at one point been negotiating with the Ober office himself, and the price that Ober had asked for was $50,000.

The problem, Peter points out, is that he himself is not buying the property. He must get his producer to buy it. Peter has emphatically indicated to his producer that he wants to do it, but the question will be (a) whether the producer shares Peter's enthusiasm for the property and (b) whether he will pay anything remotely like what you want in order to acquire it.

On this latter aspect, Peter says that it may be difficult, if not impossible, to convince a producer that a property which could have been bought so recently for $50,000. is now worth $150,000., especially when it is 15 years old, and there is no "hot" bidding for it. "Requiem For A Nun" is not a criterion, because dramatic properties always, or usually, sell for much more than novels, and "Requiem" was, at the time of its sale, a fresh property. It was, in fact, a pre-production deal, as you know, and you are aware of the maneuvering I had to do to get the price up to what we got.

In summary, therefore, we will make a sale of the property through Peter only if he can induce his producer to buy it, but it is doubtful that we would get anything like $150,000. If that fails to come through, you might well consider with Harvey the possibility of putting the property in the hands of someone like Irving Lazar,[1] with whom I have been having some recent dealings. The fact that the property is 15 years old and that no motion picture company has been interested in it would be rather against it, but, on the other hand, the renewed interest in Faulkner's works for motion picture vehicles might be in its favor.

In any event, if you would like to, perhaps we should all meet and discuss the situation as soon as we hear from Peter.

Love,
/s/ Arnold
/t/ L. Arnold Weissberger

[1] Irving Paul Lazar, a literary agent with offices in Beverly Hills and New York.

S-94 Letter from Ruth Ford to Arnold Weissberger, September 14, 1960, signed ribbon typescript, 2 pages.

Dear Arnold:

Alas, the payment on "LIGHT IN AUGUST" is due tomorrow and I (I say 'I' because this was my project, although it involves Zachary and Harvey) haven't got the money. That means Zachary hasn't got it either. When we decided to do this it seemed almost certain that Zachary would get the Herbert Tareyton T.V. job, which would have brought us in good and regular money for the next five years but, as you know, that didn't come about, and I should be old enough and smart enough to know that nothing is ever really definite regarding theatrical work.

I have been trying to think my way out of this. I have also involved Harvey in this and I feel very responsible about that too. I only have one idea and this is it. Tell me what you think of it. It is to tell whoever it is now at the Ober office, since it isn't Anne Davis, that we cannot meet the payments tomorrow (I don't imagine Harvey would want to make a payment unless we did) and that we will have to have another extension.

When the three of us bought this property we had hoped, and it was our desire, to make a personal project out of it—that is, for Harvey to write the screen play and Zachary and I to be involved in it either as actor, actress, producer, or in some way. In the meantime, it seems to be an enormous project for the three of us, since we have not really had any experience in this particular field. Loving Faulkner the way we all do, we also wanted to protect the property and see if we couldn't finally get a Faulkner film that would remain true to his work and that he would be proud of. I think my information is correct that the highest price that has been paid for any property of Faulkner's to be made into a film before "REQUIEM FOR A NUN" was $50,000. At the time we bought the property I think someone else was interested in it, but whether a firm offer had been made I don't know. Since we got the price up to $135,000 (admitting that we were able to get this price for it because it was a play first) I would like to keep Faulkner's prices somewhere up around that level—for him, of course.

Now, the proposition that I referred to is this; we could be given an extension and try to sell the property, as we are now trying to do, for as much as we can get for it, somewhere under or over $100,000, and give Faulkner a percentage of that. What percentage would you suggest, if you think this is a feasible idea? Then, of course, Ober would tack their percentage on that, so everyone stands to profit from the deal. Or they could sell it for any price over $50,000—keep all they get for it—and return our $5,000 investment to us.

The only other alternative is that, since we have failed to make our payments, they have a right, of course, to claim the property back, which means that I would be out $5,000, because I feel responsible for Harvey's half, since I got him into it and I would be the cause of him losing that money.

If you have any other ideas, please let me know, and let me know what you think of this.

Love
/s/ Ruth

P.S. Of course, another idea—which is really the best idea—is to have them just grant us another extension until the 1st January.

The latest development; I spoke to Philip Langner last night, who is co-owner of "THE NUREMBURG TRIALS" with Stanley Kramer, and they are starting filming in January. I told Philip all about "LIGHT IN AUGUST" and said that, if he liked it, he could present it to Stanley Kramer as another joint venture. He was thrilled at the idea and was rushing out to get a copy of the book to read over the weekend. I told him, if he was interested in the property, to contact you. I quoted $150,000.

S-95 Letter from Ruth Ford to Arnold Weissberger, September 19, 1960, signed ribbon typescript, 1 page.

Dear Arnold:

After our phone conversation today about "LIGHT IN AUGUST" I got to thinking. Mightn't it be better for me and Zachary to turn this property over to M.C.A.—they are our agents—and present them with the idea of selling it, with them getting 10% above $50,000. It seems to me they are in a more powerful position than Irving Lazar, and they could make a package deal out of it. They could interest a director and a star and a producer. In any case, if you don't think that M.C.A. is a better idea than Lazar, I would like to limit Lazar's exclusive to, say, three months. Also, I don't want him to quote less than $150,000 as this would be unfair to the people to whom I have quoted that price, and I think he must have a list of the people I have already contacted quoting that price, in case some of these people should be on his list and he would quote less. Here is the list,[1] if you would like to send it on to him.

Do let me know what you think about this.

Love,
/s/ Ruth

[1]The enclosed list included the following names: Ingo and Otto Preminger, Sam Spiegel, John Frankenheimer, Martin Jurow, David Susskind, Peter Glenville, John Huston and Paul Kohner, Joe Mankiewicz, Philip Langner, and Stanley Kramer.

S-96 Letter from Arnold Weissberger to Ruth Ford and Harvey Breit, September 27, 1960, signed ribbon typescript, 1 page.

Dear Ruth and Harvey:

Ivan Von Auw has called me back in connection with "Light In August." He said that he had had a letter from Faulkner, and Faulkner wanted to know whether you were simply planning to resell the property as is, or whether it was to be part of a package with the screen play. I realized what Von Auw was driving at, and I said that it had been your intention to sell the property with the screen play. Von Auw said that if you were simply reselling the property, then Faulkner felt that offering him 10% of the excess was not enough.

Faulkner was making two counter-proposals. He wanted you not to have any loss, so if you wished to drop the property now, he would pay you back the money that you had paid to him, and all rights would revert to him. If you wanted to hold on to it, he would agree to give you an extension of a whole year in selling it, but he would then want 50% of the excess over $50,000.

Will you consider this and then discuss it with me?

Warm regards.

Cordially,
/s/ Arnold
/t/ L. Arnold Weissberger

S-97 Letter from Ruth Ford to Ivan Von Auw, Jr., October 18, 1960, unsigned carbon typescript, 2 pages (1 leaf).

Dear Mr. Von Auw:

I know that you and my lawyer, Arnold Weissberger, have been dealing with the "LIGHT IN AUGUST" situation. However, I thought I might make my position clearer on this if I wrote you directly.

When my husband and Mr. Breit and I acquired this property we had the following idea in mind. All of us admiring Mr. Faulkner's work beyond bounds, and also loving him as a man beyond bounds, we wanted very much to see if we could put together a film adapted from "LIGHT IN AUGUST" that not only we would be proud of but that he would be proud of. In other words, an extraordinary film following his, Faulkner's, story and not having it turn out, as all his films have in Hollywood, a complete distortion of the original work. The three of us thought at the time that we would be able to do this. Mr. Breit was going to write the screen play, Zachary wanted to play either Joe Christmas or Hightower, and I wanted to play Lizzie [blank].[1] We wanted to choose the director and try to sell it as a package to a producer of talent and integrity. Since we acquired the property and tried to deal with it in these terms, we see that this idea is practically an impossible one. It is just something that Hollywood won't go for. To make a completely unnecessary statement and judgment, they are not interested in art or quality—only in box office. We could perhaps, by holding on to this property, get a picture made the way we want it maybe in ten years, but I don't think any of us, including Mr. Faulkner, want to wait that long and, with Khrushchev not only banging his fists but his shoes at the U.N., we might none of us even be here ten years from now! Also, my husband and I ran into money difficulties and could not meet our obligations—that is, our payments—because a television series that looked certain at the time we acquired this property, that would have made the payments not only possible but easy, did not come through.

So that is why we all think the best thing to do now is to try to sell the property simply as a property and, naturally, get all we can for it. In other words, to keep Mr. Faulkner's price up where it should be. I think I am correct in saying that, until "REQUIEM FOR A NUN" was sold for $135,000, the highest price any of his books had gotten for a screen play was $50,000, and, if I remember correctly, Mr. Faulkner got 60% of the $135,000 and the producers of the play and their backers got the other 40%.

I think Arnold Weissberger misunderstood me somewhat about the percentage. I told him we wanted to sell the property and give Mr. Faulkner a percentage. He assumed that would be 10% as that is, as you know, the percentage the "agent" gets for selling a property. However, I don't feel that any dealings that I have with Mr. Faulkner could be based solely on business, and I was going to present this proposition to him, through you of course, and let him state the percentage that he would like, which he has done at 50%, which I certainly think is more than fair to everyone concerned.

May I offer this alternative suggestion? Since none of our talents are now involved in this—that is, mine and my husband's and Mr. Breit's—we are no longer *personally* concerned in the property from that point of view but, loving and admiring the property, we would like to try to sell it for Mr. Faulkner and try to see that it gets into the best possible hands—that is, producer or director—people who love it and understand it. So let me make this proposition. Let *all* of us try to sell it—you, Mr. Weissberger and the three of us. If *we* sell it, let us take 50% over $50,000—if *you* sell it for $55,000 or more, return to us our $5,000 and keep for Mr. Faulkner all the rest, no matter what the amount is. If you think that is an acceptable idea to you and Mr. Faulkner, let me know. I think we should ask $150,000 for the property—at least, start off with that. That is just $15,000 more than was paid for "REQUIEM FOR A NUN" and I think we should point out to would-be buyers that they really paid $185,000 for "REQUIEM FOR A NUN" because, in order to make the film, they had to pay another $50,000 for "SANCTUARY," so that really made it $185,000 for the property. Of course, it is always easier to sell a property after it has become a play. That I know.

Let me have your thoughts on this.

Sincerely yours,
[no signature]

[1] Miss Ford probably meant Lena Grove.

S-98 Photostatic copy of letter from Irving Paul Lazar to Arnold Weissberger, October 20, 1960, signed typescript, 1 page.

Dear Arnold:

Still working on LIGHT IN AUGUST and don't want you to think I forgot it. Will call you when I get to New York.

The book is now being read by Richard Brooks who seems a natural to write and direct the screenplay. If he liked it, we'd be in business because I can get any kind of money budget I want for the picture. Will keep you informed.

Until then, my best.

Sincerely,

/s/ P

1502b Letter from Phil Stone to Kraig Klosson, October 21, 1960, carbon typescript with typed signature, 2 pages.

Dear Kraig:

We got your letter written Monday and were very glad to hear from you indeed.[1]

Don't forget to write us a little later on when you think you can come up here for a day or so.

As for Miss Maud, it was the best thing that could have happened. They had funeral services for the family only down at her home and buried her Saturday afternoon at 3 o'clock P.M. I was one of the pallbearers and a few people only were there because they knew the Faulkners didn't want a big crowd.

As for what Bill is going to do, I don't know. I never ask him what he is going to do anyway. I don't think he will stay in Virginia because, frankly, I think he stayed there so long that the Virginians found out he didn't know as much as they thought he knew. I saw him this morning in front of Mack Reed's drug store and spoke to him but did not stop because I was in quite a hurry at that time. Anyway, if Bill has anything he wants to say to me he will say it. So I never bother to ask him anything that is not necessary.

As for Bill speaking with his tongue in his cheek, he is not doing any such thing. He really believes all that stuff he says himself, at least he believes most of it.

There is a good deal of symbolism in what Bill has written, but a lot of it they think is there is not there at all. This is another thing that is due to their tendency to overrate Bill as a novelist. Subconsciously he may have picked up something. The vital thing for you to remember, as my wife has said, is that Bill is an empirical writer. He has no theory and, like all authors, he is a jackdaw picking up things here and there. You remember it was said that Mercury was the god of thieves and poets. I am not criticizing about that. That is perfectly legitimate.

As for the Bible, it is one of the grandest books that ever lived and has some of the grandest prose in it.

As for teaching English, I am doubtful about that. I still think you would do better if you were a mechanic in a garage where you could really pick out some material which you could use for writing novels. You won't get it from English teachers. I don't care if they are the best in the world, that is still true. Why don't you get a job in a bank where you get a regular salary? You know this is what T. S. Eliot did for a living.

You are not boring us a bit, and I wish I had time to write you a longer letter, but I am really working these days.

Above all, don't go too far the other way because Bill is still the best novelist writing in America today. I confess I don't think the standard is very high, however. That man can write and use words, and never think that he can't.

Your friend,
Phil Stone

[1] Klosson, a student at Tulane University, had recently accompanied his professor, Richard P. Adams, on a trip to Oxford to visit Phil and Emily Stone.

1503b Letter from Phil Stone to Richard P. Adams, October 31, 1960, unsigned carbon typescript, 1 page.

Dear Dick:

(I hope you don't mind me calling you by your first name. I am not given to "first-naming," but I am so much older than you are I perhaps have a right to call you by your first name.)

Thanks for your nice note of October 28. We enjoyed you and Kraig very much.

. . . .

If and when you do come to Oxford again be sure and call us and come to see us if we happen to be in town. Emily is usually here, but I am gone so much I can't tell when I am going to be away because I don't always know myself ahead of time.

With regard to my remarks about Bill's writing, please do not get the impression that I do not think he is grand, because he is. He has many beautiful talents in writing and he is still the best of the present crop in the United States. The basis of my complaint rests upon the fact that, first, the crop is not so good and, second, I get peeved because with all the ability Bill has he could have been a greater writer if he had really bothered to try. That just gripes me.

Yours truly,
[no signature]

S-99 Letter from Faulkner to Joan Williams Bowen, undated, signed autograph manuscript, 1 page, with envelope addressed in Faulkner's hand and postmarked Charlottesville, December 12, 1960.

I wrote you a letter about a month ago, then decided not to send it for a while, if at all maybe.

[no signature]

1503c Letter from Richard P. Adams to Phil Stone, December 12, 1960, signed ribbon typescript, 1 page.

Dear Mr. Stone,

I fully sympathize with your general feeling against first-naming, and because I do, I'm especially pleased that you want to make an exception of me. I consider it an honor.

I've taken the liberty of ordering a book on Faulkner which will eventually be sent to you, but the publisher is slow in furnishing it. I neither recommend

43. Photograph of Faulkner inscribed to Dorothy Oldham, February 21, 1961

nor disrecommend it, but I hope you'll enjoy reading it, and will be interested to know what you think of it, pro and con.

The other day, in the course of research on Eugene O'Neill, I ran across an article in the *American Magazine* for November, 1922, in which O'Neill was quoted as saying something about the desirability of a writer's having unlimited objectives, because he can achieve a greater success in failing to reach them than he could if he set a more modest goal. It looked like a statement that would have interested Faulkner very much if he happened to see it. Do you think he would have been likely to read that article? Do you know whether he has ever been interested in O'Neill's plays?

I hope to visit Oxford again for a day or two some time this summer. If you are there at the time, I would certainly like to see you again.

Most cordially,
/s/ Dick Adams

1503d Letter from Phil Stone to Richard P. Adams, December 14, 1960, carbon typescript with typed signature, 1 page.

Dear Dick:

Thank you very much for your nice letter of December 12.

I shall look forward to getting the book, but don't think I don't appreciate it if I take a long time to read it. Outside of law books I hardly get to read more than one book a year.

With reference to the O'Neill article, I doubt if Bill saw it and he probably wouldn't read it if he did. He has to some extent been interested in O'Neill in the past because I called his attention to him and told him this was one man who came pretty near having genius.

If you come up here any time please let me know ahead of time so I can arrange to be at home.

Thank you very much for the book.

Your friend,
Phil Stone

1961

S-100 Letter from Faulkner to Joan Williams Bowen, "Thursday," signed autograph manuscript, 1 page, with envelope addressed in Faulkner's hand and postmarked Oxford, April 22, 1961.

Dear Joan,

I found the book[1] when I got back from Venezuela yesterday. Beautiful. I am proud of you. Dont stop now. I believe, hope you are already working on the next one. Love.

Bill

[1] *The Morning and the Evening*, Joan Williams' first novel.

S-101 Letter from Faulkner to Mary Winslow Chapman, Secretary, Longreen Hunt, Germantown, Tennessee, dated "Oxford, Miss. / 3 May, 1961," signed ribbon typescript, 1 page, with envelope addressed in Faulkner's hand and postmarked Oxford, May 6, 1961.

Dear Mrs Chapman:

Notice that the subscription list is open was in the mail today.

Thank you for the chance to subscribe and do my bit to support fox hunting in our country; I would want to subscribe even if I didn't hunt.

I dont know just what my status is so I enclose the check in blank. Please fill in for whatever fits my case. Would be happy to subscribe the $75.00 even though I am not a member, if this is acceptable.

I leave for Va. Sunday, will be back in July, when I hope you will bring the hounds and mounts down here. We can do some night hill-topping with cars and see how the fox will run, and ride the country by day and see where to open it up. I suggested this to Mr Anderson last month, will communicate with him as soon as I get back from Va.

Yours sincerely,
/s/ William Faulkner
/t/ William Faulkner

1264d Letter from James W. Silver to John Cook Wyllie, August 21, 1961, carbon typescript with typed signature, 1 page.

Dear Mr. Wyllie:

From what I have heard from Tom Hammond and Paul Gaston, they must have given you an erroneous impression regarding my Faulkner manuscript[1] and my desire to take a year off to collect local impressions of Faulkner.

There was a time when I would have done the latter, and I think that it might still be done by the right person—although it is getting late. For instance, William Faulkner's mother died last spring, and she was of course a priceless source of information, for the right person, that is. In any case I am not interested in this for myself inasmuch as I am in the middle of research on a book which I hope will be really worth while.

But I have had a couple of second thoughts about the manuscript. While at the University of Virginia this summer I had a chance to look at the Faulkner holdings in the library and I am impressed with what you are doing. I'm sorry that we did not get to talk because there are some suggestions I could make that might help you fill out your Faulkner material. For instance, there are some people in this area who have Faulkner letters (Phil Mullen of Canton, for instance) who probably would never let you have them but who if approached in the right manner well let you photostat them.

To get back to my little manuscript. Mr. Massey wrote me two letters in November and December, 1956, about it, but I decided then that I would rather keep it myself. At that time I had no idea that his material would be turned over to a university library nor that the Princeton holdings would find their way to Virginia.

Anyway, I'm sending you the manuscript, for which I want $150. This price is determined from Mr. Massey's letters. If I weren't so much in need of cash, with two children in college, I would be tempted to give it to your library. But I can't at the present moment.

I would prefer, also, that neither Bill Faulkner nor his daughter Jill know

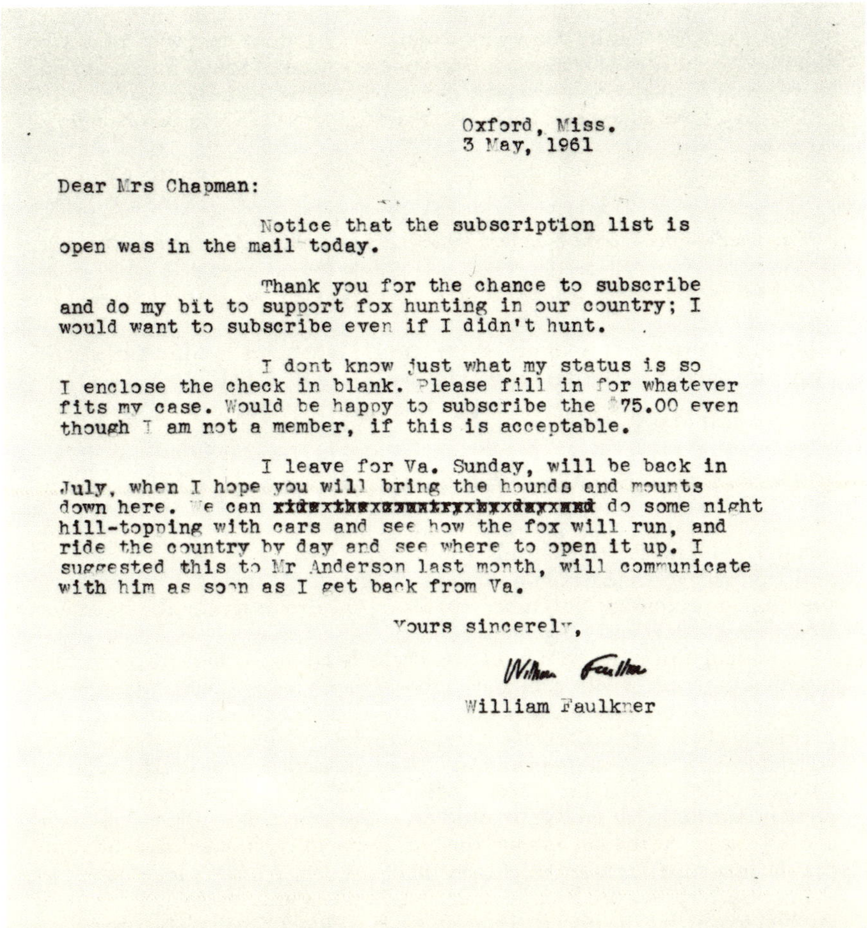

Oxford, Miss.
3 May, 1961

Dear Mrs Chapman:

Notice that the subscription list is open was in the mail today.

Thank you for the chance to subscribe and do my bit to support fox hunting in our country; I would want to subscribe even if I didn't hunt.

I dont know just what my status is so I enclose the check in blank. Please fill in for whatever fits my case. Would be happy to subscribe the $75.00 even though I am not a member, if this is acceptable.

I leave for Va. Sunday, will be back in July, when I hope you will bring the hounds and mounts down here. We can ~~ride the country by day and~~ do some night hill-topping with cars and see how the fox will run, and ride the country by day and see where to open it up. I suggested this to Mr Anderson last month, will communicate with him as soon as I get back from Va.

Yours sincerely,

William Faulkner

William Faulkner

44. Letter from Faulkner to Mary W. Chapman, with envelope (item S-101)

that I *sold* the manuscript, if you desire to purchase it. We have been intimates of the Faulkner family for twenty years, and I think my wife would be horrified at the idea of *selling* this. She was once offered $2000 for a magazine story about Faulkner and turned it down, because of the family angle.

I'll add a short statement[2] about the manuscript itself, which may be helpful to you.

Sincerely,
James W. Silver

[1]Faulkner's address to the Southern Historical Association in Memphis in November 1955.

[2]See the next item.

1264d Letter from James W. Silver "To Whom It May Concern," August 21, 1961, carbon typescript with typed signature, 1 page.

To Whom It May Concern:

I was program chairman for the 1955 meeting of the Southern Historical Association. My chief accomplishment in that position was to secure William Faulkner as a speaker. I began to work on him as early as April of 1955 and by the latter part of May he promised me that he would speak if he were in the country. At first his speech was set for an afternoon session, but when I realized that everyone would probably come to hear Faulkner, I changed it to the dinner session on November 10, 1955. On the program also appeared Benjamin E. Mays and Cecil Sims.

As we had a running battle with the Peabody Hotel for some three or four months before the meeting, largely as to whether a Negro could appear in the main banquet hall (which the people of the Mississippi Delta seem to think is peculiarly their own), there was considerable question about the meeting right down to the deadline. At first it was decided that we would have no banquet table—or speakers' table—because the hotel management was adamant in its ruling that no Negro could eat at the head table, although he could speak from it. At the last minute the management capitulated. I don't think this performance has been duplicated since.

Because I was fearful that Faulkner might not appear at the last minute, I got him to give me the enclosed speech, on November 3, a week before he was to appear. In it there is one interesting error, which I caught, and informed Faulkner about, and which he changed in his final draft. At the top of page four you will note that he writes of Burgess and Meredith or Hiss. He meant, of course, Burgess or McLean, and he changed this after I pointed it out to him. He smiled a little as he did so but said nothing.

There was a good deal of excitement at the meeting, largely because of the presence of Mr. Mays, but also because of Faulkner's appearance. The Minute Ladies (a right wing organization) tried to purchase tickets with the purpose of some sort of demonstration, but this plan was frustrated. The papers played up Faulkner and forgot Mays who, really, was the featured speaker. When he finished, a southern audience of some 700 rose and cheered him. I have never seen anything like it at one of our meetings. But the Faulkner appearance was something of a sensation, too. He spoke so quietly that I doubt if half the audience heard him. After the speech he took off by plane for New York, but his wife received threatening calls in Oxford for the next ten days. She sat with my wife and myself at the dinner.

James W. Silver

1264e Letter from Linton Massey to James W. Silver, August 30, 1961, signed ribbon typescript, 1 page.

Dear Dr. Silver:

You have no idea how much pleasure it gave me to find here in Virginia the typescript of the Faulkner speech before the Southern Historical Association in 1955, together with your own absorbing account of the circumstances relating to the occasion; my delight was only tempered by the fact I could not thank you in person, nor become acquainted during your stay in Charlottesville. Perhaps you will give me and others here another chance.

Let me hasten to reassure you as to the typescript: it is most improbable that either of the Faulkners will ever learn of its being here. I myself will be the very soul of discretion!

Had I been here I should have taken the opportunity of showing you the Faulkner collection in its entirety, for I am sure you missed seeing some of the manuscripts, the early correspondence relating to the publication of THE MARBLE FAUN, and a few unique items. I own over forty letters of early date, but these are restricted out of the author's professed wish for privacy. I should most certainly be interested in acquiring others, either the originals or photostatic copies.

Your interest in preserving material relating to Mr. Faulkner is most commendable. Miss Maud might have been willing to help, but it is now too late for this.

If I may be of assistance in any way please feel free to call upon me. In the meantime, with most sincere thanks, I am,

Cordially yours,
/s/ Linton Massey
/t/ Linton Massey

1526a Letter from James W. Silver to John Cook Wyllie, September 1, 1961, carbon typescript with typed signature, 2 pages.

Dear Mr. Wyllie:

Here is the best example that I know of of the necessity to do something about the possibilities in William Faulkner's home town.

I noticed in your inventory of Faulkner materials that you have a copy of his short story, "The Wishing Tree." I don't know what copy you have but I'm reasonably sure that you don't know one-tenth of the story behind the story. I don't profess to know all the story but I know enough to be sure that it is a fascinating one.

In the first place (I'm no Faulkner critic) I rather suspect that its presence would confound some of the Faulkner students, for "The Wishing Tree" is a fantasy, a kind of fairy tale, written solely to please a little girl.

For a long number of years I assumed that Mrs. Maude Morrow Brown (who has known "Billy" since the moment he was born) had the original copy. She had an afflicted daughter who died a couple of years after Faulkner brought to her the story. There is some question as to the date although Mrs. Brown could pinpoint that. It was somewhere between 1926 and 1929. (Mrs. Brown is now about ninety but full of wit and wisdom.) This "original" copy has a good many interpolations in Faulkner's handwriting, and on the 1st sheet has written on it, "To Margaret, from William Faulkner." I had the original in my office for years and made several copies of it. Faulkner borrowed it from "Miss Maude" in 1949[1] and made another copy for Phil Stone's son. He then sent it back to her via special delivery although the post office was farther from his house than her home. Mrs. Brown states that Faulkner told her this was her story, to do with as she pleased. On this basis, after the story had been exhibited at Princeton, I made a couple of efforts to see about the publication of the story—which was never done because of reasons too involved to go into here. My only purpose, other than a natural interest in such a human story, was to get Mrs. Brown a little money, which I'm sure she could use.

Anyway, in May of this year, I was talking one night with Faulkner's step-daughter, Victoria Franklin Fielden, who accidentally remarked that she had a copy of a short story written for her by Faulkner when he was courting her mother. This was the "Wishing Tree" and was apparently given to Mrs. Fielden on her ninth birthday,[2] in 1927. Whether the Brown copy is the original or whether the Fielden copy is the original I don't know, though I rather suspect that the Brown copy is, from internal evidence.[3] Anyway, Mrs. Fielden was shocked to discover that there was another copy in existence, and I think a bit hurt, for she had treasured this story as being hers and hers alone. Of course, Mrs. Brown has felt about the same way, particularly after the death of Margaret and after Faulkner had told her that she could do with it as she pleased.

I'm not sure that you can make much sense out of this because I'm writing in a hurry, taking time out from a paper on which I have a near deadline. But this may give you an idea as to what I had in mind when I first wrote you. I think that the story behind the "Wishing Tree" is as important as the story itself. I doubt whether Faulkner could unravel the mystery himself, and God knows I wouldn't approach him about it. On the other hand, the mystery should be solved before it is too late.

What you could get from Mrs. Brown in the way of specific information I don't know. I doubt whether you would achieve anything by correspondence but you might.

I have thought from time to time about trying to get at the bottom of the story but usually I come up with the feeling that there are too many sensitive people I know too well who are involved.

Anyway, I hope that this will give you some idea of the kind of work that could be done on Faulkner in this area—while there is still time.

Sincerely,
James W. Silver

[1]The year was 1948, not 1949.
[2]Actually her eighth birthday.
[3]Silver was mistaken: the Victoria Franklin copy, dated February 5, 1927, on the front flyleaf, was the original. See Blotner, *Faulkner: A Biography,* p. 541.

1526b Letter from James W. Silver to Linton Massey, September 3, 1961, carbon typescript with typed signature, 1 page.

Dear Mr. Massey:

The letters I write these days seem to be hurried affairs, largely because I have a deadline for a paper that must be completed before school opens.

I did enjoy your letter of August 30, partly because it indicates a real awareness of the possibilities of doing even more than has been done about the Faulkner story. The other day I wrote Mr. Wyllie some comments and I suppose that you will see them.

For several years I made what I suppose was a feeble effort to get people concerned with collecting Faulkner information while it was still available. Several times I thought that I was near success but it always seemed to elude me.

This last book by Floyd Watkins,[1] for instance, has a lot of stuff in it that is worth preserving. He picked up what he did in a summer here (he lived in my house) and in a few more visits. But he also preserved a bunch of rather obvious errors. There are many people here who will talk to an outsider like Watkins *up to a point* and then shut up. Mrs. Brown, I think, is probably one of these. Phil Stone knows a hell of a lot about Faulkner and has talked with many people but he should be quizzed over a period of weeks. It is also true that he is unreliable about a lot of things but, it seems to me, everything should be taken down (that he is willing to say) and then the truth might be sorted out later. There are many members of the older generations in Oxford who might talk and, of course, many members of the Oldham, Franklin, and Faulkner families. John Faulkner, as big an unconscious liar as he may be, could be the source of an enormous lot of information.

All this depends, in my thinking, on whether Faulkner is a really great writer. I'll be damned if I know, but apparently you think he is. *If he is* a great deal could be done to explain him—in the next few years. But, for instance, Mrs. Brown (now about 90) may die any day. Phil Stone is 69. Etc., etc.

My relation with the family has been accidental. The two step-children, Malcolm and Victoria, have been intimately associated for 25 years with my wife and myself. I have my own little collection of some 50 books by and about Faulkner, but this is just a curiosity. I have known Bill off and on for twenty or more years but don't profess to really know much about him. I think that my wife knows him about as well as a human being as anyone. In any case we are too closely associated with the family to write about any part of it. And I'm not interested in doing any of this myself simply because I'm determined to complete a book I'm working on.

But someone should collect a lot of raw material on Faulkner while it is still available.

Sincerely,
James W. Silver

[1]*Old Times in the Faulkner Country* by John B. Cullen in collaboration with Watkins (Chapel Hill: University of North Carolina Press, 1961).

1526d Letter from Linton Massey to James W. Silver, September 16, 1961, signed ribbon typescript, 2 pages.

Dear Dr. Silver:

Your fine letter of September 1st addressed to John Wyllie he promptly turned over to me for reply, out of reasons best known to him. You were concerned therein with the circumstances relating to THE WISHING TREE, and all you had to say was of the most profound interest. Most of what you said is now known to specialists. Let me say for my own part that if Mrs. Brown, who evidently needs the money, is willing to sell, then I pledge myself to buy at the current market at a price fair to her and to me. That is to say, I am prepared to be decent and entirely just. She will in this way get more money than she would if she were to sell to a dealer. If I am suspect, let John Wyllie set the price and I shall abide with his decision. From your description it would seem that the Brown copy is the original, not the Fielden. In any case I can assure you Mr. Faulkner has not forgotten the story itself; and if memory serve, he read it to a group of children a few years ago. If I may serve as a means of placing this important mss. where perhaps it ought to be, in my collection at the University of Virginia which you saw, and with the other Faulker manuscripts, also at the University, do write.

I myself obviously as you remark believe deeply in the greatness of William Faulkner as a writer. He has written many memorable books that will live in our literature; at least four of them will endure as long as our culture survives, and maybe longer. That he is an enigmatic figure in Oxford I am well aware, but in the long run this estimate of him will become, I am convinced, a puzzle to later generations. He is in some ways a writer's writer. He is often obscure. He is more frequently, profound. Anything about him that will explain his work without intruding upon him as an individual I am determined to fasten upon; and if it can be put on paper, then so much the better. All I can do, so long as purse permits, to preserve his manuscripts I shall undertake, provided I can accomplish all this without attracting attention to myself.

Unselfish and devoted friends such as you can help pursue a similar course; and the more you can do to dispel the myths, the falsehoods, the distortions, and the misrepresentations surrounding William Faulkner the better. Every creative artist makes more enemies than friends. Because they are different from you and me, because their behaviour at times is unconventional, and because, having created a world of their own they are singularly independent of this one, they are freely condemned by those who usually have no right to express any opinion whatever.

What you write is very refreshing, indeed. I am more sorry than ever I did not have the chance to meet and talk with you this summer; but there will with favoring luck be other summers and other times.

Do write me whenever you think of any matter I should know about. And if through you I may serve Mrs. Brown and help in a small way to preserve those things that ought to be preserved, do by all means let me know at once.

In the meantime, with much admiration for your courage and insights, I am,

Cordially yours,
/s/ Linton Massey
/t/ Linton Massey

1503h Letter from Richard P. Adams to Phil Stone, October 3, 1961, signed ribbon typescript, 2 pages.

Dear Mr. Stone,

The new school year is under way, and things have settled down enough so I can do some work; and I've been gathering a few more questions which I hope you won't be too busy to comment on, to whatever extent you think they warrant.

I was very much interested in what you said about your and Faulkner's interest in Eliot. As I recall, you indicated that you read *Poetry* magazine pretty regularly, and I note that Eliot had poems in three issues of *Poetry:* "The Love Song of J. Alfred Prufrock" in June, 1915, "The Boston Evening Transcript," "Aunt Helen," and "Cousin Nancy" in October, 1915, and "Conversation Galante," "La Figlia che Piange," "Mr. Apollinax," and "Morning at the Window" in September, 1916. Do you recall whether you and Faulkner read these issues, noticed any of these poems especially, or talked about Eliot as early as 1915 and 1916?

I also note that Eliot had some poems in the *Little Review* for July, 1917, and again in the issue of September, 1918; also a couple of essays on Henry James in the issue of August, 1918. Did you get the *Little Review* at that time? And again, do you recall any notice being paid to Eliot's contributions?

Did you have the good luck to get hold of a copy of the 1917 edition of *Prufrock and Other Observations?* That, of course, had the poems that had been published in *Poetry.* If not the 1917 volume, did you get the first American edition, the *Poems* of 1920?

Do you recall where and when you first saw *The Waste Land?* It was published (without the notes) in *Criterion* for October, 1922, reprinted in the *Dial* for November, 1922, and published as a book (with the notes) by Boni and Liveright in December, 1922. What did you think of it, and what was Faulkner's response to it at the time, if any?

I'm also very much interested in two of Eliot's early essays, "Tradition and the Individual Talent," published in the *Egoist* for September–October and November–December, 1919, and "Ulysses, Order, and Myth," published in the *Dial* for November, 1923. Did you get either of these magazines, and do you recall noticing either of these particular essays? Do you recall being especially impressed with any other early essays by Eliot, or by any of his critical views or pronouncements, however reported? Did you get *The Sacred Wood* either in the London edition of 1920 or the New York edition of 1921?

Don't you think I would have made a good lawyer, with all this cross examination? You will see what I'm driving at—I want to have some estimate of Eliot's influence on Faulkner, which is clearly shown by the internal evidence of Faulkner's works, but which I'd like to confirm and specify by whatever external evidence you may be able to supply. My feeling is that Eliot was a very important—perhaps the most important—literary influence Faulkner felt in the early years, and I'd like to know whether you would be inclined to agree or not.

Along the same line, I wonder if Faulkner followed up Eliot's interest in Sir James Frazer and specifically *The Golden Bough.* Did you or he have access to the complete edition? Or did you have a copy of the unabridged edition of 1923, and if so did Faulkner see it? Were you interested in any other of the Cambridge anthropologists, such as Cornford, Jane Harrison, or Lord Raglan? Did you read Jessie L. Weston's *From Ritual to Romance,* the study of the Grail legend Eliot cited in his notes to *The Waste Land?* Did Faulkner see it?

One other question, and I'll stop, at least for this time. You mentioned having given Faulkner a book by Bergson to look at, and said he handed it back without having studied it much; still, if you can recall which one it was, I'd be curious to know. The volumes of Bergson that had been translated by 1920 were *Creative Evolution, Introduction to Metaphysics, Laughter, Matter and Memory, Mind-Energy,* and *Time and Free Will* (so far as I've been able to check). Do any of these titles strike a bell? Faulkner may not have read that book carefully, but somewhere, somehow before he wrote *Soldiers' Pay,* he got hold of some ideas about time, about concreteness, and about change that are mighty like what Bergson says on those points. Incidentally, I was reading Conrad's *Chance* the other day, and noticed a direct reference to Bergson's theory of laughter, though Conrad's character didn't mention Bergson by name. I'm interested partly because Conrad was a friend of Henry James, who was a brother of William James, who influenced Bergson and who was influenced by Emerson, whose philosophical importance I feel has been underrated—and who, by one way and another (though your friend might deny it) has also influenced Faulkner. Not that I plan to make a case out of that. It's too devious. But I find it amusing.

I find, in fact, an enormous amount of amusement in all this literary detectiving, whether it really proves anything or not. I hope I'm not boring you with my endlessly involved details; and particularly I hope I'm not being impertinently intrusive in any way. If you feel that any of my questions don't deserve an answer for any reason, don't hesitate to say so, or to refuse to answer on any grounds you like, or without grounds. Whatever you feel able and willing to give me along the lines suggested by the questions I've thus far succeeded in framing will be most gratefully received, and most helpful to me in the job I'm trying to do.

Some time, I hope soon, I'll visit Oxford again, and look for better luck for me and better health for you, such that we can have a good talk. Regard to all your family.

Yours,
/s/ Dick
/t/ R. P. Adams

1503i Letter from Phil Stone to Richard P. Adams, October 4, 1961, carbon typescript with typed signature, 2 pages.

Dear Dick:

I was very glad to receive your letter of October 3, and hope that you and Mrs. Adams will drop by some time soon but please let us know as far ahead as you can.

I am going to answer your letter right now as best I can, because if I don't answer it now I don't know when I will ever get it done.

As for the second paragraph in your letter, Bill probably read all of these things because I took all the issues of *Poetry* magazine and all of them were burned when our old house burned in 1942. I am sure that Bill read most of these because I would give them to him and he probably read them all.

With regard to *The Little Review,* I took all of them from the beginning and they also burned, and I am sure that I must have frequently called Bill's attention to Eliot and anything he would write because he was the one that I told Bill at the time would stand out from all his contemporaries sooner or later. As to any particular things, I cannot remember that far back.

My recollection is, as to *Prufrock and Other Observations,* that I did have the 1917 volume, but I may not have had this because it is possible that Bill read this particular thing in the original magazine. In fact, I remember now that he did do so.

As to *The Waste Land,* we first saw it in the *Dial* for November, 1922. I know I had Bill read this.

As to the *Essays* of Eliot, I am not so sure about that except that I did have all the copies of *The Egoist* and the *Dial.* As to *The Sacred Wood,* I do not remember anything about that.

Eliot had a big influence on Bill, but Conrad Aiken had almost as much or more, as you can easily see from some of Bill's verse.

As for expecting Bill Faulkner to follow up anything by reading several books: that is impossible optimism. What he probably did was pick up a few paragraphs somewhere and use them, but I am sure he never bothered to read *The Golden Bough,* although I had a copy of it.

I am not sure as to my recollection but what probably happened is that I told Bill about it and gave it to him to read and he didn't bother about doing anything except turning through it. I am pretty sure he did not read it fully or we would have had some discussion about it.

As to Bergson, my recollection is that the volume I had was *Creative Evolution,* and I think Bill read a good deal of this because it seemed to interest him.

Literary detectiving is interesting. It is particularly interesting to me because of the conclusions drawn by a lot of people who don't know Bill, conclusions which absolutely have no basis in fact at all.

We are holding you to that promise to visit us.

Your friend,
Phil Stone

S-102 Letter from Zachary Scott to Jean Renoir, October 20, 1961, signed carbon typescript, 1 page.

Dear Jean:

Ruth and I recently acquired the rights to William Faulkner's "LIGHT IN AUGUST" and I am very anxious to see a film made of it. Have you read it and, if not, will you, and let me have your reaction to the idea? It should make a sensational film and no-one that I can imagine should direct it but yourself.[1]

Warm good wishes to you and Dido[2] and in anticipation of an early reply,

I remain,
Fondly yours,
/s/ Zachary

[1] Jean Renoir, son of the famous painter, is considered one of the greatest filmmakers in the history of the cinema. He directed nearly forty movies, including *Nana, Le Grande Illusion, Swamp Water, The Southerner, The Woman on the Beach,* and *The River.*

[2] Mrs. Renoir.

1529 Letter from Estelle Faulkner to James W. Silver, "Tuesday 21st," signed autograph manuscript, 3 pages (1 folded leaf), with envelope addressed in Mrs. Faulkner's hand and postmarked Charlottesville, November 22, 1961.

Dear Jim—

You have no idea how contrite I am, asking you to assume more responsibility for Malcolm than you've already undertaken, out of sheer kindness—I *am* sorry—

We knew that you weren't too well—but did not know about an impending operation—For God's sake take care of yourself—and tell Chester[1] to get you as good a surgeon as he did me—However, I had the good fortune to fall in love with my Jewish doctor—and you'll scarcely go to such extreme lengths—Helps though—

Indeed I do want a copy of your address at Gettysburg—and no one could persuade me that you aren't the peer of Mr. Lincoln—

Had a wonderful, long letter from Vicki yesterday—bless her heart—Tell her for me—I *will* write, and soon—Believe that Vic hit the nail on the head about Malcolm—He is frightened of change—in fact Mac hasn't been the same since they moved the medical school—That disrupted his tight little world—

God! I do worry so—not knowing what to do—except to treat him as a child, and simply take care of him—

I suppose—uncontrolled worry = ulcers—

Never mind—I'll bury myself in philosophy and come out the better woman—

We like the country place—I have plenty of leisure and [indecipherable] to paint—Come up to my show starting Saturday—I do wish you and Dutch could—Have been invited to exhibit for two weeks before a jury show, which opens on the 8th—

Never fear—your nice letter got to me right away—Thank you—

This is a note to Dutch too—so I'll ask her to kiss you, and pat you on the back for us—by way of sincere congratulations—

Really, if I had my way—you'd be president of the United States too—

Love, from all us—to Dutch and Gail and Vic and you—

Estelle—

[P. S.] Re-reading this—my sentences are as involved as Bill's

[1] Dr. Chester McLarty, an Oxford physician.

S-103 Letter from Dido Renoir to Zachary Scott, November 30, 1961, signed ribbon typescript, 1 page.

Dear Zach:

I read "Light in August" before sending the book to Jean in Vienna. I was extremely moved and impressed and anxious for Jean's reaction although I knew he would not have much time for reading during the shooting of his picture. He has now read part of the book and believes it is a very great thing. He seems terribly excited and wants me to tell you so. The locations in Vienna will be finished in a few days, then Jean will work in Paris and hope it will be less strenuous there and that he will have more time to himself.

Fond regards to Ruth.

As ever,
/s/ Dido

S-104 Letter from Jean Renoir to Mr. and Mrs. Zachary Scott, December 18 [1961], signed autograph manuscript, 1 page.

Dear Zac—dear Ruth—

My best wishes to both of you, for a lovely Christmas and a good new year. My dearest wish—and selfish—being to find—some day—all of us around a camera, shooting Light in August.

With my affection
Jean

1962

1548c Letter from Linton Massey to James W. Silver, February 4, 1962, signed ribbon typescript, 1 page.

Dear Dr. Silver:

When I saw Mr. Dain in New York he proved to be all you had represented: an earnest, dedicated, and very capable fellow embarked on a labor of love providing much glory and very little cash. It was easy to admire him and his work; and the more I saw and the longer I listened the deeper became my sense of frustration.[1]

His project is entirely outside the provisions of our charter in the Foundation,[2] so much so that a participation would in fact imperil our tax exempt status. My own position in the organization would make it highly improper for me as an individual to help him. What he wants and needs is of course a subsidy of some kind; magazine and book publishers could provide one, but he declines at this point, when his work is scarcely begun, to bind himself to either.

All I can do is thank him (which I have done) for an opportunity to see his work and to give him a little moral support. And thanks to you for putting me on to him and his work.

Sincerely,
/s/ Linton Massey
/t/ Linton Massey

[1] Dain was seeking financial support for his work in photographing Faulkner country. Silver had endorsed Dain's work to Massey.

[2] The William Faulkner Foundation was established by Faulkner in 1960 to support various philanthropic projects. Massey was one of the directors of the Foundation.

1548f Letter from Faulkner to James W. Silver, "Wednesday," signed ribbon typescript, 1 page, with envelope addressed in Faulkner's hand and postmarked Oxford, April 4, 1962.

Dear Jim:

We are leaving this afternoon, so I probably wont see you or Mr Dane (Dain?) either before that. So will you please get word to him to please dont make any more photographs on my property while we are gone, and also that I will not authorise the reprinting or publishing or disseminating of the ones he has made here (I mean on my property, of me and my animals and servants) in any form. Please impress on him that I dont want photographs of myself and home and animals etc. in newspapers or magazines or books or in the possession of strangers.

We will see you in June.

Yours,
/s/ William Faulkner

S-105 Letter from Ivan Von Auw, Jr., to Ruth Ford, April 13, 1962, signed ribbon typescript, 1 page.

Dear Miss Ford,

I'm sorry not to have acknowledged sooner your letter of March 26th, but I thought that I had better write to Mr. Faulkner and see how he felt about your proposal. He now writes me that he doesn't remember anything about the arrangements suggested in Arnold Weissberger's letter of April 7, 1959, to Harold Ober, nor do we have any information about this in the office. He adds, however, that such an arrangement might have very well been made even at his instigation and that he is willing to adhere to it if it means that, should we get a bona fide offer for one of the three books named in that letter, that is ABSALOM, ABSALOM, THE BEAR, and AS I LAY DYING, you have the right to match any offer for a period of twenty-four hours. I take it that something like this is what Arnold Weissberger meant by the right of first refusal. The practical difficulty of such an arrangement is that it's hard to get any picture producer to make a concrete offer if he knows that somebody else has the right to match it or preempt it. That is the reason why we have to make the time period so short. Would this be agreeable to you?

Sincerely yours,
/s/ Ivan Von Auw, Jr.

1553 Letter from Linton Massey to James W. Silver, April 22, 1962, signed ribbon typescript, 1 page.

Dear Dr. Silver:

Stelle Faulkner handed to me today as a good will gesture on Easter Sunday a copy of the Beer Broadside she had pestered you into finding, according to her story. In any event I am deeply grateful to you personally for whatever trouble you had to take in finding it. In order to preserve it for future generations I think I shall have it de-acidified and mounted by a paper expert we have in nearby Richmond.

I still very much hope to meet you. From all I hear, it will be my privilege from every possible viewpoint.

Again with sincere thanks, I am,

Cordially yours,
/s/ Linton Massey
/t/ Linton Massey

1554 Letter from Estelle Faulkner to James W. Silver, "Tuesday—April 23rd," signed autograph manuscript, 3 pages (1 folded leaf), with envelope addressed in Mrs. Faulkner's hand and postmarked Charlottesville, April 25, 1962.

Dear Jim—

Not being gifted with words, (among many other things) I hardly know how to thank you for sending the "Beer Broadside"—Linton was beside himself with thankfulness and am sure will write to you—

I feel very ashamed to have waited so long to write, but as excuses are the devil's own—I have more than my share—

They sent an air-force plane up from Georgia with a crew of Jews to cart

Bill, Jill, Paul and me to West Point last week—where Bill read and answered questions, as he does here[1]—

It was fun, but exhausting—Anyway, Bill and I were housed in the Presidential suite in the post hotel—and I had generals in plenty to squire me around—

When we boarded the plane to fly home, the mere major in command didn't seem quite as resplendent as I remembered him!

Easter, and three little boys got me back to earth in a hurry, and I have decided definitely on civilian life—

I see from the newspapers that we are to be guests of the Kennedys Sunday night for dinner—We are not—Bill asked me to decline—said he wouldn't go to Washington just to eat[2]—I would like to go, I think—

Haven't seen many University people yet—all that starts next month—Joe *has* been out, but as a matter of fact, nearly all our neighbors are University-gone-rural—Joe Blotner still a townsman—He sends regards—

As you may have guessed, young Will is at my elbow—so I'll send love to Dutch, Vicki and Gail—and stop—

As always
Estelle

[1] For a detailed account of Faulkner's two-day visit to the United States Military Academy on April 19–20, 1962, see *Faulkner at West Point,* ed. Joseph L. Fant, III, and Robert Ashley (New York: Random House, 1964).

[2] President John F. Kennedy had invited American Nobel Prize winners and other notables to a White House dinner.

S-106 Letter from Zachary Scott to Jean Renoir, April 30, 1962, signed carbon typescript, 1 page.

Dear Jean:

. . . .

Re "LIGHT IN AUGUST": I cannot tell you how thrilled I was to learn of your interest, and it breaks my heart at this moment to tell you that it very much looks as though the property, which we control, will be sold, and that we, or rather, my company, Volcano Productions Ltd., will not produce it. We have had a fabulously lucrative offer for the property and it is now in negotiation *but,* should anything happen that the deal does not go through, we shall adhere to our plan to go through with production on it in 1963. You, of course, would be my only choice for a director. You and the story are exactly right for each other. Should the deal go through would you mind if I hounded them with the idea of your directing it?

Ever,
/s/ Zachary

1548g Letter from Martin Dain to James W. Silver, May 3, 1962, signed ribbon typescript with autograph additions, 2 pages.

Dear Jim:

On the 29th of April I sent you a great bunch of pix most of which are for Vickie.[1] I hope you received them in good condition. I spent a lot of solid time in the darkroom on the most recent stuff and I am most pleased and in full confidence. Very soon now I shall be meeting with a potential publisher

(Europe too) and a film company. One of the partners of this particular TV film company, is most enthusiastic and hinted that they had been waiting to see if I could get to the old man. Let me assure you that I think I have enough of Faulkner around the fields with horses and dogs and Vickie to take me over the hump. I hope in the future I might be able to do something inside the house—but not with him—unless he wants to. You wanna work on that? Anyway the pix of Stone, the banker, dog trots etc are just fine. I am now about to make copies of Mrs. Brown's slides and then I shall send them back to her. I wonder if her son's article on Oxford as Jefferson has been published yet.[2] I would like to have that. I would also like to have a copy of the note that Faulkner sent you,[3] for I don't want to hide anything from publisher and I have lost the sense of that note except that he tells me to stay the hell away. Do you think the invitation to drink as we left was for the purpose of telling us first hand—in place of note?

. . . .

I want to send to Mr. & Mrs. Faulkner varied pix of Vickie and himself such as you saw plus one shot of each horse. The only good one of the brown horse happens to be with himself smiling—I'll send him that and one of the grey horse solo. Now do you think that I should include a note of apology for disturbing him or is it much too late for that—your opinion. So could I have the address please? Will send about 5 or 6 horse pix.

Thanx for the flood pix—I also missed the man when he spoke at West Point—knew nothing of it. Hope to be able to photograph the National Arts & Sciences presentation—will be on jury duty then.

Want to thank all of you for help. I'd be pretty much alone down there without you. Let me know when you're off to Oregon—& address. Haven't decided if I shall return before Oct. Want to do itinerant salesman, speak with Farley, FUDGE (?), Avent, free-trade day in Ripley.

How is the campaign? Golf?

Respects

Marty

[1]Victoria Fielden, Faulkner's step-granddaughter.

[2]Calvin S. Brown, "Faulkner's Geography and Topography," *PMLA*, 77 (December 1962), 652–659.

[3]See item 1548f, printed above.

1557a Letter from Richard P. Adams to Phil Stone, May 18, 1962, signed ribbon typescript, 3 pages.

Dear Mr. Stone,

My efforts to discover what Faulkner felt and thought when he was young continue; I work hard, I read all kinds of things I think he read, I get occasional glimpses, and I wrestle with the whole insoluble problem of what forms a young man's mind and what supplies the thrust of his ambition. I couldn't even answer that question for myself; why do I presume to try to answer it for Faulkner? Well, two reasons, maybe: first that Faulkner has furnished more materials for an answer, and second that it's a good deal more important to answer for him than for me. Anyway I keep on trying, though I don't hope to succeed very well.

And I keep asking questions. I've just finished reading all of Conrad's novels and short stories, and I note that in one of his interviews at Virginia

Faulkner names *The Nigger of the "Narcissus,"* "Falk," "The End of the Tether," and "Youth" as his favorite Conrad works to reread, says he has not reread *Victory* or *Nostromo* in years, and ignores a question on *Lord Jim.* But it seems to me clear that he has used both *Victory* and *Lord Jim* in his own work, and used them well. Do you have any recollection of particular Conrad stories that made an impression in the early days? How about *Heart of Darkness* or *The Secret Sharer?* Do you think Conrad's way of bringing characters from one book into the story of another, such as Captain Lingard, the hotel keeper Schomberg, etc., may have helped suggest Faulkner's way of doing the same thing? (Of course I know Balzac is a primary influence in that, but Conrad's stories about the sea and the islands in the East Indies add up to something like a Balzacian Human Comedy too.)

A good many other authors have written more than one book with the same setting and some of the same characters. The Old Testament, as well as the New, has some of that quality; so do Shakespeare's history plays; so do the Greek epics and tragedies. Balzac of course; also Cooper, Mark Twain, Henry James, Trollope, Hardy, Zola, and in a sense Joyce in *Ulysses,* Proust in *A la recherche du temps perdu,* and Mann in *Buddenbrooks;* definitely Wolfe in all his novels—if they can be called novels. Wolfe came too late to be a formative influence, but some of the others I'm sure Faulkner read earlier. Which of them do you think may have made some impression by 1925 or 1926; and which of them do you think may have made the most impression? Do you remember having discussions with Faulkner on the business of using characters and settings in more than one book, and looking at them from more than one point of view? Do you think it would be fair and accurate to say that he was particularly interested in authors who have used such methods as that?

I've also been looking over Faulkner's poems—I've typed out copies of all I've been able to find in print—and have been trying without any very great success to figure out what they're all about. I hope to be able to come to Oxford some time this summer, and perhaps go over some of them with you, to see what light you could throw on the meanings and feelings they embody. Meanwhile, I'll work over them by myself, in the hope of at least being able to ask intelligent questions.

Also I've recently been reading some of Faulkner's favorite poets, notably Keats and Swinburne. I had not read much of Swinburne before, and I'm finding him interesting, but rather over-whelmingly voluminous. Could you suggest some particular Swinburne poems that Faulkner especially liked? Was he interested in the tragedies? *Atalanta in Calydon? Erechtheus? Chastelard, Bothwell, Mary Stuart?* These last three might be like Balzac's *Comedie Humaine* for scope and continuity; *Bothwell* especially is long enough. Did Faulkner read any of Swinburne's essays?

Going back to Keats, did Faulkner read Keats's letters, and if so was he impressed with any of Keats's ideas in particular, such as negative capability? (It seems to me that Faulkner has the quality Keats describes by that term to a rather remarkable degree.)

About Faulkner's own poetry—he says somewhere that it was all written by the time he was 23. Perhaps you would know whether the material in *A Green[ing] Bough* was or was not all written before 1925. You will see, I'm sure, what I'm trying to do with this part of my job. Nobody has seriously studied Faulkner's very early work at all. Everybody says Oh well, yes, there's Faulkner's poetry—not much in that; let's get on to the fiction. So critics talk at some length about *Soldiers' Pay* and *Mosquitoes,* and don't really get down to business until they come to *Sartoris.* I'm not content with that. Maybe the poetry isn't Faulkner's best work; maybe, as he likes to say, he's a *failed* poet; but I'd still like to know what it was he failed to do, what it was he was trying to do, with the poetry. I suspect I may find out something in that way about what he was still trying to do when he turned to fiction. Prose, after all, is not incompatible with poetry, properly defined.

One specific question I might venture about *A Green Bough*—was it written as, and intended to be read as, one single poem, or is it a collection of more or less closely related individual poems? Does the theme of the wounded and traumatized flyer, which is explicit in the poem numbered I and seems to be implicit in those numbered XXVIII and XXXI, go all the way through the book? Or is it only one among many different themes? Is the point of view in most or all of the poems the same, or does each poem have its own point of view, or its own individual speaker? If you can give me the answer to that question (that is all one question, really), I will know much better than I do now how *A Green Bough* should be read, and what relation it might be said to have to such later works as *Soldiers' Pay* and *Sartoris.* I'm assuming, by the way, that *The Marble Faun* definitely *is* one poem—sort of a cross between Keats's "Ode on a Grecian Urn" and Mallarme's "L'Apres-Midi d'un faune"—and that it is rather closely related to *Soldiers' Pay,* where Donald Mahon is so often figured as a faun.

I hope that's not too many questions for you, all at once, and I hope you will answer as many of them as you can, and make any suggestions otherwise that may occur to you. Any advice you can give me on how to go about learning and understanding more about Faulkner's work in general, and his early work in particular, will be most deeply appreciated. I do really want to understand him in the way he would want to be understood—or maybe even a little better—if such a thing is possible.

All best wishes,

Yours,
/s/ Dick
/t/ R. P. Adams

1557b Letter from Phil Stone to Richard P. Adams, June 1, 1962, carbon typescript with typed signature, 2 pages.

Dear Dick:

Pardon me for not having answered your letter of May 18. We have been busy in court and I have been working day and night.

First, don't feel discouraged, as you sound in your first paragraph. You will get it all together one of these days and as you go longer through it I think it will be easier for you.

As for Conrad, I do not at this time remember just what parts of Conrad that Bill read, but the statement which he made is probably right. I don't remember any particular Conrad story that made an impression on him more than another. I think it quite possible that Conrad's way of bringing characters from one book into another story may have suggested this to Bill, but I do not know this. My idea is that Balzac would probably have had more influence on him than anybody else.

I confess I do not remember having any discussions with Bill on the business of using this character and settings in more than one book. In fact, I was rather opposed to it because I thought Bill was actually being lazy.

As for the poems, most of the other ones burned up in the fire that consumed my old house. Some time when you come to Oxford we can talk about that, but please let us know ahead of time and let's try to get a good cool spell because our little house is hot. I may have the air conditioners in by the middle of this summer and I may not.

As for Swinburne, he is one of the best. He is simply out of style. I don't remember what particular Swinburne poems Bill liked, but I think he did like the one about the coming of spring: "The hounds of spring on winter's traces . . ." or something like that. It was probably *Atalanta in Calydon* as much as anything else. I am sure that Bill never read any of the essays by Swinburne because I never read any of them myself.

Bill was much impressed by Keats, as I still am, but I don't remember if this is true of him now.

The material in *The Green Bough* was not all written before 1925, but most of it was during that year. As for most of Bill's poetry, it is not worth looking at anyway.

Soldiers' Pay and *Mosquitoes* are not so hot and Bill would never have got published if it had not been for Sherwood Anderson.

I think when he was writing poetry he was just writing it to get something written and get it printed, and I didn't know he was even going to try to write a novel until after *Soldiers' Pay* was in the works. I accused him of having a new sweetheart and I remember he wrote me back that he did have a beautiful sweetheart and she was 125 pages long.

The Green Bough was simply a collection of a number of poems and was never intended to be one poem. It was really an exercise. About the wounded flyer, that was never in *The Green Bough* at all.[1] The different poems are supposed to have had a different point of view but, generally, more like *The Shropshire Lad.* I would think *The Green Bough* had very little relation to any of the novels later.

The Marble Faun was one poem. In fact it was about the one-tenth of about a hundred poems. We were just trying to get something published and I had to pay for it myself, but actually it turned out that Bill and I both made money on it later as a piece worth preserving.

I confess I cannot write you about these things as well as I can tell you and I hope I get that opportunity before too long.

Your friend,
Phil Stone

[1]Stone apparently is referring to *A Green Bough* as originally conceived. The poem about the flyer ("The Lilacs") does appear as poem number I in the published version of *A Green Bough.*

1557d Letter from Phil Stone to Richard P. Adams, June 8, 1962, carbon typescript with typed signature, 2 pages.

Dear Dick:

You are getting so formal I shall have to call you "Doctor" only.

It would be better by far if you could make it up here along about the first week in August. After that I have to go really back to work again on a very large and important lawsuit. In between, it is just odds and ends that I have to get done this summer.

I think it would be a good thing if you would send me a few pages of your manuscript[1] ahead of time. I will take care of it and I can jot down lots of things that occur to me which I might not think of if I had not seen some of the manuscript. As to the cross-examination, don't worry about that. I like it that way and I like to try to tell you what you want to find out.

Best of luck,

Your friend,
Phil Stone

P.S.: Don't repeat this to anyone, but Bill has been home for a few days and I saw him on the street the other day. I have never seen him look so old before. It is not his eyes, but the skin around his eyes; looks like that of an old man, and he looks to me like he has aged about five years since I saw him a few months ago.

[1] Adams' completed manuscript was subsequently published as *Faulkner: Myth and Motion* (Princeton: Princeton University Press, 1968).

1585 Letter from Phil Stone to Faulkner, June 13, 1962, carbon typescript with typed signature, 1 page.

Dear Bill:

Thanks a whole lot for leaving for Emily and myself at the office the autographed copy of the Reivers. I know you don't like talk over the telephone, and hate it much more than I do, and I don't know when I might see you personally. So I am sending on this letter.[1]

Just one thing: Please don't be surprised if I am a long time reading it because here lately all I have time to read is law books.

Best of luck.

Your friend,
Phil Stone

[1] On a xerox copy of this letter Mrs. Emily Stone has provided the following note of explanation: "(Phil told me that he had not thanked Bill for this, so I called and thanked him. Phil may have written this after I protested at his not having thanked Bill.) EWS 6/18/81."

1558d Letter from Phil Stone to James B. Meriwether, June 15, 1962, carbon typescript with typed signature, 1 page.

Dear Jim:

Pardon me for not having answered sooner your letter of June 2. We have been so busy that I just could not get around to answering my mail generally. Also pardon me for not going more fully into the answer of your letter of June 10th. I have not received any stout packing box yet for shipping and when I do, if I can find someone to get it done for me, I shall try to get this off to you.[1] Frankly, I hate to risk it but am doing it for you. I know you will be careful but if it should happen to be gone or lost it could never be replaced.

Bill came around the other day and gave me an autographed copy, as usual, of his last book. I don't know when I shall have a chance to read it.

By the way, Bill got thrown by another horse and is having trouble with his back again. I told him he was going to break his neck one of these days.

We all send love.

Your friend,
Phil Stone

[1] Meriwether was assisting Random House in the preparation of a corrected edition of *The Hamlet* and had requested the use of the typescript of the manuscript which Faulkner presented to Philip Alston Stone in 1945.

1556d Letter from Phil Stone to Alan R. Frederiksen, June 21, 1962, carbon typescript with typed signature, 1 page.

Dear Mr. Frederiksen:

I have your note of June 20. Like a lot of things that go around these days, it has one very serious factual error.

The idea that Mr. Jacobs[1] has that I was introduced to Bill Faulkner through Mr. Stark Young is ridiculous. I was still fooling with Bill long before I took him over to meet Mr. Stark Young. Mr. Young was teaching at the University of Texas or at Amherst at the time and when he came by one summer to see his father I took Bill to see him, Mr. Young.

I am the Phil Stone they talk about but I wish, when they talk about me, they would get their facts correct. I did help him publish his first book of poems just in order to get him going. The amusing thing is that we actually made money on the thing and didn't lose any money at all because when Bill got famous I had him autograph all of them and sent them off, and he got $10 for autographing and I got $40 or $50 for each of the books.[2]

Yours truly,
Phil Stone

[1] Robert D. Jacobs, author of an article on Faulkner which Frederiksen had cited in his letter to Stone.

[2] At the bottom of a xerox copy of this letter Emily Stone has written the following comment on this last paragraph: "This is not what he had told me for years. EWS."

1586 Western Union telegram from Estelle Faulkner to Dorothy Commins, July 6, 1962, with envelope.

BILL DIED HEART ATTACK. SERVICES SATURDAY AFTERNOON

ESTELLE

1590a Letter from Hubert Starr to Phil Stone, July 6, 1962, signed ribbon typescript, 1 page, with envelope postmarked Los Angeles, July 6, 1962.

Dear Phil:

The radio this morning tells us that Bill died of a heart attack at Oxford. It's sad. Everything's sad. Life's sad.

Would you be so kind as to send me clippings from your local paper, which will tell so much more than will "Time"? I have no knowledge of Bill's wife, or of Jill.

If he were like me, he had lived too long anyway. I don't like anything that has happened since the general election of 1932; politics has become an unsavory competition in defiling the flag and trampling on the constitution.

. . . .

Best wishes from your fellow helot of the Welfare State,

/s/ Hubert

1557g Letter from Richard P. Adams to Phil Stone, July 7, 1962, signed ribbon typescript, 1 page.

Dear Phil,

I haven't been able to think of anything adequate or even appropriate to say about Faulkner's death. Perhaps it's not for me to say anything at all. It's his work rather than his life that I've concerned myself about; and I'm convinced that his work will live as long as the English language is read. I guess I feel a bit like Lincoln at Gettysburg—it's not what I say that matters, but what Faulkner did. And that will never die.

There seems no reason for me to change my plans for coming to Oxford in the first week of August, unless you prefer another time. I can imagine that you've probably been pestered half to death by newshounds, but that won't last very long. They mean well, no doubt, but they can be an unholy nuisance.

My first chapter is about done, in its very rough first-draft form. I'm going to try to go over it a bit and make a readable copy to send you as soon as possible. Later on, I'll revise it thoroughly in the light of whatever discussion we're able to have about it, and whatever further thinking I can do. I'm very dissatisfied with it as it stands. I want it to be a vivid account of how Faulkner must have felt when he started out on his career, what he must have hoped to do, and what he was trying to get at in his writing. It's not easy, and I haven't got it anywhere near what it ought to be as yet. I hope you can help me do it better. The second chapter, on Faulkner's reading and literary background, will be even harder.

Best regards,

Yours,
/s/ Dick
/t/ R. P. Adams

PS: Your remark on Faulkner's appearance[1] was all too prophetic.

[1] In the postscript of Stone's letter to Adams, June 8, 1962, printed above.

1590b Letter from Phil Stone to Hubert Starr, July 11, 1962, carbon typescript with typed signature, 1 page.

Dear Herb:

Thanks a lot for your letter of July 6. I had no idea that Bill's death would hit me as hard as it did but I have not gotten over it yet.

We do want to come to see you some time although you probably don't believe it, and one of these days we are.

I think things are going to improve so far as socialism is concerned. It may have started already.

Pardon this being so short but I still don't have a lot of pep for writing letters because of Bill.

Remember us all to Lucil.

Your friend,
Phil Stone

1596a Letter from Phil Stone to John Starr, Senior Editor, McGraw-Hill Book Company, July 12, 1962, carbon typescript with typed signature, 1 page.

Dear Mr. Starr:

I just called the office of the Chancery Clerk here and am informed that Bill's will has not yet been offered for probate. One of the deputies told me that Mr. Paul Summers, husband of Jill (Bill's daughter) said he would send down the will for probation but he has not done so yet. I shall keep checking on it and if and when that is done I shall advise you by telephone.[1]

When they left here Tuesday, Jill told me that she would be back in a week or two. I think that means that Mr. Summers will come back and bring the will and probate it at that time. I shall try to keep checking on this every day that I am not out of town and shall let you know at the earliest possible moment.

Mr. Summers is named Paul D., and is the City Attorney of Charlottesville, Virginia. Being a young man he does not have any but the usual rating as to ability, but he has the very top rating as to character and I would guess that that is correct.

Yours truly,
Phil Stone

[1] Starr had contacted Stone about the possibility of securing his assistance on a biography of Faulkner. Princeton University historian David Donald, a native Mississippian, had been selected by the publisher to do the book, while Stone would serve as the liaison with the Faulkner family and supply information on Faulkner's early life and career.

1596b Letter from Phil Stone to Paul D. Summers, July 12, 1962, carbon typescript with typed signature, 1 page.

Dear Paul:

Before you and Jill left I told Jill that there would probably be a number of publishers trying to get a life of Bill written and published. This morning I did get an inquiry over the telephone from Mr. John Starr of McGraw, Hill Book Company. I told him, as I had told Jill before, that if anything turned up by which she could get some money for a book on Bill's life (not on his personal life) and somebody got after you people, that she should communicate with me first (or you should) because if she could get something out of it and if they would let me hire the young man who would actually do it, that I would be glad to help him as much as I could in getting the actual facts about the writing of the various books through *Sanctuary* with the understanding that I would not accept any money involved. This may be sentimental, but I would just feel like I was picking Bill's corpse and I just could not do it in any other way.

When you come down please let me know when you offer the will for probate because McGraw, Hill wants to get in touch with the Executor. I suggested to Mr. Starr that he might write you direct. These publishers are in the publishing business for themselves and I would not like to see you and Jill get gypped in any sort of way.

Anything I can do down here, please let me know.

Yours truly,
Phil Stone

1598b Letter from Phil Stone to James B. Meriwether, July 17, 1962, carbon typescript with typed signature, 2 pages.

Dear Jim:

We were glad to get your letter of July 13, but ask your pardon again for taking so long to answer it, and even now I shall have to answer very briefly because we have so much here to do.

Of course I'm not entirely cleared up in my own mind now, but it is better than it was.

About the project,[1] there are several ideas which you have, but I think we had better wait a little while until we get some more offers. I got a telephone call from Mr. John Starr of McGraw Hill Book Company, but I put him off also. He had a young man at Princeton who was the very man to do the job, provided I would help him, but when I talked to him over the telephone I told him I had a young man closer who would be able to do it better to suit me.

Of course we can't hurry this in any way because that would depend on Jill and she has not yet come back from Virginia, although I expect her to be here this week. I think the best thing she and her husband can do is to wait until they get a number of offers from a number of publishers and then talk to me about and we decide what is best for them.

As for the tapes, I think that is a very good thing to do, but we won't bother about that right now.

I notice what you have written to Texas[2] and I don't think we need anybody to get up the money because I think some publisher is going to be very eager to put up the money if and when Jill agrees that this should be done.

I hope you do well with Viking and I am sure you will.

We hope to write you later, but we are both buzzing around so fast now we will have to wait for that. It might be a good thing, it seems to me, to have Emily present too, and in that way, with several tapes, I could talk out a lot of stuff for her and then she could send it to you, you two working together, without you having to trot over here all the time.

You understand, we are not figuring on making any money out of it ourselves.

Best of luck to you and yours,

Your friend,
Phil Stone

[1] Stone had suggested that he and Meriwether collaborate on a book about Faulkner. Meriwether indicated an interest in the project and suggested that they begin by taping Stone's reminiscences.

[2] Meriwether had contacted the University of Texas, which had expressed an interest in sponsoring the project.

1600b Letter from Phil Stone to Elizabeth Yeager Grosch, July 19, 1962, carbon typescript with typed signature, 4 pages.

Dear Mrs. Grosch:

Pardon me for not having answered sooner your letter of July 14, but we have a lot to do in this law office and I don't have much chance to write letters about anything else.

It was so kind of you to think of me and to send me this clipping[1] that I don't know how to thank you. I want to save it for my son, (who is 22 and graduated from Harvard this summer) because Bill was one of his godfathers.

As you may remember, nobody who knew anything about writing would bother with him at all until he became famous and, as a matter of chance, I am the only man who knows certain facts about the writing of the first six novels, ending with *Sanctuary.* Nearly all of them I had read to me from his manuscripts, and a very few of them only have I read since they went into print.

Since you were so kind I will tell you a few things that are accurate and possibly not entirely accurate in the New York Herald-Tribune article. Most of it is far more accurate than most of the things about Faulkner.

I do think that his death was probably due to the fall he got in Virginia and the one he got after he came home this summer. He was suffering a great deal from it even as late as the week before he died.

In the article it said something about his "ain'ts" and that he professed to never read reviews. I think it probably is true that Bill never read any reviews. I never caught him at it.

In the next paragraph, when they talk about Bill's sitting down in the Square of Oxford listening to the local gossips, this is quite true and the result of it is very plain. He does not do negro dialect very well, but the rhythm and exact speech and even the way of thinking of these farmers in the hill country of Mississippi is perfect.

When we get down "to New York to write," that is foolishness. He had been writing long before he went to New York and I did my best, and succeeded, to keep him away from Greenwich Village. He went up to New York in the hope that we could get somebody to notice him so he could get published, but that did not come off.

As to being identified as an "artist," he wasn't identified that way at all. In fact, he was identified locally as "Count-No-Count."

As for his education, he didn't want to take a job. He wanted to write, which he did.

Further down, about poetry, I did steer him into Joyce and Ezra Pound, but I told him by all means not to use Joyce as a model.

In the second column on page 4, Bill did not go through such a trying time because he got published in 1925 [*sic*] with *Soldiers' Pay* and by 1930 he had made a good deal of money.

He had a good time the first part of the '20s because he got a job as postmaster at the University which gave him a living and which he secured through the help of Major Oldham, Estelle's father, and myself out of family influence with Senator Pat Harrison. The truth [is he] was not fired, and I determined to not let them fire him, and that took a good deal of political pulling, too, but he ought to have been fired the second day he was postmaster because he was, undoubtedly, the world's worst postmaster.

From the standpoint of a writer, I still think *As I Lay Dying* is the best-written book he has ever done.

As for *Sanctuary,* that may amuse you. He had run out of something to write about and I happened to know the background of all of that and he was just writing something to be writing, but it is not true that it was written for money because Bill didn't think he would get any money out of it and neither did I. I told him it would not be a good book and that the day of the shocker had passed, and I was wrong on both counts. I have read *Sanctuary* since (having read it only in the manuscript first) one day when I had some flu, and it is a damn good book, one of the best from the writer's standpoint that he has ever done.

The rest of the stuff I admit I could not stand. It was very dull and Bill repeated himself so much, and I don't think he has done any book since *Sanctuary* that has been anything like as good as it could have been.

By the way, his acceptance speech for the Nobel Prize was a rehash of something he had written before.

The Snopes business was actually generated around 1924 and 1925, and nearly all of the incidents I gave him, and some of the characters I invented for him, as in *Sartoris. Sartoris* is really factual and we thought sure it would sell and get him a lot of money but it also fell flat. That was the time, in desperation, that I suggested to him to write anything he wanted to, any way he pleased, and perhaps he would get prestige and later could make some money. That was the day when he said he didn't know why he kept on writing—he supposed he did it just to stay out of work, that he was sure he would never make any money writing and was quite sure he would never receive any recognition. I felt the same way at that particular time (I can pick the spot on the University campus where we stood and talked about it) but I didn't dare tell Bill because I was the only one who believed he could do anything, and I was afraid if I told him he would lose heart. I should have known better. You can no more stop a professional from writing than you can stop a dope fiend from taking dope. That is the final test of the difference between amateurs and the pros. I know that very well because I have two in my family still, a wife and a son. Whatever you do, don't let yourself get hooked up with any writer.

Yours truly,
Phil Stone

P.S.: . . . .

P.P.S.: Oxford, Mississippi, is not in the "back country," as you probably know. They have had a university here for something around 120 years. But, New York generally thinks that anything south of the Potomac River and west of the Allegheny Mountains is back country.

[1] From the *New York Herald Tribune,* July 7, 1962.

1601b Letter from Phil Stone to H. Edward Richardson, July 19, 1962, carbon typescript with typed signature, 1 page.

Dear Mr. Richardson:

Pardon me for not having answered sooner your letter of July 15.[1] We have been very busy here in this law office and Bill's death stopped everything for me for a while. I can't promise anybody any appointment to go over this stuff because there is so much of it and because we have so much to get done the rest of July and in August.

Perhaps, if you have a series of factual questions (not his personal life) that you wish answered, I would have a better chance to answer them for you if you would just write them out and mail them to me.

I would like to help any Southerner and anybody interested in Faulkner, but you have no idea how much of this stuff people try to bring me into every single day. If I answered all of them and gave them all the information and time they wanted, I couldn't even make a living.

Don't say I said so, because I live here, but the best hotel in Oxford is the Alumni House at the University. The next one is probably a motel which is about a mile west of the University of Mississippi on Mississippi Highway No. 6.

Yours truly,
Phil Stone

[1]Richardson, who was completing a doctoral dissertation at the University of Southern California entitled "The Early Faulkner," had requested an interview with Stone. Richardson's research was subsequently published as *William Faulkner: The Journey to Self-Discovery* (Columbia: University of Missouri Press, 1969).

1596e Letter from Phil Stone to John Starr, July 21, 1962, carbon typescript with typed signature, 1 page.

Dear Mr. Starr:

I have your letter of July 17 and appreciate it, and will also appreciate reading some of the stuff Mr. Donald has done.

I quite agree that the important biography should not be done by a literary critic, but I am not sure what they mean by "biography." If they are talking about a personal biography, I am not interested in that and would be interested only in the writing of the first six novels in which I had such a large part and of which there are things which only Bill and myself knew.

I will be glad to hear from you at any time. This morning I got a letter from Mr. Summers, Bill's son-in-law, at Charlottesville, and he said that Jill (Bill's daughter) and her mother would be back down here about August 1. I have kept my word to you by checking the courthouse records, and up to this morning there has been no petition filed for the probation of Bill's will. I don't know who wrote it and who is the executor because I didn't want to have anything to do with it, as I told Bill some years ago. It would be too sad a job for me.

As to when I can agree for Mr. Donald to visit me, that is just beyond my guess at the present time because we are very busy here and I just don't know ahead of time when I can have some time. I shall be glad to pass him over to Mrs. Faulkner or to Jill, either, if he happens to run into [them], provided they want to talk to him.

I have not yet read the copy of *The Reivers*. Bill always gives us an autographed copy, but all I read is law books.

Yours truly,
Phil Stone

1596f Letter from Phil Stone to Paul D. Summers, July 21, 1962, carbon typescript with typed signature, 1 page.

Dear Paul:

I have your little note of July 18.

Personally, I see no reason for us to hurry about doing anything about Bill's life. In fact, all I am interested in doing anything about, unless Jill thinks otherwise, is Bill's writing life for the first six novels that were published. I just want to be sure that nobody takes advantage of her if she wants it done, or if she needs the money to have it done, I shall be glad to help although I would not do the actual writing. As far as his personal life is concerned, I am just not interested in putting any of that in a book, but I also would help with that if you and Jill think otherwise.

I am looking forward to seeing you and I hope you can drop me a line several days before you come, because we are going to run into a pretty heavy load along about the first of August because I was so hit by Bill's death that I am now only beginning to get something done. Of course that is silly, but I don't seem to be able to help it yet.

Your friend,
Phil Stone

1557-1 Letter from Richard P. Adams to Emily and Phil Stone, August 10, 1962, signed ribbon typescript, 1 page.

Dear Emily and Phil,

I want to thank you both for the kindness and hospitality with which you made my visit to Oxford pleasant; and then for all you have done to help my work along. If the first chapter is, or ever will be, worth people's time to read, it will be to a large extent because of your help and encouragement.

The second is going slowly and laboriously at present. The problem, I suspect, is that in trying to figure out what is important in Faulkner's literary background I very quickly get into intangibles; and I'm reluctant to take the plunge, admit that my thinking, like most of my evidence, is not very objective, and put my best judgment on the line, right or wrong. But I've about got to the point of admitting to myself that it has to be done sooner or later, and might as well be now. Yes; in fact I think this afternoon I'll throw away what I've done and start over, on a frankly subjective basis—giving my reasons.

I made my pilgrimage to Faulkner's grave, which was terribly bare and raw. Then I took your advice and sat around by the courthouse for a while and listened. You're absolutely right, of course, about the miraculous way Faulkner caught the tone and rhythm of people's talk.

. . . .

Yours,
/s/ Dick
/t/ R. P. Adams

1596h Letter from Phil Stone to John Starr, August 20, 1962, carbon typescript with typed signature, 1 page.

Dear Mr. Starr:

Pardon me for not having answered sooner your letter of August 15.

As for Mr. Donald coming down any time before September 15, I don't see how in the world I could get time to see him. We are going into one very important court now and we go right from that into another court here and then to another court in another county.

Estelle is still here, but Jill has gone back to Virginia and probably won't be back for several weeks. I would want you to discuss the matter directly with her or her husband before I would commit myself to anything about it, and not then if Jill objects.

The Virginia lawyers who attempted to file Bill's will here, knowing nothing about the law in Mississippi, have got the thing where they can't proceed yet, and I don't know what they will do. If and when I find out I shall let you know.

Yours truly,
Phil Stone

1607a Letter from Baldwin Harper, an official of the Voice of America, to Phil Stone, September 5, 1962, signed ribbon typescript, 1 page.

My Dear Mr. Stone:

The Voice of America is at present engaged in developing a documentary program on William Faulkner.

We understand that you were an early friend of Mr. Faulkner's—one of the first to believe in his great talents.

We wonder if you would be willing to voice a short taped recording, covering your early association with Mr. Faulkner? Your contribution would prove of great value in our Worldwide English programs and in many of the other thirty-seven languages in which the Voice of America currently broadcasts.

If you agree to this request, we could have a technician from the local Oxford station come to your home and record the material.

Please telephone me collect at WOrth 3-3456, in Washington, D. C. or use the enclosed stamped, self-addressed envelope to advise me of your decision.

Your kind cooperation will be greatly appreciated.

Sincerely,
/s/ Baldwin Harper
/t/ Baldwin Harper
Acting Chief
Special Events
Broadcasting Service

1607b Letter from Phil Stone to Baldwin Harper, September 13, 1962, carbon typescript with typed signature, 1 page.

Dear Mr. Harper:

Please forgive me for not having answered sooner your letter of September 5. I am in court now in a case that has already taken five days and will probably take another week and I do not have time to do anything else.

As for me being an early friend of Bill Faulkner's, and being one of the first to believe in his great talent, I was the only one who believed in it for twelve years and I know a world of stuff that nobody else knows because nobody else bothered with him until he got famous.

I would not care to voice a tape recording. In fact I get so tired people worrying me about Bill that I have gone under a cover. Also I would not be interested making any money out of it. Some day, some time, I may bother myself to do this, but I am certainly not going to do it until Jill (his daughter) approves of it and that may be a long time because I am so busy now I have still not read Bill's last book, although he brought me, as usual, an author's first edition autographed copy.

Just now I am still a little too shocked by his death.

Yours truly,
Phil Stone

1609b Letter from Phil Stone to Edmond L. Volpe, September 18, 1962, carbon typescript with typed signature, 1 page.

Dear Mr. Volpe:

I was very glad to get your nice letter of September 15, but for the present and for several months, I shall not have any time to do anything about Bill.[1] Frankly, I think I may have to go a long time before I could do anything very accurate and in proper order because Bill's death hit me much harder than I anticipated that it would.

So don't bother about any tape recorder yet. I enjoyed seeing you and hope you can come to see us again.

Yours truly,
Phil Stone

[1] Volpe had offered to assist Stone in tape recording his reminiscences about Faulkner.

1412n Letter from Albert Erskine to James W. Silver, October 3, 1962, signed ribbon typescript, 1 page.

Dear Professor Silver:

I am sorry to bother you with this small matter, but I hope you can be of help to us in it.

I have recently heard that there is some possibility that Mrs. Calvin Brown will make further efforts to achieve the publication of THE WISHING TREE by William Faulkner, in the mistaken belief that his death changes the legal status of the manuscript. I do not even know if this is true, but since you wrote to us on her behalf in 1959, it seems best for me to convey this information to you. If you could pass it along to her, I would appreciate it; if you think it better that I write to her direct, please let me know and I shall do so.

The fact of the matter is that the possession of the manuscript does not give its possessor any publication rights whatever; the death of the author does not change this. THE WISHING TREE now belongs to the Estate of William Faulkner and can be published only with the Estate's consent. What I fear is that Mrs. Brown might get herself in difficulties if she presented the manuscript to a publisher not fully aware of this, or one who chose to risk ignoring it.

As you probably know, Bill apparently saw no harm in making double use of this little story which he had written for and presented to Victoria Franklin a number of years before he gave it to Margaret Brown. But even if he had given it to twenty little girls, it would not change the legal situation which I have described above.

I have heard many nice things about you from a number of sources, and I hope someday to have the pleasure of meeting you. Meantime, I hope this letter reaches you in an atmosphere of peace and quiet.

Sincerely yours,
/s/ Albert Erskine
/t/ Albert Erskine

1611a Letter from Carvel Collins to Phil Stone, October 5, 1962, unsigned ribbon typescript with autograph postscript, 1 page.

Dear Phil,

It was a great pleasure to see you and Emily and Araminta. . . .

It is hard for me to imagine what Oxford must be like now that it has become an army encampment.[1] I wish I could sit for an evening with you two and hear the straight dope about it all.

I had hoped that as soon as we got home I would be able to send you a copy of the little volume of William Faulkner's early prose and poetry which the Atlantic Monthly Press is publishing. But I find it will not be out until October thirtieth. (I forgot to say during our hurried visit last week that the volume quotes with great profit the extremely perceptive prediction about William Faulkner's future work which you made in your preface to *The Marble Faun.*)

We are looking forward to seeing you this winter—with time to give you warning and with a bottle of Jack Daniels. Meanwhile, we wish all of you all good things.

As ever,
[no signature]

P.S. Is it possible for you to let me know the wording of the tombstone inscription in the Savannah cemetery which both Emily and William Faulkner by coincidence copied out?

[1] Federal troops had been sent to the Ole Miss campus to ensure the safety of James Meredith, the first black to be enrolled in the university.

1612b Letter from Phil Stone to Elizabeth M. Kerr, October 9, 1962, carbon typescript with typed signature, 1 page.

Dear Miss Kerr:

Your letter of October 5 came while I was out of town in court.

We have so much to do that we are all behind, and for me to help anybody complete a book on William Faulkner, or take part in it or even discuss it, I simply do not have time and probably will not have time for months, perhaps never.

We have so much to do here that when that is over I have had enough. In addition to that I have so many people from all parts of the country writing to me about Bill I just don't have time to answer most of the letters. Also his death was a good deal of a shock to me and I shall just have to ask you to excuse me from going into that subject any time soon.

Yours truly,
Phil Stone

1963

S-107 Letter from Ivan Von Auw, Jr., to Ruth Ford, February 15, 1963, signed ribbon typescript, 1 page.

Dear Miss Ford,

The Robert Flynn adaptation of AS I LAY DYING[1] to be presented at the Dallas Theatre Center is the same one that I spoke to you about before. I don't know why the script was sent to Harold Clurman. We did have a request from Robert Flynn to be allowed to try to dispose of professional stage rights, but I sent the script to Mrs. Summers and she has not agreed to its being released for the professional stage. Frankly, neither our office or Mrs. Summers thought it was a very good adaptation. All that Mr. Flynn is allowed to do is to present it in the Dallas Theatre Center. I don't have a copy of the script here, but since Mrs. Summers doesn't like it there wouldn't be much point in my sending it to you anyway, I suppose.

As to the LIGHT IN AUGUST movie contract, this still has not been signed. Mrs. Summers has some questions about the terms and plans to discuss them with me on her next trip to New York which should be fairly soon.

Sincerely yours,
/s/ Ivan Von Auw, Jr.

[1]Entitled *The Journey to Jefferson.*

S-108 Western Union telegram from Martin Rosen to Ruth Ford, March 20, 1963.

PURSUANT TO AGREEMENT BETWEEN YOURSELF AND WILLIAM FAULKNER,[1] PLEASE BE ADVISED YOU HAVE 24 HOURS TO MEET BASIC TERMS OF FOLLOWING BONA FIDE OFFER ON MOTION PICTURE SALE OF "AS I LAY DYING":

1. $10,000 FOR 18 MONTH OPTION AGAINST $75,000.
2. REVERSION OF ALL RIGHTS FIVE YEARS FROM EXERCISE OF OPTION IF PRINCIPAL PHOTOGRAPHY HAS NOT COMMENCED.
3. 6% TO 100% OF PROFITS.
4. NO SEQUEL, NO REMAKE, NO LIVE, NO FILM TV RIGHTS.
5. 50% OF ALL PROFITS IN EVENT OF RESALE

MARTIN ROSEN ARTISTS AGENCY CORP NEW YORK

[1]See letter from Ivan Von Auw, Jr., to Ruth Ford, April 13, 1962, printed in this volume.

S-109 Letter from Ruth Ford to Robert Glenn, September 17, 1963, unsigned carbon typescript, 1 page.

Dear Bob:

Thanks for your long and interesting letter.[1] To get to the point: first of all this project would have to be approved by William Faulkner's daughter and some kind of contract or deal or terms worked out. This sounds like a very, very interesting project. At this particular time I don't have the time to work on it to any extent. If I alone were tackling something like this, I would have to give myself a year to get it together. In fact, I would have to re-read everything that Faulkner has ever written. It is very difficult to excerpt from Faulkner—that is, out of context.

If we get permission to do this, I would want it to be a collaboration between you and me. I am sure that Faulkner's daughter would want final approval of the script. Then, after her approval, I would want approval.

So I will present this idea to Faulkner's literary agent, who will then pass it on to his daughter and when I hear I will get back to you.

[no signature]

[1]Glenn, a director, had written to Miss Ford on September 15, 1963, proposing a two-person show (for Miss Ford and Zachary Scott) based on Faulkner's life and works.

1966

S-110 Letter from Evans Harrington to James W. Silver, October 3, 1966, signed ribbon typescript, 2 pages.

Dear Jim,

Here's the Dick Adams article, brief, saying nothing that you can't find from reading Faulkner himself in the Gwynn and Blotner FAULKNER IN THE UNIVERSITY, but serving the useful function of summarizing and crystallizing it in handy form. My one demurrer is that he seems to make this concept of change as good, or at least inevitable, a clear-cut and fully accepted thing in Faulkner's mind during the major part of Faulkner's career. I rather think this is what Faulkner finally came to, after agonizing efforts (like Quentin Compson or Ike McCaslin or Joe Christmas, etc.) to find some better solution. True, Faulkner himself in his late years pronounced Ike as not the best kind of man; and he praised Ratliff as a healthy adjuster to life. But if the *good* characters are only those Adams cites—Byron Bunch, Dilsey, Ratliff, *et al.*—why are they usually fringe characters? How can Faulkner have spent so much heroic sympathy—even empathy—on Quentin Compson, Ike, Joe Christmas, etc.? I'm not saying that the concept Adams advances isn't what finally emerges from Faulkner's works, even THE SOUND AND THE FURY and other relatively early ones. I'm simply calling attention to the fact that the concept is not so easily, happily, neatly delivered in the works; in fact, it emerges as a tortured, grim, infinitely ironic, at least half-despairing residue of the furious struggles to establish other truths. So that those who point to the despair and nostalgia in Faulkner are not, as Adams says, completely wrong. Those elements are fully as present in the works as is the acceptance of "life-as-change." And *that* is why, I maintain, that the British Runner who tries "to do something about it" is, precisely and symbolically, divided down the middle—one-half whole and smiling, the other an anguished scar. That runner could symbolize not only the best kind of man, as the novel implies and Adams and I seem to agree; but also all of Faulkner's strongest work. At the end, having been through all those novels, he may have told boys in college classrooms rather mildly that life is change and change is, in that sense, good; but in the throes of those novels he was constantly grappling with—against—that truth. Because, of course, change is also, and more obviously than any philosophical acceptance of it, the complete destruction and death of all we have known, all we cherished as well as all we didn't care about. I think that struggle in Faulkner was what gave the books such furious power.

I think also the same sort of complexity, of refusal and/or inability to accept a clear-cut solution, pervades every important aspect of Faulkner's work—including, maybe particularly, that of the Negro. He *wasn't* simply good or bad, sinned against or sinning, stronger or weaker than we. He was many individuals, all of them men, shaped as malleably by heredity and environment as other men, and also facing some particular shaping factors—of color and history—that some other kinds of men didn't have to face. So he could range from a Dilsey to a Lucas Beauchamp to a Butch Beauchamp. And Faulkner could make wildly contradictory statements about his race in isolated public pronouncements (contradictory at least on the surface, maybe at bottom). But read him closely and you'll find, I believe, that he tried to see the Negro as a human being "living-in-motion" just as he did the white man; and against a Popeye there's a Butch Beauchamp; against a Lena Grove or Byron Bunch, a Dilsey; against an L. Q. C. McCaslin, a Lucas Beauchamp, etc.

. . . .

Best,
/s/ Evans

A COLLECTOR'S SENSE OF HISTORY

I

History is an ocean's shore. And each of us has pleasured in speculating on its evolving fascinations. In fact, without realizing, we spend our entire lives shuffling along its scattered beach, sifting detritus in an effort to make sense of its ever-changing wash. And at best, our results are mere fumblings in dimness, because the ceaseless flux makes definitive explanations and absolute answers fatuous and irreducible. We walk the shoreline, picking up strange shapes and placing them in memory-buckets, our repositories for experience. Just when we believe we've picked clean the shore and can return home to do a kind of Darwinian cataloguing from which we might extrapolate universal conclusions, the ocean crashes in or gently laps again, not merely erasing, but changing the model, the shapes, the matrix itself. The intricate, elaborate constructs for skywalks, spacebridges, God-ladders, and dreamdomes surmounting and spanning our sandcastle visions of Carcassonne and Kenilworth crumble in the natural progression time engenders.

Furthermore, the ocean changes second to millisecond to microsecond, infinitely; it never returns to its former shape; not even a single pattern or design repeats itself over the entire course of eternity. The facile notion that humans can arrest and plot Understanding or that they can confirm and fix History becomes an absurdly colossal delusion. Yet, though we are made privy only to the residue, the spewed refuse of time and circumstance, we go on trying, as though the ordering were itself sufficient to give meaning to our existence. Intuition persuades us that the actual ocean contains all there is to ascertain and understand, if we might just discover how to reduce it to quantifiable formulae. Those of us who consider ourselves poets, historians, philosophers, teachers, in the best sense, realize that this is too colossal and too presumptuous a task; we content ourselves with fragments, partial truths, reasonable speculations. We accept the tentative as satisfactory, realizing that the "history" we fashion in any given generation is incomplete and ever edging toward revision and redefinition.

II

Some see history differently; to them it resembles not so much an ocean's shore as an intricately-laced intercostal waterway system—man-made, alterable, technologically sophisticated and ever responsive to utilitarianism. Requiring complete answers and explanations without exceptions, these persons frequently eschew straight lines or prescribed channels, rather zig and zag with formidable, if circuitous, versatility, often arriving at destinations unreachable by natural modes.

Within this group are those who contribute to salutary ends by their willingness to take liberties. That history appears incomplete, truncated, does not deter them; they accommodate it, accepting "stories" exhumed from the past, no matter how recent, as bits of the Apocrypha—myths, fables, allegories, parables. Eager to proclaim definitive conclusions, they refuse to accept the Myths they create as myths, the Fables as fables, Truth as truth.

To them, history based on "facts" is secondary and ultimately irrelevant to their capacity to instruct, to inspire in future generations special respect for the worthiness of moralistic continuity. Whether events really occurred or were invented is not as significant as the irrefragable fact that they do "exist" in the here and now. What counts is that they have survived in a mythopoeic suspension, a metaphorical time-warp as actions and events, exemplary and heroic and noble, as people and places converging in permanent arrest. In essence, what they "factually" create from the unverifiable past is almost always merely a projection of themselves; a salutary exercise. History for these believers is a process of reducing the massive evidence of human activity in a particular era to a sensible, patterned, microcosmic reflection of the universe.

Within this milieu, there is a group of thinkers and writers who focus on a narrower, although no less significant level of sentient endeavor: individual human history. They, like their allies, subjectify from the objective materials at hand, or mythicize; nor do they reject, when necessary to reinforce their conclusions, fashioning from the unknown or illusional the "desired," regardless whether the facts are present or non-existent. What they emerge with is a reflection of the universe that has shaped all of them who have spent the time and energy to extract and interpret from myriad "knowns" an "historical truth": To see the universal in the individual is the ultimate goal of the fictionist, biographer, social, art, and literary historian, as well as the cinematographer, psychiatrist, clinical scientist, and the Speaker of the House.

What then are the reasons for studying history, allowing ourselves to be fascinated and cajoled and persuaded by histories, biographies, religious tracts, T.V. and movie documentaries, if indeed, they perpetuate myths, slanted conclusions, biased fabrications, inventions of one kind or another? How does one learn to discern the intellectual "Y" (Why?) at which fact and fiction part ways in the name of substantiating a particular theory or pet bias? How does one make proper judgments? I suspect there is no recognized, authoritative handbook on the subject. Yet, for the inquiry into the lives of public figures who have made contributions to society during the past hundred and fifty years, I believe there is hope of approximating substantive truths. Discovering the "true" nature of events, circumstances surrounding them, persons connected with them, depends to a great degree on dealing directly with FACTS without being tempted to tamper, embroider, hyperbolize, extrude into gold-woven chains possibilities intended to remain fragile threads.

III

As a deep sea diver or marine biologist descends into regions hithertofore unfathomed in hopes of discovering new or exotic species, so too can each of us who wants to know new and newer truths dig into the troves of materials yet undiscovered. Frequently, letters, manuscripts, logs and diaries, inscribed or hand-made books, first editions, photographs, legal documents, as well as other vaguely related physical objects, can be found in trunks sequestered in attics or "stored" in museum and library basements and lairs, domestic nooks, bank deposit boxes, and "hiding places" long since hidden from remembering—artifacts lost or forgotten, waiting to be sifted, recognized, authenticated. Most commonly, materials of supreme interest to the collector, as well as scholar, still reside with the original recipient or their children or relatives—objects gathering dust on obscure shelves, in dim closets, in frames on desks, coffee tables, bedside stands, shoe boxes; objects originally given out of love, objects waiting to be discovered and seized by "sleuthsayers."

Once found and acquired by the collector, precious objects must be sifted, given validity by becoming a piece of the greater, now-more-complete design. The discoverer must not be willing to accept them on faith. Instead, he must be patently skeptical at the outset, challenging, even contentious, if necessary, in assaying the evidence before cataloguing and making it available to the public.

In a very personal sense, I am ever compelled to question what I read and be critical, even dubious about what I inspect and listen to and record. I have been doubly skeptical in regard to the curious case of William Faulkner, a radical enigma even to himself throughout his enigmatic life. For at least the last decade, I have realized that for scholars to see Faulkner in an accurate historical and biographical context, they must treat randomly surfacing details of Faulkner's life (not necessarily his literature) with even more care than they may have done previously. To do this, they must either gather for themselves, or, in most cases, rely on others to give the facts as they *were* and *are* through more fastidiously documented dissertations, bibliographies, reminiscences, biographies, interviews and articles.

I am convinced that for all the "factual information" now both current and fashionable, there yet exists much more still very much retrievable, definitely accessible. To date, far too much factual detail has been withheld for various reasons, or lifted from its contextual nests, distorted, fashioned ultimately into stories calculated to please readers and satisfy obligations of those who have devoted years creating mythic proportions. As critical, judicious readers, we must be alert to quicksand beneath many well-intentioned biographies and psychobiographies, literary histories and affectionate reminiscences. We should demand nothing less than that our subject be brought to life in all his eloquence, grace, and nobility counterpoised by his grossest posturings, the whole accomplished against the most authentically recreated Zeitgeist possible.

It has been almost exclusively to the life and literary career of William Faulkner that I have directed my attentions since 1960; on numerous occasions during the past ten years I have played the role of "sleuthsayer," excited in each new sally forth with the hope of discovering and seizing another revelatory letter or group by which to further factualize William Faulkner's career. My travels have taken me to Emily Stone in Montgomery, Alabama; Phil Mullen in Osceola, Arkansas; Joan Williams in Memphis and Oxford; Dorothy B. Commins in Princeton; Jim Silver in Cape Coral and Dunedin, Florida; Vance Carter Broach in Tulsa; and Ruth Ford in New York City. Booksellers Glenn Horowitz of NYC, Maurice Neville of Santa Barbara, and Diana Crump of Memphis have also provided a few of the letters in the Brodsky collection.

The journeys have been dynamic, not static; the acquisition of the letters has been inspired by an overriding desire on my part to get to know better the man who wrote *The Sound and the Fury, Absalom, Absalom!* and *Go Down, Moses.* And, to a degree, I have succeeded in gaining insight not only by sharing in some of his private thoughts expressed in his letters, but by sharing in those written by others about Faulkner. Furthermore, I have had the additional privilege of getting to know many of those who wrote or received the letters, or, at least, family members of those original correspondents who themselves have had recollections to share with me. The results of my commitment are evidenced, in part, by the contents of this volume.

Even when confronted by facts expressed in letters, we, as wary readers, must recognize the nature of public and private guises within a "private" letter. Obviously, there are layers within layers of meaning and implication within these letters by various persons orbiting in the Faulkner "cosmos." Each letter, while expressing information, is also one form of persuasion and manipulation: the writer is concerned, above all, with impressing and imposing upon his recipient, either subtlely or undisguised, a particular point of view. Therefore, we must read and sift the facts carefully if we are to gain the fullest resonance from each one.

Still, only by consulting actual artifacts, either first hand, or by going back to an author's sources, can we be sure, or more certain, that what we are being asked to believe by a journalist, biographer, documentary cinematographer, or historian is verifiable, therefore accurate. It is to this end that my collaborator and I have striven, and will continue to strive, to set before the public, more materials than were previously available in print or in public repositories. It has been my resolute choice and pleasure and my unarguable responsibility to act in this manner; not in hope of discrediting existing work, but to fix a more reliable record by which future scholars and enthusiasts of William Faulkner's literature might better appreciate the astounding gifts which this solitary and lonely genius bequeathed to all of us.

Finally, we must question: at what point do History and poetic Myth become one, distinct from and immune to human fabrication and tampering? I suggest that this convergence cannot occur before virtually all of the available artifacts have been accounted for, considered, then presented in a form untainted by speculative interpretation; not until artifact and fact merge indistinguishably. Conclusive artifacts (in this case, the approximately 500 letters transcribed in this volume) should not necessarily nurture conclusive interpretations; rather, they should foster an intellectual atmosphere in which continuing interest and research and discovery can flourish.

Louis Daniel Brodsky
Farmington, Missouri
September 7, 1981
August 13, 1983

INDEX

Dear Dorothy and Sue: The lab ...

all right, but I was right about ...
it. I am already sick to the ...
[illegible] have become for. ...
them entire Hollywood line ...
have it Xmas, Stockholm ...
last got back tonight.

Have had no word ...
everything is all right ...
about the money ...
[illegible] $2500 ...
Bank. Oxford ...
[illegible]: last ...
[illegible] ...